Copyright © 2021 Reuben A. Bauer
All Rights Reserved

ISBN: 978-1-990265-08-2

Then and Now

Printed in Canada
No part of this publication may be reproduced, stored in a retrieval system or transmitted, in any form or by any means, electronic, mechanical, photocopying, recording or otherwise, without the prior written permission of the publisher and /or copyright holder.

First Edition: July 1995
Second Edition: June 2021

Additional Copies may be purchased from:
W.C.H.F.
#374-9768-170 Street
Edmonton, Alberta
CANADA, T5T 5L4

Typeset and Printed by
Heritage Books – Canada
#374, 9768-170 Street
Edmonton, Alberta
Canada, T5T 5L4

Acknowledgements:

I wish to acknowledge and express my thanks to many people who have helped in any way with this book. A special 'thank-you' to:

-The pioneers who came to the districts;
-The people who contributed written articles, family histories, pictures and documents.
-The Manitoba Provincial Archives;
-The Provincial Land Titles Office;
-The Shellmouth Municipality Office;
-The Roblin Review and Russell Banner for help in researching old papers;
-The typist and proof readers;
-The artist, Marlene Shearer, who took the time to do the front cover;
-To all individuals who donated time and labour and helped in collecting materials;
-The purchasers who wish to own this book;
-The publisher, Marcon Consulting (Uvisco Press), who made an excellent job of producing, printing and publishing this book;
-And to my husband, Tom, who has put up without a wife for the past six months.

There probably are others to whom we owe a debt of gratitude. To anyone who has been missed I apologize. Your omission was not intentional. My thanks to you all. I appreciate your contribution no matter how small.

Sincerely,

Betty Bauereiss

Dropmore Homecoming

Dedication:

This history is dedicated to the many pioneer families who were among the first to settle in the Shellmouth Municipality at that time known as the R.M. of Shell River. Some of these pioneers arrived in the late 1800's before the railroad was built through this area. We owe them much for the sacrifices they made and for their perseverances in making these communities.

This book is a tribute to all who came here in the early days. They laid the foundation on which others have been able to build. Generations to come will reap the benefits of their labours. I hope you enjoy reading the histories and that they will bring back many fond memories.

How the "Homecoming" Came About:

I have been working on gathering the history of the Dropmore District for about two years in preparation for the R.M. of Shellmouth Centennial coming in the year 2008.

Then on October 14, 1994, a public meeting was held in Dropmore for the organization of a Dropmore Homecoming of all residents and former residents of Dropmore, Castleavery, Grainsby and Rochedale School Districts.

The long weekend of August 4, 5, and 6th of 1995 was set for the Homecoming. Various committees were set up and the ball started to roll.

I have tried to be as accurate as possible. Many families will have been missed as they did not all respond to the request for family histories. To all that have contributed to our history, in work, thought or deed, thank-you!

The signage for the Dropmore Homecoming 1995

About the Author

    Betty Bauereiss, was born Betty Anne Halwas, on the 27th of August, 1947, to Hermann (deceased) and Alvina Halwas. She was raised on a farm south of Inglis, Manitoba. She received her education in the Public School and High School in Inglis.

    In 1964, she married Tom Bauereiss, also a resident of Inglis. The couple moved to Winnipeg, where Tom was employed with a construction company. Their first child, a daughter, Darlene, was born there in 1965. Since both Tom and Betty loved the land, they moved back to Inglis in 1966, where they began farming. It was there in 1968, that their first son, Brett, was born. It was in the spring of 1968, that they first rented land in the Dropmore area and then moved to a farm which they purchased in 1970. By 1972, they had a second son, Carman.

    Up to that point, Betty had been kept busy tending to her home duties and helping Tom in the farming operation. She has, nonetheless, been kept busy through her involvements with many community-minded projects such as: the Community Club, 4-H, the Dropmore Chicks, curling, dancing, cross country skiing, horseback riding, walking, reading and gardening, to name just a few. She also enjoys her children and two grandsons.

    Besides her personal pursuits, two years ago, Betty ventured into a new business. She opened a skin-care business and is now a Mary Kay Consultant.

    Her interest in reading history books of other communities, has led Betty into collecting stories and pictures about her community. The more books she read, the more excited and curious she got about the Dropmore area. When the community decided to hold a Homecoming, "I realized my opportunity had come", she says. She also realized that if this collection of material was to be become a book, it had to be done now.

    When she began, little did she know how complicated it would be to write a book. Nevertheless, she maintains that she has enjoyed the challenge of this book and hopes that it will be a treasured memory for all who read it.

TABLE OF CONTENTS

Acknowledgements i

Dropmore Homecoming iii

Sign for the Dropmore Homecoming iv

About the Author v

Letter from the R.M. of Shellmouth 1

Maps of R.M. of Shellmouth 2

Dropmore Cenotaph 6

SECTION ONE - Historical Flashbacks to Events and Other Happenings

    Picture of train arriving in Dropmoe 8

    Rural Municipality of Shell River 9

    Rural Municipality of Shellmouth 10

    Aerial view of Dropmore 14

    Dropmore History 15

    Rochedale History 19

    Castleavery School 20

    Dropmore School 23

    Grainsby School 24

    Rochedale School 25

    Post Offices 27

    Castleavery Church 28

    Community Activities 29

    4-H Assiniboine Sewing Club 32

    Dropmore Hall and Community Club 33

    Businesses 34

Railways, Elevators and Station...35

Entertainment..35

The Dropmore Chicks..36

Bridges..41

Rural Telephones...42

Pyott's West Campground..43

Kilman Enterprises...44

Rivendell Cross Country Ski Club..45

Frank Skinner's Dream...46

SECTION TWO - Historical Family Ties in Our Communities
Family Stories..51
(see Index of Families at the back)

SECTION THREE - Historical Recollections in Photo Memory
After the horse and wagon...242
Buildings of the Past..244
By-gone school days...247
Community activities..250
Farming in the past..253
Our prized livestock...259
People tell the story...261
When horse was King..272
Visit Our community..275

SECTION FOUR - Historic Archival Reprints
Blueprints of the past..283

Family Index..298

Alvin Zimmer
Reeve of RM of Shellmouth
Shellmouth, Manitoba

Greetings from Alvin Zimmer:

On behalf of the R.M. of Shellmouth, I would like to express greetings to the Dropmore area on the occasion of their homecoming.

Dropmore has played an important role in the development of the R.M. of Shellmouth over the years. The R.M. of Shellmouth council meetings were held in Dropmore from 1921 - 1967.

I particularly wish to convey our gratitude to those people who worked hard over the years to make their area a better place to live.

Best wishes to all

Alvin Zimmer
Reeve
R.M. of Shellmouth

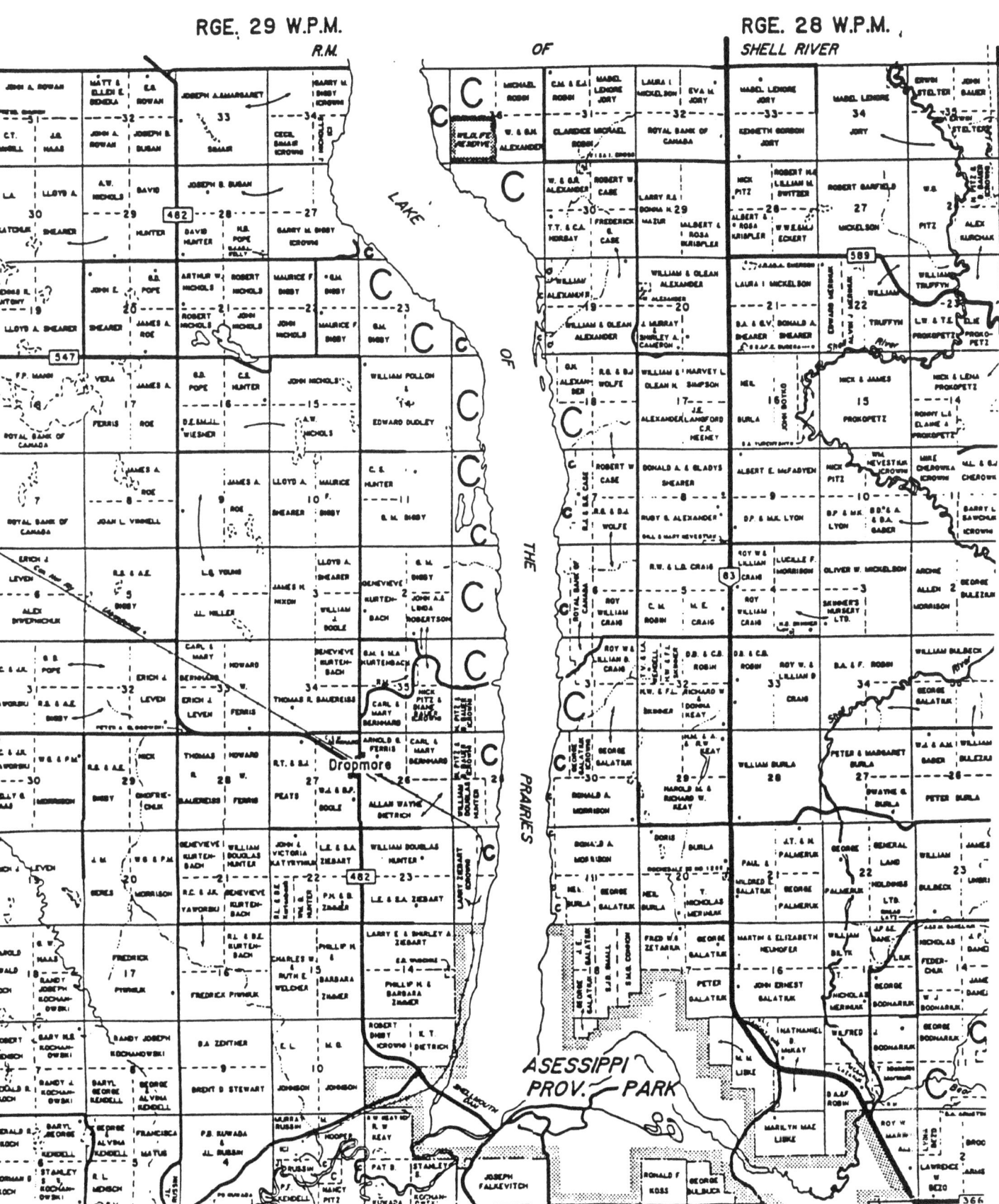

Military Service

World War I

Bradley-Hunt, Basil
Brown, Fred
Burell, Samuel
Clark, Corpl. Kenneth A.
Ferris, William
Goodbun, Oscar
Gray, Pte. John
Gysin, Major Leonard S.
Heather, Pte. Hugh Bertram P.P.C.L.I.
Hunt, Bert
Hunt, Pte. Arthur Winter
Hunt, Pte. Frank
Leflar, Lce. Corpl. Ira A.
Cameron, Roger
Nevill, Lt. Ralph
Pope, Ernest
Theobald, Corpl. Ernest
Watson, Lce. Corpl. William Douglas
White, Art
White, Frank

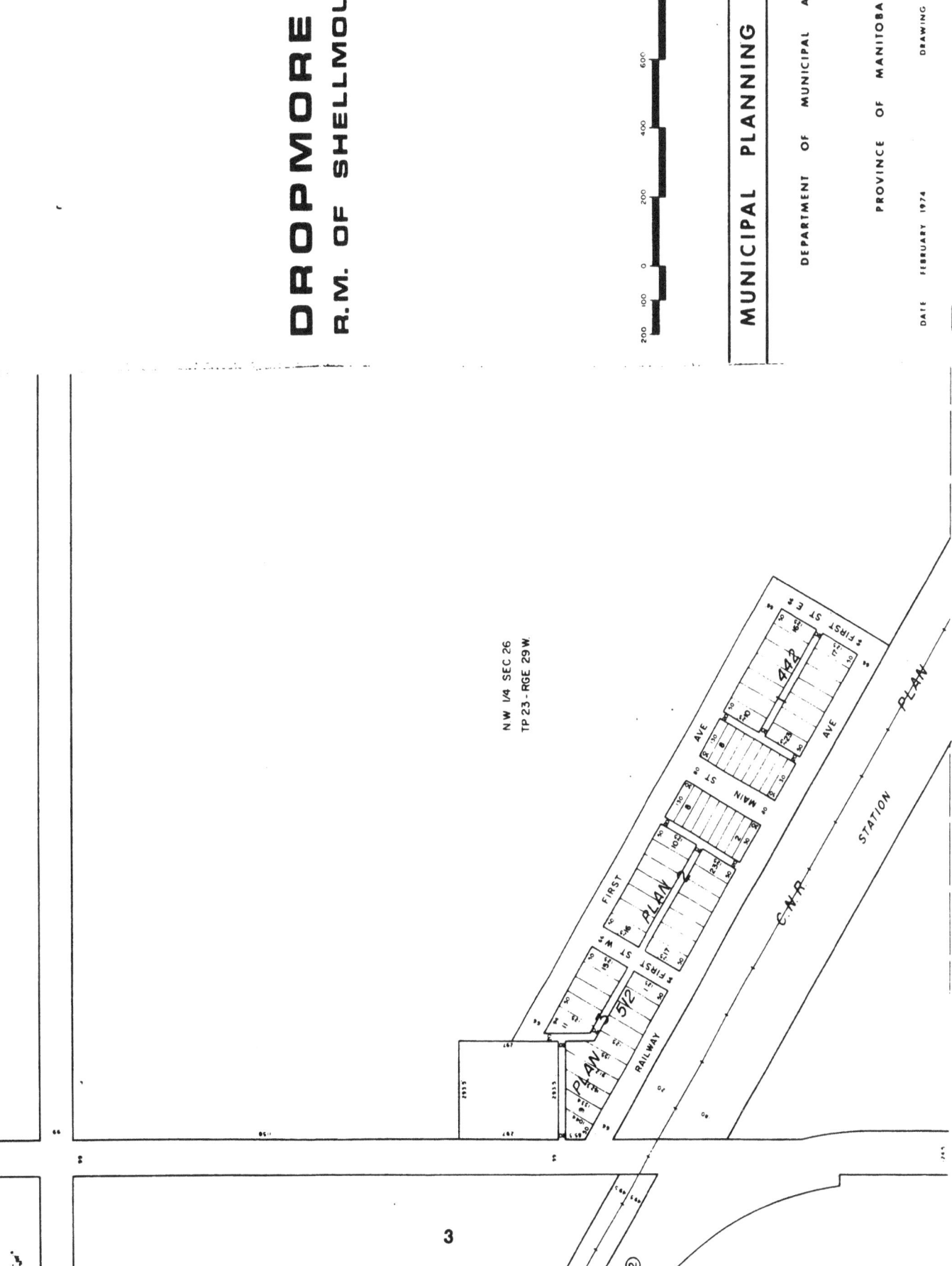

World War II

Alexander, K.
Comfort, H.
Cox, Bert
Dalle, Henry
Dietrich, Paul
Farncombe, Charlie
Ferris, Art
Ferris, Bill
Ferris, Stan
Ferris, Victor
Gilhooley, Bill
Gilhooley, R.
Goodbun, R.
Hansen, A.
Hodgson, Thos R.
Hunter, Dave
Hunter, Jim
Jones, Harold
Keay, H.M.
Kolstad, Leonard
Kruger, Ron
Leflar, Bryce
Leflar, Roy
Lewis, M.
Morrison, Earl
Moster, Harold
Nerbas, Rupert
Nichols, Jack
Petz, George
Piwniuk, Bill
Piwniuk, John
Piwniuk, Peter
Rawlings, John Jack
Rawlings, Walter
Richardson, Fred
Robb, E
Robb, George
Roe, Eva
Seeback, Ed
Shearer, Isobel
Spies, Ted
Ziebart, John
Zimmer, Frank

The unveiling of the War Memorial in Dropmore, Manitoba, (circa) 1919

The Dropmore Cenotaph as it appears today

Section One

Historical Flashbacks to Events and Other Happenings in

Castleavery
Dropmore
Grainsby
Rochedale

This picture shows the train stopping in Dropmore, Manitoba (circa) 1920.

Rural Municipality of Shell River

Reeves
1884 - 1895	Alexander Stewart
1896 - 1897	James Richardson
1898 -	Alexander Stewart

Councillors

1884
- R. J. Brooks
- Francis Nixon
- Thomas McLennan
- Matthew Whaley
- Thomas C. Gerrard

1885
- Matthew Whaley
- Thomas Gerrard
- Joseph Dugan
- Thomas Tod
- I. McDougal
- W. Adams

1886
- Matthew Whaley
- Joseph Dugan
- Archibald Buie
- Thomas Tod
- Mervyn Hewitt
- Peter Wallace

1887
- Mervyn Hewitt
- Archibald Buie
- Robert Murray
- Peter Wallace
- Joseph Dugan
- Matthew Whaley

1888
- MacDonald
- Joseph Copley
- J. H. Kines
- Peter Wallace
- Matthew Whaley
- Joseph Dugan

1889
- MacDonald
- Joseph Copley
- Matthew Whaley
- J. H. Kines
- John Simpson
- Joseph Dugan

1890 January
- Joseph Copley
- J. H. Kines
- John Simpson
- Joseph Dugan

October
- Walter Gordon
- William Denmark
- J. H. Kines
- Joseph Dugan

1891 January
- Joseph Dugan
- Peter McDougall
- William Denmark

April
- Walter Gordon
- Johnson replaced Gordon

1892
- Joseph Dugan
- William Denmark
- Thomas McLennan
- Peter McDougall

1893 - 1896
- William Denmark
- Thomas McLennan
- Peter McDougall
- Johnstone

1897 - 1898
- Peter McDougall
- Thomas McLennan
- Allbright
- Mitchell

Secretary - Treasurers

1884	Alfred Crebbin
1884 (April) - 1885	A. G. Venables
1886	Henry Teulon
1887 - 1898	William S. Wallace

Minutes of the Shell River Municipality from the year 1899 - 1907 may be obtained from the Shell River Municipal Office.

Rural Municipality of Shellmouth

Reeves

1908 - 1918	Thomas McLennan
1919 - 1920	John McEwan
1921 - 1922	Thomas McLennan
1922 - 1925	John McEwan
1926 - 1963	E. H. Armstrong
1964 - 1975 (Oct.)	H. M. Mench
1975 - 1992	E. A. Mench
1992 (Nov.) to Present	Alvin Zimmer

Rural Municipality of Shellmouth

Councillors

1908	John T. Adams William Denmark	A. H. Ferriss George Ford
1909	Thomas McLennan John T. Adams Joseph Dugan	George Ford O. W. Goodbun
1910	Thomas McLennan John T. Adams William Denmark	Joseph Dugan George Ford

1911	Thomas McLennan John T. Adams William Denmark	O. W. Goodbun George Ford
1912	Thomas McLennan O. W. Goodbun George Ford	Joseph Dugan Robert Beatty
1913 - 1915	Thomas McLennan R. W. Patterson George Ford	Joseph Dugan Robert Beatty
1916	Thomas McLennan R. W. Patterson John McEwan	Joseph Dugan Robert Beatty
1917 - 1918	Thomas McLennan Robert Beatty John McEwan	William Barry Joseph Dugan
1919	G. H. Cammidge William Skinner	William Barry Joseph Dugan
1920	William Barry Joseph Dugan	Herbert J. Adams William Skinner
1921	Robert H. Beatty John L. Bryant	Joseph Dugan William Skinner
1922 - 1925	Annie Robin John Bryant	Joseph Dugan William Skinner
1926 - 1927	William Skinner H. J. Adams	John L. Bryant Joseph Dugan
1928 - 1929	H. J. Adams James Craig John L. Bryant	Joseph Dugan Sudbury
1932	Sudbury Joseph Dugan	H. J. Adams John McEwan
1933 - 1934	Francis Garnett	H. J. Adams John McEwan
1935 - 1936	H. J. Adams Garnett	Nicholls John McEwan
1937 - 1938	John McEwan H. J. Adams	Nicholls L. C. Elliott
1939	John McEwan H. J. Adams	L. C. Elliott H. A. Rowan
1940 - 1942	H. J. Adams L. C. Elliott	H. A. Rowan William Craig

1943 - 1944	William Craig Lloyd	H. J. Adams H. A. Rowan
1945	William Craig Sudbury	H. A. Rowan H. J. Adams
1946	William Craig H. A. Rowan	Sudbury Hansen
1947	William Craig H. A. Rowan	Hansen L. C. Elliott
1948	William Craig L. C. Elliott	Hansen Ferris
1949	Hansen William Craig	Ferris J. G. Langford
1950 - 1951	Ziprick William Craig	Ferris J. G. Langford
1952 - 1960	J. G. Langford Robin	William Craig Ferris
1961 - 1965	J. G. Langford N. D. McKay	William Craig Ferris
1966 - 1968	J. G. Langford William Burla	Bill Ferris N.D. McKay
1969 - 1972	William Burla N. D. McKay	John Robertson Rudy Nerbas
1973 - 1975	N. D. McKay J. Piwniuk	John Robertson William Burla
1976	N. D. McKay Gene Nerbas	John Robertson William Burla
1977 - 1984	N. D. McKay Gene Nerbas	William Burla Maurice Digby
1984 - 1989	N.D. McKay Gene Nerbas	William Burla Tom Bauereiss
1989 - 1992	Alvin Zimmer Cyril Sudbury	Tom Bauereiss William Burla
1992 - Present	Randy Fingas Gene Nerbas	Tom Bauereiss Rick Keay

Secretary-Treasurers

1908 - 1920	Fred Richardson
1921 - 1924	George Hunt
1925 - 1937	W. S. W. Newsholms
1937 - 1946	B. Bradley Hunt
1947 - 1963	D. A. Bradley-Hunt
1964 - 1967	C. Joel Stauffer
1968 - 1976	E. M. Paterson
1976 (Sept.) - 1982 (June)	Conrad M. Nicholson
1982 (June)	Raymond G. Bomback
1982 (July)	Dianne Ungarian (Assistant)

From 1884 - 1920, the council meetings were held in a variety of places, most of them being at the Assessippi Town Hall. In 1921 - 1967, the meetings were held in Dropmore. Then the council meetings were held in Inglis, 1968, in the new municipal office.

A new seal was purchased in 1908. It was to be two inches in diameter and on the face of it "Shellmouth Municipality" with Maple Leaves enclosing a horse's head and a sheaf of oats. This is the same seal that is still used today.

On December 9, 1913, a fire destroyed the house of F. G. Richard, who was the clerk at the time and where the municipal office was located. Cash in the amount of $150 and $1500 in drafts were burnt. Some books and papers were destroyed that were in the desk. Papers in the safe were badly singed. The R. M. of Shellmouth took loss of money that was burnt.

In June, 1982, the offices of the Boulton and Shellmouth municipalities amalgamated into one office which is located in the R. M. of Shellmouth office.

In 1992 a new municipal office was built which houses both Shellmouth and Boulton municipalities.

Receipt from R. M. of Shellmouth from A. Goodbun for taxes.

An aerial view of Dropmore, Manitoba and the surrounding countryside taken in the early 1980's.

Dropmore History

Compiled by Lloyd Leflar 1963

GEOGRAPHY AND TOPOGRAPHY

Area being Townships 23 and 24 in Range 28 and 29 West to land on west side of Assiniboine River, originally gently rolling prairie with a few scattered poplar bluffs. Land on east side of the Assiniboine Valley mostly covered with heavy poplar timber.

The Assiniboine River, which takes its rise in Nut Mountain, flows south through a deep valley along the eastern sections of Townships 23 and 24, Range 29, and is joined by the Shell River on Sec. 12-23-29. The Assiniboine River turns slightly west at this point. This area was formerly part of Shell River Municipality, but was divided in 1908, the southern portion taking a the name of Shellmouth. Local districts included are Castleavery, Rochedale, Grainsby and Dropmore and village.

INDIANS AND EARLY PIONEERS

No Indian reserves are included, and except for a few roving bands who passed through the districts in early years digging Seneca Root or trapping fur, Indians were seldom seen.

The earliest pioneers arrived in 1883. Among the first to arrive was Joseph Dugan, accompanied by two daughters and two sons. This party came directly from Ireland, arriving in Brandon in June. Brandon was the head of the railway at that time. Mr. Dugan purchased a team of oxen, a wagon and supplies and started the journey west to their homestead. They travelled northwest by way of Shoal Lake, Rossburn and Birdtail, and stopped at Rossburn while Mr. Dugan went south to Birtle to make entry for his homestead - NW 1/4 28-24-29, and continued their journey by way of Russell which consisted of two stores, a post office, and one or two small dwellings. They arrived at Shellmouth on 12 July, and here were joined by two more new settlers, each of whom had an ox team and wagon. Names of these men were Alex McIntyre of Brandon and Duncan Gordon of Rossburn. The only building in Shellmouth at that time was Major Boulton's shack near the site of the old bridge. The party crossed the river on a scow, which took about three hours time, and proceeded north about twelve miles. No dwellings or settlers were seen in travelling this distance. Camp was made on the new homestead where the family lived in tents until October.

Mr. A. McIntyre settled on the SW 1/4 of 24-24-29, while Mr. D. Gordon took the SE-1/4 of 28-28-20. These were apparently the first homesteads taken up in this township.

Mr. Dugan's family built a house of logs and had to travel to Birtle to obtain lumber for roofing, windows, etc. Only rough lumber was to be had.

After completing the house, Mr. Dugan returned to Ireland and brought out Mrs. Dugan, a daughter and a son in the spring of 1884. They were met at Minnedosa with the ox team, by his sons Joe and Frank. Minnedosa was then the end of the Manitoba Northwestern Railway line just under construction. It was expected at this time that the Manitoba Northwestern Railway would pass through Rossburn and Shell River area, and settlers continued to come into the district and take up land.

Among these early settlers were William Anderson's family, the Albright Bros., John and Walter Robertson and John Birnies. Mr. Birnie located in the Assiniboine Valley at the site of the present Birnie Bridge. Many other settlers followed and most of the homesteads in the Townships 24 and north portion of 23, Range 29 were taken up.

As the land on the east side of the Assiniboine River was mostly heavily timbered, settlement of this came later. Mr. John Skinner and family settled on the west bank of the Shell River in the early nineties where they are still ranching.

In 1885, the Manitoba Northwestern Railway Company was given a land grant of 6,400 acres of land for each mile of line built from Portage la Prairie, Manitoba to a point on the Saskatchewan River, twenty miles south of Prince Albert. This line did not follow the route through Rossburn and Shell River as was first expected, and many of the settlers in the Shell River area abandoned their homesteads and moved elsewhere. These lands which were abandoned were cancelled back to the Dominion Land department. Those who remained in the District took up ranching. They were in most cases the first pioneers who came in and settled along the Assiniboine River. With plenty of hay and water in the Assiniboine Valley, plus an abundance of prairie land for pasture, it was ideal country for ranching. Since there was no demand for grain, owing to lack of transportation, very little land was cultivated.

A drought which began in 1889 and continued until 1892 resulted in an acute shortage of feed during the winter of 1892. Spring was extremely late in coming, and many cattle perished. Some of the ranchers constructed crude snow plows to scrape snow off the grass in sloughs and low places. R. Albright, who had only a few cattle shovelled snow off the grass in order to help out his feed supplies and so managed to save all his stock. One rancher told me later that he recalled leaving a door of a rancher's shack which stood a few miles north of where MacNutt town stands today, and walked for seventy yards on dead cattle without once stepping on the ground.

The following spring some settlers who had located in the district north of MacNutt moved to the Assiniboine Valley. Among these were D.C. Stewart, Sandy Stewart, Doc Baker, Jack and Captain James Anderson (later called Anderson's east to distinguish between this family and Wm. Anderson's family who continued to reside a few miles west). During this dry spell, the Assiniboine River stopped running, the only water being in the deeper parts. P.N. Patterson who now resides in Shellmouth recalls riding a pony up the bed of the Shell River for several miles at that time, the river bed being quite dry.

TRAVEL AND ROADS

Roads in early days were only prairie trails. Since there were no fences, trails were made in whatever direction people wished to go (as the crow flies). Travel on foot was not uncommon. Oxen or horses and wagons were used for long trips, also saddle ponies as horses became more plentiful. Oxen were less common and seldom seen after 1900, except those used by Ukrainian settlers. Road grading was started around 1905.

The first bridge at Shellmouth was built in 1885, and the bridge at Birnie's Crossing was built in 1905. Scows had been operated at Shellmouth, Birnie's Crossing and other points along the Assiniboine previous to this. The first bridge on the river at Dropmore was built in 1908, and a modern bridge replaced the old wooden bridge at Birnie's Crossing recently. A new modern bridge was also built at Dropmore three years ago in 1960. Trunk roads are all graded, gravelled and maintained for winter travel at the present time. No. 83 Highway runs through the east side of the municipality.

The first car in this district appeared in 1912, and was owned by Alex McDonough of Russell. Cars came into general use in 1916-17. The first plane to pass over the district was seen in 1921.

LOCAL GOVERNMENT

The Municipality of Shell River came into being about 1886. As fire destroyed all municipal books and records sometime about 1909, it is difficult to determine exact dates. The first Council seems to have been elected sometime in the 1890's with A. Stewart as Reeve and R.W. Patterson, J. Mitchell, Geo. Ford and Geo. Watson as Councillors. Municipal Office was at Shellmouth with William Wallace as Secretary-Treasurer.

Meetings were occasionally held in Roblin. Some other Reeves who followed were: J. Gil, T. McLennan, John McEwan, and H. Armstrong in the given order. The Municipality of Shell River was divided at the north line of Township 24, about 1908, the southern portion taking the name of Shellmouth.

SCHOOLS

The first school to be built was Castleavery in 1885. This building was constructed of logs with planks for seats and desks. A young man named Nat Minnish was teacher. It is difficult to understand how early schools like Castleavery were financed, unless it was by local settlers. Dominion Statutes of 1885 state a grant of $30,000 was made to Manitoba Public Schools in 1886. This was the first year in which such grants seem to have been made available.

Grainsby School District was organized in 1904, with the school located on Sec. 33-23-29. The first trustees were Wm. Ferris, Wm. Wardle, and Alex Hunt with Ira Leflar as Secretary treasurer.

Rochedale School was built in about 1905. This school was only open in the summer months for the first years. Trustees were F.G. Richardson, A. Gilchrist, and R.H. Keay.

Grainsby School District was divided in 1911 and the east half became Dropmore School District with a new school being built in Dropmore Village. This building was replaced by a modern school in 1952.

Miss Yeates (now Mrs. D.G. Stewart) who resides in Shellmouth and who was engaged as a teacher at Castleavery for the term of 1900, recalls that she had to wait while new desks were being set up on the first day of school that term. This would indicate that seats and desks of planks were still in use up to that date.

INDUSTRIES, STORES, HOSPITALS, ETC.

A small sawmill, a brick kiln, store and flour mill were started as Asessippi in the late eighties or early nineties by J. Gill who later moved to Roblin when the railroad was built through that district. Many of the early settlers bought lumber and bricks there for their building. Joe Dugan opened a small store on his farm in 1885. Previous to this, early settlers sometimes went to Moosomin, Saskatchewan for supplies, travelling by ox team and wagon.

T.C. Gerrard opened a store in Shellmouth in 1889. A sawmill was also in operation here about that date, operated by two men. One of them was named Mitchell. The logs sawn were floated down the Assiniboine and Shell Rivers from the Duck and Riding Mountains.

Hanbury Lumber Co. also carried on cutting logs in the Duck and Riding Mountains for several years, floating their logs down the Assiniboine River to their sawmill at Brandon. The last log drive to go down the river was in 1903.

Mr. Gerrard opened a creamery in Shellmouth in 1903 with Chris Paulson in charge. Cream was hauled from as far north as Township 25. The creamery was later sold to Smellie Bros. of Russell who closed it soon after.

When Mr. Gill of Asessippi left to go to Roblin, the brick kiln and sawmill were discontinued. Mr. T. McLennan took over the store and flour mill. These two closed later when the CPR extended their line north and the town of Inglis came into being. The Post Office was moved to Inglis.

During the dry seasons of 1889 and early '90's prospectors were at work along the Shell River in search of Gold. Some of the old timers tell of returns of $2.00 to $3.00 per day being made. Remnants of some of the old rockers sluice boxes can still be found along the Shell River.

F.L. Skinner, youngest son of Mr. and Mrs. John Skinner, who were among the early settlers in the Rochedale district, operated a plant nursery on the land taken up by his father in 1895, and has won many prizes and awards as well as the Degree of Doctor of Horticulture for his work in plant breeding, particularly roses and lilies. Dr. Skinner ships plants, shrubs, etc. to many parts of the world. The Skinner's Nursery is located at Craig's Corner, one mile east of No. 83 Highway.

In 1912, Guy Ferris and Wm. Longden were manufacturing cement blocks for buildings or foundations with a machine powered by a treadmill on NW 1/4 of 16-24-29. War broke out a year later and this enterprise was ended. A building of these blocks stands on this land today, which is now owned by John Pope.

No hospitals are in this municipality, but Township 24 in Range 28 and 29 are included in Roblin Hospital District.

CHURCHES

The first church in this area was built in the Castleavery district. This came about as a result of a tragic accident which happened on the farm of R. Albright in the fall of 1889, in which three men were instantly killed and two more were seriously injured, when a steam boiler which was being used to thresh, exploded. Those killed were Frank Dugan, a young man named Foulerton and a man named McLennan. Joe Dugan, Jr.. had his leg broken in two places while G. McDonald lost the sight of one eye. Doctors were called in from Russell and Saltcoats to attend the injured. Either of these towns were thirty miles distance. Sometime later Mrs. Foulerton who lived in England sent a sum of money to be used to build a church in memory of her son who was killed This church, which was constructed of logs was built sometime later in the Castleavery cemetery. It was later burned by prairie fire. The Castleavery cemetery is one of the oldest for many miles around and is still in use.

Church was held in Grainsby School and Dropmore Community Hall until a church was built in Dropmore in 1953. This is a community church serving Castleavery, Dropmore, Grainsby and Rochedale Districts.

The Shellmouth Church was built in 1904.

FRATERNAL ORGANIZATIONS AND CLUBS

A Ladies Community Club comprised of the ladies of Rochedale, Dropmore, Castleavery, and Grainsby looked after the organization and refreshments of concerts, dances and other social events. Dropmore districts also have a Curling Club and large rink. A bonspiel is arranged every winter.

In earlier years local baseball and football teams were organized in each district, and contests were staged at local picnics and sports days. Horse races, polo, etc., provided entertainment, but of late these have been discontinued as sport has become more professional.

Castleavery also has a curling rink and hold an annual 'spiel. A large Community Hall located in Dropmore is sponsored by the four districts, Rochedale, Dropmore, Castleavery and Grainsby. Grainsby School has been closed for four years for lack of sufficient pupils.

MILITARY ACTION

H.W. Albright, one of the early pioneers of Castleavery, served as a member of Major Boulton's Scouts in the last Riel Rebellion. O.W. Goodbun served in Lord Strathcona's Horse in the Boer War. Mr. Goodbun returned to farm in the Dropmore district for a number of years and later moved to British Columbia where he died some years later.

A Rifle Club was organized at Dropmore in 1910. Officers were A.H. Goodbun, H.V. Ferris, Secretary - Ira A. Leflar. Many of the younger members of this club enlisted in the early part of World War I. About twenty men in all left Dropmore. The first two to go were Leonard Gysin and H.H. Heather of Castleavery District. Both of these men were killed in action. Names of those killed in action can be found on a monument erected to their memory in the Dropmore School yard. Many young men also left the district to take part in World War II. Many of those also made the supreme sacrifice.

RAILROADS

When the CNR started to push its main line west toward the coast about the turn of the century, the word came that a line would be built from Neepawa through the Rossburn district to Russell and west to Yorkton, interest was again roused in the homestead lands in the Shell River area. Prior to this, a few new settlers had come in to take up ranching, but settlement was practically at a standstill. The few who had taken up land included C. Langley, J. Shearer and a man named Pelton who located in the Assiniboine Valley on land formerly occupied by S. Stewart. But in 1901 homesteaders began to take interest again and in 1902 a real rush started. My father G.M. Leflar and brother homesteaded the west 1/4 section of 28-23-29 early in June and stated at that time that most of the land in Township 23 was still open, but when they visited the district to look over their land six weeks later, they reported most of the land was taken up. In 1903 saw settlers busy breaking land and erecting buildings on their new farms. Most of the buildings were of logs, but with new settlers coming, several sawmills were put in operation along the edge of the Riding Mountains where settlers could take cut logs to be sawn into lumber. Each for the fee of .25 cents, each homesteader could get a permit which entitled him to cut logs to the amount of 10,250 ft. board measure of lumber to construct buildings on his homestead. Mill operators charged $3.00 to $6.00 for sawing the logs into lumber. Settlers were also allowed a certain number of fence posts, rails, and logs and farmers spent their winters taking out lumber, posts, wood, etc. It was not uncommon to see a string of teams, ten times or more long in the early morning going to the bush or returning late in the evening. Those were the days of thick fur coats, lumbermen's socks and buckskin moccasins.

The Canadian Northern Railway did not reach Dropmore district until 1909. Grading along the Assiniboine Valley started in 1907 but the steel was not laid until 1909. A grain elevator was built in Dropmore by the British American Co. in October, 1909, and opened for business in November. The first carload of grain to leave the district by the new railroad was loaded at a cutbank about three miles south of Dropmore in June, 1909 by O.W. Goodbun.

J.C. Smith opened a store in Dropmore in September, 1909, and a Post Office in 1910 when Castleavery Post Office was closed. E.T. Lewis opened a store in Dropmore in 1910. Mr. Lewis had been among the early settlers of the '80's but had moved when the Manitoba Northwestern Railroad bypassed the district.

The coming of the Canadian National Railway and building of the new bridge on the Assiniboine River enabled the settlers of Rochedale to deliver their grain to Dropmore and saved the long hauls to Russell or Roblin.

Since much of the land on the east side of the Assiniboine River was covered with heavy poplar bush, the work of bringing it under cultivation progressed somewhat slower than did the prairie lands on the west side.

A local branch of the Grain Growers Association was formed at Dropmore, later a United Grain Growers elevator was built. Directors of this elevator were J.G. Richardson, Wm. Skinner, John McEwan, Joseph Dugan, Alex Hunt and H.V. Ferris. This elevator burned down in 1928 and was rebuilt the same year. It was later purchased by Dropmore Local Pool Association.

FINAL SUMMARY

In writing this I have sometimes wandered outside the borders of the District. This has been necessary because these stores or other industries played a part in supplying the wants of new settlers in the districts of which I write. Shellmouth Post Office, Store and Creamery served the people of Dropmore and Grainsby districts until the coming of the railway in 1909.

In the short time permitted it has not been possible to write a history of the district. The history of the Castleavery District which began more than eighty years ago and is one of the oldest settlements in the Shell River area, is a story in itself. Castleavery was named by Mrs. Dugan, Sr., and her daughters in memory of their old homes in Ireland.

In this short and somewhat disjointed sketch I have endeavored to give an insight into the lives of these new settlers and the many problems they faced in establishing their new homes. Nor has it been possible to mention all the people involved. The first and in many cases second generations have now passed on and many of the family names have disappeared from the Assessment Roll. It is to be regretted that with the building of the Shellmouth Dam, the last of these historic old ranching sites, which in many cases represent the toil of two or more generations, will disappear and be forgotten.

I wish also to acknowledge information and assistance given me by the following persons: Mrs. A. Johnson-Shellmouth, R.J. Lewis-Dropmore; John Robertson Jr.-Dropmore; E. Morrison-Dropmore; P.N. Patterson-Shellmouth

VILLAGE OF DROPMORE
Submitted by: Betty Johnson (Rawlings)

This bit of Dropmore history has been compiled from my Mother's notes ---Elizabeth Rawlings (nee Hunt) who lived all her life in the Dropmore/Grainsby districts.

When the railroad came through in 1909, a village started to grow. Once the BA elevator, loading platform and small station were built, farmers were relieved of having to haul their grain to Langenburg, Roblin or Russell. Farmers either hauled grain to the elevator or organized a hauling bee to load a grain car from the platform. Later, the United Grain Growers also built an elevator. They were eventually replaced by Manitoba Pool. A new train station was built in 1921 and a station agent was employed. There was a local train and express from Winnipeg to Yorkton, Saskatchewan, as well as freight trains. Cattle were shipped to Winnipeg by train. A section crew worked out of Dropmore for many years.

During the late teens and early 1920's, there was quite a business section in the village. It included two stores, post office, municipal office, lumber yard, deep well, Imperial Oil filling station and bulk sales, blacksmith shop, garage, veterans hall, butcher shop, outdoor rink and school. A community hall was built from the veteran's hall and garage. It wasn't long before it boasted a maple floor and stage. A curling rink with two sheets of ice was built in 1950 with all volunteer labour. Reg Lewis arranged the work crews and the ladies of the district served the lunches. A lot of improvements have been made to both the rink and hall over the years. The annual bonspiel was always well patronized and the hall has been the location for many dances, concerts and community gatherings. Both facilities have been a credit to the community.

A church was built in 1953 with volunteer labour except for the inside work. The first service was held on Good Friday, 1954. A lot of items were donated by local citizens including the organ, pulpit, and chairs. A very active women's group was formed in 1952 representing Dropmore, Grainsby, Castleavery, and Rochedale. These women were tireless fund raisers and were able to raise money for the maple floor, pews and carpet along with many other things in the church.

As the years passed, the blacksmith shop closed and the Municipal Office moved to Inglis. The elevators were torn down, as was the train station and even the railroad tracks. The school closed and students were bussed to Roblin. The Grainsby School was purchased by W.G. Ferris and moved to his farmyard. The Castleavery Ladies' Club purchased their school and used it as a community centre. The Dropmore School was bought by Mr. and Mrs. Charlie Bernhard who transformed it and the school yard into a very attractive home.

Over time, the one remaining store closed as did the filling station, the church, and the post office. Many other buildings are gone and most of the residents. Like so many little prairie towns and villages, Dropmore has all but disappeared. The memories, however, live on in the hearts of those who grew up there.

Rochedale History
by Bill & Alice Keay 1995

In the 1870's, the Hudson Bay Co. and the British Government were negotiating land claims, which resulted in the Hudson Bay and Northwest Territories being transferred to Canada, with part of it becoming the Province of Manitoba, and the remaining part placed under Territorial Government.

Manitoba was set up in the County system, but with the influx of settlers this system did not prove satisfactory, then it was changed to Municipalities.

This area was known as the Shell River Municipality from 1884 to 1907. It extended from the Duck Mountain Forest Reserve on the north, to the Russell Municipality on the South. The Council meetings were held in Roblin. With horse and buggy being the mode of travel, it was too long a trip and too time consuming for the Reeve and Councillors, so in 1907 it split up into the R.M. of Shell River and R.M. of Shellmouth.

This put Rochedale District in the R. M. of Shellmouth. Some of the first settlers arrived in the late 1800's. Among these we find such names as Richardson, Todd, Gilchrist, Lougheed, Patterson, Hackman, Keay, Cameron, Farquardson, Skinner, Bassil, Temple, Halpin, Lloyd, Craig and Wilson. No doubt we have missed some. Then, a little later, there were many more who settled in the area.

Some of the children of these first settlers walked through the Shell River Valley to Asessippi School to get what little education they had.

Then the Rochedale School S.D. No. 1268 was formed in 1905 and a school built on the site where the cairn stands today. In 1953 a new school was built on the same site. Miss Helen Skinner was the first teacher in 1905.

Like most School Districts, the school is sort of the "hub of the district", where all activities seem to take place. It was used for church services down through the years. The first Minister was The Rev. Stevenson, who had been sent to Canada by the Irish Presbyterian Mission Board, to serve the three Mission stations of Shellmouth, Rochedale, and Asessippi in 1913. He held services every Sunday at all three locations for five years until his death in 1918. In the following years there were many different ministers who took the services.

Some of the first settlers, who in later years passed away, are laid to rest in Rochedale Cemetery which is located 1 1/2 miles west and 3/4 mile south of the school site on the brow of the hill overlooking the valley where the Shell River joins the Assiniboine River. This is a very scenic and peaceful location.

There were numerous social events held in the school, where everyone enjoyed themselves. The school children's Christmas concert with Santa and all the trimmings, was a big event for both children and parents. Then there were card parties, social evenings, dances. Some winters, the more active members would get together and put on a 3-act play. We enjoyed ourselves as much as the audience, but no actor was ever called to Hollywood.

In the early 1900's, the younger men had a very good soccer team and would take in a number of Sport's Days where there were Soccer Tournaments and usually came home with the top prize. It did not do much for the district, because not many people knew where Rochedale was and couldn't find it on a map.

Then when Frank Skinner, a self taught Horticulturist went into the Horticulture Nursery business and became known around the world for his plants and trees, which brought him many awards and the title of Dr. Skinner, Rochedale was well known.

The women of the District had quite an active W. I. group in earlier years, which in later years the name was changed to Rochedale Ladies Club. They looked after the social events and school picnics, with the proceeds if there were any, being donated to some charitable cause.

As most of you know, the district is located between the two valleys of the Shell and Assiniboine Rivers, which means lots of grazing land and hay meadows, so it was a natural for mixed farming. Most families were self-sustaining, growing grain, feed, cattle, hogs, chickens and big gardens. So they had their own, meat, dairy products, eggs and vegetables and wild fruit was usually plentiful, and for a change there was wild fowl. In the summer time the Beef Ring looked after the fresh meat supply which was greatly appreciated.

Then in the 1960's when there was a population up-surge and the country school children were ready for high school, there was no place for them to go, as the town schools were filled, so that was the start of the School Divisions so all children would have an equal chance.

This finally led to the closing of the country schools and end of social life in the district, as parents naturally had to help support the children's social events in the towns.

I am sure we all benefited in some small way from this country school social life which the present and future generations will miss.

I guess that is what progress is all about.

Castleavery School No. 416 (SW 20-24-29)

The School District of Castleavery No. 416, formed on August 5, 1885, was to consist of the following land: Section 2 to 11 inclusive, 14 to 22 inclusive, 27 to 34 inclusive in Twp. 24, Range 29 West, and those portions of 1, 12, 13, 23, 24, 26 and 35 lying and being on the west side of the Assiniboine River in the same township and range. The district was readjusted from time to time. The Intermountain School Division No. 36 included the School District of

Castleavery No. 416 in Ward 3, effective April 1, 1967.

The first Castleavery School was built of logs in 1885 on SW 1/4 of 20-24-29 where John Shearer now resides. It is believed that Jane Dugan and Nat Minnish were the first teachers. Some of the students who went to that school were: Albert Shearer, James Shearer, Maggie Shearer (now Mrs. Arthur Nichols), Bert Hunt, and some of the older members of the Thomas Langley family who lived on the NW quarter of 18-24-29. Planks were used for seats and desks, as there were no desks. Slates and slate pencils were used, as there were no pencils and scribblers as yet. The first teachers were: Jane Dugan (Mrs. George Hunt), Mr. Nat Minnish, Mrs. Clara Watson 1896, Miss Nellie Skinner (Mrs. Fred Richardson) 1897 - 1898.

Castleavery Pupils of 1927
(L-R) Dorothy Nichols, Edward Jones, Harold Jones, John Hunter, Dave Hunter, Earl Morrison, Cedric Rowan. (Center) Irma Shearer, Jim Hunter, Jean Birnie, Babe Comfort, Trix Shearer, Ida Ferriss, Nan Comfort, George Hunter, (Back Row) Sam Comfort, Essie Farncombe, Annie Shearer, Joyce Ferriss, Peggy Hunter, Bill Hunter, Ronnie Morrison.

Castleavery Pupils of 1933-1935.

Castleavery School with Eva Roe about 1943.

In 1905, a new school was built on SE 1/4 of 28-24-29, the last Castleavery School site. It was used as a Community Centre since the closure in 1965. Then in 1986 Neil Kelly purchased the school site for a summer cottage.

Castleavery Pupils of 1933-1935(?)

New Castleavery School.

Castleavery Pupils in about 1951 or 1952. Remember sitting around stove with coats and boots, talking, reading while ink bottles thawed on top of stove.

Castleavery Pupils of 1963
(Top L) Dan Sawchuk, Ellais Sawchuk, Greg Hunter, Corey Bauming, Donald Rowan, Ian Hunter (Bottom) Brenda Simair, Faye Digby, Florette Simair.

Castleavery School #41

Year	Teachers	Salary
1896	Clara Watson	
1897 per month	Clara Watson	$35
1898 per month	Miss N. Skinner	$35
1899 per month	Miss N. Skinner	$30
1900 per 6 months	Miss N. Skinner	$180
1901	Mr. MacDonald	
1902	Mr. MacDonald	
1903	Miss Florence Yeates (Mrs. Duncan Stewart)	
1904-1905	New school built	
1906	Miss Mabel Evans	$315
1907	Miss Lydia Simpson	$400
1908	Miss Millicent Hodgson	
1909	?	
1910	Miss Mitchell (Mrs. James Hunter)	
1911	Miss Mitchell	
1912	Miss Longden (Mrs. Harry Rowan)	
1913	S. E. Longden (Aug.-Dec.) Hattie MacDonald (Jan.-Mar.)	$495
1914	Anna J. McLean	$650
1915	Anna J. McLean (Aug.-Dec.) N. Singleton (Jan.-June)	$600
1916-18	Jessie Margaret Mowat	$600-$700
1919	Stella M. White	$1000
1920	blank register	
1921	Margaret E. Cochrane	$1000
1922	Alice Dodge (Aug.-Mar.) Marion Reid (Apr.-June)	$961
1923-24	Marion Reid (Mrs. Hillard Ferriss)	$800
1925	Helen J. Lind (Aug.-Dec.) Agnes Spencer (Jan.-June)	$800-$850
1926	E. M. Hedley	$890
1927-29	George Pearson	$873
1930	register missing Mr. Fred McCauley	
1931-32	A. B. Thom	
1933-34	Florence Kirkpatrick	$500
1935-37	Isobel Stewart	$500-$550
1938-39	Joan Glover	$500
1940-41	Mary E. Patterson	$500-$650
1942	Ivy Soderstrom (permit)	$700
1943	Donalda M. Bell (permit)	$800
1944	Doreen Day (permit)	$850
1945	Lillian Ellerington (permit)	$825
1946	?	
1947	Mary B. Budz (permit)	$950
1948-49	Alice M. Trickett	$1400-1600
1950	Mrs. Annetta C. Lett (Aug.-Nov.) Lillian Gabrielson (Dec.-June) (permit)	$1700
1951-52	Don Webb	$1800
1953-54	Elizabeth Taylor	$2200-2500
1955-56	Marlene Laliberte	$2500
1957-58	Michael Kozinski	$2700
1959	Marlene Websdale	$2900
1960-61	Elaine Trakalo	$3000
1962-63	Hollie Andrew	$2800
1964	Jean Stovin	$3000
1965	school closed	

To Commemorate the Castleavery School No. 416, a cairn now stands to the east of the school building.

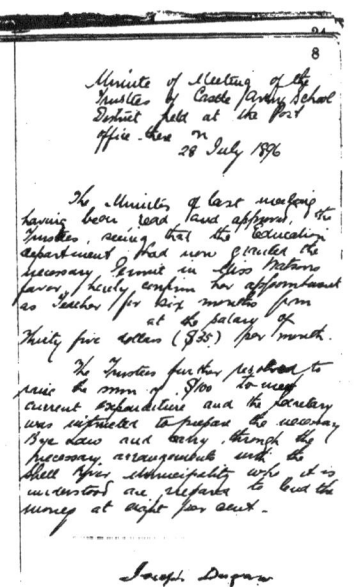

A sample record of Minutes from Castleavery School Board 1896.

Castleavery School Cairn.

Dropmore School No. 1558 (Dropmore)

The School District of Dropmore No. 1558, formed on February 18, 1911 by By-Law No. 46 of the Council of the R.M. of Shellmouth, was to consist of the following lands: Assiniboine River in Sections 12, 13, 24, 25, 36, all in Twp. 23, Range 29; sections 2, 3, and all lands west of the Assiniboine River in section 1, Twp. 24, Range 29 W. The district was readjusted from time to time and, effective April 1, 1959, an Order by the Minister to establish The Intermountain School Division No. 36 included the School District of Dropmore No. 1558 in Ward 3. Effective April 1, 1967, the Intermountain School Division No. 36 was declared to be a division within the meaning of Section 443 of the Public Schools Act by order of the Minister dated March 11, 1967.

Old Dropmore School, 1911.

Dropmore School Pupils of 1944-1945.

Dropmore School and Pupils of 1948 -1949 (Back Row) Doreen Barnett, Marie Barnett, ? , ? , ? (Middle Row) Murray Robertson, ? , ? , Bill Robertson, ? , ? , (Front Row) Doug Hunter, Bird, Bird, Bird, Betty Goodbun, Alice Goodbun, Reg Robertson, Gene Nelson.

A new school built in 1952 by this school was closed in 1968. The children are now taken by bus to Roblin for their education.

New Dropmore School built in 1952.

In 1946 a private school for Grade X helped educate five students. Bessie Munro was the teacher. The pupils were Bob and Jessie Pyott, Ivan and Anne Rowan, and Evelyn Brown. These classes were held in the former Andy Francis' Store.

Dropmore Private School 1945-1946 with Bessie Munro as the teacher.

Grainsby School Pupils of 1943.

Grainsby School No. 1294

by Mildred Rawlings

The first Grainsby School was built in 1904. In August 1918 it was burnt and a new one replaced it built by Mr. G. N. Leflar. While the school was being built, classes were held in Mr. William Wardle's log house.

The school was closed in 1960. In 1964 the school was sold to Bill Ferris and moved to his farm where it was turned into a shed.

Grainsby School.

Grainsby School Pupils of 1936.

Teachers of Grainsby School

1905	Hugh W. Keele and Emily Turner
1906-7	Miss E. Turner, Florence McClare and J. M. Davidson
1908-9	A.S. Bishop, Percy M. Baldwin
1909-10	Annie McDougall, Violet E. Leflar
1911-12	Annie Hodgson
1913-14	Christina Fletcher
1914-15	Emma Henderson
1915-16	Emma Henderson
1918-19	A. E. Cameron
1919-20	Olive Charbonneau
1920-21	Stella White
1921-22	Leslie Langford
1922-23	Florence Henderson
1924-25	Bentina Erlendson, Mabel F. Cook
1925-26	Dorothy Nuttall
1926-27	Mabel F. Cook
1927-28	Jean W. Woodhull
1928-29	Mildred Belton
1929-30	Winnifred Harvey
1930-31	Malcolm Gillies
1931-32	Malcolm Gillies
1932-33	Malcolm Gillies
1933-34	Kennatha Statham
1934-35	Kennatha Statham
1935-36	Kennatha Statham
1936-37	Kennatha Statham
1937-38	Florentine Menzies
1938-39	Florentine Menzies
1939-40	Florentine Menzies
1940-41	Violet Lewis
1941-42	Lucie Brooks
1942-43	Orma Mack and Flo Hunter
1943-44	Flo Hunter

1944-45	Dorothy Baxter
1945-46	
1946-50	School closed
1950-51	Margaret Dillabough
1951-52	Freda Bradley-Hunt
1952-53	Myron Shykitka
1953-54	Mrs. Lietz
1954-55	Mrs. Thirza Smith
1955-56	Mrs. Thirza Smith
1956-57	Mrs. Thirza Smith
1957-58	Mrs. Margaret Kendrick
1958-59	Mrs. Margaret Kendrick

School closed. Some names in the school registers throughout the years: Leflar, Ferris, Cowles, Hunt, Wilson, Smith, Elridge, Fraser, Herbert, Spiess, Berndt, Wardle, Carmichael, Craig, Goodbun, Rawlings, Bowels, Reich, Langley, Larsen, Bagnall, Gloump, Moore, Koch, Yaworski, Bieber, Nerbas, Zamzow, Morrison, McFadyen, Dalle, Cooper, Beals, Yasinsky, Haberstock, Wishart, Slemmon, Moster, Ostrowka, Wirth, Bessel, Piwniuk, Bolton, Trupp, Threinen, Sopp, Seebach, Kruger.

Rochedale School District No. 1268

The Rochedale District got its name from Mr. Halpin who named the district after his hometown in Rochedale, England.

The first school was built in 1905 by Mr. Darcy Johnson of Boggy Creek.

The first teacher was Miss Helen Skinner. The first families were: Gilchrist, Richardson, Lougheed, Farquardson, Hackman and Cameron.

In 1925 the W. I. improved the heating system in the school and started a circulating library. Also, a porch was built on at that time and two new doors put on.

On July 20, 1936, the ratepayers passed a resolution that an addition be built, 12' x 18' and the cost not to exceed $325.00.

In 1952, a discussion was held regarding consolidation at Russell but nothing further developed and in 1953 a new school was authorized by the ratepayers. Mr. A. Robinson of Dauphin was awarded the contract and the new school was opened in October 1953.

The main events of the school year were the Christmas Concerts, Field Days in Inglis and the last day of school, a School Picnic.

With the consolidation of the schools in 1967, the children were bused to Inglis for their education.

The school was moved to Inglis, and used as a classroom until 1979 - 80. Then the Inglis Hi-Liters used it for a few years as their meeting room and finally Norman Liske bought it and moved it to his farm for a workshop.

In 1985, a cairn was erected and dedication was in July 1990, at the Rochedale reunion.

Rochedale Cairn marks the location of the original school site.

Rochedale S.D. #1268

Rochedale name given by Mr. Halpin who came from Rochedale in England. The teacher of Rochedale School before 1915 was Barbara MacLennan

Year	Teachers	Trustee
1915	Gladys Kerr	John Bassil
	Margaret Hopper	F.G. Richardson
		William Skinner
1916	Margaret Hopper	Wm. Skinner
		J. Bassil
		F.G. Richardson
1917	Mary Hodgson	F.G. Richardson
		J. Bassil
		G. Robb
1918	Gladys V. Kerr	F.G. Richardson
		J. Bassil
		G. Robb
1919	Mary Mills	George Robb
	Gladys Rae	Jonathan Bassil
		Mrs. J. Lloyd
1920	Marg. McMurray	George Robb
		C. Cooke
		Mrs. J. Lloyd

Year	Name	Officers
1921	Lily Donaghue	C. Cooke / George Robb / R. A. Hammond
1922	Lily Donaghue	R. Hammond / C. Cooke / George Robb
1923	Margaret Irvine	Mrs. Skinner / G. Keay / R. Hammond
1924	A.M. Goodbrand / W.E. Chalmers	F.G. Richardson / G. Keay / R. Hammond
1925	W.E. Chalmers	F.G. Richardson / G. Keay / George Duncan
1926	Benjamin Franklin, Privat	George Duncan / J. Craig / F.G. Richardson
1927	B.F. Privat	George Duncan / Jas. Craig / Mrs. Jas. Lloyd
1928	Jane Anderson	Jack Bassil / James Craig / Mrs. J. Lloyd
1929	Eunice Bullard	Jack Bassil / James Craig / Mrs. J. Lloyd
1930	Gladys Mitchell	Jas. Craig / J. Bassil / C. Cook
1931	Margaret Way	C. Cook / J. Bassil / J. Craig
1932	Florence Kirkpatrick	J. Craig / J. Bassil / T. Langley
1933	Evelyn Tarrant	R. Hammond / J. Craig / J. Bassil
1934	Evelyn Tarrant	R. Hammond / G. Robb / J. Bassil
1935	Evelyn Tarrant	R. Hammond / G. Robb / J. Bassil
1936	Pearl Porter	J. Bassil / R. Hammond / G. Robb
1937	Pearl Porter	Geo. Robb / G. Craig / J. Bassil
1938	Pearl Porter	J.D. Goodbun / W. Craig / Geo. Robb
1939	Margaret Arnott	Geo. Robb / W. Craig / J.D. Goodbun
1940	Margaret Arnott	Geo. Robb / W. Craig / J.D. Goodbun
1941	Margaret Arnott	W. Craig / Wm. Skinner / J.D. Goodbun
1942	Margaret Cameron	Wm. Skinner / Wm. Craig / J.D. Goodbun
1943	Margaret Cameron	W. Craig / W. Skinner / J. Goodbun
1944	Margaret Cameron	W. Craig / G. Choropita / R. Morrison
1945	Gladys Mickilson	W. Craig / Geo. Choropita / R. Morrison
1946	Mavis Dillin	W. Craig / G.W. Choropita / Ronnie Morrison
1947	Irene Lovas	W. Craig / Ronnie Morrison / G.W. Choropita
1948	Esther Jeffrey	W. Craig / G. W. Choropita / R. Morrison

1949 Irene Lovas
1950 Irene Lovas
1951 Irene Lovas
1952 Ruby Kolstad
1953 Ruby Kolstad
1954 Freda Robin
     G. K. Breckman
1955 Margaret Cameron
1956 Margaret Cameron
1957 Winona Keating
1958 Winona Keating
1959 Jeanne Matchett
1960 Joyce Price
1961 Alice Kulchycki
1962 Patricia E. Fedirchuk
1963 Marion Werschler
1964 Marion Werschler
1965 Marion Werschler
1966 Marion Werschler
1967 Marion Werschler
1968 Marion Werschler

Rochedale Class of 1943
(Back) ?, Eva Hammond, (3rd row) John Palmeriuk, Nelson Hackman, Eli Palmeriuk, Andy Evanisky (2nd row) George Hackman, Doug Goodbun, Roy Craig, Bill McKay, Johnny Hackman (Front) Jean Cameron, Annie Palmeriuk, Francis May, Nancy Cheropita, Helen Cheropita.

Rochedale School Pupils.

Rochedale School Girls only.

Rochedale School Boys only.

Post Offices
Castleavery and Dropmore

The first post office opened on April 1, 1885 in the Castleavery district. Mr. Dugan had the post office in his store. This post office operated until 1910 when it was closed and relocated to Dropmore.

Mr. Edward (Barney) Lewis had the post office in his little store on the corner from 1910 - 1934 when he passed away.

Then Mr. Bradley-Hunt took over the store and post office until 1941 when he took on the position as Secretary-Treasurer of the municipal office.

Reg. and Francis Lewis took over the post office in 1941 till 1965 when George Petz had the post-master duties. George passed away in 1978 and his wife Anne ran the post office till she retired to Roblin in 1992. Presently we get our mail delivered to rural boxes situated next to the hall.

Dropmore Post Office.

Rural Post Boxes.

Castleavery Church

The first Castleavery Church was built in 1889 because of a terrible accident. A boiler of the steam engine exploded and killed Frank Dugan and J. Fullerton.

Mrs. Fullerton sent a sum of money from England to build a church in memory of her son. The log church was built in the cemetery. This church was later destroyed by a prairie fire in 1918. To date the cemetery is still being used and it is the oldest cemetery in the district.

Dropmore United Church (1954-1985)

In 1952, a meeting was held to discuss plans for a church for Dropmore and districts. Previous to this, services were held in the hall.

Work was started in 1953. Most of this was volunteer labour by members from the four districts, but a great deal of material was also donated. Reg Lewis built the pulpit for the church.

The first service was held on Good Friday in 1954 and the Dedication Service was held August 1, 1954.

There were thirty-one years of regular services, Sunday School, weddings, funerals, baptisms, confirmations, etc. but due to a dwindling population, the church closed, with the final service on June 9, 1985.

The building was bought by the Neuhofer family and moved to the Beautiful Lake Farm at Shellmouth and is now known as the Church Caffee.

Castleavery Church - 1886.

Castleavery Cemetery and Cairn.

Castleavery Cemetery.

Fond memories of our little Dropmore Church with the Lewis's home in the background.

Dropmore Cemetery.

Rochedale Cemetery.

Community Activities

Hockey was played on an open-air rink in Dropmore, around 1930, under Harry Gilhooley's direction, taking in tournaments in Russell, Roblin and Shellmouth.

Castleavery curling rink was one sheet of ice constructed in 1948 on Art Nichols' farm near Longdon Lake. Flooding was done with a pump and gas motor. Gasoline lanterns were used for lighting until 1951 when hydro came to the area. A wood burning stove warmed the waiting room. The doors closed in 1964 and the rocks were sold to San Clara Curling Club. The rink still stands today and is being used as a storage shed by the Nichols' Bros.

A curling rink with two sheets of ice was built in 1950 in Dropmore. Propane heaters were put in, in 1973 making curling a lot more comfortable, also electric heat replaced the wood burning stove in the waiting room. Water was piped to the rink in 1979. In 1988, all lunches during the bonspiel were served in the hall.

Curlers came from miles around to participate in the annual bonspiel held in January, with many a good meal coming from the so-called kitchen.

Lack of interest closed the rink for a couple of years. Then again, curling picked up and the rink was opened again. The last few years have lacked for curlers, but the rink remains open to date.

In summer, baseball and football attracted many young and old players. Contests were held at the local picnics and sports' days.

In the 1900's, the young men of the Rochedale District had a very good soccer team. They would take in a number of sports' days and tournaments and bring home the top prizes.

Dropmore Hockey Club in the 1930's: (L-R) Alvin Robb, Jesse Wardle, Sam Comfort, Jack Rawlings, Syd Finkbeiner, Cliff Woods, Donnie, Jim and Buzz Lewis.

Castleavery Curling Rink.

Castleavery Curling Rink.

The workmen at the Castleavery Curling Rink having their lunch break.

Another view of the workers at the Castleavery Curling Rink.

Construction of the Dropmore Curling Rink.

Workmen busy at putting up the scaffolding on the Dropmore Curling Rink.

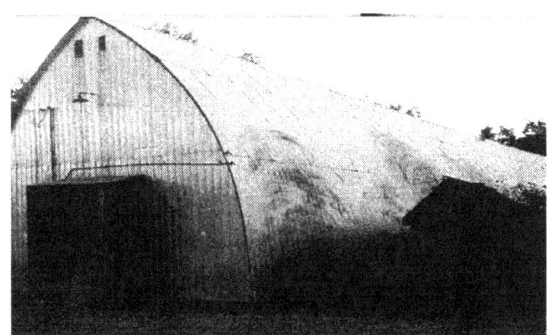
The exterior of he Dropmore Curling Rink as of 1991.

Some members of our community in a good 'spiel at the Dropmore Curling Rink.

The Dropmore Football team before 1914: (Back row) Jack Bryant, Ernest Teobald, A.H. Goodbun (Ike), Leonard Gysin, Ralph Neville, Guy Neville, O.W. Goodbun (Bun). (2nd Row) Sid Wishart, Edgar Comfort, Jim Lloyd, Basil Bradley-Hunt. (Front row) Arthur Colicott, Jim Langford.

More of the Dropmore Team.

Rochedale Rangers Football Club, North West Champs Pratt Cup Winners In 1930. (L-R Back) Jim Reid, Jack MacLeod, Nat McKay, Sandy Craig, Jim Robertson, Sid Otto, John Robertson. (2nd row) George Beamin, Jim Craig, Martin Woods, John, Willie and Peter Craig.

The 4-H of Assiniboine Sewing Club
by Florentine Hunter

The club was organized in 1957. The leaders were: Mrs. Florentine Hunter, Mrs. Irma Hunter and Mrs. N. Bauming.

The officers of the sewing club were: President: Ann Robertson, Vice-President: Linda Nielson, Secretary-Treasurer: Erla Morrison and Club Reporter: Lorraine Kruger.

The original members were: Ann Robertson, Irene Robertson, Isabel Hunter, Betty Rawlings, Linda Neilson, Evelyn Draga, Sandra Wardle, Lorraine Kruger, Erla Morrison, Charlene Bernhard, Marion Hunter, Sharon Rowan, Elle Maudsley, Janet Maudsley, Patsy Kennedy.

The meetings were held in Grainsby School, after school on Fridays. The first meeting was held on Sept. 24, 1957. Attending that meeting was Velma Reid, Home Economist, and Harold Boughton, Agriculture Representative, to help us organize.

The girls soon learned their basics, the threading of a needle, and tying a knot was fun to learn. It wasn't long until lovely samples and good books were done.

This was not all work. We had parties; the Christmas Party was always fun. One year, we all went sliding down the hills and then went back to Dropmore for lunch. We put on a couple of whist drives to help out our finances. One winter we had square dancing. Harry Oliphant came and led. What a great time was had!

We made some lovely displays for achievement and rallies, such as "4'H Leads the Way", "Better Living", and "Make Canada Safe For All".

Some girls were awarded trips to various places such as Saskatchewan, New Brunswick, Prince Edward Island and Nova Scotia. Also, an award was given to go to camp. That was a fun time!

A short while after, we organized the girls and leaders from Rochedale, too. Among the leaders to help them were: Mrs. Marge McNeil, and Mrs. Helen Skinner. New members were: Isabel Skinner, Marilyn Parmentier, Jackie MacLeod, Jayne McNeil, Lorna McNeil, Diane Burla, Theresa Burla, Sharon Zetariuk, Sheila Zetariuk.

The name of the club was changed to Assiniboine Sonnets. The girls were into French now and "sonnets' meant Belles. Achievement Night was the highlight of the year. It was held in the Dropmore Hall. Their work was all beautifully displayed and judged by the Home Economist. Ribbons were awarded and we always had our fair share of red ribbons, some purple and the rest were blue.

We had a good program in the evening. Demonstrations were given, there was some speaking, singing, etc. A guest speaker, a Home Economist, spoke.

Our first uniforms were white blouses with blue skirts. Rally days were held in the summer. We marched, gave demonstrations, etc. Our keenest competition was from the Girl's Club at Binscarth and Russell. Some of us received 12 year certificates before we finished.

This was, I think, the most rewarding work I have done.

Assiniboine Sewing Club

Assiniboine 4-H Sewing Club.

The Inglis Clothing Club.

A 4-H Rally.

4-H History
Assiniboine 4-H Club
Roblin Ag. Rep. Area

The Assiniboine 4-H Beef Club was organized in the fall of 1954 with 16 members registered.

Murray Shearer and Maurice Digby were the first leaders with Murray Robertson as President, Garry Digby as Vice-President and Robert Digby as Secretary. John Hunter became leader after Murray Shearer's retirement.

4-H meetings were held in the Castleavery School, and for many years, achievements were held at the farm of Maurice Digby. At the first achievement, eight calves were shown. The judge, Keith McComb, congratulated the boys and girls for their first showing and the good work they had done. Achievements were always special days for the whole district, as most of the spring work was shut down for two or three hours while everyone turned out to view the calves, give their opinions and have a good visit over lunch (which all the mothers contributed to).

After the show was over, the calves were loaded and trucked to Dauphin where they competed the next day against other clubs for overall best calf and showmanship. All club members dressed alike for these occasions and placed their own club banners in front of the stalls.

In 1959, the swine project was introduced and existed for three years, along with a heifer project.

Rallies were also very important and were held at the local fair in either Roblin or Russell. Public speaking and demonstrations were activities in the club that everyone participated in. Several gold watches, plaques and trophies were awarded to club members for their participation in 4-H activities and achievements.

The John Norquay trophy was awarded to Top Showman for Manitoba and was awarded at the Brandon Fair. It was held for one year in our club.

There were also two trips to the Toronto Royal, one to Port Alberni and several exchange trips to the USA and other parts of Canada.

In 1967, the beef club shut down as there were not enough boys and girls of age to keep it going.

As others became interested in a Pony Club, reorganization took place around 1971 with the two clubs joining together to form the Assiniboine Beef and Pony Club, with eighteen members.

Fred Piwniuk and Gen Kurtenbach were the leaders with achievement day being held in Roblin.

During the mid 70's, projects like conservation, handicrafts, home design and junior leader were being taught. There was another name change to the club, "Assiniboine 4-H Club", with approximately 20 members.

In the 80's, with few members, the beef club joined with the Inglis Club and the club was called "Inglis 4-H Beef Club". By the mid 80's the members of the beef club joined together with the Cromarty Club to form the MB/SK Club. This club is still active today.

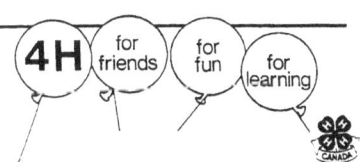
The 4-H Logo Card.

The Man.-Sask. Beef Club Achievement in 1987.

The calf scramble in Brandon, MB in 1987.

Dropmore Hall and Community Club
by Phyllis Morrison

In 1919, the Veterans built a small hall for them to hold meetings in and in 1923, Leflar's Garage was moved and added on to the Veteran's Hall - thus it became the Dropmore Hall. The Veteran's Hall became the stage part of the hall.

In 1963, a meeting was held and the Dropmore Community Club was formed. This consisted of the Ladies Community Club, the Men's Sport's Club and the Board of Trade. The Dropmore Community Club became responsible for the Hall and it has continued that way ever since.

In 1975, the Community Club was split into "work groups". This has worked well in our community, as everyone shares the responsibility for putting on dances, caretaking and mowing grass etc. We continue to take turns as groups, putting on dances and the Community Christmas Party. We have the co-operation of the whole community when it comes to funerals, showers, farewells, parties etc.

In November 1976, a motion was made to build a 30 x 30 addition on the east side of the hall and to bring water to the outside of the hall. This project was completed in 1979.

The dance floor is the original one, being sanded and revarnished in 1979. In 1983, the old part of the hall was repanelled and the ceiling painted.

Many fund raising projects - including snowmobile poker derbies, dances, suppers, raffles, etc. were taken on, to raise money to build the addition, paint, panel and re-side the hall. Most of the work was done by local volunteers.

During the week of the Curling Bonspiel, a bar is set up and meals are served from the hall, with the week winding up with the Bonspiel Dance - this is our fun for all week.

We continue to have dances, community Christmas party, anniversaries, showers, birthdays, farewells, meetings, etc. at the hall.

I have been Secretary-Treasurer since 1976. Many a good time has been had in the hall. The population of rural areas has diminished drastically and our area is no exception. We are fortunate to have had good support from many friends in surrounding communities for which we are thankful. They keep coming back for our good old "Dropmore Hospitality".

Here is a picture of the old Dropmore Hall.

Here is the old Dropmore Hall refurbished with new siding.

Businesses

In 1909, Jack Smith opened a general store which was operated by Remus and Harems.

Edward (Barney) Lewis built a small store in 1912 and on Dec. 12, 1929, Mr. and Mrs. Bradley-Hunt took over this store along with the post office. (This store was on the corner south of the church.)

A butcher shop, along with groceries was built around 1920 and run by Tom Langley, then Sid Wishart and last by Morgan's. This butcher shop was torn down by the Craig's and the lumber was used to build houses. Later, the church was built on this place.

In 1920, E. T. Lewis built a larger general store and the post office was moved there also, later taken over by his son Reg. Around 1926, Jim Wong had a cafe in part of the Lewis' store. In 1950, this store was sold to Dave Bushko and the post office was moved to the house next to the store owned by Reg. Lewis. Dave Bushko was a fine tailor. Many men from near and far wore a suit made by Dave. He closed the store in the late '60's and moved the store to the Big Lewis house which he had bought. In 1971 he moved to Dauphin. After several years, he retired in 1983 to Dropmore. In 1984 he passed away and is laid to rest at Beulah.

The Lewis General Store in 1947.

George Petz's Store.

George Petz had a small store in the old municipal office.

Dan Smith had a blacksmith shop, then Mel Watson, and Billy Longden until 1940. Later Alec Ralston operated it. (this blacksmith shop was north of the well). Later, the shop was moved to Doole's.

Leflar's built a garage in 1920. This garage still stands today as part of the Dropmore Hall.

On the west end of town, Bob Hunt had a filling station and in 1927, Walter Rawlings took over the Esso filling station and ran it until he retired in 1979. He also operated a grain and fuel trucking service for a number of years.

The Dropmore filling station.

The Union Bank of Canada rented the Municipal Office for a bank under the supervision of the Russell office. It was managed by C. R. Ivey with Ettie Hunt assisting. This bank was in operation for about two years.

About 1920, a deep well was drilled by Britton Ferris to supply the village with water. A small pump house was put over it and in 1981 a new pump house was built.

Theo Burrows had a lumber yard managed by Joe Larsen in 1921. There was also a pool room for a short while.

This is Britton Ferris with his water well-drilling operation. He drilled wells in the Dropmore area.

Railway, Elevators, and Station

In 1909 the Canadian National Railway was built along with a small station.

The first elevator was built in 1909 by the British American Company with Mr. Harems as the grain buyer.

Mr. O. W. Goodbun hauled the first load of grain.

In 1916, the Grain Growers opened an elevator. In 1927 the British American elevator burned down and a new one was built.

Then in 1928 the Pool and Grain Growers elevators were destroyed by fire and rebuilt. The grain buyers at that time were Mr. Grundy in the Pool and Mr. Bill Moore in the Grain Growers. Many bushels of grain were bought at these elevators.

The train made its last run in 1971. The station was torn down and the freight shed moved to Calder, SK. The tracks were taken out and the elevators were pulled down in 1972. Now, the farmers truck their grain to alternate points in Manitoba and Saskatchewan.

Some of the grain buyers were: Mr. Harem, British American; Wright 1911-21; Rod McIntosh (G.G.) 1916; Sid Finkbeiner (Pool); Garnet Rusk (Pool); Pete Robinson (B.A.); Buchanan (B.A.); Herity (G.G.); Pearce (G.G.); McNish (G.G.), Dinty Moore (G.G.); White (Pool); Early (Pool); Joe Brown (Pool); Hyslop (Pool); Buick (G.G.); Sutherland (G.G.); Harvey Munro (Pool); Anderson (Pool); W.R. Robb (G.G. and Pool); W. Nielson (Pool); Colin Wilson (Pool).

The British American Grain Elevator Co. located in Dropmore in (circa) 1909.

The Dropmore Railway Station.

The Pool grain elevators in Dropmore.

The old steam engine on the railway track running through Dropmore.

Entertainment

The Dropmore Orchestra consisted of Jessie Wardle on violin, Reg Lewis on drums and saxophone; Cedric Rowan on clarinet and piano, along with Beatrice Wood, while she was teaching here. They played for many a dance in Dropmore.

The make-believe orchestra consisting of (L-R) John Dalle, Albert Manweiler, Harold Jones and Henry Schneider.

The Dropmore Orchestra (Back Row) Ernie Johnson, Jessie Wardle (Front Row) Cedric Rowan, Reg Lewis.

The Parklanders Orchestra (L-R) Charlie Bernhard, Harry Driedger, Fred Piwniuk, Harry Muir and Harold Schrader.

The Rochedale Drama Club.

The Dropmore Chicks
by Elizabeth Roe

In October of 1979, the Shellmouth Municipality provided the money for a banquet to honour the Senior Citizens of Dropmore and nearby districts.

Twenty ladies gathered at the Dropmore Hall to plan the entertainment. At first the majority felt the schoolchildren of the area could provide the entertainment. Now who was going to lead them and plan the program? Liz Roe piped up and said, "Why can't we ladies, just for once, provide the entertainment, ourselves!"

Reluctance and self doubt were obvious at first. Then, slowly, the ladies began to thinking, "Why not?"

Liz Roe and Edith Mann planned the program with suggestions and music supplied by Curtis Campbell, Music Consultant for Yorkdale School Division in Yorkton, SK. Edith and I sat up late at night writing the words to the songs and doing a lot of giggling over some of the silly phrases we accidentally created, but wisely didn't use. The practices took place at the Roe home. Man! Did we practise!

The night of the program, we wore period costumes - long dresses. The program was a success! After the program, while we were still embued with success, someone said, "Why don't we do this again!" Edith said that Togo was looking for new entertainment for their Seniors' Christmas Program. Did we want to go? Everyone shouted, "Yes!"

Caroline Hunter jokingly said, "We should have a name for our group." This was serious business! Several very proper titles were suggested such as "The Dropmore Ladies" and "The Assiniboine Valley Ladies".

Elaine Digby turned to the group and said, "Let's call ourselves, 'The Dropmore Chicks'!"

We performed in Togo, four consecutive years, beginning in 1979. For our first performance we chose old, favourite songs that had a Christmas theme. Since the stage wasn't very high, I sat to direct the choir. Edith Mann did a superb job of introducing the numbers and keeping the program moving along smoothly. At the end of the program, Erma Baumung said, "I know Liz Roe and Edith Mann, but I don't know anyone else. Please introduce the husbands as well as the ladies!"

Edith proceeded to do so. Lloyd Shearer wasn't there: but when Edith introduced Marlene Shearer, four of our men stood up. Edith said, "You have to watch those guys. They're tricky!"

In our second Program at Togo, we performed in the new hall. Edith and I made up a song about the men in Togo: Bert Franklin, Archie Parker, Howard Wilson, Phil Hern, Harv McMurray, Orville Wilson and Bill Harper. All of them enjoyed the ribbing and attention. We also accompanied our singing with ukuleles which added a nice touch. But we badly bombed out in our singing of "The Little Drummer Boy". Betty Bauereiss and Caroline Hunter, clad in long underwear doing a frolicsome dance while the rest of us sang, "Vinter Undervear" helped restore our spirits. Marla Mann capped that act with her beautiful playing of "The Music Box Dancer" and "The Pied Piper".

In our third and fourth programs in Togo, along with our singing of sacred songs, interspersed with lively rollicking tunes, we had a beautiful reading by Phyllis Morrison entitled, "Friends", and a Cockney rendition of Cinderella given by Elinor Digby, that had everyone roaring, including the "Chicks". The people of Togo appreciated our efforts and treated us very well.

In August, 1980, we sang four songs at the Yorkton Threshermen's Reunion. One song in particular was giving us a lot of trouble. We went over and over it until we felt we could sing it without a mistake. That day, just as we got to that part of the song, the train passed through Yorkton and the "Woo, Woo" of the train whistle drowned out our words. Marilyn Roe, on guitar, was our source of music.

Once, we sang two songs at the MacNutt Fall Concert. We made the mistake of forming a straight line across the stage. The acoustics were poor in the rink. As a result, the altos couldn't hear the sopranos and our harmony wasn't as good as it could have been. In our first song, we paid tribute to Roland Wagner and John Melnick.

We had a ball at the Shellmouth Centennial in 1982. We dressed up in gowns and Native costume, reminiscent of 1882. Fred Piwniuk, with his big green wagon and nicely decked out horses, was our transportation. We took part in the parade, singing our hearts out and clowning when the opportunity arose.

The night of our performance at the Russell Leisure Club was a very cold, icy-road night. Two carloads of "Chicks", struck out for Russell. I rode in Gen Kurtenbach's car. Most of the time, I kept my eyes shut and prayed because the car took some wicked slides. But Gen was a good driver and we got there. The Seniors really enjoyed the program, particularly our harmonizing in "The Farmer's Song and "Amazing Grace", and our jolly rendition of "Tie Me Kangaroo Down" with Janie Wiesner melodiously shouting, "Altogether Now!" to get the Seniors to join in singing the chorus.

At the Elks Hall in Russell we had a great time! Caroline Hunter and Betty Bauereiss did their "Vinter Underwear" number which brought the house down. The people were amazed that girls our age could play the ukuleles so well! We were too, but, we weren't admitting it. After our program ended, no one wanted to go home. A group of people, including many of us, gathered around the piano and sang song after song. That was the night Ada Dugan accidentally forgot her ukulele on the trunk of Marlene Shearer's car. She was a bit upset about it when she got home: but nothing could be done about it then. Next morning, Ada got a phone call from a nice Russell lady who had found the ukulele intact. Ada had put her name, address and phone number on the ukulele case!

The year we took part in the entertainment for the Russell Rural Fair we again had Fred Piwniuk with his wagon and horses to transport us. Just before joining the parade, Fred had to pull up to a filling station to get air for a sad looking tire. At the fairgrounds we performed on an open air stage with the aid of one standing microphone. Our audience was a good thirty feet away from us. I doubt if anyone heard us even though we were in good shouting form.

We put on five concerts in Roblin. Our first concert was for a Ladies Curling Bonspiel. We'd written a curling play that supposedly involved Maggie Cameron. Mrs. Souter, and Ellen Robertson, acted out by our Chicks. Of course, Ellen was ragging Maggie about hitting the "wee hoose". Maggie couldn't see the reason for hitting any house. And Mrs. Bowley was yelling at Mrs. Souter, "You're too narrow!"

Maggie replies, "I dinna think so!"

Another song we sang had the words, "Three little words you'll hear in your sleep are so important - "Sweep! Sweep! Sweep!"

Then we visited and entertained at the Roblin Residences. One song we made up was about Mr. Souter, Mrs. Laurie, Mrs. Ben Alexander, Mrs. Comrie, Mrs. Britcher, and Mrs. Anne Lunan. They loved it! Many of us, until this time, didn't realize how much the Seniors appreciate just a wee bit of attention. Another of our songs was, "Smile Awhile". We ended each verse with the words, "Reach right out shake his/her hand and smile." While singing, we too walked through the seniors shaking hands and smiling at them. After our program we were treated to a sumptuous lunch.

Next, we performed for the residents of Maple Manor. Again we wrote a song about a few of the residents: Mrs. Maguire, Edith

Andrews, Mrs. Staples, Mr. Arnott, Mr. Stauffer, and Annie Short. They loved it. Again we were treated to a delicious lunch. Then to end the evening, Vivian Ward played the piano and everyone sang Christmas carols. What a lovely evening of fellowship.

A few days later we performed for the residents of Crocus Court. Mr. Dixon, the oldest resident, had been a British soldier in the Boer War. We had changed many of the words in "Marching to Pretoria" to enhance his part in that war. Well! He didn't want to come out of his room. He was embarrassed about his appearance, felt he was too crippled to be in our company. I went in to see him and told him we had written a song just for him. Would he please come out and listen to us sing the one song. He thought it over for a minute, then grudgingly consented. I wheeled him out and all the Chicks made a point of saying "hello" to him. He enjoyed his song and the attention so much that he decided to stay for the whole program! Of course we made a point of making a fuss over all the residents. Many hummed along as we sang. They may have forgotten some of the words but they still remembered the melodies.

Our last performance in Roblin was for their Moonshine Daze. We dressed as tramps. Olive Digby introduced the songs and all of us hammed it up. We sang three songs: "Moonshine Daze", "I Want A Crop", and "Happiness is Free".

We performed three times in Inglis, MB. The first time was part of a Variety Show in the Inglis Centre. One of the songs we sang was a made up song called the "Inglis Polka" in which we sang about the Mackenzies, Kopetskys, Kosses, Liskes, Zipricks and Bombachs. There was a gentle line of ribbing running through it which amused the audience: "Another name for Inglis town would be Liskeville. There's more of them than ever, what's happened to the pill?"

The next time we sang three songs at the Inglis Ladies Curling Banquet. They were "Happiness is Free", "O Lord Tell Our Skip Not To Mumble", and "Down In The Valley". Then one of the Chicks read 'The Ten Commandments of a Curler'. I liked the ninth commandment: "Thou shalt have no discourse with thine adversary while his foot is in the hack and his hand is on the rock, but if thou wilt, thou can'st pray for him."

Our last performance in Inglis was to honour Mr. Wally Mackenzie on his retirement from political life. When I peeked through the stage curtains and saw all those MLA's sitting in the front rows, I almost swallowed my tongue. But I soon realized that the other Chicks were nervous too. I calmed down. We performed without a hitch. One of our songs involved a bit of clowning and the use of signs which amused the audience.

We performed for three showers in our Dropmore Hall. They were for Diane Shearer, Charlotte Kurtenbach, and Marla Mann. We made up songs about each girl and her future husband, nothing serious, just gentle teasing.

Perhaps the most enjoyable programs we ever planned were the ones in our own community. Sometimes we played a small part in the program. Other times we were asked to plan the entire program. I'm talking about wedding anniversaries. Not only the Chicks took part, we dragged men in too if we could.

The first 25th anniversary program was for Jim and Liz Roe. I prepared all the cakes, slices and fillings for the sandwiches. Marilyn, our daughter, was to look after the raw veggies. She told me she had asked Caroline Hunter and Edith Mann to help her. What she didn't tell me was that all the Chicks were helping and under Edith Mann's direction had even planned and practised for a program. And this was August 17th when every farmer is running six ways at once. The memory of that program will always remain dear to us. The mock wedding with Marlene Shearer as groom, Dave Wiesner as the bride, Caroline Hunter as a bridesmaid and Marv Bernhard as a very serious preacher, was absolutely hilarious. But when Irv Young, all decked out in a fancy gown, rose and so piously sang "O Promise Me", straining his voice to the limit to reach the high notes, but not quite succeeding, we thought we'd die laughing. It was so funny!

Lloyd and Marlene Shearer's 25th anniversary occurred in 1982. Elaine Digby, Mary Bernhard, Caroline Hunter, and I gathered in Mary Bernhard's kitchen to write the words for some songs. My job was to write the introductions to the songs. We did a lot of laughing over the goofy rhymes we sometimes created: but, in no time we had a program. Now all the Chicks had to do was practise for at least two weeks to perfect it. On the anniversary evening we sang several songs, one of which was "The Shearer History" sung to the tune of "Mocking Bird Hill": 'Tra la la Tweedle dee dee. At home Lloyd's a slave! He has to cook his meals in a microwave!' Marlene had just started her job as a crop adjuster and we had to needle her about that too!

Our first forty-fifth anniversary was for Olive and Maurice Digby. I was called to the Garry Digby home about ten o'clock one evening. With Elinor and Garry giving me ideas and lots of coffee, I finished writing the program by one-thirty a.m. It consisted of scribbles and crossed out phrases throughout, accompanied we hoped with some good descriptions and dialogue. It took Elinor about five minutes, using the typewriter and carbon paper, to make three copies. Faye Orr read the program over three times, and on the evening of the performance she handled the job of mistress of ceremonies like a pro. We sang and played a medley of old time, favourite songs. Elinor recited "Rindercella" which was hilarious as usual. After singing a 'roast' song we decided to save face by singing "Amazing Grace."

      Then there was the fiftieth anniversary for Jim and Florence Robertson which was a real hoot! We made up some dandy songs about their courting days. Jim was quite a runner as a young man. Florence never had a chance! Of course we had to have a mock wedding. Maggie Cameron was the preacher and with her Scottish drawl, she was very funny. Mervyn Kelly was the blushing bride. The things Maggie was saying would have made any bride blush!. Olive Digby was the groom. She was a great actress! Barb Kelly was the anxious father of the bride. Anxious to get rid of her, that is!

      John and Violet Robertson's fortieth anniversary also had a mock wedding. Bill Doole was the bridesmaid. Walter Kurtenbach was the bride. Maurice Digby was the father of the bride and Mary Bernhard was a very convincing preacher. Bill waltzed in first, looking very demur. Then in came Walter looking more embarrassed than anything else. Maurice rushed to assist the 'bride' up the aisle and almost fell over Walter. Irv Young's rendition of "O Promise Me" cracked us all up. He sounded like a baying coyote. And we didn't hesitate to remind John that he'd backed into a well during one dating session.

      Irvin and Viola Young's fortieth anniversary was supposed to be a secret. Elinor and Garry Digby invited them over for supper. The neighbours and friends got there first and hid their cars behind the barn. Naturally the Youngs were very surprised and happy to see us all there. I can still remember seeing the tears in Viola's eyes when she spotted her daughter, Leah, who had really planned the surprise along with the help of a few neighbours. The Chicks entertained in a very relaxed manner, singing the tunes we knew Irv and Vi liked. Leah, herself regaled us with stories of her escapades in Saskatoon.

      The fiftieth anniversary of Joe and Maggie Simair took place on a nice, warm day in summer. The whole Simair family was there including Joe's sister, some of Maggie's brothers and sisters and also the gentleman who had been Joe's best man. Our program contained a poem called 'Maggie's Window' which spoke of the many changes Maggie witnessed as she often gazed out that window throughout the years. Our songs revealed their kind nature as well as their love for fun. In one song, we jokingly referred to Joe's dislike of school and the naughty tricks he often played on women. It was not unusual for a visiting woman to find a piece of wood, a small potato, or a stone in her overshoe when she went to go home.

      Bob and Elaine Digby celebrated their twenty-fifth anniversary in 1987. We sang "We've Been Working On the Cattle", - 'We've been working on the cattle. All the whole d-- day. We just have to get them ready. The show's on Saturday!', "Down In The Valley" - 'From this valley we soon will be leaving. We'll not miss the steep hill or no phones.', "It's A Small World", - 'It's a time to honour their 25th year', and "Elaine", sung to the tune of "Daisy! Daisy!" and using almost the same words except she wasn't riding any bicycle! Their children and nieces put on a play that was very funny. Reg Robertson's talk on Bobby's fishing and boating techniques had us all in stitches.

      Bill and Buryle Doole celebrated their fortieth anniversary on June 6, 1986. We sang three songs: "Blue Bird On Your Window Sill"- 'In Feb. '43, Bill blew into town to find a place to hang his hat and carefully look around'! etc.: "Casey Jones"- 'Come ye folks, if you want to hear; a story about some folks so dear. He really didn't give a darn. They raised their kids on strawberry jam etc.': and "Irish Eyes Are Smiling". I also read a poem about a dedicated farmer named Bill Doole who had to get off his farm binder and search for a missing chain in the grass. He was without doubt a praying man who never swore! Since Bill had taken part in so many mock weddings we were out to get even! Irv Young played the bride. Caroline Hunter was the groom, and our own special preacher, Marv Bernhard, tied the knot. With Irv cooing, Caroline protesting, and Mary scolding, it was hilarious. Dancing, food and "bubbly" completed a perfect evening. We put on a surprise twenty-fifty anniversary for Edith and Fred Mann's at Ada Dugan's farm. Relatives of both Fred and Edith were there. There was an outdoor picnic lunch supplied by the community. We ate and visited. Then we went indoors to entertain the Manns. We sang a number of their favourite tunes. One was a beautiful German song sung by Jutta and Erich Levens. Of course we had to sing, "When Irish Eyes are Smiling" for Edith, along

Our performance in October, 1979 for the Seniors of Dropmore and nearby districts.
(L-R) Marlene Shearer, Elaine Digby, Gen Kurtenbach, Betty Ferris. Edith Mann, Mary Bernhard (hidden), Anne Petz, Liz Roe, Eleanor Digby, Phyllis Morrison, Pauley Dietrich, Buryle Doole and Caroline Hunter.

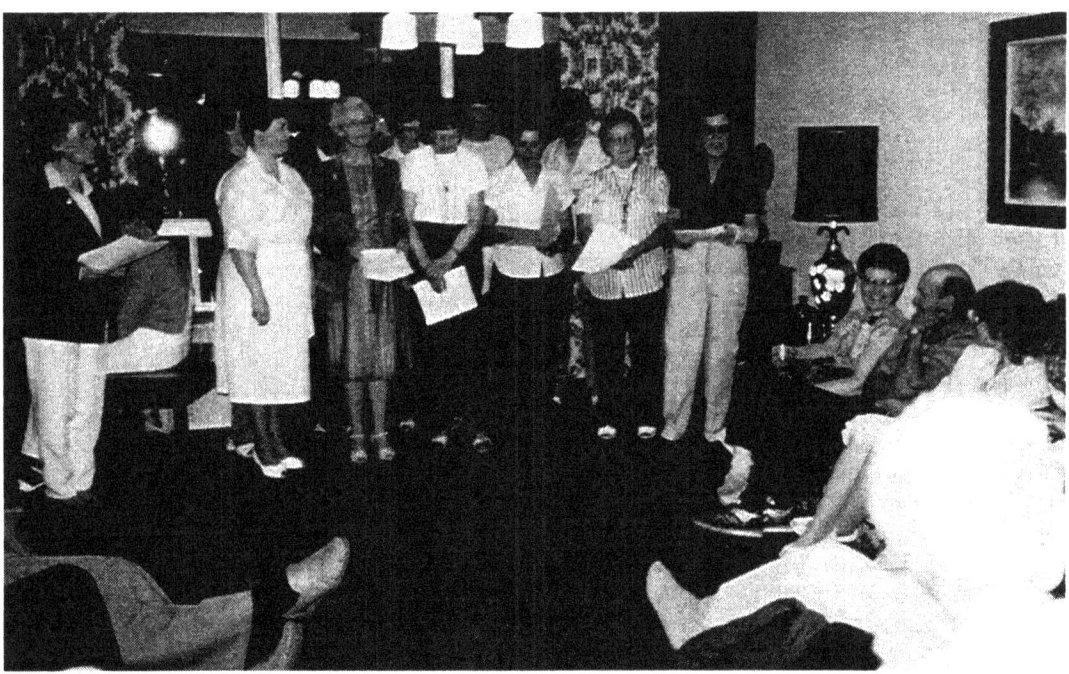

Performing for Fred and Edith Mann's 25th Wedding Anniversary at Ada Dugan's home.
(Back row L-R) Ada Dugan, Eleanor Digby, Buryle Doole, Elaine Digby, Betty Bauereiss. (Front row L-R) Janie Wiesner, Viola Young, Caroline Hunter, Phyllis Morrison, Mary Bernhard and Liz Roe.

with other favourites tunes. Our last performance as "The Dropmore Chicks" occurred in the spring of 1989. It was a Farewell for Caroline Hunter who was moving to Roblin, MB. Janie Wiesner was in charge of the program. We sang two songs. One was made up about Caroline and how Roblin would have to watch out because Caroline was a girl full of pep! Next, we sang Caroline's favourite song: "Little Green Valley". Then everybody sang "For She's A Jolly Good Fellow". And most of us were in tears. We hated to see her leave the district. She had never missed a singing practice. Besides, she was that rarity, an alto singer!

Tribute must be paid to the wonderful ladies who played the piano or guitar to accompany us in our singing. Marlene Shearer and Marilyn Roe accompanied us a few times on guitar when a piano wasn't available. Marla Mann was our first accompanist on piano and she even played a few piano solos to liven up our repertoire. Betty Ferris and Marlene Shearer took turns playing the piano with Betty finally ending up doing most of it when Marlene started working at her new job. Without these ladies, our choir would never have got off the ground.

On behalf of the Dropmore Chicks I'd like to end with the words we used so often to end almost all of the programs: "So here's to you. May your skies be blue. And your love blest. That's our best to you!"

Bridges

The first bridge over the Assiniboine River at Dropmore was built of wood in 1908. A new steel bridge replaced the wood one in 1960.

The wooden bridge at Dropmore.

Pyott's Bridge

To meet the growing demands for safe and convenient crossings over the Assiniboine River, more bridges were needed. In 1905, the scow used for many years to cross the Assiniboine at Castleavery was replaced by a Warren Truss Bridge and further north, a modern wooden structure was built at Pyotts on Sec. 2-25-29.

A second bridge at Pyotts was built in 1938 and damaged by the flood of 1956. This bridge was then replaced in 1956 with a steel bridge.

With the completion of the Shellmouth Dam, this last bridge was taken apart and moved.

The first Pyott Bridge built in 1905.

The Pyott Bridge washed out..

Another view of the wash out at Pyott's Bridge.

The second Pyott Bridge built in 1938.

The third Pyott Bridge built in 1956.

Rural Telephones
The first telephones were in 1912 in this area.

In 1913 there were 91 telephones listed from the Russell exchange.

The Inglis Telephone Office was opened in Nov. 1954 with the Dial System. Dropmore was under the Inglis listings.

In 1975, Russell Dial System office was opened, and in July of 1991, cable was buried for private lines. All multi-party lines were deregulated in Oct. 24, 1991. The ending of an era of people listening in on the neighbours' calls. Now, everyone enjoys a private line with many modern "calling" features available.

Hydro
Manitoba Hydro came to the Village around 1947 and the rural areas were connected in the early 1950's. This gave many the opportunity to have the luxuries of a fridge and a deep freeze, doing away with the ice houses.

Stockyard
The stockyard and boarding platform were built east of the elevators, so farmers were able to load their cattle and ship them to Winnipeg by rail.

Nurses
Jessie Anderson R.N.
Isobel (Dugan) Johnson R.N.
Both graduated from St. Boniface Hospital. They worked in the area under the direction of Dr. Shaw and Dr. Brownlee.

Jessie Anderson, R.N.

Isobel (Dugan) Johnson, R.N. graduated in 1927.

Shellmouth Dam Project
Construction of the Shellmouth Dam on the Assiniboine River near the mouth of the Shell River started in 1964. The lake is called "Lake of the Prairies" and the park known as Asessippi Provincial Park" officially opened July 8, 1973.

The Dam.

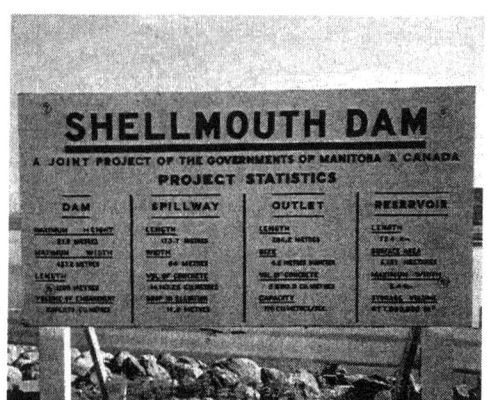

Shellmouth Dam Project Sign.

Pyott's west campground - aerial view taken in 1988.

The control at the dam.

Pyott's west campground - aerial view taken in 1990.

This lake is the largest man made lake on the prairies. It is 40 miles long, a mile and half wide and approximately 70 feet deep in places. The purpose of this dam is for water conservation and flood control. It brought changes to the valley from agriculture to tourism.

Pyott's West Campground
by Mervyn and Barb Kelly

In 1986, we, Mervyn and Barb Kelly started the Pyott's West Campground. It is situated on the west side of Lake of the Prairies where Robert Pyott had lived until the valley was flooded (SE-3-25-29W R.M. of Shell River).

The first summer was spent clearing lots for seasonal campers, getting hydro to the sites along with sewage disposal and roads. Buildings were put up as needed. In 1986 camping fees were $4.00 per night.

We now have electrical and non electrical sites, 75 seasonal sites, lake shore lots along with group sites. A playground for the children. A convenience store at the campground to supply you with all your needs. Along with boat and motor rentals.

We offer "Family Fun in the Sun" from the middle of May to the end of September.

Equipment shed at the campground.

Campers enjoying the nice weather.

Entertainment with Tera Lynn Moore.

Ice still on the lake.

Kilman Enterprises Ltd.

Kilman Enterprises is owned by Lorne and Myra and Jim and Annette Mansell of Russell.

Kilman bought the land (N24-23-29) comprising of 115 acres of lake front property from crown lands in the spring of 1994. Kilman had been working on a proposal for a cottage, tourism and recreation development since 1989.

This land had originally been homesteaded by Archibald Henry Goodbun. They called the homestead the "Maze". His son Archie and Cora (Larsen) then lived there until they sold it to George Dietrich. The Dietrich family farmed the Maze until the inception of the Shellmouth Dam, at which time it was purchased by the government.

Upon gaining title to the land, Kilman surveyed and built a road and subdivision of twenty-six lake front lots. By October 1st, 1994, only three of these lots remained. In Spring of 1995, Kilman surveyed another subdivision of six lake front lots. To date two of those have been sold.

By 1997 Kilman proposes to have four rental cottages and a lodge in operation. The lodge will be situated where the Goodbun and Dietrich yard site was.

Kilman would like to keep the development as "environmentally friendly" as possible. There are many wild flowers, trees and wildlife that create aesthetic value. Nature hikes and cross country trails will be available along the valley.

The Kilman Property - 1993, an aerial photo of the yard site and the 115 acres.

Road construction going down to the lake development.

KILMAN COTTAGE DEVELOPMENT

LAKE OF THE PRAIRIES

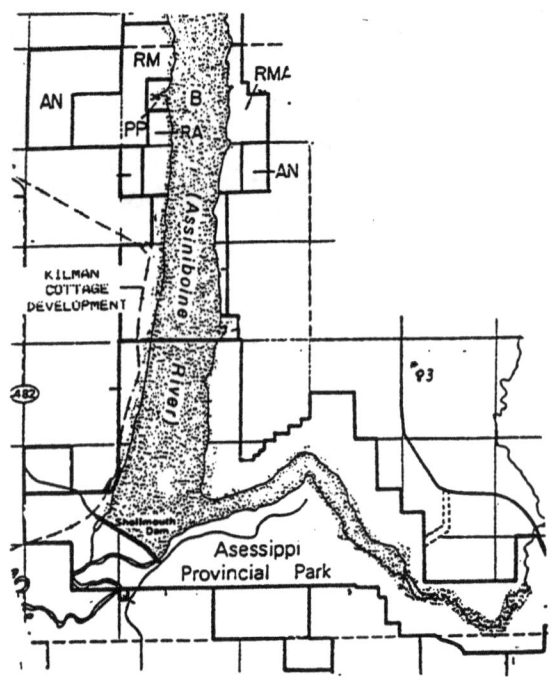

KILMAN ENTERPRISES LTD.

 Jim & Annette Mansell
Tel. # 1-204-773-2157
Lorne & Myra Kilkenny
Tel. # 1-204-773-2765

A portion of the brochure illustrating the Kilman Development..

Rivendell Cross Country Ski Club
by Isobel Wendell

Rivendell Cross Country Ski Club was born out of the Shell Hills Ski Club, which was initiated and run by Bob Pritschau. Bob, a great ski enthusiast passed away after a long fight with cancer. His gentle ways and contributions to cross country skiing will be remembered by all the area's skiers.

The Rivendell Ski Club members developed 10 kilometres of trail in 1992. We moved a small house to the trail head. With a little renovating, this became our Club House. A wood fire keeps the Club House warm on weekends. We also purchased Bob's rental skis. We charge a small trail fee to help to cover some of the expenses of maintaining, packing and tracking the trails. For those who do not have equipment of their own, we rent skis, boots and poles. In our first year of operation our trails were skied by more than 500 skiers.

We added 6 kilometres in 1993 and for the 1994 season we had 22 kilometres of packed and tracked trails. Two Team Canada Olympic coaches have been on Rivendell trails. Both were excited to find this calibre of trail being developed in rural Manitoba.

The Rivendell facility is located 32 kilometres north of Russell and 20 kilometres south of Roblin along the scenic Assiniboine Valley. The original 10 kilometres of trails follow the crest of the east side of the valley. The newer trails take skiers into the more challenging hills within the valley. The terrain provides skiers with both interesting challenges and beautiful views, and has inspired our club members to get out and ski a lot.

Our Club has hosted Club and Regional Races. Several different groups of school children have skied Rivendell. In 1995 we ran a successful children's program on Saturday mornings. We hope to expand on this program in the coming season. But best of all are those clear winter nights when the moon is full. We meet at the Club House and ski in groups. The winter nights have a deep quiet. Sometimes the trees and the snow along the trail sparkle in the light of the moon and it truly is a Winter Wonderland, or in the words of one five-year-old night skier, "a fairyland." We meet back at the Club House for hot chocolate and a visit, a perfect prairie winter evening.

The development and maintenance of the Rivendell trails and Club programs and events have been possible only through the enthusiasm, dedication and hard work of all of the Rivendell Cross Country Ski Club members. Bob

Mickelson, Doug Lyon, and Tim Wendell have spent countless hours developing and maintaining the trails. The Neuhofer families, John Skinner, Marlene Lyon, Jo-anne Hamilton, Hugh Skinner, the Gregoires, Debbie St. Germaine, and the rest of the Wendells along with Bob, Doug, Tim and other Club members have planted trees, worked on the Club house, cleared trails, mowed trails, organized and run various programs and events, and donated time, equipment and furnishings.

The Rivendell Cross Country Ski Club enthusiastically promotes Cross Country Skiing. We encourage everyone, no matter what your age or ability, to enjoy the prairie winter by getting out there and skiing. See you on the trail.

Youngsters playing on a hill.

Club House at the Rivendell and Country Ski Club.

(L-R) John Skinner, behind Bob Michelson, Doug Lyon, and Isobel Wendell.

Frank Skinner's Dream
taken from "The Western People"

Towering over the farmland, 13 miles south of Roblin, MB, is a tall stand of spruce, pine, poplar and cottonwood. The trees were planted 50 or more years ago by pioneer horticulturist Frank Leith Skinner.

Although Skinner died 28 years ago, the huge stand of trees is more than a memorial to him. Within the enclosure, hidden from the road, are rows of tiny nursery trees, plots of perennials, pots of seedlings, and greenhouses full of newly rooted cuttings.

In the past 22 years, Skinner's Hardy Plant Nursery has been revived by his son, Hugh. It is a difficult and sometimes unprofitable task to keep a nursery running in a rural area, isolated from large centres of population. But keeping Frank Skinner's legacy alive is important to both his children and his widow.

Frank Leith Skinner came to Canada in 1895 at the age of 13. His father, John Skinner, was a fish merchant in Scotland who broke during a big disruption in the fish markets. His mother, Isabella, kept the family together, and in her mid-50s brought her eight children and her husband to the Dropmore area of west central Manitoba to start a new life as homesteaders. Two of the older children had preceded the family to the area.

But gardening in Manitoba was discouraging. Few European varieties of trees or perennials would grow. Skinner's first experiments crossing hardy native varieties with imported trees and plants started him on his lifelong work as a horticulturist.

Skinner's formal schooling ended when the family moved to Canada. In this new country, Helen Skinner said, "he went to school about two days and decided he knew more than the teacher. That was quite characteristic."

From then on, he educated himself. Most of the books and papers he collected were about plants, and since he loved them, he found it easy to learn.

As a young man, Skinner was sickly (he lost the use of part of one lung through pneumonia) but that did not stop him from establishing a homestead and farming with his brother. In 1907 they built a two-storey wooden house and Frank began planting trees around it. Eventually he took over the cattle part of the business while his brother grew the grain.

In 1909, Skinner joined the Manitoba Horticulture Society and was soon presenting papers to society meetings. He met provincial and Dominion horticulturists, who encouraged his work. He began corresponding with horticulturists from around the world and collecting seeds and cuttings. He was particularly interested in plants from parts of Asia which had latitude and climate similar to that on the Canadian prairies. When Skinner eventually visited botanical gardens in the United States, Great Britain and Europe with whom he had corresponded for years, he knew so much about plant breeding he had no trouble talking to researchers with PhDs.

When farming markets started to drop in the 1920's Skinner decided to establish a Hardy Plant Nursery. Sales of plants from the nursery would support his hobby of plant breeding. His land, on the northern edge of what was then considered suitable for farming, was ideal for developing plants that could grow throughout the Prairies. Since the nursery was so isolated, it had to be primarily a mail-order business.

Many of the large trees now growing on the site were planted in the 1930's. "That was a time when a lot of people would work for board and a meal and not too much cash," said Hugh Skinner.

Frank Skinner eventually introduced 248 plant species to the prairies. He had improved upon 144 of them himself. Of particular importance were the trees he developed for windbreaks and shade, including fast-growing poplars, but Skinner also developed trees for fruit and for beauty. With a twig from the Arnold Arboretum at Harvard University in Boston, he grew the first hardy pear on the prairies. By crossing French lilac with Korean seedlings, he developed early blooming, heavily perfumed bushes.

Because Skinner loved roses and found few that would grow in Western Canada, he crossed strains imported from Scotland with wild Manitoba roses. He also imported roses from Manchuria and the Soviet Union and bred them selectively to develop hardy varieties. He was well known for his work with lilies and in 1933 won an award for his Lilium Maxiwill, developed when he crossed a Korean with a Chinese lily. Skinner's lily had both the sturdy stem of the Korean and the delicate beauty of the Chinese.

"Frank had to be a dreamer to be a plant breeder in this country," Helen said. One of his biggest problems was that his plant varieties could not be patented. He spent many years and a great deal of money developing a variety until it was ready to market. By the time he was through that process the larger commercial operations could have it in production and sell it for less money.

Skinner was always a quiet man and remained a bachelor until he was in his mid-60s. Then Helen Cumming came to the nursery to visit her brother, who was running the business while Skinner concentrated on plant breeding. Helen had stayed at home to look after her parents and after they died, she trained as a nurse. When her brother's wife died, leaving several children, she came to Dropmore to see if she could be of any help. When she went back to Winnipeg to work as a nurse, she and Frank Skinner corresponded and visited back and forth. In 1947, when he was 65 and she was 33, they were married. Over the next eleven years they had five children.

Frank Skinner wrote numerous articles and a book about plant breeding. In 1947, in recognition of his work as a horticulturist, he received an honorary LL. D degree from the University of Manitoba. Earlier, he had been honoured with an M.B.E. Years ago, at a convention in Cleveland, Ohio, the United States Plant Propagators' Society praised Dr. Skinner by announcing that he had "done more for hardy plants than anyone on this continent."

"Both in North America and Overseas, Dr. Skinner is recognized as a leading authority on plant hardiness. By crossing flowers and grafting fruit trees, he has enabled those living in the colder parts of Canada and the United States to enjoy gardens and orchards in locations where cultivation was once impossible."

He always encouraged young plant breeders, including his children. Two of them, his son Hugh and daughter Heather, eventually studied horticulture at University.

In 1972, Frank Skinner's second oldest son, Hugh, graduated from the University of Manitoba, with a degree in horticulture. He began working at the nursery part time in 1972, and in 1977 he moved back to operate the nursery full time.

It took quite a while to get started again, and he had a lot to learn. One of his biggest jobs was clearing away the old nursery stock that had gone wild. He left the huge trees around the old homestead; it looks like a jungle with cedars, caragena, honeysuckle, scotch pine and white spruce towering over the Russian thistle around their trunks.

Plant markets have changed since Frank Skinner's time. Years ago, most plants were dug out of the field and sold in the spring. Now, many plants are grown and sold in pots, which means they can be transplanted at any time of the year without disturbing their roots. Hugh Skinner sells about half of his plants directly to gardeners, and the other half to distributors. His biggest market is trees and shrubs, although he also has a popular collection of perennials. Some of the plant markets were developed by his father, and although the official title of his business is Skinner's Nursery Ltd., he also calls it, "The Home of Dropmore Hardy Plants."

Skinner keeps 30 acres cultivated and maintains another 20 acres of grounds. He uses a rotation system to keep the soil fertile, growing two crops of nursery stock, then a crop of alfalfa which he plows under. Most of his plants grow in the fields; his greenhouses are used only for propagation and rooting. He uses a water-saving trickle irrigation system, installed underground near the plant roots, because the nursery is on a high point of land and his only source of water is dugouts.

Sometimes, Hugh finds the business discouraging. Our market in this area is rather limited. He is so busy running the business, he has little time for plant breeding, other than experiments with new varieties from universities and research stations.

Frank Skinner Arboretum Trail

In 1994, with sponsorship of the Roblin Soil Conservation Corp., The Canada/Manitoba Forestry Agreement and the Assiniboine Birdtail Soil and Water Conservation Association, Hugh Skinner began developing the Frank Skinner Arboretum Trail. In the Fall of 1994, the Frank Skinner Arboretum Corp., a non-profit corporation was formed to oversee development of the trail. The trail is to honour Frank and to allow better public access to the diverse and magnificent trees which are growing on the nursery site.

The trail begins in the yard of the first Skinner family home on the property where Scots, Pine, Larch, and Spruce, some planted as early as 1912, tower to 80-90 feet. The walk combines areas of native poplar and willow with landscaped areas which are planted with more exotic plants. The native areas show a variety of wild flowers including lady-slippers, wood violets, wintergreen, and ferns. The landscaped areas display trees such as Red Pine from the Whiteshell in Eastern Manitoba, Rocky Mountain Douglas Fir from Jasper, Alberta, Dahurian Larch from Eastern Siberia, Mongolian Linden from Mongolia and Swedish Columnar Aspen from Sweden.

At the south end of the walk is the Historical Greenhouse Selection Site where Frank Skinner started his seedlings in a small greenhouse and later transplanted them for testing.

In 1995, work has continued on the trail with sponsorship of the Manitoba Sustainable Development Fund. Program development has begun with the co-operation of Assiniboine Community College. The Skinner family hope that you will walk along the trails and enjoy the peace of nature and that you will be able to take part in programs at the trail.

Located on Highway 83
23 km south of Roblin
or
31 km north of Russell,
MB

Trail is open during daylight hours
Spring to Fall
Free of Charge - Donations Accepted

Skinner Nursery and home, 1947 (courtesy Manitoba Archives).

Dr. Frank Skinner and his famous Lily.

Mrs. Helen Skinner and son Hugh unveil Plaque honoring Dr. Skinner, 1967.

Section Two

Historical Family ties to our Communities in

Castleavery
Dropmore
Grainsby
Rochedale

John Allan Anderson Family

John Allan Anderson, born 17th August, 1860, in Sterling, Scotland. He married Christian Skinner, daughter of John Skinner and Isabella Scott-Bernie, born 18th May, 1870, in Roseharty, Scotland, on August 4th, 1897.

John Allan Anderson and his brother Jim came to Canada from Scotland, landing in Halifax, NS. on May 24th, 1881. They homesteaded in Foxwarren, MB. originally. They were among the first settlers in the Castleavery district and began farming there in 1886. They were known as the Valley Andersons to differentiate them from two brothers with the same names who had homesteaded near MacNutt, Sk.

Their three children, Gilbert, Jessie and Allan, none of whom married, stayed on the Castleavery homestead until 1966. The erection of the Shellmouth Dam flooded the Assiniboine Valley, including the Anderson farm. They then retired to Roblin, MB. The three children were all born in Castleavery.

Gilbert Allan was born June 8th, 1898. Gilbert died from a stroke August 30th, 1967. Gilbert loved the outdoors, doing a great deal of hunting and trapping.

Jessie Bella was born December 20th, 1899. She graduated from the St. Boniface School of Nursing in 1927. Besides practising her profession in Winnipeg, Jessie nursed at The Pas, MB and in Vancouver, B.C. Jessie died on November 6th, 1981.

John Allan was born July 5th, 1901. Allan spent most of his life on the family farm, with the exception of two summers when he went north to work on the construction of the Hudson Bay Railway from The Pas, MB to Churchill, MB. Allan also had a great love of the outdoors. He made many trips to Kindersley, SK to hunt geese. He also looked forward to elk and moose hunting trips to a cabin in the Duck Mountains with others from the community. Allan passed away on October 23, 1993.

Gilbert and Allan were noted for their Aberdeen Angus cattle. When they shipped a carload of calves, Mr. Spigelman, the Roblin Cattle buyer, would notify a cattle buyer in Iowa the day the Anderson cattle would be on sale in Winnipeg. Many times that buyer would arrive to buy the Anderson calves, often topping the market by as much as .05 cents per pound.

Jake & Lydia Andres & Family

by Ken and Lorraine Andres

Mr. & Mrs. Jake Andres and family moved from 6 miles west of MacNutt, SK to the Fred Andres farm which they purchased in the fall of 1949. They had a family of three children: Ken, Patricia, Gerald.

This farm was located 3 miles east of the Village of MacNutt, SK on the Manitoba border.

Jack and Lydia farmed in the area from 1949 to 1965 when Jake became ill and had to stop his farming practice.

Ken and Pat went to the dances in Dropmore and a great time was always had. In the winter they went with a team and van. Sometimes they would drive along the railroad track which was a much shorter route.

Ken and Lorraine farmed in the MacNutt area for many years and have recently moved to Saltcoats in October, 1994.

Patricia and Melvin Berezowski reside in Kamsack, SK. Gerald and Elaine live in Saskatoon, SK.

Jake died on April 20, 1988. Lydia died on February 23, 1991.

James Atkinson

by Arthur Atkinson

Hello, my name is Arthur Atkinson. My grandfather, James Atkinson (1864-1941) and my Grandmother Ruth (Ingleton) (1866-1933), homesteaded in the Roblin District.

Pictured here are Mr. & Mrs. James Atkinson at Shellmouth taken on July 4th, 1926.

On arriving in Canada from Leeds, England, via the USA, James joined the Federal Force being assembled to confront the Metis at Duck Lake. His duty included the care and preparedness of five horses for the use of General Middleton.

His name is listed among the soldiers at the museum at Duck Lake. Somehow I am aware he was given a medal when they returned to Winnipeg. My father was said to believe the quarter section where he was born and raised on was made available to his father at that time. My father's sister, Mrs. Dorothy Morris, Portage, MB. lives only a few miles from that land site and may be able to confirm that.

My father, William Charles Atkinson (1894-1976) was born at McGregor, MB., Image Creek District and married Hilda Temple (1895-1987) on January 2, 1915 at Endcliff, MB.

My mother's family, Arthur and Elizabeth (Ward) Temple had arrived in Russel, MB. in 1909 from Wales in hopes of improving Arthur's health. Grandfather Temple passed away November 2, 1909 leaving Hilda, Nellie, Harriet (known as Sis.), Sydney, Jack and May. Sis's family, Amy, Russel and Marie Meadows grew up in Russell, MB.

My sister Ruth (1915-), brother James (1917-1987) and brother William, (known as Gordon) (1919-1976), were born in Russell, MB. Following the family's move to Valparaiso, SK in 1926, Harold (1926-1991), Fay (1936-) and myself, Arthur (1940-) were added to the family.

Father and mother often spoke of the "Skinner Place" and they wintered cattle on the Todd Ranch. One winter my father suffered multiple fractured bones in a sleigh wreck on the hill leading to their home in the valley. Dad was laid up for several months while mom was left with all the chores.

My grandparents had 3 other children. Ruth - Mrs. Albert Jones was shot and killed on June 10, 1926 at the Jones farm leaving Harold, Dorothy, Elizabeth, (Mrs. Len Bowly, Russell, MB.) and Ivan. Sarah Ester -- Mrs. Langley (1899-1992), Yorkton, SK. Dorothy -- Mrs. George Morris (1906-), Portage, MB.

Grandfather's brother, Tom, settled in the Swan River area. Grandfather's sister, Mary Atkinson, married Joe Longden of Chicago and some of your readers would be familiar with that family. Ella --- born at Bagot, married Gilbert Ferris. Their children, Hilliard, Vera, Oliver, Shirly, Leonard, Joyce, Ida and Gordon. (Much of this information was given me by Mae (Ball) Ferris, Swan River, MB. Sarah Edna -- married Harry Rowan. They farmed at Dropmore before moving to Armstong, BC in 1947. One son, Orland, serves as a missionary in Brazil.

My father and mother moved to the Valparaiso, SK area in 1926. Dad worked on the Highway #3 grade. They bought a quarter section, a place mother called "the Willows".

Mom suffered with T.B. for many years. The hospital bills rendered expansion dreams impossible. As a consequence I am a young 55 year old with the memories of growing up on a horse farm, without electricity or telephone.

In 1952 we visited Dropmore area and Roblin to view my grandparents gravesites and we also visited many of the Ferris families. In Russell, time was spent with the Meadows and a trip to Grandpa and Grandma Temple's graves.

My wife Jean and I have 3 children. Todd, a student at Oxford University, England. Scott, our adopted son, Edmonton, AB. Kimberly, a florist and a mother of two, living in Lethbridge, AB.

We are presently serving our Lord at the Eston Bible Institute, where I give direction to the current Campus Expansion. Jean and I served in Pastoral ministry in Esterhazy, SK, Creston, BC and finally in North Battleford, SK.

Elizabeth Ruth Atkinson

by Mrs. Lester Salm (Ruth Atkinson)

Elizabeth Ruth Atkinson was born in Russell, MB on September 28, 1915 and raised in the hills of their homestead by Rochedale School. She started school from Gramma's house. Castlevery had closed and she went to Roblin School by van operated by cousin Walter Payne. Then in 1923 Jim started school so they could go together to Rochedale School a distance of 2.3 miles. Up the hill and round the cemetery (scary). In 1924 they moved to Shellmouth and Dad went to build railway bridges and Mum and 3 kids lived in a rented house in Shellmouth. Then we moved stock by railway to Tisdale and from there out to 80 acres which Dad bought. We started school in the fall of 1926 at Berlin School in Saskatchewan.

The Bassil Family

by the Family

Jack Bassil (1875-1965) came to Canada from London, England in 1901 with his cousin, George Church. He got a job working on the farm for Mr. & Mrs. Harry Smith of Silverton, MB. He took a load of cattle by boat to England to sell for Harry Smith. On his way back here by boat, he met his future wife, Tamar Burrell (1879-1935), who was coming to Winnipeg from London, England to visit her two brothers, William and Edward Burrell. As the years went by, they crossed paths with Tamar Burrell again in the Rochedale District, where Tamar's parents came to live. Jack and Tamar were married in Russell, September 4, 1906. They took up residence and farmed in

(L-R) Mary Burrell (Tamar's mother), Jack Bassil, and his wife, Tamar (Burrell) Bassil.

Rochedale where Neil Burla and family now reside. Jack and Tamar had four children, Reg, Florence, Winnifred and Violet. All the children attended school in Rochedale. Several years after Tamar's death, Jack moved to Winnipeg in 1945.

Here are the children of Jack and Tamar Bassil (Back Row) Reg Bassil, (Front Row L-R) Florence (Bassil) Robertson, Violet (Bassil) Robertson, Winnifred (Bassil) Preece..

Walter Reginald was born November 23, 1907. he attended school in Rochedale, then in later years went to Nokomis, SK and worked for a year. Then he rode the train to Churchill where he worked for two years, and returned to Nokomis for another year; then, back home to farm in the district. On October 24, 1936 he married Winona Goodbun. They worked on the farm. Their son, Richard was born August 18, 1937. That year they moved to Alberta and farmed in the Innisfail-- Didsbury areas. Their daughter, Ann was born September 2, 1938. In 1951 they moved to Calgary where Reg worked for a company repairing dirt moving construction machinery until 1974 when he retired. In 1989 they moved to Edmonton, where they now reside. Their son, Richard and wife Jill and family live in Edmonton, and daughter, Ann and husband Bob Anderson and family live in Ontario.

Florence Mary was born at home on July 28, 1912. Florence attended school at Rochedale and Inglis. She worked at Skinner's Nursery where she first met her future husband. She then worked in Russell for a short time before going to Winnipeg in 1929. Florence was employed at the YMCA for several years before returning to marry Jim Robertson and begin a new life as a farmer's wife. Florence and Jim spent many enjoyable years farming and raising their five children in the Dropmore district. Florence currently resides in Roblin.

Winnifred was born on October 8, 1914. With her sister Violet, they would ski the area and into the Assiniboine valley. She left her home in Rochedale and went to Winnipeg in 1937 to work. There she met Harry Preece. They came home to be married in August, 1949. After they wed they returned to Winnipeg. Harry has since passed away. Winnifred currently resides in Winnipeg.

Violet was born September 9, 1918. In 1937, she went to Winnipeg with Winnifred to find work. After working for three years, she returned home for a holiday. At that time, Jack and Kay Goodbun required help, so she worked for them until 1942. In July 1942 she married John S. Robertson and they moved to the farm at Dropmore. She helped John on the farm and they raised four children: Ann, Irene, Joan and Allan. They retired to Russell in 1984, and she maintains a home there.

Tom Bauereiss

by Betty Bauereiss

Tom (1945), Betty (1947), Darlene (1965) and baby Brett (1968) came from Inglis to Dropmore in the spring of 1968. We rented the former Earl Morrison farm 8-24-29 owned by Joan Vinnell. Settling into the district was easy as the neighbors were very friendly. The card parties and suppers in the Castleavery School, and the curling and dancing in Dropmore kept our social life busy.

In 1970 we purchased the Watt Ferris farm 34-23-29. With this move many improvements were made. As there were only 3 trees on the yard, a shelter belt was started to protect us from the winter elements. In the fall of 1970 Darlene started school in Roblin. That was the start of the school bus reign.

In Dec. 1972, our second son Carman was born. We increased our farm by purchasing the W1/2 of 28-23-29.

Carman on Rusty.

Our life seemed to have settled into a pattern of raising our children, general farm work, and social events in the district.

When we moved to the Dropmore district our neighbors The Ferris', Mr. and Mrs. Bill Ferris and Howard and Betty Ferris became like family to us, also A.W. Nichols, fondly known as Junior. These people were referred to as our "Dropmore Family". We became involved with the hall and rink, spending many hours dancing and curling. The children grew up and one by one have gone their own ways.

Darlene married Grant Andrews (1958), son of Merlin and June Andrews. In 1983 they had a son Justin Grant born Oct. 23, 1983. In March 1984 a farm accident took Grant's life and in the fall Darlene moved her house trailer to Inglis and started working in Russell at the Russell Banner in 1985.

Also in the fall of 1984 Tom took on the job as Councillor of Ward 3 in the RM of Shellmouth.

July 11, 1987 Darlene married Garth Jackson (1963), son of Stan and Carol Jackson. They live on a farm south-east of Inglis, raising purebred Charolais cattle as well as grain farming and raising commercial cattle. Justin goes to school in Inglis. Darlene still works part time at the Russell Banner.

Brett had various jobs for a few years. Then in 1988 he started working for the Paterson Elevator in Cracknell. In 1990 he was transferred to Lang, SK. As housing was a problem, he lived in Yellow Grass, SK and commuted to work. In 1991 a house became available in Lang and Brett and friend Jennifer moved there.

On August 1, 1992 Brett married Jennifer Burla (1972), daughter of Peter and Margaret Burla, they have a son Seth Thomas born Dec. 22, 1992. In 1994 Brett again was transferred to Indian Head, SK as Assistant Manager for Patterson Elevator.

In 1990 Carman joined the Armed Forces, but after his basic training decided that wasn't what he wanted to do. He also worked at various other jobs. He farms with us in the summer and worked on the pipeline in Northern Alberta for the winter.

The love of the land has kept our children close to the farm. Brett and Jennifer purchased the Arnold Ferris farm SW 1/4 26-23-29 and the Charlie Bernhard farm SW 23-35-29 and the north 1/2 of NE 1/4 27-23-29 and Carman purchased the E 1/2 of 28-23-29 from Howard Ferris. Tom and I are still on the farm and plan on staying here for a while yet.

The Bauereiss Family.

Andy and Noreen Bauming

by Beryl Robertson

Andy and Noreen Bauming moved to section 16-24-29 of Castleavery in 1943 with children Beryl and Don. The family was Canadian of German heritage and culture. They lived four miles away, south side of Salt Lake before moving to their new home. Son, Corey, was born in 1952.

Andy built a log home for the family. He became the barber, butcher, vet for the community. He never hesitated to help others until he died in 1963.

Noreen left the farm, worked in Winnipeg, never remarried. Died in 1987.

The brothers and cousins of Bill Robertson dressed up cart and pony to take Bill and his bride Beryl from the United Church (in background) to the Hall in Dropmore on their wedding day.

Beryl lives in Toronto with 22 year-old daughter, Meredith. She continues to work in hospital, enjoys taking courses and workshops.

Don lives in Lorette, near Winnipeg. Happily married to Betty with their 16 year old daughter, Leah, and is working as a cabinet maker.

Corey lives in Winnipeg, drives his own taxi, when not working full time at Pioneer Electric. He has a 17 year old son, Jess, and an 8 year old daughter, Chantil, that he lives for.

Children of this time lived a very simple life. They were expected to do their share of chores around the home. Because there was no television, they were creative, finding things to do and to play with, like make-believe school, store, or being Mom and Dad to their brothers and sisters. I remember playing with mud pies, and at Christmas time, gifts were usually just one thing like a doll, a watch, skates, or a wagon.

Party telephones were a source of entertainment for many by listening. Transportation was by horse and sleigh, wagon, or walking.

Remember the family travelling to town by horse and van for mail, supplies, and entertainment. We always looked forward to having shelled peanuts to eat coming home.

The whole family attended the gatherings of Fowl Suppers, Turkey Shoots, Summer School Picnics, Barn Dances, Amateur Night, Christmas concerts, Big New Years' Eve Dance, Weddings, Funerals, Church, and Bees for harvest or building (when everyone turned out to help in some way).

Our entertainment was curling, skating, dancing, tobogganing, wiener roasts, swimming, Saturday night shows (movies), and gatherings at our friends and family's houses.

Harold Beals Family

by Dorothy Coulter

Ida Maud (Cooper) Beals was born in Harrowby, MB on April 4, 1910. Her father, William Cooper, ran a livery stable there for some years. Ida was the eldest of 11 children. Their next move was to Langenburg where they ran the hotel and the livery stable. They must have done well because William Cooper owned the first car in that town --- a Ford. Ida worked very hard helping them run the family home. Then when the livery stable business declined because more cars came, they moved to Shellmouth where they bought what they called the 'Langford place'. Ida and her brothers and sisters went to school at Shellmouth. That was only for a awhile and they moved to Dropmore to farm where Ida and Harold met.

Walter and Harold Beals in their Hard Ball outfits. This picture was taken before 1929.

On December 16, 1930 Ida married Harold Beals who had moved to Canada from College Spring, Iowa about 1916. He farmed with his brother Walter. The two of them were great ball players and played with the Dropmore Club and surrounding towns. On Dec. 25, 1931 their first child was born, Harold Glenn. On May 26, 1933 a daughter, Dorothy Amelia came. Harold and Ida moved to Shortdale where he farmed for about 15 years. Keith was born April 19, 1936; Yvonne was born Feb. 4, 1944; and Frederick Harold on Aug. 19, 1945. Yvonne and Freddie burned to death on the family farm in the barn loft where they were playing on June 30, 1949. That fall Harold and Ida sold out and moved their family to Bowsman. They bought more land and settled in the Brierley District. Two more children were born -- Thelma Gwendelyn on Dec. 28, 1950 and Lawrence Bartley on July 9, 1953.

The Harold Beals Family. The 50th Anniversary for (seated) Ida and Harold Beals.(Back Row L-R) Kieth, Thelma, Bartley, Dorothy and Glenn.

In 1970 they sold the farm and moved into Bowsman where they lived for a number of years. In 1983, Harold passed away and a year or two later Ida moved into the Personal Care in Swan River where she still resides.

Walter Beals Family History

by Pauline Ferris

Walter West Beals Sr. was born on November 6, 1894 in College Springs, Iowa, USA. He lost his father at an early age, leaving his mother, younger brother and sister, so he took a man's place very early in life.

When he graduated from college his class motto was, "We will make a path or find one" and looking back, over his life, we believe he took this to heart and made his path to the North. Martha Ann Dow was born June 9, 1896 in College Springs, Iowa, USA and received her education there. In 1916 Walter Beals and Martha Dow were married. They were only married a few weeks when a neighbor, Luther Johnson came over. He told them he had bought some land in Canada and he would like them to go with him and he would help them get started in this wonderful country. After talking it over they decided to accept, and they ordered an immigrant car to arrive in a week. They packed their implements, a team of buckskin horses, cows, a team of mules, a barrel of canned fruit, and whatever else it took to start from scratch to farm in a new country.

It was a three week trip, it seemed endless for a young bride of a few weeks and who had left family and friends. They were lonesome and homesick, but never once in all the years they lived in MB, did they ever talk of going back, they loved their adopted country.

There was many a funny story told and jokes played on hired men over the mules they brought up with them. While the men would be feeding their horses, one of the mules would bray, and there was nearly always a race for the barn door to get out. It was a very startling sound, but they lived for many years and their's was a wonderful source of power.

Walter and his wife settled down in a two room house in the Castleavery District on Section 15. They lived there for a few years and then moved to a farm 3/4 miles east of Grainsby School.

They had good crops and certainly thought they had found the land of plenty. Walter played hard ball with the Dropmore hard Ball team; he was a very talented pitcher. He had also been joined in farming by his brother Harold, who now played catcher for the same team. Walter's pitching came to an end in 1929 when he accidentally got his hand caught in a wood saw and was never able to pitch again, but it never dimmed his love for the game. His love of sports was inherited by his children and grandchildren.

Walter threshed many years for neighbors in and around the district and Mrs. Beals often baked bread and cooked meals for the bachelors in the area, Jack and Watt Ferris and Lloyd Lefler, for example.

But the good years weren't to last. The drought had hit the prairies and after seven years of no rain and three of being hailed out, they began to look to the north again. The summer of 1934, Mr. Beals accompanied by his brother-in-law, John Dow, drove a team and wagon to the Swan River Valley, made a deal for a quarter section of land,

From (L-R) the Walter Beals Family. Nadine Olson, Helen de Groot, Marjorie Graham, Walter Jr., Mae Cook, Dale, Alyce Mullin, Arthur, Kay Christensen, Pauline Ferriss, Walter and Martha. Taken in 1972.

three miles east of Bowsman in the Croppertop District. Mr. Dow bought a quarter directly east of the Beals quarter. They spent six weeks putting up hay and bought a house from the Burrows Mill and moved it on their land. He arrived home in good spirits, ready for another move and very happy with the land and new neighbors where we were going to live. Mrs. Beals and her daughters had also been busy picking what berries there were and canning vegetables besides cooking for the bachelor neighbors when the threshers were at their place. They also had cows to milk and poultry to look after.

They moved by horses and wagons. He built a big crate on the back of one of the hay racks and loaded the turkeys his wife had raised and wouldn't leave behind. They drove the herd of cattle, so had cows to milk night and morning, also all the milk they wanted to use. He was accompanied by his six daughters, who helped drive the cattle, drive a wagon team, and make meals when they stopped to rest the horses and cows. He also had help from John Dow who moved his stock and belongings at the same time. Harry Ferris, a neighbor from Dropmore, also made the trip and helped out.

He had one big worry and that was the road through the mountains. It was a clay road with no gravel. If it rained he was in trouble, but he was lucky and had lovely weather the full week he was on the road.

Bartley and Lila Carmichael drove Mrs. Beals and her two small sons Walter Jr. and Art by car and when they landed in Bowsman there was no sign of Mr. Beals and the rest of the family. They had stopped over in Kenville at Burnett Ralston's and became acquainted with their new neighbors, one mile from the farm where she was going to spend the next 31 years of her life. Two weeks after she arrived in the Valley she gave birth to her ninth child, a 9 lb son Dale and two years later their tenth child arrived, another little girl Kay. Our Dad always said, "His family was his fortune" and he always made us feel as though that were true. So again they had to start a new life. With a big family and both older in years, but, with the help of wonderful neighbors and the pioneer spirit they both had, they managed to make a good living. It was all man power, logs to cut for barns, wood to cut for stoves, grubbing by axe. There was never much time for parties in those days. Mrs. Beals always raised her chickens, hatched from an incubator and kept warm by a wood burning stove, so when she got a coal burning brooder she was really pleased. One night it decided to act up and she spent the entire night in the brooder house to keep it running. When she arrived in the house at breakfast time, everyone burst out laughing. She looked as if she might have driven a freight train as she was black from coal dust and not too happy.

They continued to farm until 1965, when they decided their farming years were over. They bought a small house in Bowsman where they spent a very happy retirement and they both enjoyed good health and it was truly their "Golden Years".

Mr. and Mrs. Beals enjoyed their large family of seven girls, Mae, Marjorie, Helen, Alyce, Pauline, Nadine, Kay and three boys Walter Jr., Art and Dale.

Mae married Carl Cook of Bowsman and Mae passed away in February, 1979.

Marjorie married Ted Graham, Bowsman. They now live in Thompson.

Helen married George DeGroot, Bowsman. George passed away in August.

Alyce married Cliff Mullin, Bowsman. They now live in Swan River.

Pauline married Gordon Ferris, Bowsman.

Nadine married Gotthard Olson, Bowsman. Gotthard passed away in June 1994.

Walter Jr. married Myrna Colbert, Bowsman.

Art married Doreen Ruach of Brunkild. They now live in Winnipeg.

Dale lives in Dawson Creek, BC.

Kay married John Christensen, Swan River.

The grandchildren and great grandchildren always loved to go to Grandma and Grandpa Beals. One little great grandson said, "Do you know why I like to go to Grandma and Grandpa Beals? Because they always have "soft butter", that's why!" On any evening you wanted to stop by, there was nearly always someone around the kitchen table having coffee, toast and "soft" butter.

Mr. and Mrs. Beals celebrated their 59th anniversary. Mr. Beals passed away in May 1975 and Mrs. Beals passed away in June 1977. They left many descendants with a close bond, and family re-unions are held every three to five years in Bowsman.

Charlie and Mary (Zimmer) Bernhard

by Charlie Bernhard

The Bernhard family moved to Dropmore in spring of 1946 from Killaley, SK.

The Zimmer family moved to Dropmore from Strathclair, MB in the fall of the same year. During those first few years there were a lot of house parities, dances, etc. and in summer there were ball games, picnics and fishing in the Assiniboine River.

Charlie and I met that first year and we got married the next fall in October 27, 1947, and we took up farming west of Dropmore.

Our first child Charlene, was born September 11, 1948. For her first grade years she went to Grainsby School.

In June 1957, we had a set back. We lost our home to a fire. With the kindness and help of

Charlie and Mary Bernhard.

our relatives, friends and neighbours we weathered that storm.

Our second child, Sheldon, was born September 3, 1957. He got his early education at Dropmore School. Both Charlene and Sheldon finished their education at Roblin.

We then moved to a farm closer to Dropmore and also purchased the Dropmore School and renovated it and landscaped the yard, where we lived until July of this year.

Charlene and Ron Wall, Jayson and Janelle

After high school Charlene went to Winnipeg to a business college to continue her education. She was employed as a secretary in an insurance company. In August 5th, 1972 she got married to Ron Wall who is employed as a carpenter. After some years Charlene stopped working to be a full time mother. They have two children Jayson and Janelle. Now that her children are grown up she is back in the work force. She now works at the Assiniboine Medical Clinic in Laboratory Accounts Dept.

Sheldon also went to Winnipeg and now is employed at Manitoba Telephone System as an audio visual specialist. He got married to Debby Bezo in August 5th 1978. Debby is employed as a pharmacy technician. They now live on an acreage near Stonewall, MB and both commute to their

Sheldon, Debby and Aron Bernhard.

jobs in the city. They have one son, Aron, who attends grade school at Stonewall, MB.

We have lived close to Lake of the Prairies and we have enjoyed fishing, camping and the outdoors in summer. Through the years, Charlie has acquired eleven master angler awards for some of the large fish he has caught.

I have enjoyed various crafts and quilting and have made hundreds of quilts through the years.

Charlie and his Master Angler.

We have been retired for several years and we have enjoyed gardening which also includes various fruit trees, shrubs and flowers.

We sold our farms this past year and moved to Stonewall, MB in July, 1995 where we will be close to our children and grandchildren.

Johann Frederick Bieber and Katherina (Wirth, Goeres) Bieber

by Mary (Bieber) Peter

Johann Frederick Bieber (1878 - 1957) and Katherina Wirth Goeres (1884 - 1975) immigrated to Canada from Landestreu, Galacia, Austria in the late 1890's. Prior to her marriage to Johann Frederick, Katherina, at age 16 in Austria, met and married her first husband, Albert Goeres, and in 1902 set sail for Canada, arriving in Halifax by boat, along with her half brothers and sister. Katherine and Albert settled down in the Castleavery District of Saskatchewan.

Upon the first years of their settling in this area, there was a terrible drought. Barrels of water had to be hauled for miles, often as far as Shellmouth, MB, a distance of 14 miles, and all hauling was done by oxen and wagon. Some muskeg areas were so dry that huge cracks appeared, and cattle often disappeared when they fell in, only to be found weeks later dead, a great loss to these early struggling pioneer farmers.

Government aid had encouraged the coming of more settlers, and each homesteader was given a grant of one cow, one dozen chickens, one yoke of oxen with harness, a single plow, an axe, a store of several iron cooking utensils and five bushels of seed wheat. The homestead of 160 acres was purchased for ten dollars. This was repaid to the government, over a period of years, with farm goods. As one of the first settlers in this area, Katherine and Albert endured many hardships as they farmed their homestead.

On October 12, 1902, a daughter was born to Katherina and Albert and they named her Elizabeth. When Elizabeth was two years of age, Albert (who was many years older than Katherina) passed away and Katherina was left alone with her little daughter to face the many formidable tasks and hardships of surviving on their homestead. Clearing land, farming with oxen, hauling stones off the land and trying to raise enough produce to support her daughter, became almost impossible for Katherina. She relates how, one day, as she was working in the fields with her oxen in the dry, dusty, drought conditions of 1906, the animals were slow and cumbersome. They decided to go in a direction of their own choosing. They headed directly into a muddy lake to cool off. In vain, Katherina tried desperately to control them, but eventually she gave up in despair. She merely got dragged along into the muddy mire. From that moment on, she knew within her heart that she had reached the "end of the rope" and could no longer manage this situation alone.

Little did she realize that God was already preparing for her the help she would need. In 1906, Johann Frederick Bieber, a handsome young bachelor of the area, came to Canada from Landestreu, Galicia, Austria with his parents, George and Maria (Kendal) Bieber and siblings. He and Katherina became acquainted, and on November 25, 1906, they were married in MacNutt SK.

Johann Frederick Bieber, known as "Fred" or "Fritz" as he was more commonly known, and Katherina Wirth Goeres, or Katherine as she was more commonly known, had both been raised as Lutherans and were married in the local Lutheran Church. A short time after their marriage they had a change of religious conviction through two missionary "Evangelists" called the Vosse Brothers who came through MacNutt, SK. Fred and Katherine came to the knowledge of the Gospel of Jesus Christ, accepted Him and were baptised. Along with Fred and Katherine, other families of the area identified with them in this new missionary zeal, namely: Haberstocks, Wershlers, G. Adams, J. Dresslers, J. Mundts, J. Burkarts, Jobs and others. The church services were often held in the home of Danny Dressler Sr.'s large log house or in different homes. This fellowship was a close-knit one and these families experienced God's love for one another as one family of God.

The union of Fred and Katherina Bieber resulted in the birth of nine children, six sons and three daughters.

On October 26, 1908, Edward was born, a baby brother for Elizabeth, who by this time was six years of age. Edward was their pride and joy. His father named him "Edward Bieber, Throne Prince". He followed his father everywhere he could. It was after the birth of Edward, that Fred and Katherine decided to leave the farm and move into McNutt. Until the early 1900's early settlers travelled by ox carts or horses to Langenburg, Russell or Saltcoats to do most of their business. A trip to Langenburg was long and difficult. Therefore, the early settlers decided on a smaller trading centre on the site of which is now the village of McNutt. During the early 1900's a number of businesses were set up on the south side of the village.

My father, Fred Bieber built a blacksmith shop in MacNutt. It was on the spot where Mrs. Merril Rathgeber resided. It was moved in 1909 to the spot where Cornelius Garage now stands. Fred Bieber operated this black smith shop for a short time, then in 1914, sold it to Mr. D. Fisher. Fred also built a house on the corner of the lot south of his blacksmith shop. The house was just a few blocks from the school. He also constructed a livery stable on the property of Cornelius' Garage. The livery stable was sold to his brother-in-law,

Katherine and Fred Bieber with the first four of their ten children. Picture taken (circa) 1911.

Adolf Becker. Later on, it was sold, and dismantled in order to build the Cornelius Garage.

On August 25, 1910, in the new home built by Fred, their first set of twins were born and they named them Mary and George. These were the first set of twins, born in the Village. They were named Mary and George, after their grandparents, as well as after King George V and Queen Mary, who had been crowned that same year. George, as an infant, was not well and when he suffered convulsions, Katherine prayed for God to restore him to health or to take him to heaven. Her prayers were answered and he did recover but he didn't walk until almost two years of age. My mother related to me how she would ask me, Mary, to take George for a walk and I would take him by the hand and he would slide along, even if it was through mud puddles, resulting in George and I looking like mud balls. Because we were the first twins born in the Village we were honoured with a set of silver cups, spoons, knives and forks and also a silver bracelet for each. The gentleman delivering these keep-sakes was Mr. Thomas MacNutt, after whom the town of MacNutt was named. He was a well-respected citizen, who served as a County Coroner and the local Justice of the Peace.

Fred was very ambitious and a real entrepreneur. He began a hardware, then a grocery and finally a general store, where both groceries and hardware were handled. He was always busy, aiming at making a comfortable living for his growing family.

On August 13, 1912, another son was added to the Bieber clan. This dark-haired baby was named Rudolph. In addition to raising her family, Katherina tried to help Fred in running the store. Her cousin, Millie Rickert, often came to help her. Elizabeth was also becoming a great help as she was now approaching her teens, and she enjoyed looking after her younger brothers and sister.

The General Store business was a challenge to my parents. Because their customers were of Ukrainian, German and English descent, Mother did alot of talking using her hands for sign language. She and my father tried to learn the English language but German, their Mother language came easiest.

The "Spanish Flu" or influenza broke out at the time Fred had the store business. The family had now moved into the same building which had living quarters at the back and upstairs. The town was quarantined. The poolroom run by William Lindenbach, our uncle, had to be closed at six o'clock. All houses containing the Flu were to be quarantined and a fine of fifty dollars was to be imposed for any infringement of this law. In his store, Fred had a large, high coal and wood heater to heat the building. He would keep his store disinfected by putting creoline in a container on top of the stove. The smell wasn't very pleasant but Fred and Katherina were thankful to God that their family were spared the serious results of the Flu.

Around 1912, the first school opened in the second floor of the Rudolf Andres Store. If my memory serves me correct, it's the store my father, Fred bought later. The school remained there for about a year. Miss Sylvia M. Bowles was the first teacher. She certainly had her hands full. Some of the children were ten years of age and had never been to school. Mr. Gibson, a young Irish immigrant, was the first principal. He was a stern disciplinarian and soon had everyone in order. I can still recall coming to school late and getting the strap. Mr. Gibson left school teaching to join the Army and he died later of meningitis in a military hospital in England. My sister Elizabeth, was one of the first students to attend this school, as well as my brother Edward. Our cousins, Katie and Elizabeth Becker also attended, as well as about forty-six other children.

The new two-storey school was built in 1913 by Emerson Bass of Grandview, along with Bob Thomson.

On April 18, 1915, Albert, son number four, was born and he was followed on September 7, 1917 by Adolph William. After the birth of Adolph, my parents decided, with their large growing family to sell the business and move out to the wide open spaces. Their move was to Dropmore, MB. Although Dropmore was small in size, it was big in spirit! The people were very active as farmers and businessmen. The Biebers purchased a three quarter section of land in the Grainsby District, right on the Saskatchewan border. It was eight miles from McNutt, four miles from the village of Dropmore, six miles from the Shellmouth and about fifty miles from Yorkton. With the move came much work in building a new home (the family had moved into an old one room shack) in 1919. Dad hired a carpenter, Mr. E. Bass to construct our home.

This was our home built in Dropmore, MB in 1918.

Although times were hard, Fred and Katharine always had enough food and clothing for their family. They built up a herd of cattle, horses, pigs, chickens, turkeys and geese, Horses were used to plow and work the land. The children were all expected to pitch in, either in caring for siblings or in helping with the farming or gardening. Mother and Dad used to plant a big garden, potatoes (half an acre), mangles (for the cattle in the winter), rhubarb, raspberries as well as many vegetables. We would go out to pick Saskatoon berries and Mother canned everything and preserved it in half gallon jars. She would also can pork and beans, pork, beef and fish, as well as chicken raised on the farm. We had no refrigerator or freezer. There was no running water in the house and no electricity. We used coal oil lamps and a huge "alladin" hung in the front room. Washing was done with hand turning and later a machine and hand wringer. The water for the laundry was heated on the stove in a boiler. We carried water from a well, quite a walk from the house. We hauled water, even for the garden when it didn't rain. We had a beautiful flower garden in front of our house. Even though we had no modern conveniences, we all enjoyed living on the farm. In addition to the farm work, Dad had quite a number of bee hives which he enjoyed looking after. He extracted the honey from the combs and stored it in five gallon crocks. Needless to say, we had all the honey (and honeycomb) we could eat!

Our parents taught us all to work, do chores, feed stock, milk cows, help Dad pick up rocks from the fields and clear the land. Gophers were a real pest in the early days on the prairie, so the Government paid a bounty of a cent a tail, to get rid of them. My brothers took an active part in this campaign and the competition was keen as to who would have the most tails. All the tails they managed to capture, were kept in a box while waiting for the trip to town to turn them in for the reward.

Since father was a blacksmith, and could make almost anything, he fashioned a little digger, shaped like a hand with the thumb sticking out. With this digger, the boys would go out into the fields and dig Senneca roots. These roots were dug, washed and laid out to dry. When dry they were sold in town for thirty-five cents per pound.

It was into this rural setting that the youngest son, Frederick, or "Fred" was born on November 20, 1919. Fred was a very active, daring youngster. One late evening, the family all came in from threshing after a hard, long day out on the land. "Freddie" was missing, so we all hurried back into the dark night to look for him. We found him, fast asleep under some sheaves near the threshing machine. Another time we found him asleep in a manger in the barn. On another frightening occasion, we heard a loud cry coming from the direction of the barn. When the family reached the barn, they found Freddie lying on the ground with a bleeding face. He had ventured too close to a young colt and tried to stroke his hind legs. The colt kicked and broke Fred's nose. Another anecdote I remember about fearless Freddie was the time he disappeared and was found grunting, stuck in a badger hole!

Much to the joy of Fred and Katharine, another set of twins was welcomed into the family. The date was March 31, 1923 when Minnie and Annie arrived and completed the Bieber family of ten. Now that the other siblings were older, we were able to help Mother care for these two babies.

Fred and Katherine Bieber Family with their ten children in (circa) 1927.

As busy as Fred and Katharine were, raising and caring for their family of ten children, they did not neglect reading the Bible and having morning and evening devotions. All the children sat around the table while each had a Bible in hand and took turns reading the day's scripture passage. They were encouraged to memorize a verse every day. They usually sang hymns around the organ. Often times, they were unable to go to church because of inclement weather, so their parents would gather them together and Dad would read the stories of Joseph, David and Goliath or Ruth. The stories were so interesting that they would beg him to go on and on and on, until they heard the whole story. I remember that after Dad was through and we had had family prayer, we would go out into the yard to play games, with Dad leading the pack. How well I remember playing "stealing sticks", or "croquet", or "sheep, sheep, come over", or "prisoner's base".

Fred Bieber with all his boys.

As the children continued to grow, school was a vital part of their lives, and several of the younger Bieber children attended Grainsby School. Some of the older ones were attending school elsewhere, after receiving what they could get at Grainsby.

The first Grainsby School burned down in 1916 and school lessons were given in an old discarded home of William Wardle's until the next school was built. The new- one-roomed school was built, I believe in 1917. It had one classroom from grades one to grade nine. In the summer, the Bieber children walked to school, a distance of one and a half miles. In the winter they drove to school with horses and sleigh. Fred had built a closed-in caboose on the sleigh which was warm and comfortable. It had a window in the front and a door in the back. With all the blizzards in the Manitoba winter months, they found riding in this caboose a luxury. They did upset several times, but were able to scramble or roll out at the back door into the deep snow. There were often six at a time in the caboose as well as a cousin, Mary Haberstock who came along. Roads, at that time were not ploughed out and the snow was several feet deep. When it rained, it made getting to school very treacherous.

In the summer, recess and lunch hours were often spent chasing gophers with school friends. They would take pails, fill them with water and dump the water into the gopher holes to drown them out. When the gophers came out, the children would chase them with clubs. Ball was also played often. The one-roomed school was special to the students. On the average it had about 13 to 15 students. Fred would often say to his children,"I can't give you a big inheritance, but I want you to have an education." Although some of the Bieber children did not finish high school, four did and became school teachers, and some went into business.

I clearly remember some of the electrical storms experienced while our family lived on the farm in Dropmore. On one occasion I stayed home with my oldest brother, Edward, while the rest of the family had gone to church. It was in 1935 and I can recall the day in which a tornado destroyed Dad's implement shed, which housed his threshing outfit and other farm implements. There were posts cemented into the ground about six feet. When Ed and I saw the approaching storm, we took refuge in the house. When it did strike, we were afraid and asked the Lord to protect us. After the storm was over, those cement posts were ripped out of the ground and the roof was lifted off but we were saved. Another time, when the family was all together in the house, a severe storm came up just as I was carrying the dishes into the china cabinet. I saw a streak of light in our front room. I yelled out, "Fire"! The lightning had struck our house. It ruined the top half of the chimney and knocked some plaster off the wall upstairs. On the window sill was a plant. Underneath that plant a splinter was taken out of the sill and half the plant was dead. God had spared our lives again and we all thanked Him for His protection and safety.

Fred Bieber riding on his Titan tractor pulling the threshing machine which has Rudolph, Adolph and Albert sitting on top.

How the years in Dropmore did fly! Three of the oldest Bieber boys, Edward, Rudolph and Albert were now going to Normal School (Teacher's College) and Elizabeth and George had left to go work.

Because the boys were not available to help with farming, Fred and Katharine decided it was time to move. The farm was too much for Fred alone, so he decided he would rent the farm out, sell everything on auction and move to BC.

Since this was the depression time of the early 1930's, the auction sale did not result in great profits. Cows sold for eleven to twelve dollars, turkeys for thirty-five cents, chickens for twenty-five cents or less and horses for very cheap. The sale started early in the morning and lasted until eleven at night. Dad made only $1800.00 from that sale.

Fred built a big van on the back of his truck, all that was possible to take along was loaded on the back and the Bieber Family left Dropmore, a home that had given them so many beautiful memories. They arrived in Medicine Hat, AB in 1935. Here they were made so welcome by their cousins, Mary and John Burkart, that they decided to stay.

They rented an older house on Balmoral Street in which they lived a short time before moving into a larger house on the same street. Father was offered the sale of thirty lots at fifteen dollars per lot, but money was so scarce at that time he didn't buy them. Instead, he bought a large three-storey building, did some renovating and made the front part into a grocery store. It had three bedrooms in it with a kitchen and living room. The upstairs rooms, eleven in number, were rented out. He also rented some irrigated land on the outskirts of town and began market gardening. He bought a truck and hauled vegetables as far away as Calgary and surrounding areas. With gardening, looking after the rooming house and the grocery store, we were all kept very busy. At this time, Mary, Minnie, Annie Fred and Adolph were the only children still at home. The other boys were at teacher's college, teaching or working.

Katherine and Fred Bieber lived out their retiring years in Vernon, B.C.

In the late 1940's, my parents, Fred and Katherine, along with Minnie and Annie sold their business in Medicine Hat, AB and moved to Vernon, BC. Here they had a market garden raising many fruits and vegetables on their acreage on the outskirts of Vernon. On their retirement, they moved into a smaller house in Vernon where they resided until Fred's death on February 28, 1957. Katherine then moved in with her daughter, Mary and Adolph Peter, who lived in Vernon. She lived a vibrant, happy life until God called her to be with Him on November 12, 1977 at the age of 91.

My parents, Fred and Katherine Bieber left their family a great heritage. They modelled for their children and grandchildren how to earn a responsible living. They were always concerned about the stability of the Family. Their efforts helped shape a wonderful example of an upright, moral life-style and a commitment to God. At each family reunion, their memory enhances our celebrations. We remember them with great fondness, and know that because of their deep abiding faith in God, we will see them again!

The descendants and in-laws of Fred and Katherine Bieber in a second reunion held in 1993. The only surving children of Fred and Katherine are shown here in the center of this picture.(Standing 3rd row from the back) Rudolph, Mary, Annie and Minnie.

Please Note: The reader may wonder what happened to the rest of the Bieber Clan. The following will give a very brief summary of their whereabouts.

Elizabeth (Goeres) Bieber married Ephriam Hude and they had five children, Lorne, Rita, Don, Norman and Bert. Elizabeth passed away on Aug. 18, 1968 and is buried in Lethbridge, AB.

Edward Bieber took his formal training at Normal School in Calgary and taught for twelve years in a one-roomed school at Sunbeam, AB. He completed his B.Sc. degree during summer school courses and in 1941 became a Principal of the East Coulee High School in East Coulee, AB. During his four years at East Coulee he met and married Vera Sondar on July 7, 1945. Later that year, Edward and his brother Fred, jointly purchased a general store at Ranier, AB. In September 1948, the partnership was dissolved and Ed and his wife moved on to Rolling Hills, AB, where they operated a general store, post office and a garage, later branching into farming and a feed lot operation. They had two sons: Robert obtained his Engineering Degree at the University of Calgary and now is a project engineer for Avery Lawrence Co. in Singapore. Grant received a B.Sc.in Computer Science from Calgary University and works for the City of Calgary at City Hall. Their only daughter, Shelley, graduated from the University of Calgary with a Bachelor of Commerce Degree. She also has her ARCT Performer's degree in piano. In 1976, Ed suffered a stroke which left him very immobile. On July 8, 1977 he went home to be with His Lord. Vera, who still resides in Medicine Hat, calls him a "Prince Among Men" and treasures the wonderful memories the family has of a caring, thoughtful and loving, husband and father.

George Bieber, twin brother to Mary (Bieber) Peter, married Leah Gehring. She died after the birth of their only child, Leonard. He then married Hilda (Lay) Bell, who had two children, Ernie and Lorne by a previous marriage. George and Hilda had one son, Kenneth, who was born Jan 3,1956. Kenneth took University training in Calgary, married a teacher, Sandra May, and they have three children. George and Hilda spent many years in Fernie, BC and Medicine Hat, AB. George passed away on September 16, 1979, and Hilda on July 11, 1988.

Rudolph, after attending Bible College in Medicine Hat, and Normal School Teachers' Training in Calgary, taught school in various communities throughout Alberta. It was at one particular two-roomed school in Landen, AB, that he announced to his class that he would be going to Medicine Hat to bring back his valentine. When he

The survivving Bieber children are (L-R) Mary Peter, Annie Roth, Minnie Arnold and Rudolph Bieber. Missing from this picture is Adolph (Bill) Bieber.

returned with his wife, Edna Fredericks, a big welcome celebration was put on for them. Before moving to Red Deer, where he taught for about seven years, Rudolph and Edna lived in Southern Alberta for seven years. There, he was a principal for two years at Bow Island and then five years at Burdett, AB. Rudolph and Edna were blessed with six children, five girls and one boy. Ruth Elaine was born on July 4, 1945. She married Rodney Penner in 1967 and they reside on Quadra Island, BC. They have five children who have all attended Trinity Western University or Three Hills Bible College. Their oldest daughter, Lynette is in her second year of medical studies at the University of BC.

Marlene and Marian were twin daughters, born to Rudolph and Edna. Marion, a school teacher, married Arthur Nowell on June 28, 1980. They reside in Seattle, WA where Arthur is a researcher at the University.

Marlene, a nurse, resides in Portland, OR with her husband, John McKenzie and three children. Lois, their fourth daughter married Harold Strohschein of Red Deer, AB. They have two sons, Bradley and Darren both attend Briercrest Bible Institute. Wanda married Kenneth Annett of Red Deer on May 6, 1972. Wanda is a lab technician and Ken is a Treasury Branch Bank supervisor. They reside in Edmonton, AB with their three children, Kelsey, a student at NAIT, and Michael and Robert still at home. Brian, their only son, married Heather Cotnam, a nurse on July 11, 1981. Brian is a principal of an elementary school in Red Deer, AB. He and Heather have one son, Mark, born on 24 Aug. 1988.

Albert Bieber became a school teacher and taught in Alberta schools for many years. He married Mary Schweigert on Aug. 20, 1949 and they have three sons, Bruce, Marwin and Douglas, and one daughter, Barbara. Albert retired from teaching and enjoyed a relaxed life, caring for his home and garden and visiting friends and relatives with Mary. Albert passed away on October 16, 1993. His quiet, gentle manner is missed by the family.

Adolph Bieber moved to Vernon in 1946 and here he met Irene Scheutz. They were married in 1949.They then moved to Ranier and Brooks AB, where they operated a grocery store and owned two school buses. Their children, Jim, Norman and Wendy were born in Alberta. In 1958, the family moved back to Lumby, BC where "Bill" owned a school bus and also set up the "Family Cafe". Keith, their youngest son was born in Lumby. Bill and Irene are now retired in Vernon. Their son Jim, a fireman and ambulance driver, married Cathy Rachwalski of Vernon. They have five children. Norman completed one year of Bible School in Vancouver and then married Sharon Rogolsky, a Vancouver school teacher. They now reside in Salmon Arm, BC with their four children.

Keith, their youngest son, married Pamela Reeve on May 9, 1987. He and Pamela live in Vernon. Wendy, their only daughter, married Elwin Brown, a finishing carpenter. They live in Kelowna, BC with their two daughters, Carleen and Barbara, and son, Douglas.

Fred Bieber, the youngest of the six Bieber brothers, married Martha Lust in 1941 in Medicine Hat, AB. Following in the business tradition of his father, Fred and Martha for many years, operated a store business in Brooks Alberta before moving to Calgary. They were blessed with four children, Bill, David, Roger and Marion. Their oldest son, Bill is a medical doctor in Calgary. Fred and Martha, along with their family were very active members of their church in Brooks, The Free Evangelical Church. In 1973, Fred became ill and he died of cancer on June 29, 1973, Martha passed away on October 15, 1982. Their family miss them dearly.

The family stories of Mary, Annie and Minnie Bieber are found in separate stories in the Bieber History.

Descendants of Fred Bieber who became teachers: (Back row L-R) Albert Bieber, Rudolph Bieber, Karen Rothe, Darlene Smithson, Minnie Arnold, Dennis Peter, Nova Gould, Lorne Peter, Linda Golby, Brian Bieber, Cheryl Fenske, Ruth Bauer, Ruth Penner, Vern Roth.

Mary (Bieber) Peter

by Mary (Bieber) Peter
edited by Ruth (Peter) Bauer

While the Frederich Bieber Family were still living in Dropmore, MB, an immigrant family, Julius and Paulina (Krinke) Peter arrived from Germany. They stayed with friends of our family for several weeks and then moved to a homestead in Prince George, BC. At that time, I didn't realize that their eldest son, Adolph would, one day, become my husband.

Our wedding on December 27, 1939, in Medicine Hat was very simple, but beautiful. At that time, Adolph was living near Prince George, BC on the Red Rock Farm. After the wedding we returned to Red Rock to live. As was the custom in those days, we lived with my husband's family and I learned much about pioneering life, working hard and being thankful to God for His daily provisions and care. In the Spring of 1940, Adolph and I moved to our own three bedroom new home, just seven miles from Prince George.

The Wedding of Mary Bieber and Adolph Peter.

Adolph was a hard worker and together we cleared more land, got some more cattle and things went well. We grew clover for seed and in the winter, Adolph took his teams of horses and went into the bush to skid logs to the sawmill. We had caring neighbours and friends and we began Christian church gatherings in our home.
We lived in Prince George for six years. Although we enjoyed our home and farm, we had heard many stories of the warm climate, good farming, lots of fruit and many friends who lived in the Okanagan Valley in BC, so after selling our farm, cattle, horses and machinery we loaded our car, furniture and household goods into a boxcar and took the train to Vernon, arriving there in December of 1946.

In Vernon, we bought a farm about six miles out of town, and again we were into gardening. It was at that time that my mother and father, Frederick and Catherine Bieber moved to Vernon from Medicine Hat. They along with Minnie, Annie and Adolph, moved to our farm and stayed with us for about six months until Mom and Dad bought their own acreage closer to Vernon. My parents were a great help to us, and we benefited from all of their farming and market gardening experiences from their Dropmore and Medicine Hat days. They decided that we work together in shares. Minnie, my sister was an excellent secretary, and we all did well, enjoying the love of our large extended family.

Adolph and I made two other moves in Vernon, both onto larger mixed farms with fruit trees, market gardening, haying and dairying. To supplement our income when farm prices fluctuated, Adolph also took on labouring jobs in Vernon and surrounding area. He worked at different times at a sawmill, at an ice plant, and at a fruit packing plant. We were blessed to have extended family living in Vernon. There were my parents, Frederick and Katherine Bieber; my sister (one of the Bieber twins born in Dropmore), Ernest and Annie (Bieber) Roth; and my brother, Adolph (Bill) and Irene (Scheutz) Bieber living in Lumby, a small community some twenty-two miles from Vernon. My sister Minnie (Bieber) Arnold, and her family lived in Vernon for shorter periods when her husband, Lawrence was our church pastor.

Adolph and I were blessed with six children, each one of them a special gift from God. **Lorne Frederick** was born on Aug. 7, 1940 in Prince George, BC. After getting his early schooling in Vernon, BC, he attended the University of BC to obtain his Bachelor of Science and Bachelor of Education degrees. He married Janet Houghton, also a teacher. They reside in Vernon, where Lorne teaches high school math. They have three children: Justin, attending Gardiner Bible College, Sarah, enrolling in Okanagan College, and Rebekah, in grade 10.

Ruth Meriam, was born on Jan. 29, 1942, in Prince George, BC. She completed formal schooling in Vernon, and then went on to the University of BC to obtain her Bachelor of Education (Elementary) degree. She taught school in Vernon for several years. She married Reuben Bauer of Stony Plain, AB, and they live in Spruce Grove, AB, where both she and Reuben teach school. They have two children, Simone attending University of AB in second year of Bachelor of Music Program and Jonathan, attending North American Baptist College in first year Bachelor of Arts Program.

Four generations with (L-R) Ruth (Peter) Bauer, Great Grandmother Katherine Bieber holding great granddaugther Simone Bauer, and Grandma Mary (Bieber) Peter in 1975.

The Peter Family: Janet & Lorne Peter (holding Rebekah), Darlene & Lee Smithson, Ingrid & Allan Peter, Mary & Adolph Peter, Karen & Dennis Peter (holding David), Ruth & Reuben Bauer. Grandchildren: Christopher Smithson, Jonathan Bauer, Carla Smithson, Simone Bauer, Sarah Peter, Nathan Peter.

Wedding of the Youngest. Lorne & Janet Peter, Adolph & Mary Peter (Parents) Allan & Ingrid Peter, Darlene & Lee Smithson, Karen & Dennis Peter, Ruth & Reuben Bauer.

Darlene Minnie and **Eileen Annie**, twin girls, were born in Prince George, BC, on February, 5, 1944. They were named in honour of their Bieber Aunts, Minnie and Annie. They both grew up in Vernon. Darlene became a teacher, receiving her training at the University of BC. She married Lee Smithson, a teacher from Alberta and taught school briefly in Alberta. They now reside on a large farm near Camrose, AB where they raise Red Angus cattle. They have three children; Carla has just completed her Master of Arts in English Literature and is now on the Campus Crusade staff at the University of Calgary. Christopher obtained his Bachelor of Arts from King's University in Edmonton and is presently attending Seminary at North American Baptist College in Edmonton. In 1982, Darlene and Lee adopted Darlene's nephew, Nathan, aged five. He was the only surviving family member in a car accident that killed his parents and brother. Nathan is now nineteen and is a weekday resident of Rehoboth Homes, an adult rehabilitation center in Stony Plain, AB. He comes home each weekend.

Eileen completed her Practical Nurses' training in St. Joseph's Hospital in Victoria, BC. She nursed in Kelowna, BC, then attended Gardiner Bible College in Camrose, AB. After completing a Medical Record's Librarian Course in Edmonton she was employed as a personal medical secretary to Dr. Hanson of the Hanson Medical Laboratories in Alberta. In 1970, Eileen married Arnold Glassford, a grain farmer from Saskatchewan and they moved to the farm in Adanac. After a short illness with a brain tumour, Eileen passed on to be with the Lord whom she loved and served. She was just thirty-two years of age at the time of her death, but her memorial service and the memories of lives she touched with her caring nature and gentle servanthood, are a living example of her faith in God.

Dennis Wayne was born in Vernon, BC on August 7, 1947. He also attended the University of British Columbia and completed his Bachelor of Science Degree followed by an Education Degree. He taught school in Kamloops, BC and married Karen Goshulak of Chilliwack, a colleague who was teaching in Merritt, BC. Following their marriage, Dennis and Karen both taught school in Kamloops, interspersed with frequent summer school courses in Vancouver for Dennis, who was completing his Master's Degree in counselling psychology, and Karen, who took music courses to enhance her school music teaching. They had two sons, Nathan age 5 and David age 2. It was following one of their summer school courses in 1982, while Dennis and Karen were on a family holiday to visit family and friends, that they met with a tragic car accident. Dennis and Karen were killed on August 1, 1982 and David passed on to be with Jesus one week later, August 6, 1982. Nathan survived the accident, but sustained permanent injury. He was adopted by the Smithson Family, Dennis' sister, Darlene and husband, Lee. He is now 19 years of age. Dennis, Karen and David are buried in the Pleasant Valley Cemetery in Vernon, BC. How beautiful are the memories we have of Dennis and Karen, their enthusiastic and encouraging nature, their musical talents and their love for their families and for God. We miss them!

Allan Kenneth Edward, our chosen adopted son was born on May 2, 1957. He attended school in Vernon, then moved to Grand Prairie to work. He married Ingrid Baron of Vernon on August 19, 1976. They are now divorced. Allan is working in Vernon again.

During the latter years, of her life and after the death of my father, Frederick Bieber, my mother, Katherine Bieber came to live in our home. It was a great privilege to care for her. She was a wonderful example of faith in God and we all miss her. She died in 1975 after a brief illness.

Adolph, my beloved husband of 49 years, passed away on June 13, 1987, just a few short months before our 50th Wedding Anniversary. After his death, I sold the farm we lived on and now live in an apartment in Vernon. I am still in good health and love to spend time with my children and grandchildren. I am also involved in church activities, volunteering in the local thrift shop and ministering to the "old" folk in the senior citizen homes around Vernon.

Mr. and Mrs. Adolph and Mary (Bieber) Peter in retirement in Vernon, BC.

Minnie (Bieber) Arnold "Reflections"

by Minnie (Bieber) Arnold

Memories are gifts from God. It is with gratitude that I reflect on my years spent on the farm at Dropmore, MB. Being the second youngest of a family of ten children, placed me on the receiving end of much pampering and loving. Life was good, and provided many opportunities for work, play, and skill development such as riding horses and milking cows. One task in particular which my twin sister Annie and I did during the summer holidays was to herd our cattle on the road allowance. To help pass the time we devised our own games using small stones. On another occasion, paralyzed with fear, I "flew", across the field, arrived home breathlessly, minus one shoe, and explained that a coyote was out there. Upon investigation, my father, gun in hand, discovered that it was only the neighbour's dog.

My sister Mary, unravelled the string from an old threshing machine belt and roped off an area in the woods for our playhouse. Much time was spent in this outdoor setting. I recall, also, going down the lean-to of the barn on a shovel and landing on the hay stack below. Looking back now, we probably consider that as a dangerous activity. Because we were a large family, we never lacked for players during the games' times in our yard.

The twins Minnie and Annie riding their favorite horse helping their older brother, Rudolph with a stone-boat loaded with manure to be spread on the fields.

The first school experience I recall was participating in a Christmas concert. Some very small children and I had to march around in a circle, stiff-legged, waddling from side to side singing the following ditty to the tune of Yankee Doodle; "Oh we are Santa's Christmas dolls. We're fine as we can be-o. Perhaps you'll find us hanging high, Upon the Christmas tree-o". Chorus: "Fa-la-la-la, Christmas dolls, Don't you think we're dandy. We are Santa's Christmas dolls, O we are sweet as candy". As I recall now, perhaps we were guest participants for this Yankee Doodle Christmas march.

Our Mom, Katherine Bieber and my twin sister Annie on the right. Note our stylish 1927 beeline hats.

Here is Minnie's Report Card.

I still have a one page report card issued by Miss W. I. Harvey, which states: "Grainsby School, Easter examination, April 17, 1930, Minnie Bieber." The subjects were reading, writing, arithmetic, drawing, and handwork, with a percentage mark obtained for each. I also have, as a prized possession, a booklet containing my report cards from Malcolm Gillies and Kennatha Statham. I remember Malcolm Gillies out on the school yard supervising the students during recess and also participating in their games, such as soccer,

The twins (L-R) Annie and Minnie. Talking about herding cattle... here is one that didn't get away!

baseball and anti-anti-over. One day, after recess, he questioned my behaviour because I kept chasing one girl. I replied, "I don't like her!" So much for the golden rule.

One type of discipline was to make a girl sit with a boy. This was very convenient because of the double desks in our school room. I don't recall there was a rush to obtain misdemeanour points. The blackboards sometimes had beautiful borders on them. By using a chalk-filled brush and perforated stencils the design was "powdered onto the board." These pin-pricked outlines were then filled in with coloured chalk. Although the library cupboard in the school contained a limited supply of books, we all looked forward to the times the teacher read to us. One story about a two-headed animal called "The Pushmi-Pullyu" will always remain etched in my memory. I don't remember a thing about the story itself, but the name stuck. I was curious so I phoned the Edmonton Public Library to see what they could tell me about the "Pushmi-Pullyu", and this is what they told me: "It is found in the story of Dr. Doolittle by Hugh Lofting. Dr. Doolittle received a Pushmi-Pullya, a rare llama with a head on each end, as a gift to help him raise money for his journey, in search of the great sea snail." Well, I guess I'll have to read the book if I want to know the end of the story. I appreciated this information.

My father's Model-T Ford was used for pleasure, shopping, attending worship, berry picking, or for visiting friends or relatives in Shellmouth, Dropmore, Langenburg, MacNutt, Bersina and yes, also for optometric needs in Russell.

My father learned his blacksmith trade while a soldier in the Austrian Army. He was very proficient in his own blacksmith shop as he repaired and fashioned tools for himself and his neighbours. In my mind's eye I can still see the sparks fly as he removed the hot plowshare from the fire, placed it on the anvil, struck it with his hammer, and then plunged it into cold water.

The picture of my father with his head enclosed in a white, screened, window cage, as he gently worked with his bees, is a memory I treasure. Dad assembled all of his own frames by putting one sheet of waxy film inside of a frame. The bees formed their own combs and filled them with honey. What a learning experience for us as we watched the process from frame to bee to hive to honey. At first Dad tried to winter the bees by giving them sugared water from a perforated pail. He found this method of preserving bees not very successful, so each spring he ordered a new supply of bees. I found it fascinating to learn that the queen bee was kept in a compartment, separate from the worker bees. During the summertime season, Dad would take each frame out of its hive, search out the drones, and destroy them. If he found two queen bees in one box, he would take out one of the queens and put her into another hive to start a new colony. This prevented them from swarming. As a teacher today, I would give anything to return to my childhood memories and share a field trip with my students to my Dad's blacksmith shop or bee apiary.

On one of our many berry-picking excursions to wooded areas, I recall my brothers and sisters shouting to each other to keep in contact. The wooded areas were very dense and it would have been very easy to get lost.

One day, my Father felt the time had arrived to move the Family to greener pastures. Being a practical man, he first made the trip to Lula Island (now Richmond), BC. to scout out a suitable and profitable environment in which to move his family. Upon his return, I was enthralled with the world-shattering news my father related, "You just need to move a switch on the wall and the lights go on!" Now that's progress from the lowly kerosene lamps!

He also said, "I saw a lady typing without looking at the keys and she was talking at the same time!" Wow, what marvellous magic for a ten year old!

I'm grateful to my parents, Fred and Katherine Bieber, for their devotion to God and the wonderful legacy they have handed down to their children. We did leave the farm in Dropmore and, moved to the Okanagan Valley, BC, after a ten year stop-over in Medicine Hat, where my father owned and operated a grocery store.

In Vernon, I met my husband Lawrence, whose chosen vocation was the pastoral ministry. Lawrence studied for his church ministry at Bible College in Camrose, AB and Anderson, IN. He also completed his Bachelor of Education degree. This further University training enhanced his church ministry. Most of his pastorates were in Calgary and Edmonton

My chosen vocation was that of a public school teacher. I have a Bachelor of Education degree from the University of Calgary and taught school in Calgary and Edmonton for over twenty years.

Lawrence and Minnie with their grown daughters (L-R) Nova, Karen, Lawrence, Minnie and Cheryl.

Our family of three girls. (L-R) Lawrence holding Cheryl, Nova (standing between us) Karen and Minnie.

We have three daughters. Karen obtained her Bachelor of Education degree from the University of Alberta. She married Wayne Rothe on March 23, 1979. She is a music teacher in Spruce Grove and Wayne was employed in public relations. Because of his excellent writing skills, he was an editor for various publications. He now has his own business. They have two children, Jordan and Chelsea.

Nova, our second daughter also trained to become a teacher at the University of Alberta and obtained her Bachelor of Education degree. Nova is a music teacher. She married Daniel Gould on August 23, 1975. They have three children: Nathan, Aaron and Rebecca. Dan's work experience has been that of a buyer, including a sixteen month contract with the International Monetary Fund in Washington, D.C. Nova and Dan spent one year living in Arlington, Virginia. Dan commuted to his job in Washington, a twenty- minute Metro ride and Nova taught Kindergarten and ESL in Virginia. Lawrence and I had the privilege of spending two weeks with them and really enjoyed the beautiful area. We visited many of the historic sites. Nova and Dan have now returned to Edmonton where Nova will continue to teach for the Edmonton Public School System and Dan hopes to continue his work as a buyer.

Our youngest daughter, Cheryl is an elementary school teacher in Crossfield, AB. She too, received her Bachelor's degree in Education from the University of Alberta. On July 4, 1981, she married Marc Fenske, a junior high school teacher from Calgary who is noted for his wonderful sense of humour with his students. They reside in Airdre, AB with their two children, Mariah, and Kassandra.

Lawrence and Minnie (Bieber) Arnold are retired now, both enjoying good health. They travel a lot and greatly enjoy life.

Lawrence and I are both retired but our lives are busier than ever. We have done extensive travelling to many parts of Canada and the United States. We enjoy World Adventure Tours, Symphony Concerts, Rosebud Dinner Theatres, and weekly church commitments. From time to time, Lawrence enjoys filling in as a relief pastor in neighbouring churches. We are a very close-knit family and delight in our children and grandchildren. We are fortunate that they all live within easy commuting distance. When we have our family gatherings, we sound like a "Teacher's Convention", with all our mutual teacher's training. We are grateful that all of our children are actively committed to God and the churches where they worship. God has blessed us richly. My chapter closes, but the list of memories lives on...and on... and on.

The Arnold Family: (L-R) Daniel & Nova Gould, Marc & Cheryl Fenske, Wayne & Karen Rothe, Lawrence & Minnie Arnold. The grandchildren: (Back row L-R) Jordan Rothe, Aaron Gould, Nathan Gould. (Front row L-R) Rebecca Gould, Mariah Fenske and Chelsea Rothe.

The Wedding of Ernest Roth and Annie Bieber.

Annie (Bieber) Roth

by Annie Roth

As the youngest member of the Fred Bieber Family of ten, I'd like to relate some incidents that I recall from my early years, growing up with my 6 older brothers and 3 older sisters. These events would come under the numbers of 7 and 8 on a scale of 1 to 10, I presume...i.e. "Miraculous Escape From Fatal Injury During a Severe Electrical Storm." Also, recalling exciting times, visiting the places of interest at the fair in Yorkton or Russell and the Experimental Farms.

As a child of 8 or 9, I remember very vividly the severe lightning and thunderstorms we often experienced on the farm near Dropmore. One very hot July or August summer day, a terrible storm was "brewing" overhead. A streak of lightning hit our house with a deafening sound that knocked the plaster off the closet wall (upstairs), zigzagged across the room where my youngest brother Fred was sleeping, then made its way down the wall (downstairs), where it took a splinter of wood out from a houseplant where it was sitting on a window sill. Half of the plant wilted - the other half was untouched. "Almost like magic", no one was injured during this fateful lightning bolt for which we all were "exceedingly" grateful and thankful to God for sparing our lives! The fear of this traumatic event stayed with me for a long time and I dreaded every thunderstorm that came along, holding my breath every time I'd see a streak of "fork" lightning, wondering, hoping and praying it wouldn't strike our house again!!!

The Roth Children (L-R) Vern, Allan, baby David in the carriage and Linda.

Another "adventurous" family get-together I remember participating in was "berry picking" time in August or September - going down the Shellmouth Hill with all its winding "merry loops" in Dad's old Model T Ford car was an adventure in itself. With as many of the family that could fit in the car, one or two standing on the running board, holding on the sides was a "sight to behold" - you can well imagine. But we made it safely down - down to the beautiful "Assiniboine Valley" where luscious beautiful ripe berries of every variety were growing - ready to be picked by eager hands. It was such a delight for us all to do this "together" as a family. Talking, laughing, picking pails and pails of juicy Saskatoons, cranberries, chokecherries, pincherries, into our buckets which we all would so much enjoy in the cold winter months as canned fruit, and jams and jellies were preserved by Mom and her family members, sorting and cleaning the berries. You can be sure we all enjoyed our coffee break time - it was great. Mother always had sandwiches, homemade "kuchen", cookies and cake to go along with our coffee and berries, juicy sweet, Saskatoons- mmm-so good--how well I remember this eventful day.

I must go on and tell of the times Dad would take us to Mr. Skinner's experimental horticultural farm. To me, as a little girl of about 9 or 10 - it seemed like heaven! The air was filled with a beautiful aroma of honey from the bees buzzing about, gathering honey from the flowering fruit trees and flowers just everywhere!! My Dad really loved coming here where he learned alot about tree growing and flowers. I remember the beautiful Sweet Williams, and holy hocks, and nasturtiums, flox, and sweet clover we used to have around our house along with the hives of bees that my Dad would raise for honey, year round. He was a great lover of bees and had a honey extractor that we used to extract our winter's supply of honey for the family year round. I used to love to chew the beeswax, filled with honey as Dad would trim off the thin layer of wax from off the frames before putting them in the extractor to draw out the honey. What "beautiful" sweet memories I have of this happy event!! Before leaving this part of my story, I'd like to add - I believe my Dad got a good part of his "bee-keeping" training from Mr. Skinner's valuable knowledge and enthusiasm. Also from a "Mr. Millar" who also was very knowledgeable in raising bees. I'm pleased that my Dad, Fred Bieber, had the courage and incentive to take up this valuable hobby that benefited our whole family.

Dad was a real "family man" and I recall how he used to read us stories from the Bible, after the evening meal, stories like Daniel, Joseph, Moses, Abraham, all Bible characters who lived and died like courageous heroes.. These stories stuck with us and we remember them today. After our Bible reading and prayer and hymn time, Dad would come outside with us and play all kinds of games!

The Roths today - (L-R) Vern, Ernie, Annie, Linda, Allan and missing from the picture is David.

With these "happy memories" I'd like to close my Bieber memories of Dropmore with this special quote: "Happiness is Homemade"! It was so in our family of 10 with 2 sets of twins.!

Please note: Annie left Dropmore in 1934 when The Biebers moved to Medicine Hat and then to Vernon, BC. Annie married Ernest "Ernie" Roth in Vernon, B.C. on August 4, 1948. Ernie was active in dairy and mixed farming and in his later years worked with a building contracting firm. They have four children all happily married: Allan, a realtor in Agassiz, BC, Linda, a school teacher in Richmond, BC, Vern, a teacher in Spruce Grove, AB and David, a supervisor in a building contracting firm in Vernon, BC.

Annie and Ernie are retired and live in Vernon, BC where they enjoy their church involvements, their many friends and visits from their children and ten grandchildren.

Frank and Doris Bird

by Daphne Villers

Frank and Doris Bird.

Frank came to Manitoba from Norfolk, England in 1912. He worked on farms until the outbreak of WW1, when he enlisted in the 43rd Cameron Highlanders. He was on active service in France until he was wounded at Parthenay. Frank married Doris Newman in Warwick County, Birmingham, England. They came to Canada in March, 1930, to the Dropmore area. They farmed in Grainsby and Dropmore area until 1950, when they moved to Vista, MB.

All of their children went to high school and most of them worked in nursing and secretarial areas. They had 12 children, 46 grandchildren and 45 great grand-children.

Frank and Doris enjoyed a trip back to England to visit their many relatives.

The children are Mary (Bucklaschuk), Joan (Pattison), Jean (Hanmore), Rose, (Bonin), Daphne, (Villers), Violet (Stouffer), Ruth (Robertson), Lucy (Cummingham), Anne (Dann), Ted Bird, David Bird and Sylvia (Farley).

Frank passed away April 5, 1983, Doris passed away January 10, 1986. and Joan passed away January 16, 1986.

Mabel (Cook) Bird

by Mabel Bird (1902 - Present)

I came to teach at Grainsby School in January 1924 after Miss Erlandson resigned. I was there until June but had to go to Winnipeg Normal School to get a second class certificate to replace the 3 year third class which had expired. After a year I came back to Grainsby for a year.

I married Victor Bird in December, 1927. I also taught in Dropmore in 1932. We moved from Dropmore in 1940 going to Endcliffe where I was Secretary-Treasurer of Endcliffe, S.D. until 1952 when I went back teaching for another thirteen years. When I retired, we moved to Edmonton where I did substitute teaching for six years until I was seventy.

Victor passed away in 1987.

My later years were spent with Senior Citizens' Clubs and visiting friends in hospitals and nursing homes and traveling far and near.

John Birnie Family

by Jean Morrison

John Birnie was born on October 13, 1858, in Rosehearty, Aberdeenshire, Scotland. His father, John Birnie was a ship's carpenter. He died at sea, of yellow fever we think, leaving his wife and son in Scotland. She later married John Skinner in 1860.

John Birnie attended school and later worked on farms, etc.. In 1882, like so many others, he struck off for this new land, Canada, where there was free land (a homestead). He got a job with the C.P.Railway and worked west of Winnipeg near Westbourne.

He used to tell us about the big snowstorms and the huge drifts of snow that blocked the railway and of the difficult time they had getting the snowplow through. Then he worked on the "Bell Farms" near Indian Head, NWT. They had a huge round barn for the horses. We don't know how long he was there. So, off he went looking for a homestead and located one near Togo, SK, where he met up with Ernest Thompson

Seton (the author of many children's books and a naturalist) who was looking for a homestead too.

They batched together one winter. John gave up that homestead and he met up with James Mitchell who was also seeking good hay and pasture land. They came to the Castleavery district. John Birnie located on 2-25-29. Mitchells located across the Assiniboine River. This was a good place to be in 1888 and 1889, as those were the dry years.

In 1889 John's sister, Christian Skinner came out to keep house for him. That was before there was a bridge across the river. There was a scow built to cross the river and she learned to operate that too. The rest of the Skinner family came out in 1895, and John helped get them settled in the Rochedale district.

John married Marjory Anderson Pyott in October, 1910. They lived for awhile at the Birnie Bridge, later called Pyott's and now Pyott's Point campground. They moved to 2-24-29 near Dropmore. They later built the present house where they lived until 1948.

They were both interested in community affairs. John was involved with the Dropmore Rifle Club. He loved to hunt and had some specimens mounted - a moose, elk and deer as well as a bearskin. He told us many interesting stories about hunting.

He served several years on the school board and was a member of the United Grain Growers. They were very interested in gardening and grew Colorado Blue Spruce from seed, which took years and years. I believe there are still some on the farm, also many lovely rose, etc.. Marjory was very interested in needlework. She was a seamstress in Scotland, had served her apprenticeship and was employed before she and her brother, William Pyott, came out to help William Anderson at Clova in 1905. The Pyott family came out later to Clova and later settled at the bridge.

Marjory worked very hard for the community and church, doing sewing, baking and helping with teas. During both wars she did knitting and worked on committees for the hall. She enjoyed music and singing. She was also a member of the Red Cross there and in Armstrong, BC.

John and Marjory had a family of two: John Pyott, born in 1912 and Jean in 1921. They both attended school in Dropmore. We were all fond of horses and kept quite a few. John took an electrical course by correspondence. He liked hunting and music. John married Vera Johstone in October, 1944. They lived on the home farm. John Edward was born in May 1946. His grandfather really enjoyed him for those few months. John Birnie Sr. passed away in September, 1946.

The family moved to Armstrong, BC in 1948 and lived in Granny Pyott's old home.

John and Vera had four of a family: Leslie Allen born in 1949, Marjory Caroline in 1953 and Robert James in 1955 all in Armstrong, BC. By this time they had moved to a dairy farm just out of Armstrong.

Marjory did enjoy her grandchildren and continued working for the local Ladies' Church group. After suffering a stroke, she had to go to a nursing home. She passed away in 1971 and was laid to rest near other members of the Pyott family, in Armstrong.

John Birnie passed away in July 1985 and Vera in December 1990. Ed and his family live in Surrey, BC and Leslie, Marjory and Robert remain in the Okanogan Valley.

Jean married Earl Morrison in 1943 and lived on 8-24-29. They had one daughter Janet Erla, born in 1944. They farmed until 1966, when they moved to Brandon and still reside there.

Basil Bradley-Hunt Family

By the Family

Our dad, Basil Bradley-Hunt came from England in 1910 to the Dropmore district, to his step-cousin, O.W. Goodbun, who farmed on Sec. 14-22-29. He enlisted in the 1st C.M.R.'s early in 1915, served in England and France, where he was taken prisoner on June 2nd, 1916. After a period of time in a hospital in Germany, he was sent to Russia, then later back to a small village in Germany where he and five other soldiers worked on farms. They were billeted with a farmer and his wife, who were extremely kind to them and shared their meagre rations with them. After the Armistice

Basil and Dorothy Bradley-Hunt.

(L-R) Don & Freda Robin, Phil & Barb Zimmer, Joyce & Barb McMurchy.

was declared, he worked in London in the office where they arranged for the transportation of the Canadian troops back to Canada.

In July of 1919, our dad and mother, Dorothy Neeld, were married. He came back to Canada and after getting his discharge. He worked for Tim Goodbun in the Royston district until our mother came to Canada in the spring of 1920. By the time she came, he had acquired land on Sec. 22-23-29, where they built their house and farmed until 1930. They moved to the village of Dropmore and operated a general store until 1937 when our dad was appointed secretary treasurer of the R.M. of Shellmouth, a position he held until his sudden death in 1947. Our mother was asked to take on the work, which she did and stayed until her retirement in 1964. She continued to live in her home in Dropmore until a very few years ago, when she moved to The Banner County in Russell, where in her 97th year she still resides.

Joyce married Henry Turner, a grain buyer in 1944. Henry had a son, Rae from a previous marriage, and Henry and Joyce had a daughter, Linda and a son Gerry. Rae married Julie Van Mackelberg from Deloraine. They live in Boissevain, have a family of three, Kim, Brad and Todd, and now have five grandsons. Linda married Bill Naughton from Woodnorth, MB. They presently live in North Battleford, and have a son Derek, and a daughter, Sandra. Gerry married Beverly Chopey from Calgary, they have a daughter Kristine, and daughter, Janice. They live near Edmonton. Henry passed away suddenly in 1963, and Joyce was remarried to Bob McMurchy, a farmer from Reston. They resided on the farm until the spring of 1994, when Bob sold the farm. They built a home in Virden and retired there in October 1994.

Barbara married Phil Zimmer in 1951 and they lived on their farm until they sold in 1992. They retired to Russell, where they are enjoying their retirement. Their history is elsewhere in this book.

Freda and Don Robin were married in 1952 and live on Sec. 33-23-28 in the Rochedale district. They have a family of three, Brad, Lori and Sally. Brad is on the home farm, and married to Brenda Petz. They have a family of two, Kiley and Kristy. Lori works in Calgary, Sally is married to Charlie Linski. They have a family of two, Alice and Gabriel, and live in Winnipeg. The Robin history is also elsewhere in this book.

Brown Family

by Audrey Loewen

Alfred William George Brown

Alfred William George Brown - born May 24, 1888 came from Brighton, England to Canada in 1911. He retired in 1958 to Brandon, Manitoba. He moved to Winnipeg in 1964. During the First World War, he served overseas with the R.C.H.A. 1914-1918.

Ida Mary Brown

Ida Mary Brown - born November 17, 1896, came from Devon, England to Canada in 1919. She was in her early 20s. In 1920 they settled on the Warburton Farm, just East of Dropmore, S.E. sec. 26 township 23, 29 W.I. Rural Municipality of Shellmouth, MB, the farm bordered both sides of the railway. This was the birth farm for five children, William Wilfred, Eveline Mary, and Audrey Winnifred and two children which died at birth. In the mid 1930s they moved to the Brewer Farm, just south of Dropmore Cemetery S.E. 27-23-29 W.

The Brown Family - Alfred and Ida, Evelyn, Wilfred and Audrey.

Alfred and Ida got married in Russell, MB. driving the distance by horse and buggy.

Alfred Brown home south of Dropmore.

Our first home was a two storey wood farm home, as was our second. When the work was done and the ice froze, the winters were spent skating on a slough which Dad and Wilfred cleaned off. People came from Tummell, Shellmouth, Inglis and the surrounding area for a hockey game every Sunday. Many dances were enjoyed in the Dropmore Hall.

Wilfred Brown and his Black Angus cattle.

Ida enjoyed knitting, crocheting and making quilts. They raised turkeys and Black Angus cattle. They enjoyed farm life until health forced them to retire to Brandon, MB. Mrs. Brown lived 43 years in Dropmore and then moved to Brandon in 1955 and lived there for eight years. Mrs. Brown died in Brandon in March of 1963 at the age of 68 years.

Mrs. Brown drove a 1929 Durant car before getting a new model which was a 1949 Plymouth.

Mr. Brown moved to Winnipeg in 1964 to live with his youngest daughter Audrey until 1970. He then moved into the Legion Towers. He worked as a Commissionaire in Brandon and in the

Ida Brown & Reg Rowland beside the 1929 Durant car.

English Gardens in Winnipeg, until his death in June 1973 at the age of 84 years. The Brown's three living children are William Wilfred, Eveline Mary and Audrey Winnifred.

The Brown children - Wilfred, Evelyn and Audrey.

William Wilfred

William Wilfred - the oldest took his education in Dropmore. He worked on the farm with his father. In 1958 he moved to Brandon and worked for Simplot's Plant in Carberry, MB. He spent many years working for Poole Construction and retired from Poole Construction in Calgary as a Superintendent.

Wilfred has three boys --Danny who is married to Lenore and has three children. He lives in Calgary, AB. Danny is a Foreman doing construction surrounding the Calgary area. Chuck also living in Calgary is a painter and has a Rock band. Chuck is single. Thomas, who is still going to school, lives in Vernon, BC.

Today Wilfred still does some construction work, but prefers to take it easy. He enjoys fishing and mostly hunting in the fall of the year. He

Wilfred Brown loves to hunt.

spends a lot of time with his children and grandchildren in Calgary. Thomas is able to get away from his school studies in Vernon, BC to spend time with his father.

Eveline Mary

Eveline Mary - the second oldest attended school in Dropmore, Grades 1-8. Grade 9 in the old Francis Store. High School 10 and 11 in Shellmouth. A business course in Brandon, worked at the Law firm of Stordy, Alder and Buckingham.

Eveline was married in the farm home south of Dropmore to Mike Pulak of Dauphin, MB. in July 1953. Mike worked in Roblin for Roblin Auto Body and also Hughes Motors, before moving to Brandon in 1949 to work for Canadian Motors. In 1981, they moved from Brandon to Penticton, BC where Mike worked for A & J Auto Body in Summerland, BC. He is now retired, but caretakes a Mobile Home Park.

Mike and Eveline's Family, Kenneth Robert, Michael James, Patricia Ann & her husband, Lance Isackson.

We have 3 children: Patricia Ann married to Lance Isackson, now living in Vancouver, BC. Michael James, single living in Brandon, MB. Kenneth Robert, single, living in Penticton, BC. Both are sports minded.

Since the winters are milder and the summers are warm, we very much enjoy our surroundings and the beautiful fresh fruit.

Audrey Winnifred

Audrey Winnifred - third youngest living. Attended school at Dropmore until Grade VIII. She then took her Grade IX at Tamarisk (Grandview) and finished her education in Brandon, MB.

Audrey Brown going riding on her horse.

Audrey worked for the RCMP for two and a half years in Brandon and in 1956 moved to Winnipeg to work for the law there. She also worked for the Winnipeg Tribune for many years. In 1970 she moved with her husband Abram to BC. She immediately started working for Canada Customs at the coast and has worked all the Ports from the coast right across to the Port of Osoyoos, BC. She is presently the Senior Customs Inspector at the Port of Penticton in the Okanagan Valley in BC.

Abram Loewen.

Audrey married Abram Loewen in 1968. Abram has four children from a previous marriage.

Oldest - Karen is married to Jeff now living in Rock Falls, Illinois and has three children.

Second Oldest - Claudette is married to Pat, living in Westburne, Manitoba and has four children.

Third Youngest - Bonnie is married to Sandy, living in Selkirk, Manitoba and has five children.

Third Youngest - Jeff, is married to Debbie, living in Winnipeg and has two children.

Our children - Susan married to Michael lives in Winnipeg and has one child.

Helen married to Mark, lives in Victoria, B.C. and has one child.

This makes a total of six children and sixteen grandchildren.

Audrey Loewen in her uniform of a Customs Officer.

Abe and Audrey love to fish and go boating. We both belong to the Royal Canadian Legion and the Eagle's Club. Audrey is very active in the Ladies Auxiliary of the Royal Canadian Legion and is presently the Sgt. at Arms. She loves to attend conventions. Abe recently retired from the BC Corp. of Commissionaires due to ill health and now enjoys making crafts, etc. at home.

J. Agnes Burgess

Thoughts on Castleavery School 1932-1933

by Mrs. J. A. Burgess (Agnes Thom)

I taught in the Castleavery School for two years and have most pleasant memories of that time.

The two mile walk to the school gave me lots of time to think about the day to enjoy or to reflect on yesterday.

The school, one large room with a teacher's room in one corner, chalk, blackboards, some double desks, an organ, outdoor plumbing, grades I to IX for 16 pupils became my responsibility. It was a busy time trying to reach out and help each child with his studies.

Christmas concerts were inevitable - always a joy to the children and parents. Finding suitable programs was difficult with such a variety of ages but when the great day arrived, everyone was in the spirit and enjoyed the event.

One morning when I pulled out the drawer of my desk, I gazed into a new mouse nest and hairless baby mice. I went screaming out the door and the boys got rid of the problem.

My pupils were:
JIM ROE, EVA ROE, JEAN CASE, JACK NICHOLS, HOWARD COMFORT, DOROTHY JONES, BETH JONES, ISABEL SHEARER, GORDON FERRIS, DURWARD ROWAN, DOROTHY NICHOLS, JOHN HUNTER, HAROLD JONES, IRMA SHEARER, MARGARET COMFORT, DAVID HUNTER, and April Beginners - ILENE ROE, DOUGLAS DOW, PAT NICHOLS & DONNIE SHEARER.

Some of my pupils are here for this homecoming - they might even be grandparents by now.

Mr. and Mrs. Walter Robertson.

I can honestly say the two years with these children were enjoyable and memorable.

I boarded with Mr. & Mrs. Walter Robertson, better known as Mr. & Mrs. "R". There was a kitchen-living room, scullery and steps at least 12 inches high, which led to three bedrooms that were not sound proof. One morning I heard Walter say, "What day is this Helen?" "It's Christmas tree day you silly cuddy," she said.

There was another room attached to the kitchen area - the "parlour". Its furniture included an organ that apparently Mrs. R. played quite well at one time; she also trained the school children to sing for their Christmas concerts. During my time, this room was never used socially. It wasn't heated so was used to keep food from spoiling.

My bed had a straw mattress and by the end of the week I had made a sort of hollow where I could lie comfortably. When I returned from having spent the weekend in Russell, Mrs. R had shaken up the mattress and it took me all week again to round out my "hollow spot".

We were having supper one night when the Watkin's man arrived. He was on his knees on the floor, opening up his bag of wares when I saw Walter pick up a big bone from his plate. It had been in a meat pie. He disappeared with it into the scullery. When he came back, he whispered to me that the Watkin's man might think that he was the dog around there.

Mrs. R. was very superstitious. Whenever there was a new moon, she would go outside, flip up her outside layer of skirts and turn a coin in a hidden pocket. This meant that she would never be poor. It would be disastrous to look at a new moon through glass.

One day I forgot my lunch and went back for it. She made me sit down and count to 10 or I would have bad luck.

Friday the 13th was fatal. They hardly moved off their chairs.

Those were the days when you had your own "ring" on the telephone. Mrs. R. enjoyed everyone's "rings". How else do you know what is going on in your community at age 70?

We played a card game called "500" - it couldn't end until someone reached the magic number - 500 - even if you played until 1:00 A.M.

Mrs. R. used to give special callers a "drink". Walter always smacked his lips and told the visitors to be sure to call again as that was the only time she would pour him a "drink".

We often tobogganed on a hill and were invited to Comforts for supper. I can still see Mr. Comfort sharpening the butcher knife as he prepared to cut thick slices of beef from a huge roast.

House parties were popular. We went to one at Richardsons on the highway in a big sleigh box. It was 8 A.M. when we arrived back to Dugan's home. I couldn't get to bed fast enough but Isabel washed the kitchen floor first.

Dances at Dropmore were enjoyable to which we travelled 8 miles by horse and cutter.

I went for a ride in a democrat with Mr. & Mrs. R. to visit the Andersons in the valley. I was terrified as we drove down the hill. I thought the horses wouldn't be able to hold back the democrat or they would gallop and we would be thrown out.

Mrs. R was a good cook and I enjoyed her meals that were baked in a quaint old wooden stove.

Mr. R. was a quiet man. Mrs. R. was the leader and Mr. R. always seemed to fall in line.

Mr. R. was born in 1865 in Scotland. He had 2 brothers, John and Jim and one sister Mary. She got married to Henry Allbright. He died in 1936.

Mrs. R., nee Helen Jane McIntyre was born in Scotland in 1864. After Walter's death, she lived in Roblin with Mr. & Mrs. John Hill until her death in 1946. Their funeral services were both held in their old farm home of 52 years in Castleavery.

Teaching and living with Mr. & Mrs. R. in a friendly district makes Castleavery special to me.

Congratulations to the Dropmore Homecoming '95 Committee.

Peter and Margaret Burla

Peter was the seventh child of George and Zanferia Burla. He was born August 4, 1929, in the Shellmouth Municipality. He got his education at the Shell Bank School and worked on his Dad's family farm. At the age of twenty he went out to work at various places, the Ontario Mine, Northern Manitoba Railroad, and driving gravel trucks.

Peter and Margaret Burla.

On July 19, 1959 he married Margaret Lungal, the oldest daughter of George and Jessie Lungal. Margaret was born August 6, 1938 in the Boulton Municipality. We moved to Dauphin, and Peter worked as a painter. In 1963 we moved back to farm, the Burla homestead where we presently reside.

We were blessed with five children. Barb was born October 18, 1960. She was married

February 28, 1981 to Layton Bezan. They have four children, Brett, Carter, Morgan, and Kirby. They presently reside on a farm north of Regina, Saskatchewan. Our second daughter, Joanne was born September 30, 1962. She married Ed Myslichuk of Roblin on August 12, 1989. They have a foster child, Crystal. On May 21, 1964, we had our first son, Dwayne. Dwayne presently works at Clements and cattle farms. Jennifer was born May 13, 1972. She married Brett Bauereiss on August 2, 1992. They were blessed with a son, Seth Thomas on December 22, 1992. They presently reside in Indian Head, SK. Our youngest son, Robert was born December 8, 1973. Robert attended University of Brandon for three years. He is presently employed with UGG Seed in Roblin. All of our children attended school in Inglis and went on to graduate from Major Pratt in Russell.

Peter and Margaret Burla Family.

Vera (Burla) Paulenko

Vera was the second oldest daughter of George & Zanferia Burla, born on August 5, 1917. She had her education of grade four at Shell Bank School.

In 1943, she worked at the Russell Hospital and also at home.

At the age of 23, on July 22, 1945, she married Matt Paulenko. Matt was the oldest child of Elie and Polly Paulenko.

They made their nesting place on the farm that they had bought with four acres of cultivation, the SW 27-24-27 in the Blue Wing District. They worked hard and cleared the land by hand and horse to grow wheat, barley and oats.

Matt and Vera had two sons: Edward was born October 15, 1945 and attended the Blue Wing School.

Kenneth was born November 25, 1952. They were both baptized in the Shell Valley Church.

In 1955 their farming ended when Matt was too sick and was hospitalized. They moved to Dauphin, MB in 1955, where they took up interior decorating and painting. Vera also worked at the Locker Plant for the next 16 years and then helped Matt paint for the next 4 years.

Vera was a great cook, baked her own bread, was a great gardener and spent hours sewing her own house dresses. She also sewed for the neighbour's children.

They enjoyed the fellowship of their good neighbours and relatives and spent hours quilting in her basement.

In 1982, due to poor health, Matt was forced to retire and they bought a house in Inglis, where they made their home.

Matt passed away on Nov. 7, 1984. Their son Kenneth passed away on Sept. 29, 1973 and their son Edward on Nov. 8, 1986.

Vera still resides in Inglis.

Bartley and Lyla Carmicheal

Bartley and Lyla Carmichael

Bartley came from the United States in 1907 with his parents and settled on S 1/2 of 5-24-29. He married Lyla Davidson of Dropmore in 1927. Her father was the station agent in Dropmore. Lyla had a sister, Tuggy Davidson and a brother Clyde.

They were very active in community affairs in Grainsby and later in Dropmore.

They moved to Russell for a short time, then to Brandon, and Bartley passed away June 1969. Lyla lived in a suite for a number of years still coming back to visit friends often.

Lyla passed away November of 1984. They had no family but were friends to many. Miss Nora Yoemens, Lyla's aunt lived with them.

All are buried in Dropmore Cemetery.

Iris Chernesky

by Iris Chernesky

My mother was Anna Dalle and my father was Reginald Baggs.

I was only 5 years old when I went to school at Rochedale, with my Aunt Matilda Case (Dalle). There is so very little I remember, only that my grandfather lived at the Lougheed farm. His name was Charles Dalle.

As for pictures, we don't have any. Our house burned on the farm in Saskatoon and we lost everything.

My mother, Anna Baggs passed away March 19, 1988 and is laid to rest in the Dropmore Cemetery.

James Boyd Craig Family

by Maggie Cameron (nee Craig)

Dad, Jas. Boyd Craig was born at East Kilbride, Scotland, May 26, 1871. Mother, Jeanie Lindsay Morrison was born Jan. 17, 1874.

They were married in 1901. They had six children - Maggie, Willie, John, Jim and Alexander (Sandy) who were all born in Scotland, and Peter who was born in Canada (the only Canuck in the family).

Dad came to Canada in 1911, intending to settle in Edmonton, AB as he had cousins there. He also had an uncle, aunt and cousins in Birtle so decided to visit them first and a school chum in Rochedale. He stayed in Birtle for a while.

One of the cows they were milking was so wild it would nearly kick the stars out of heaven. But, Dad thought he could handle her, but every one had a good laugh, when it kicked every button off his vest.

Craig House

He settled down in Rochedale and farmed for the rest of his life on Section 5-24-28.

Mother and family came out to Canada the following year, 1912. We were to sail on the Titanic, but due to Sandy (2 yrs old) developing measles, we were quarantined for 2 weeks, otherwise we would have had a watery grave.

It took real courage for Mother to leave home and country with 5 youngsters 2 to 9 years old. We had to walk 3 miles to school, summer and winter. Our mode of transportation was horse and buggy or cutter. Dropmore was our nearest town.

The years ahead were a struggle for our parents, of course kids never notice these things. A minister came to the Rochedale school every Friday afternoon and we had Sunday School.

As years went by, we got involved in different things in the district, such as Christmas concerts, plays (which I really liked), house parties, skating parties and the boys with their soccer.

From a very young age the boys spent their summer holiday at the rivers swimming, rafting and so on. The older boys taught the younger ones to swim on a "sink or swim" basis with none of this Red Cross stuff. One time at the river, cows came along and chewed up their clothes. Some would have a chewed shirt to put on and no pants and others, pants and no shirt.

In their teen days, their greatest interest (besides girls and dancing) was their soccer and my five brothers were all in it, along with the local boys who worked at Skinner's Nursery. They named their team "The Rochedale Rangers". They won the North-West League in 1930-31 and '32 and also the Pratt Cup. They went to the "Sport Days" for miles around.

Dad passed away in 1952 and Mother in 1954. Both are resting in the Deer Park Cemetery at Tummell.

I, Maggie, married Ben Cameron on Jan. 11, 1933. We had one daughter - Margaret Jean, born in 1935. Ben stopped farming in 1965 and we moved to Roblin in October 1975. Ben passed away December 3, 1975.

Willie married Gladys Rawlings in 1934 and they had one son - Roy.

John married Mabel McFadyen and lived on the home farm. John passed away October 4, 1978.

Jim married Lois Howe October 7, 1939. They have one daughter - Marilynn.

Alexander (Sandy) married Beatrice Jory. They have two children, Harvey and Shirley.

Peter married Margaret Jamieson May 24, 1941. They live in Vernon, BC and have a son named Lynn and a daughter, Sheila.

Charles and Elisabeth Dalle

by Bill McKay

Charlemagne Dalle was born about 1862, a Walloon of Brussels, Belgium. Elisabeth Birkett was a bonnie maiden, born about 1876, in Blackpool, England. They met and married in Trent, Minnesota on December 15, 1897 and it is thought that they farmed in Marshall, Minnesota. The lure of cheap farmland attracted them to the Dropmore - Castleavery area in 1913. How they moved on prairie trails to their new home in the Assiniboine Valley with eight tiny tots is beyond imagination. They settled in a very tiny house and within a few years the family grew to five boys and six girls. It is said that the children took turns going to school and shared the clothes they had. Tragedy struck this family most cruelly when my mother, Rosalie, was just five years old. Her mother, Elisabeth, choked on tea and died. Charles remained in his home and raised the family with the help of his daughters. As the family grew up, the girls left home to marry and establish their own families. The boys worked for the neighbours and the youngest, Charles Jr. remained in the family home to help.

Grandpa Charlemaine Dalle.

In his senior years, Charles Sr. moved to Inglis to live with his daughter, Emma Richardson, and finally with his daughter, Rosalie McKay, in Asessippi - Rochedale, until his passing on November 2, 1947. He was a kind and gentle man, a loving father, speaking evil of no one and I believe his legacy is that he passed on this gentle, loving spirit to his children.

(L-R) Ed Dalle, Anna Baggs, Matilda Case and John Dalle.

These children are:

Henry served in World War II, as a cook in the United States Army as he was still a citizen of that country. On his return, he bought a farm in partnership with his brother Charles Jr. This farm was in the Assiniboine Valley, south and west of the Dropmore Bridge. Henry got lonely so he hired a housekeeper and made the beautiful mistake of falling in love with her. He married Ethel Jane Kamper in 1952 and moved to Roblin in 1963. They did not have children for the idea came too late. Ethel had adult children from an earlier marriage.

August remained single and worked for farmers in the Dropmore - Blue Wing areas.

Edward Frederick survived a gun accident in his youth while reaching for his rifle on the hayrack. He lost his left arm but he lived an exuberant life, fishing and hunting. He learned how to use all handled tools and he managed electrical wiring with his one hand. Late in life, he married Hilda May Rodgers of Makaroff and they lived in Roblin. Ironically, while out on a Sunday drive, he and his wife were killed in a car accident. He had driven vehicles all of his life and at age 80, it finally caught up with him.

John Charles remained single. He loved big motorcycles and would go riding with his brother-in-law, Bill Case. John was striken with cancer and died in Roblin, January 1968.

Charles Jr., the youngest son, also remained single. He was a cattleman and a labourer, living most of his life in the Assiniboine Valley and then later, on his small ranch southeast of Roblin.

Emma Marie married Ben Richardson and they lived in Inglis for many years, raising a family of one boy, Earol, and four girls, Jean McInnis, Lois McGregor, Merle Switzer and

Margaret MacIntyre. Emma and Ben lived out their senior years on the west coast of British Columbia.

Edith left home at an early age and married Elmer Phillips of Sturgis, Saskatchewan. They raised a large family. Her whereabouts remained unknown for many years. Her brother, John, located her and brought her back into the family. She lived in Roblin for a time and is now in a Senior Citizen Residence in Wynyard, Saskatchewan.

Anna married Reginald Baggs and they lived in Springside, Saskatchewan all of their lives. They had two children, Iris and Reginald Jr.

Mary Louise married Oscar Johnson and they farmed in the Assiniboine Valley. They did not have children. Later in life, she married George Steffler.

Frank and Rosalie McKay.

Frank McKay and Rosalie Dalle married November, 1933.

Rosalie married Frank McKay in November 1933. He was a handsome man with a quick temper, but he was also quick to forgive and forget. Frank was a jackknife carpenter, a handyman and a woodsman with a reputation for marksmanship. In 1942, they settled on a small farm at the hilltop of the Shell River on Highway 83. The house was constructed from salvaged wood and materials from Bide-A-Wee filling station, owned by Archie Gilchrist. The family consisted of five boys, William, Lenard, Alvin, Peter, Edward and two girls, Gladys Johnstone and Margaret Goods. My brothers, sisters and I attended Asessippi and Rochedale Schools. At the end of the school year, the Dropmore School would invite the Rochedale School to a Field Day and a picnic. They were a larger school and those big bullies usually beat us in the Softball Event. We took our winnings in the Track Events and that is where I got my money for ice cream and soda pop treats.

Matilda, the youngest of the family, married Bill Case. They farmed at the top of the hill along the Assiniboine. Bill had a Fairbanks Morse engine and in the winter, he would cut stovewood for many of his neighbours. On Sundays, he and his brother-in-law would go riding their motorcycles. Bill was killed in a car accident in 1955. Matilda now lives in Roblin.

Emile Flammond, a resident of Shellmouth, tells the story of trapping muskrats with Bill Case. They were out on the trapline near Dropmore when they found a den of skunks. The decision was made to take these skunks for pelts so the boys started digging into the burrow. Emile broke into the nest and heaved the skunks out to Bill. The operation ended with eighteen pelts. They telephoned Jack Melanski, a fur dealer, who met them right away and bought the lot for $4.25 a piece. Emile, newly married to Julia Lefort, went home to his bride, proud as punch of his good fortune. She was taken aback by the skunk odour and insisted that he bathe and change in the shed before coming into the house. Seven daughters later, they are still happily married and still living in Shellmouth.

I have given an account of this family as accurately as I can recall it. They were a very poor family. How poor were they? The boys would go out in the morning and pick up the rabbit tracks to make soup. In the fall, they would freeze the dog until spring to save feeding it. And that's the truth.

THE HERITAGE BOOK 1994
Mother's Day

A man can build a mansion
Or a tiny cottage fair,
But it's not the hallowed place called "Home"
'Til Mother's dwelling there.

A man can build a mansion
With a high and spacious dome,
But no man in this world can build
That precious thing called "Home."

A man can build a mansion
Carting treasures o'er the foam,
Yes, a man can build the building
But a woman makes it "Home."

PRAYER FOR THIS HOUSE

May nothing evil cross this door,
And may ill-fortune never pry
About these windows; may the roar
And rains go by.

Strengthened by faith, the rafters will
Withstand the battering of the storm.
This hearth, though all the world grow chill,
Will keep you warm.

Peace shall walk softly through these rooms,
Touching your lips with holy wine,
Till every casual corner blooms
Into a shrine.

Laughter shall drown the raucous shout
And, though the sheltering walls are thin,
May they be strong to keep hate out
And hold love in.

Louis Untermeyer

Matilda (Dalle) Case

by Matilda (Dalle) Case

My father, Charles Dalle, came from Belgium. He was born in 1863. He was one of a large family. In 1893 he migrated to the United States. He earned his trip by being a valet to Mr. Barton Van Caseele. He farmed in the United States until 1913 and then moved to Canada. While farming in the United States of America, he met an English lady, Elisabeth Birkett. He married her in 1896 and raised eleven children, eight were born in the United States: Emma, Edith, Henry, Anna, Edward, August, Mary and John, and three in Canada: Rose, Charlie and Matilda. In 1912 it was impossible to rent land and buying was a very high price. Lawyers would buy land in Canada and sell to the local farmers. My father was one of them. He came to Canada in the winter of 1912-1913 and looked some land over, and in the Spring of 1913 he brought his family, livestock and machinery by train to Dropmore, Manitoba, Canada. Our first home was on south west 1/4 section, 10 township 24, Range 29.

The third place was south west 1/4 section 36, township 23, Range 29. It was on this place I was born in 1919 and my mother died in 1921.

In the Fall of 1921, the next move was to North East 1/4 of Section 4 Township 24, Range 29. This place was home for 10 years. On this place we lost a lot of cattle due to lightning, and crops to frost.

In 1931 we moved to the Rochedale District. We were always three miles from School. In the summer we walked, and in the winter we had a team and sleigh with an open grain box. I lived at home until I married William Case Jr. in 1940 and raised a family. I will leave space for each to write their own family story. The year is 1995. My home is at Roblin, Manitoba, Canada.

Katherine Dietrich

by Katherine (Zimmer) Dietrich

I'm Katherine Dietrich (Zimmer). My Dad Joseph Zimmer. Brothers - Frank, Philip. Sisters - Pauline, Mary. And I moved to Dropmore in 1946. We all pitched in with the farm work. And everything went fine. We must have made the right move, we all got married to someone around Dropmore. That's where I met Harold Dietrich. In

Kay and Harold Dietrich.

1950 Harold and I went to Winnipeg to find work. At first I got a job as housekeeping. Harold worked outside of Winnipeg at a cattle ranch. A year later I rented my own suite and worked at a candy factory. Harold quit the ranch and got a job at Consolidated Plate Glass as a shipper. We got married in May 1952. I continued to work at the candy factory til 1956. We bought a house on Strathcona St. and moved in a month before our son Kirk was born. Two and a half years later our daughter Heather was born. Ill health forced Harold to quit work in 1974. He passed away in Dec. 1979.

Kirk Dietrich, Debbie Miller, Courtney and Sarah.

Kirk worked for Manitoba Hydro as a journeyman lineman for 15 years before moving into the purchasing department as a research analyst He married Debbie Miller. They have two girls: Sarah - 9 and Courtney - 6.

Heather Dietrich and David Manion.

Heather worked at the Health Science Centre as an X-ray technologist for three years. She moved to Toronto, ON. She worked at different jobs, and is presently working at Toronto Harbourfront Centre. She's happily involved with the man in her life, David Manion. He works for the C.B.C. I still live on Strathcona St. I enjoy sewing, gardening, and do alot of crafts, mostly dolls.

Mervin and Joan Dietrich

by Mervin Dietrich

Mervin Heinrich Dietrich was born on October 26, 1930 in Dropmore on Section 14-23-29. Mervin lived and farmed with his parents in the Dropmore area for 28 years. On August 6, 1954 he married Joan Barbara Ann Mitschke (July 12, 1938), of Marchwell, SK. They continued to farm until 1958 when Mervin and Joan moved to Chilliwack, BC. They enjoyed many happy years of marriage. After Joan's death on October 6, 1994, Mervin continues to live in Yarrow, BC. He greatly enjoys his grandsons and being close to his children.

Brian Mervin was born on June, 20, 1955. He married Penny Lynne Preston on April 26, 1986. They have two sons, Logan born on February 12, 1991 and Conner born on July 18, 1993. Brian is a driller and restores cars. They reside in Yarrow, BC.

Bonnie Joan was born on March 6, 1958. She married Jim Henry Block on May 9, 1979. They have one son Derrick, born May 29, 1981. They now live in Revelstoke, BC.

Perry Mitchell was born on January 3, 1960. Perry owns a furniture store called Dietrich's Oak Gallery in Chilliwack, BC, where he also resides.

Paul and Pauline Dietrich

by Pauline (Zimmer) Dietrich

Paul Adam Dietrich was born on April 11, 1926 in MacNutt, SK. His parents, Henry Dietrich and Margaretha Kitsch were married on July 10, 1917. They farmed in the Homeland School District by MacNutt, SK. In 1930 they moved to the Dropmore area and continued to farm. Their family is Elsie (Adam), George, Jacob, Clara (Ziebart), Paul, Harold, Mervin, Milfred. Paul attended the Dropmore School. In 1944 he enlisted in the Army.

Pauline Elizabeth Zimmer was born on July 21, 1926 in Grayson, Sask. My parents were Appolonia Exner and Joseph Zimmer in Bukovina, Austria. My family is Anton, John, Joseph, Julia (Rieger), Frank, Katie (Dietrich), Philip, Mary (Bernhard). In 1928, the family moved to Grenfell, SK and farmed here for 10 years. Because of the drought, grasshoppers and poor crops, we moved to Shoal Lake, MB, and then to Strathclair where we continued to farm for ten years. In 1944, our Mother died of a stroke. My

Dad, Frank, Philip, Katie, Mary and I moved to Dropmore in 1946. On October 18, 1948 I married Paul, who lived three miles from our place. We moved to a farm one and a half miles south west of Dropmore, that Paul had purchased from Emil Hetter in 1947. Paul and I lived here for 37 years.

Paul Dietrich driving the Dropmore Transfer.

As well as farming, Paul drove the Dropmore Transfer to Winnipeg. Later he drove a school bus route from Dropmore to Roblin for which he received a 14 year Safety Driving Certificate. After his death on November 7, 1985, I sold the farm and enjoyed the tour of Austria where our family originated. On September 26, 1987 I married Albert Ernest Sudbury (July 15, 1922) a farmer and woodcarver from Shellmouth. We reside in Russell, Man. Our children are:

Patrick Paul was born in Russell on January 4, 1950. He received his Plumbing Degree from Red River and ACC Colleges. Pat worked as a plumber in the Roblin and Russell areas and is now employed with Centra Gas since 1985. On March 3, 1979 Pat married Mae Framingham (June 11, 1960) of Roblin. Mae is employed with the Royal Bank of Canada in Roblin and they have two children, Nolan Jon born March 8, 1982 and Daphne Jan born March 1, 1984. They reside in Roblin and enjoy downhill skiing and travelling in Canada and USA.

Paulette Gloria was born on March 17, 1951 at the Dietrich farm. She worked as a secretary at London Life Insurance in Winnipeg. On November 4, 1972 she married Rodney Lawrence Mushumanski (May 15, 1947) at Russell. Paulette worked for Sears, Prairie Picture Framing, and Activity Therapist at the Care Home. They have two children, Ryan Shawn born May 28, 1975 and Ashley Rae born May 28, 1979. They live on a farm by Russell and specialize in grain farming.

Patricia Margaret was born on December 11, 1952. In 1970 she moved to Shoal Lake, Man. and worked as a secretary for a Law Office. Since 1973, she has been administrative secretary for the Department of Agriculture. Patricia married Earl James Spraggs (April 3, 1947) on March 11, 1972. They have one daughter, Lindsay Dawn, born September 2, 1978. They presently grain farm and raise Simmental cattle in the Shoal Lake area.

At Phyllis & Dale Cornelius' Wedding-taken June 29, 1985 at our farm in Dropmore. (L-R) Patrick, Pamela, Pearle, Pauline, bride Phyllis, Paul, Penny, Patricia and Paulette. Children of Paul and Pauline Dietrich.

Pamela Hilda was born in Russell on January 25, 1959. After graduating from Roblin she worked as a typist at the Roblin Review. She moved to Shoal Lake and has worked as a secretary for the Department of Natural Resources since 1980. On July 4, 1987 Pam married Lawrence Thomas Chastko (December 9, 1947) of Shoal Lake. They have a farm partnership diversified into beef and dairy cattle, and hog operation.

Phyllis Darlene was born on March 1, 1961. In 1980 she graduated from a Cosmetology Course at Brandon ACC. For eight years she was a hair stylist in Russell. On June 29, 1985 Phyllis married Albert Dale Cornelius (Dec. 29, 1958) of MacNutt SK. Dale is employed with the CNR and Phyllis is hairdressing. They have two children, Hillary Dale born September 21, 1988 and Jordan John Paul born May 5, 1992. They reside in Churchbridge, SK.

Pearle Kathryn born February 6, 1963 married Terry Grant Miller (August 8, 1963) of Roblin on November 14, 1980. They were the last couple to be married in the Dropmore United Church. They moved to Williams Lake, BC where their only son Christopher William Paul was born on March 31, 1981. In 1982 they returned to Roblin where Pearle was employed with the Robinson Store. In 1990 she was promoted to Managerial Position. Terry is employed with Roblin Tire Service. Pearle has also completed a three year Remedial Massage Therapy Course. They reside in Roblin.

Penny-Ann Mary was born on September 23, 1964. After graduating from Roblin, she worked for the Cox's Food Store in Russell. On November 12, 1983 Penny married Kevin Lynn Shappert (October 21, 1963) of MacNutt. They have one daughter Paylyn Penny born November 6, 1992. Penny and Kevin have a diversified farm of cattle, sheep, and grain farming in the MacNutt area.

Phillip and Margaret Dietrich

by Esther (Dietrich) Fieseler

Mom and Dad 40th Anniversary.

Phillip and Margaret Dietrich arrived on the Archie Goodbun farm in 1928 from MacNutt, Saskatchewan area. They came to Canada from Austria when they were 6 and 7 years old. Brother Norman was born in the big brick house and Ruben was born in the Bill Hunter house. There were 5 school lunches packed at one time to attend Dropmore school. Otto, Sarah, Edgar, Roland and Lawrence (being twins), Reinhold, Herbert, and Esther were the older ones. Reinhold said at 13 years old he had to quit school and plow the fields. In 1938 the family moved to Grandview, MB. Esther remained having married Alfred Fieseler.

Alfred Fieseler - 1911.

Alfred Fieseler rented the N-1/2 of 23-23-29 in 1934. He married Esther Dietrich in 1938. In 1938 the farm sold to Bill Hunter. Alfred and Esther moved to Pipestone, MB to run a Red and White store. In 1944 we moved to the Fieseler

Esther and Alfred Fieseler - 1945.

farm north of Langenburg, SK. and raised 2 children - Bernard and Myrna. They both live in Edmonton. We are retired in Langenburg, SK. Reinhold and Herb live in Grandview. Otto deceased in 1979. Sarah retired in Grandview. Edgar in Duncan, BC. Roland deceased 1994. Lawrence in Roblin. Norm in Winnipeg, and Ruben in Surrey, BC. Phillip passed away in 1987 in Grandview, MB as did Margaret who passed away in 1981.

Bernie, Arlene, Darryl, Colleen, Robyn Fieseler.

Myrna Pilon.

Keri Ann Pilon.

Craig Joseph Pilon.

Ott's last leave - Norman, Rueben, Lawrence, Mom (Margaret), Otto, Esther, Roland, Sarah, Dad (Phillip), Herbert, Edgar and Reinhold - 1937.

At the Phillip Dietrich home. (F.R.) George, Hanz, Herb Dietrich. (B.R) Lillian Spiess, Willie Nerbas, Esther Dietrich, Henry Nerbas, Otto Dietrich in front of Henry, Lena Spiess, Reinhold Dietrich, Elsie Dietrich - 1932..

Alfred and Esther Fieseler - 1945.

Faye Digby

Faye, daughter and youngest child of Maurice and Olive Digby, was born on March 7, 1951 in Roblin, MB. She attended elementary school in Castleavery, and graduated from Roblin High School in 1968.

During her school years, Faye was actively involved in the 4-H Program both as a member and a leader. Among other awards, Faye won the Gold Watch Award, and a trip to Michigan.

After graduation from High School, Faye attended Brandon University and received her Teachers' Certificate, then taught in Russell, Manitoba from 1970 to 1972. On July 15, 1972, Faye married Tom Orr, a member of the RCMP, and youngest son of Allan and Alice Orr of Swastika, ON.

Faye and Tom then lived in Rossburn, MB, where Faye continued to teach. In 1974 they moved to Clear Lake, and on January 16, 1975, son Chad was born, and on January 16, 1977, daughter Dianna was born.

In 1978, the family moved to Flin Flon, MB, where they remained for four years prior to moving to Winnipeg in 1982. The Orr family remain in Winnipeg, where Tom works out of the RCMP Headquarters.

Since 1985, Faye has worked as an Insurance Broker with Jean York Insurance Agency Ltd. and continues to further her education through courses with the Insurance Institute of Canada. Chad graduated from Oak Park High School, Winnipeg, in 1993 and is presently working on a Physical Education Degree attending the University of Manitoba. Deanna will graduate from Oak Park High School in June 1995, and has been accepted into the University of Manitoba for the 1995-1996 term.

Family and friends in the Castleavery and Dropmore area continue to be an anchor and "home base" for the Orr family.

Garry Digby

Garry Digby was born the second son of Maurice and Olive (nee Sharp) Digby at Springside, Saskatchewan on March 1, 1943.

In the fall of 1947 the family moved to the Castleavery District of Manitoba where Maurice bought the Harry Rowan farm (SE 22-24-29).

Garry took his entire elementary education at Castleavery School where most of the time he was the only person in his grade. After grade nine, Garry boarded in Tummell where he took his grade 10, then was bussed to Roblin for his final two years at Goose Lake High.

Garry was involved with curling, at the Castleavery Rink, from the age of 11. The Assiniboine 4-H Club was the other main interest. Through it he won many awards including the Gold Watch, a provincial trip to Alberta and a national trip to Toronto in 1961.

After leaving school in 1961, Garry remained on the family farm with his father. In 1966 he purchased the former Herb Maudsley farm (NE 22-24-29). Today the farm encompasses several sections of Crown and private land formerly owned by Jim and Murray Robertson, Allan and Gilbert Anderson, as well as some on Pyott's.

In addition to grain farming, the Digbys have a commercial cow/calf herd and feedlot operation. Garry, like all of the Digby family, has always been proud of raising quality beef cattle.

For the past 21 years, first with Garry's parents, then on their own, Garry and Eleanor have hosted international agricultural exchange trainees. These young men, ranging in age from 18 - 30 have come from England, France, Sweden, Denmark, Germany, Switzerland, Australia, New Zealand and Iceland.

This has proven to be an interesting and educational experience for the family. Many humorous, and frustrating moments were experienced by the family as they endeavoured to converse with young men who could speak no English.

Community activities that have kept Garry busy over the years are: Secretary-Treasurer of the Dropmore United Church for 17 years, helping lead the Assiniboine 4-H Beef Club for three years, leading the Man-Sask 4-H Beef Club for the past six years and representing the R. M. of Shellmouth on the Roblin and District Veterinary Board for the past 17 years.

In June, 1969 Garry married Eleanor Schwartz of Moose Jaw. They settled on the Herb Maudsley farm site at the top of the Anderson Hill, where they built a new home in 1980.

During the first years of their marriage, Eleanor worked for the Roblin Recreation Commission as they endeavoured to build a recreation complex. When this fell through, she worked as secretary at the Royal Bank for one year before being employed by the Department of Agriculture in Roblin where she remained for six years. She chose to stay home to raise their family.

This couple were blessed with three sons: Trevor, born February 10, 1977; Tyler, born February 20, 1978; and Aaron, born October, 9, 1980.

Garry Digby Family (L-R) Tyler, Trevor, Aaron, Eleanor and Garry.

The boys attended Roblin Elementary School. Tyler and Aaron are presently enrolled in Goose Lake High from which Trevor graduated in June, 1995.

The boys are active in 4-H and a wide range of sports. They have made their parents proud by being recipients of a large number of both academic and athletic awards throughout their school years.

Maurice and Olive Digby

To begin the Digby story it is appropriate to first take a brief look at where the family came from and how they ended up settling in the Castleavery District. The Digby family that moved to Canada has been traced back to the Milton, Northamptonshire area of England where Digby ancestors lived in the late 17th century. While some of the Digbys still live in Milton, a branch of the family moved to the Leicester area. It was from Leicester that Sam Digby came to Canada in 1902 and settled in the Springside district of Saskatchewan. In 1903 Sam was followed by his wife Annie and their young son Ernie. Their second son Maurice was born in 1910.

Sam Digby had moved to Canada because of ill health. He farmed in the Springside area until 1914 at which time he died. Annie Digby and her son Ernie continued to farm until 1921 when Ernie passed away. With the help of a hired hand Annie Digby was able to farm until her young son Maurice took over.

In 1938 Maurice Digby married Olive Sharp. Olive was the eldest child of Robert and Elizabeth Sharp. Maurice and Olive were soon blessed with three sons; Robert, Garry and Wayne. Maurice and Olive, in addition to the farm, were active in the community. Maurice served as secretary of the Crossroads School District, President of the Springside Telephone System and President of the Springside Liberal Association, among other activities.

Maurice and Olive remained in the Springside area until 1947. In the fall of 1947 Maurice, Olive and family along with Maurice's mother Annie moved to the Castleavery District. They settled on the Harry Rowan farm (SE 22-24-29) on the west side of the Assiniboine Valley.

The Digby family quickly settled into the Castleavery District. They were continually amazed at the hospitality of their many new friends.

In 1949 Olive's brother Alfred Sharp moved to the Dropmore District to farm on the Birnie place. Later that year Alfred drowned while swimming with friends in the Assiniboine River near Shellmouth.

Grandma Digby passed away in March of 1950. A year later, in March of 1951, Maurice and Olive completed their family with the birth of a daughter, Faye.

The Digby family maintained an active schedule. In addition to the many community, church, school and sporting activities they were involved in the 4-H movement. Maurice helped in starting the Assiniboine 4-H Club and served as a leader for 15 years. All the children were involved in 4-H activities and benefited from this involvement. Throughout the years the family maintained a keen interest in the beef cattle business raising and exhibiting purebred shorthorn cattle.

Maurice and Olive continued to farm until their son Garry took over the farm. From 1977 to 1984 Maurice was a councillor for the R. M. of Shellmouth. Olive was involved in the Castleavery Ladies Club and a member of the Dropmore Ladies Church Group. They retired to Roblin and lived there until Olive passed away on June 22, 1989. Maurice continued to live in their home until he passed away March 7, 1991.

Robert and Elaine Digby

Robert Digby, the eldest son of Maurice and Olive Digby of Springside SK was born Jan. 1939 in Yorkton, SK. He attended the Crossroads School near Springside until their family moved to the Castleavery District in 1947. He then attended the public school at Castleavery and went to MacNutt for high school. He also took a one year Agriculture Diploma Course in Brandon. Following his Ag course he returned to the farm and worked with his dad. He also spent a number of years trucking cattle to Winnipeg with Jack Ferris'

The Robert Digby Family.

transfer. In 1961 when the drought hit, local farmers moved machinery to The Pas to put up hay. Trucking became a full time job in 1961 as hay was hauled from the north and straw trucked from the south.

In 1961, Bob married Elaine Morrison of MacNutt, a daughter of Wilbert and Anne Morrison. They started farming on the George Kennedy farm in the Cupar district. They purchased the Bartley Carmichael farm in 1966 and moved into the Dropmore Community. In 1969 they bought the Lloyd Leflar farm.

Bob and Elaine grain farmed and ran a commercial cow herd. In the 70's they sold the commercial cows and bought a herd of purebred Charolais cattle. Their farm then became known as Rolling D Charolais. Rob and Elaine continued to grain farm and in the 70's Reg Robertson became and continues to be a grain farming partner.

Bob and Elaine have five children, Cheryl in 1961, Brian in 1962, Donna in 1963, Barbara in 1967, and Jason in 1974. Except for Cheryl, who took grade one in Dropmore, the children attended school in Roblin. After finishing high school, both Cheryl and Donna attended college in Brandon.

Cheryl married Keith Elder of Roblin in 1986. They have two children, a daughter, Brooke born in 1988 and Clark born in 1991. Cheryl and Keith grain farm and raise purebred Charolais cattle as Silverwood Charolais. Cheryl is also a business partner "In Good Taste Catering".

Brian married Linda Laliberte of Boggy Creek in 1993. They operate Lonesome Eagle Farm, a saw-mill operation near the Duck Mountains and raise cattle as well. They have one daughter, Brailyn born in 1995.

Donna married Carman Jackson of Inglis in 1984. They grain farm and raise purebred Charolais and Simmental cattle under the name of High Bluff Stock Farm. They have four daughters: Erin born in 1985, Fawn in 1986, Haylan in 1988 and Autumn in 1990.

Barb and her son Graham (born in 1987), farm together with Albert Holopina in the Shell Valley area. They have a mixed farm as well as raising purebred Charolais known as Rockland Charolais. Barb also works as a herdswoman for High Bluff Stock Farm.

Jason has been working on the farm since he finished high school. He is interested in the cattle business and also is starting in the purebred Charolais business.

4-H Clubs have played a big part in the lives of the Digby's. Grandpa (Maurice Digby) was instrumental in starting the Assiniboine 4-H Beef Club and was a 4-H leader for many years. Bob also was a 4-H Beef Club leader for many years, first with the Assiniboine Beef Club and then with the Inglis Beef Club. From early childhood, the Digby family has been involved with cattle, on the farm, with 4-H and through purebred shows and sales. All of the family remains actively involved in the cattle industry. Jason has just returned from spending the winter on a large Charolais farm in Sweden. Our family's first 4th generation 4-Her, Erin Jackson will participate in her first 4-H beef achievement in June of 1995.

When the family was not busy with cattle, they would try to find time for the many outdoor activities they enjoyed: camping, fishing, hunting, curling, water-skiing, and snowmobiling.

Family and friends are very important to us and are always welcome in our homes. We enjoy visiting with and entertaining our many good friends. Our family has grown from five to seventeen so it isn't hard to find a reason to get a celebration going. We have always been active workers and supporters of all community events and are grateful to have lived and raised our family in the best community in the country.

Wayne and Phyllis Digby

Wayne Digby was a Christmas Baby born December 24, 1945 in Yorkton, the third child of Maurice and Olive Digby. Wayne attended Castleavery Elementary School, Tummell, and Roblin Collegiate. Growing up, Wayne was very involved in sports, 4-H and Student Council activities. Following the completion of High School, Wayne attended the University of Manitoba where he received his Bachelor of Science in Agriculture.

In May of 1968 Wayne married Phyllis Petz, eldest daughter of George and Anne Petz of Dropmore. That same spring Wayne began work as Assistant Agricultural Representative in Carman. Phyllis taught school in Roland. In 1969 Wayne and Phyllis moved to Arborg where Wayne took on the position of 4-H and Youth Specialist for the Interlake. While in Arborg Wayne and Phyllis were blessed with two February babies. Shauna Marie born February 27, 1970 and Todd Ryan born February 24, 1972.

From 1972 to 1977 the Digby family lived first in Swan River and then Russell. In these locations Wayne worked as rural Development Counsellor for the Manitoba Department of Agriculture.

In 1977 the Digby's accepted a CUSO placement in Botswana, Africa. While there Wayne worked with the Agricultural Information Unit of the Ministry of Agricultural and Phyllis taught at an international school.

Wayne and Phyllis returned to Canada in late 1979 and Wayne took on the position of Agricultural representative at Killarney while Phyllis worked for the Royal Bank. Another move was in store for the Digby's in 1985 when Wayne became Regional Director for the Southwest Region with Manitoba Agriculture in Brandon. While in Brandon Phyllis has worked for the Brandon School Division.

With much patience Shauna and Todd have followed their parents, completing their High School and first University Degrees in Brandon. Shauna is now taking her Masters in Psychology at Carlton University in Ottawa and Todd is at the University of Alberta in Edmonton taking his Masters in Library Science and Information Studies.

Bill and Buryle Doole

William Doole was born April 25, 1915 in R.M. of Wallace, Section 18-12-27 at Elkhorn, Manitoba. His parents Robert and Elizabeth (her father John Browne and mother, Mary Ann Kelso) Doole, as a young bride and groom came to Canada in 1910 from County Antrim and County Derry in Ireland. They were blessed with a family of five: Bob 1911, Mollie 1913, Bill 1915, Jim 1917 and George 1922.

They worked on farms in the Two Creeks and Uno districts and rented land near Elkhorn where Bill was born. A couple of years later they bought land 1 1/2 miles N.W. of Two Creeks where the family farmed for the next 70 years. The family all attended Ross Consolidated School at Two Creeks, built in 1915. The school still stands high on a hill on the east side of Highway 83 a few miles north of No. 1 Highway and is used as a Community Centre today.

Bill worked on the home farm and in the Harmsworth and Melita districts until 1943 when he answered an advertisement for farm work in the Roblin area. He arrived in Roblin by train on the frosty morning of February 19, 1943. His destination was Mrs. H. R. Mitchell's farm where he worked until the war was over and Jack, her son, had returned home. He then worked in Hughes' garage in Roblin before deciding to start farming on his own in 1945. At this time he started cleaning grain in the Roblin area and later built his own grain cleaning outfit on sleighs and moved from farm to farm; in later years it was set up on the home farm. During these 30 years he cleaned many bushels of grain.

Buryle Stauffer was born March 17, 1925 on S.E. 1/4 33-25-28 in Shell River Municipality S.E. of Roblin. She was the oldest of Earl and

Hazel (De La Mare) Stauffer's family of five: Orton 1926, Marjorie (Doole) 1928, Hugh 1930 and Calvin 1941. This family is the 8th generation of Stauffers in America, the Stauffer family history, though sketchy, goes back to 827 AD in Switzerland. Descendants of these early families came to America from Holland on the Mayflower in 1738 and settled in Pennsylvania, U.S.A. Then around 1800 as United Empire Loyalists they came to Waterloo Township in Upper Canada as Pioneers in a new settlement near Lucknow, Ontario. Over 100 years later, Earl Stauffer at 15 years of age came west to Roblin in 1913, with his parents Joel and Edith (Racher) Stauffer and family. They settled on S.E. 33-25-28 where Orton and Hugh live today.

Hazel De La Mare was born May 5, 1905 on S.W. 1/4 34-25-28 in Shell River Municipality S.E. of Roblin; her father William was born in Quebec City in 1856. Their family had come to Canada from Guernsey in the Channel Islands where their family tree dates back to 1650. They moved to Des Moines, Iowa where William and Lucy were married and then to Fairhope, Alabama before coming back to Canada in 1900, first to Shoal Lake where her parents, the Laughton's lived, then on to Roblin in 1903 with their family of three. Hazel (Buryle's mother) was born 2 years later on the new homestead. She attended school in Roblin, being one of the first pupils to attend the Primary School No. 1238 after Consolidation in 1912.

Earl and Hazel Stauffer were married March 26, 1924 and their family grew up during the "Dirty Thirties". We never felt any hardships; though I'm sure our parents had many worries. We were always happy and healthy; making our own fun with family and neighbors.

Buryle attended school in Roblin and after graduating was employed in the office of Smellie Bros. Creamery in Roblin. She participated in the United Church, Young Peoples' group and Women's Institute; took courses in woodworking and St. John's Ambulance. Bill and Buryle belonged to Athletic Groups and took part in many sports winter and summer, softball being the favorite.

Bill and Buryle were married June 5, 1946 and started farming in the Tummell District 1/2 mile south of the church which we attended and walked to especially in winter when roads were blocked. We did enjoy these first 3 years in a friendly, neighborly community where there were quilting, wood sawing and poultry dressing bees, also lots of entertainment with dances, concerts, house and card parties. We particularly remember the party telephone line with 14 families, including the country store. In following years at Dropmore there were also many on one line but not 14. Can you imagine how long some of the individual rings were? Like 3 long - 4 short!

In August of 1947 we lost our infant daughter, Donna Lynn. Then on February 13, 1949 our first son Leslie Earle arrived; the temperature was - 40 degrees F at 1:00 AM when we left for Russell. No heater in the car then!

October, 1949 we moved to Dropmore to S.W. 1/4 2-24-29 (the Birnie Place). That first winter in Dropmore we curled with Jim and John Robertson at Castleavery, on their new one sheet curling rink, our first experience with curling! There was lots of snow that year and when the roads blocked for vehicles we drove about 8 miles in the open sleigh through fields, first to John R. and then on to Jim's after changing teams. Leslie about one year, was looked after by Violet or Florence and sometimes Mrs. Nichols and family. There were lots of good memories there, with the gas lanterns for light at the rink, dimming and sometimes going out during a game; but hospitality everywhere and a great start at learning to curl. The long trip home was very entertaining, stopping first at Nichols then the two Robertson homes for coffee and to warm up arriving home at 3 or 4 a.m. to a frozen house. Les survived through it all and enjoyed the attention everywhere we stopped. The Robertson families were great neighbors.

The next summer, 1950, the Dropmore Curling Rink was built, all the community turned out to have it ready to open that winter. The church was also a community effort and opened in 1953.

Our first crop in Dropmore was badly frozen on August 16, 1950 when the temperature dropped to 16 degrees F (-10 degrees C), only part of a wagon load of frozen wheat was salvaged to feed the cattle along with straw, and hay from the valley. In 1951 there was a good crop but most of it stayed in the swath until spring due to a wet cold fall and early snow. Cattle prices were slightly higher about this time and with cream cheques coming in, we managed. After a warm, early spring in 1952 Bill finished combining on April 25 (his birthday) when the temperature was 80 degrees F (27 degrees C). We had fresh rhubarb pie for dinner that day!

Our second son Verne William arrived June 16, 1953. In September of that year electricity came to the area north of Dropmore. For the years prior to this we used a home power plant for lighting the big house and barn.

We enjoyed 6 years on the Birnie Place with house parties, cards, curling and good neighbors. In October of 1955 we settled on S.E. 1/4 27-23-29, the Brown Place, again surrounded by many good neighbors and friends. The winter of

1955-1956 was the year of the "big" snow and it was a continual struggle for Bill to haul feed from the Birnie Place and valley for the livestock. The snow started on Hallowe'en and by the end of November all roads were blocked and it continued to snow and storm all winter.

Les and Verne on bikes.

Our daughter, Hazel Elizabeth was welcomed into the family on April 12, 1964. When she was 3 1/2 years old all the family went through a traumatic experience when a calf died of rabies.

The Doole family was involved in 4-H for 28 years, showing 4-H commercial cattle at Dauphin, Foxwarren and Roblin. The Beef Club always took top priority, but they were involved in Swine, Handicrafts, and Conservation Clubs. All 3 members of the family took part in the Calf Scramble at Brandon Winter Fair and all were successful in catching a calf. They also were involved in 4-h exchange trips to USA and all across Canada. Participation in public speaking was a highlight, with Hazel competing at Provincial Level in Winnipeg in 1979. The Doole family was the third generation in 4-H, starting with Grandmother (Hazel Stauffer) in 1917, then Mother (Buryle) in the late thirties and our family since 1958.

Our boys attended schools in Dropmore and Roblin. Hazel attended Roblin schools as Dropmore school closed in 1968. A note of interest here is the fact that she was the third generation to start school in the same room in the old Public School in Roblin. Her grandmother Hazel Stauffer went into this room after several school districts consolidated around 1912 or 1913, and her mother Buryle Doole started there in 1931.

Mixed farming through the years with grain, cattle, horses, pigs, and poultry as well as a big garden kept the family fed and clothed. Many changes were made on the farm through the years. In the late fifties, the old blacksmith shop from Dropmore was moved and used for a barn, then in 1968, with the flooding of the valley Bill, purchased the big barn on the former Archie Goodbun and George Dietrich place in the valley and moved it over the ice on the lake in the winter of 1969. In 1971, when the Pool Elevator was to be taken down, Bill bought the office and shed and moved it to the farm for a shop. The old house which had been the lumber yard house in Dropmore, had been moved to the farm sometime in the thirties. In 1971 and 1972 we built our new home and really enjoyed the running water and many more conveniences.

The Doole Family..

The family participated in all community activities through the years including church, curling and 4-H. Bill served on the elevator, school, church, rink and hall boards as well as 14 years on the board of Roblin Residences Inc. at Roblin. Buryle was also involved with the RDCG Ladies Church Club, curling club, 4-H and Dropmore Chicks during the 10 to 11 years they were active.

Buryle and Bill's 40th Anniversary.

Bill never retired from farming but rented the land out for three years for health reasons prior to 1991. He then went back farming until his death on June 1, 1994. The following little verse personifies Bill;

After Glow

I'd like the memory of me to be a happy one.
I'd like to leave an after glow of smiles, when life is done.
I'd like to leave an echo whispering softly down the ways,
Of happy times and laughing times and bright and sunny days.
I'd take the tears of those who grieve, to dry before the sun
Of happy memories that I leave when life is done.

Bill always looked forward to visits from his family, including 12 grandchildren, friends and neighbors.

Buryle is still on the farm with help from her daughter and son-in-law, Hazel and Mickey Minchuk, many good friends and neighbors. What a great community!

Hazel (Doole) Minchuk

by Hazel Minchuk

On April 12, 1964, Hazel Elizabeth was born to William John Anderson and Buryle Patricia Doole (nee: Stauffer) in the Roblin & District Hospital.

I was raised on our family farm just a 1/4 mile south of Dropmore on Highway #482: SE 27-23-29 W. I grew up with two older brothers, Leslie Earl (1949) and Verne William (1953), who a few years later called me "Little Miss Tag Along"!

Mom's brother, Calvin Stauffer lived with us for 4 years. Apparently being the baby of the family and the only girl, I was spoiled. But standing in my shoes, I was only spoiled with love.

I remember our farm filled with chickens, pigs, horses, cattle, a dog and lots of cats, all of which were pets, not wild animals. That is, of course, until our pet, pail-fed calf, contacted rabies. At 3 1/2 years old I could not understand why all my pets had to be put to sleep-FOREVER. My entire family had to go to the Roblin Hospital every morning for fourteen days to receive a needle in the abdomen. At first I was the brave one, but bravery turned into a very sore tummy. After a few days I was quite willing to let everyone else go ahead of me.

On April 11, 1970 (the next day I would turn six years old) Leslie married Pamela Frazer from Kamloops, B.C. Verne married Barbara Dyer from Binscarth, MB on June 26, 1976. Thank you to the four of them for giving me eight nieces and nephews. I'm very proud of each one-Douglas, Michelle, Earl, Sheila, Kerry, Jereme, Toney and Jodey.

4-H was a very big part of our family. The beef club took top priority. Mom and Dad took great pride in our achievements, and even when the crop wasn't quite in, or the garden needed seeding, they always took time our for the Annual Fat Stock Show and Sale. They were involved in 4-H for 28 years.

I was also involved in the Handicraft and Conservation Clubs. I held several executive positions including President, Vice President, Secretary, Treasurer and Newspaper Reporter. Many hours were spent working on speeches for Public Speaking Competition. A special thank you goes out to Mrs. Elizabeth Roe for her many hours of wisdom and encouragement which helped me to better my speaking talents. I competed locally, as well as at District and Regional levels. In 1979 I competed at Provincial level in Winnipeg.

Another highlight of 4-H was the Brandon Winter Fair when I competed in the Esso Purebred Heifer Calf Scramble. After successfully catching a calf, I received money to go towards purchasing a heifer which would be shown at the Fair the following year. Both brothers had successfully caught a calf in scrambles before-so I had to live up to my "Little Miss Tag Along" name.

The 4-H Trips took me by bus to Winnipeg for a Conference, to Nanton, Alberta and Forman, North Dakota, U.S.A. for Exchange Student Trips. I went by train to Gillam, MB on an exchange. By air I went to Toronto, Ontario for the National 4-H Conference and to St. John's, Newfoundland on an exchange. Many of the friends that I made, I still communicate with. There will always be a special place in my heart for the "Nelson" family from North Dakota. They really made me feel like a part of their family.

I spent many hours at the Dropmore Curling Rink. I enjoyed the get together that the ladies had before the Bonspiel to make hamburgers. Except when they made me cut the onions - I always cried!

The Dropmore Hall was a popular meeting place. There were the annual Christmas concerts and in later years the Christmas parties. I helped with skits, poems, well wishes and games for bridal showers. Dropmore always had huge crowds and fabulous midnight meals at their dances. And when Bill and Buryle, Paul and Pauley had a turn at mowing the grass at the hall, one could be sure that Pearle, Penny and Hazel were not far behind on their bicycles.

I attended the United Church in Dropmore and helped with the Sunday School program for a couple of years. The Dropmore School closed in 1968. I went to Roblin by bus at 7:40 a.m. and arrived home at 5:00 p.m. I couldn't have been too bad - the same bus driver put up with me for all 12 years. (Paul Dietrich - may he rest in peace.) On Tuesday, March 7, 1972 Roblin's original high school burned. This was the same school that my mother (Buryle) and her mother (Hazel Stauffer nee: DeLaMare) had attended.

In June of 1982 I graduated from Roblin Goose Lake High School. Following graduation I helped my folks on the family farm for two years. I worked for Sid's Custom Glass in Russell for a brief period. In January 1984 I took a position as an Office Clerk at the Parkway Co-op Office in Roblin. I worked full time for two years.

Mickey Andrew Minchuk was born at the Yorkton Union Hospital on March 15, 1957 to Norman and Alma Minchuk (nee: Gamble). He was raised in Wroxton, Dilke, and Regina, Saskatchewan. Mickey was the third of four children: Murray (1951), Darlene Fry (1953), Mickey (1957), and Barry (1959). Mickey has worked from Sundre, Alberta to Hunter River, Prince Edward Island.

In June, 1986, Mickey and Hazel ventured to a little French Village called Forget, Saskatchewan to run the Hotel. After receiving legal custody, Mickey's two children came to live with us in June of 1987. Raeleen Candice was born May 15, 1978 and Michael Norman was born on March 1, 1981.

Hazel and Mickey's Wedding.

Mickey and Hazel were united in marriage on October 10, 1987. We took our Honeymoon in May of '88. We travelled to see Hazel's family in North Dakota. Then we travelled through North Dakota, Montana, and up into Alberta to see friends and family.

Jennifer Hazel was born October 22, 1988 at the St. Joseph's Hospital in Estevan, Saskatchewan. Jennifer (Jenni) was named after her mother and her great-grandmother Hazel May Stauffer (DeLaMare).

In June of 1989, we moved back to the Roblin area. Hazel was employed at Mitchell's Drug Store in Roblin in August 1989 and continues her duties there to date, with only a short break in employment from January - September of 1992. This break was due to the much waited arrival of Andrew Mickey. He was born on January 22, 1992 at the Yorkton Union Hospital. Andrew was named after his father and his great-grandfather Andrew Minchuk. Andrew was born on weedless Wednesday, to a smoke free family; thus he is a member of the smokebusters of Saskatchewan.

Mickey, Hazel, Andrew, Jennifer and Michael.

Mickey was employed at P & S Texaco in October 1989 - April 1990. He then went to work for Schmollinger Carpentry of Roblin. Anyone having had work done by Mickey and Don (Schmollinger) know that you hear the radio and the whistling above their work.

Cecil Andrew Galbraith, better known as "Bud" or "Uncle Buck" has lived with us since the fall of 1987. He is retired farmer from the Forget - Kisby, Saskatchewan area. He was born on May 2, 1928 on the family farm near Kisby.

Raeleen is living in Winnipeg, and is currently employed in the city.

Michael attends Goose Lake High School in Roblin. He, has had teachers that Hazel had, during her school days.

Jennifer and Andrew attend the Roblin Elementary School.

All of us enjoy skating, skidooing, fishing, quad rides, boating, camping, hunting, sports and nature. I curl with the Roblin Evening Ladies Club. Mickey and Hazel take in a few bonspiels each year.

I spent many hours of my childhood out in the yard, the field or the barns with my dad. I played the gopher: the chore boy! I loved every minute of it - from cleaning barns to delivering calves, running for parts or changing the points in the old truck. Unfortunately, Dad passed to rest on June 1, 1994. Although I do not wish him back to the great pain and suffering, I sure do miss the hugs, the talks and the big smile that always greeted you. We love you and miss you Dad.

Suddenly on April 18, 1995, Ordella Henderson passed away. She may not have been a blood relation - but when she asked me to be her adopted grand-daughter there was no hesitation. "Grandma" Henderson, you will be missed by all who knew you.

Favorite Things

My life is full of simple pleasures.
The kinds of joy that are hard to measure.
The scent of evening stock in the air,
The smell of my daughter's fresh washed hair.
The sight of clothes hanging on the line,
The taste of homemade chokecherry wine.

A field of grain rippling in the breeze,
The glow of sunset on a summer eve.
A row of jars sitting on a shelf,
The satisfaction of "I did it myself".
A conversation with my curious boys,
The look of my house when I've picked up the toys.

A newborn kitten, the smell of hay,
The happy weariness at the end of the day.
A flock of geese, flowers wild,
My husband a carpenter, his work so mild.
Strawberries eaten while warm from the sun,
The swift, smooth grace of a deer on the run.

There are some who would think my life is narrow.
But it is I who pity them.
They've never stood barefoot in a fresh-ploughed furrow,
Nor watched the rise of the sun.
The special joys of my simple life,
Makes me glad I'm a woman, a mother, a wife!

--Hazel Minchuk

Les and Pam Doole

by Les and Pam Doole
Once upon a time, in a well known land far, far away, a boy was born on February 13, 1949 in the Russell Hospital to Bill and Buryle Doole of Tummell, Manitoba. His name was Leslie Earle. In October of that year we moved to the Birnie Place of Dropmore where we lived for six years. I started school, and then we moved south of Dropmore to the Brown Farm where Mom lives today.

Four years of riding the bus for 35 miles a day, each way, saw me through high school at Roblin Collegiate. In the fall of 1967, I took a heavy duty mechanic's course at Manitoba Institute of Technology in Winnipeg. During one of the weekend trips home in July of 1968, I met Pamela Fraser of Squam Bay, BC who was staying with neighbors on a 4-H exchange trip.

After completing the course at M.I.T., I took a job as mechanic at Co-op Implements in Outlook, Saskatchewan where I was employed four and one half years. Pam and I were married on April 11, 1970. While in Outlook we had two children: Douglas James born June 4, 1970 and Michelle Diane on November 20, 1972.

In December 1973 we moved to Red Deer, Alberta where I was employed as a mechanic with Case Power and Equipment. After one and one half years I was promoted to Service Manager, a position I held for eight years. In October of 1977 we decided to build a house which turned out to be a very rewarding and educational experience. After many headaches and a lot of fun we moved into our first "owned" home. A year later on March 4, 1979 we were "blessed" with our second son Earl William. Still employed with Case, I started selling farm equipment and later construction equipment. For five years, things went well and the slumping economy brought another change to our lives.

Les, Pam, Douglas, Michelle and Earl.

Leaving the family behind, Grande Prairie and a job selling heavy equipment with Blackwood Hodge, was the destination. After three long months of motel living, we bought a house and the family could finally join me. Leaving a cold and snowy Red Deer behind, on December 1, 1988 Pam, the kids and I headed north. Warm sunny weather greeted us when we arrived at our new home and with help of friends from Valleyview we soon unloaded and moved in. We still live in Grande Prairie and I am employed with Union Tractor Ltd.

Pam is currently employed at the Prairie Haven Motel as a Housekeeper and is involved doing volunteer work with the Grande Prairie Balloon Club, the Canadian Red Cross, Canadian Cancer Society, Alberta Lung Association and Alberta Junior Forest Wardens.

Douglas graduated from High School at Red Deer in 1988 and in September moved to Edmonton where he attended the University of Alberta. After four years of hard work and little sleep he received his BSc in Computer Science with first class honors. In May of 1992 he moved to Toronto, Ontario where he is currently employed by IBM Canada as a computer software developer.

In 1990 Michelle graduated from High School in Grande Prairie and then worked for a year at "Just for Kids Daycare". She continued her education at Grande Prairie Regional College where she completed two years of Early Childhood Development. Upon graduation at the top of her class she opened "Michelle's Family Dayhome" where up to 30 children a month attend for love, attention, fun and games.

Earl lives at home and is in Grade 10 at Grande Prairie High School. He has worked part time at a convenience store, spent a summer herding sheep in north eastern BC and is currently working part time as a waiter in the Golden Inn Dining Room. Other interests include girls, cars, skiing and camping.

Verne Doole

The fall of 1974 I went to Brandon to take Automotive mechanics training at ACC. After completion of this level I was employed with Clements in Russell.

I married Barb Dyer of Binscarth in 1976. We moved to Swan River soon after, where I was employed with Hunt Motors. Here, our daughters, Sheila Anne, December 12, 1976 and Kerry Lynne, February 22, 1979 were born.

We moved to Crossfield, Alberta in July 1980 where I was employed at Universal Ford in Calgary. Our son, Jereme Michael was born April 9, 1982.

We moved to Estevan, October 1982 after a couple of months at the Lyle Keating farm. I was employed by Trout Chev Olds here. Our twin boys were born here January 2, 1984 (Joey Ray and Toney Lee).

(Back Row) Verne, Kerry, Sheila, Barb (Front Row) Toney, Jereme, Joey.

I am now employed by Hirsch Construction in Estevan.

We've enjoyed the Estevan area and welcome friends and relatives to visit us here.

Florence (Kirkpatrick) Dougherty

I taught school at Rochedale for the year 1932 - 33. My name then was Florence Kirkpatrick, and I boarded at the Richardson home.

I'm afraid I cannot recall the names of all the pupils I have taught. Maybe some of them will identify themselves and their classmates. The ones I can recall are: Violet Basil, two Lougheed sisters, two or three Hammond sisters, Eddie Robb, Archie, Billy, Teddy and Isabel Lloyd.

Then I taught at Castleavery for the next two years, 1933 - 35, and boarded with Mrs. Dugan. Again, I'm afraid I cannot recall all the names - but some are Dorothy, Jack and Pat Nichol, Irma, Isobel and Jim Shearer, Dorothy, Beth and Ivar Jones, Durward and ? Rowan, Howard Comfort, David and Buster Hunter, Ilene, Jim and ? Roe, Jessie Pyott, Douglas ? with the very curly hair. He once tried to scare me at recess time by advancing slowly toward me with a little garter snake dangling over a stick. It absolutely nonplussed him when I picked the snake off the stick and let it go down into the grass.

I have enjoyed reminiscing about those years, and I hope the Homecoming will be a great success. I now reside in West Vancouver, BC. My best wishes to any who may remember me so long ago.

Joseph Dugan I

by Isabelle Dugan Johnson and Ada Dugan

Dugan Family and Friends
A.H.Goodbun, George Hunt, Joe Dugan holding Hilda White, John Dugan and D.A.Goodbun. (2nd row) Maggie Dugan (Mrs. J. Anderson) (3rd row) Jane Dugan (Mrs. George Hunt) holding a G. White child, Mr. J.Dugan Sr. holding Jerry White, Mrs. Jane Dugan Sr., Anna Dugan (Mrs. S. White) holding Aileen Hunt, Tommy Garrat holding Harold Hunt. (Bottom row) Frank White, Ted White and Joe Hunt.

Joseph Dugan of Castleavery, Newtownnards, County Down, Ireland (born in 1833) married Jane Hay Boyle of Ballyrickard, Comber, County Down, Ireland in 1856. Their first home was "Lough View Farm", Castleavery, Newtownards, and just a few miles west of the Irish Sea.

The aftermath of the potato famine of 1845-1847 caused the worst disaster in Irish history. Almost a million tenant farmers died when cruel landlords evicted them if they couldn't pay their rents. Another million people, mostly men, emigrated to Britain, Canada, Australia, or the USA.

Fortunately for his employees, the 3rd Marquis of Londonderry who owned the Scrabo Quarry and much of the land around Newtownards, was a kind and thoughtful landlord. He took care of his employees! Scrabo Tower built in 1858 by grateful employees to his memory stands imposingly on Scrabo Hill at the head of Strangford Lough. Joseph I had held a 99 year lease to operate the Scrabo Quarry. The death of the 3rd Marquis of Londonderry in 1858 broke the lease. Joseph no longer had control of the quarry; but he still held a responsible position, likely that of an overseer, for all "building stone" sale bills bear his name for the next few years.

Sometime in the early sixties, Joseph and a friend, Ken, went to Australia. Since Jane suffered from a debilitating bone disease, Joseph did not wish to be away too long. He and Ken expected to find silver without any difficulty. No such luck! In disgust, Joseph headed back to Ireland after giving his share of the claim, along with the cart and donkey to Ken (As payment twenty-three years later, Ken sent to Joseph and Jane, who were now in Canada, a silver tea set which is still on display in the Dugan home.).

Joseph Dugan I and Family
(Standing L-R) Frank Dugan, Joseph Dugan II (Seated L-R) Maggie (Margaret Taylor Anderson) Dugan, Joseph Dugan I, Anna (White) Dugan.

Joseph I returned to the quarry as a labourer, but soon rose to his former position. He also continued to farm.

Gradually, new laws guaranteed fair rents, protected tenants from eviction and gave them the right to sell their property.

Although Joseph I continued working in the quarry, he sold "Lough View Farm" and purchased a larger farm with a beautiful, spacious home named "Killynether" which was a little closer to Belfast. He also bought several shares in a brewery in Newtownards. For almost eighteen years, his brewery shares were profitable, farm produce sold well, and his job in the quarry was satisfying, especially when his son Joseph II joined the quarry labour force.

By the end of 1882, business was once again on the decline in Ireland due to continuing emigration, particularly of young men; and competition from highly developed British industries.

I wish now to enclose a quote taken from the Newtownard newspaper of May 28, 1883 spoken by Mr. P. Mackintosh, Esq., J.P. Chairman of the Testimonial Committee who along with other prominent gentlemen from Newtownards visited the Dugan home before Joseph's departure for Canada - "As an employer of labour, Mr. Dugan secured not only the best services, but also the attachment of all whom he employed. He served his community at different times as a representative of his community on different boards. He also served in public office. And for twenty years he held the honoured position of Ruling Elder of the First Presbyterian Church of Ireland, Congregation of Newtownards."

It was much more sensible for Joseph I to sell his shares in business along with Killynether and emigrate to Canada. There the Homestead Act provided any person over 21 who was a citizen, the right to obtain the title to 160 acres of public land if he paid ten dollars, lived on the land for three years, and improved it. With three growing sons, what better lure could a man have!

In late May, 1883, Joseph I along with his two sons, Francis and Joseph II, and his daughters, Anna and Margaret, set sail for Canada, probably docking in Montreal. They arrived in Brandon by train, in mid June. There they purchased a wagon and a team of oxen. With the wagons loaded with trunks and groceries, they headed for Shoal Lake. Here they purchased a cow which Margaret had to lead. For the sake of the animals as well as themselves, they travelled in the morning and late evening and rested during the heat of the day. When they reached Rossburn, the family rested for two weeks, while Joseph I went on to Birtle to enter his land claim. Pioneers in Rossburn showed the Dugans how to construct a log building. They resumed their journey via Birdtail and Russell with Anna carrying her new cat "Toodles".

All Russell consisted of, was two stores: Hudson's Bay and Denmarks, a Post Office, and a few other buildings.

They camped at Beautiful Lake and crossed the Assiniboine River near the bridge at Shellmouth, July 12, 1883. Shellmouth consisted of one abode, Major Boulton's shack near the Shell River.

With new settlers, Alex McIntyre of Brandon and Duncan Gordon of Rossburn, they rested that night near the Shellmouth hills. Arriving at their homestead (NW 1/4 28-24-29) the next evening, they pitched their tents and set up camp. (It's interesting to note that Duncan Gordon was the first man to own the land on which the last two Castleavery schools were built and the land was always referred to as "Duncan Gordon's".

Soon the Dugans began building their new homes, a log building 18' x 26'. A trip to Birtle was made to secure roofing, windows and doors. They moved into their new home in October, 1883.

In November, Joseph Dugan I returned to Ireland. In the spring of 1884 he arrived in Minnedosa (to where the railway now reached) with his wife, Jane, oldest daughter, Jane, and youngest son, John. Here Joseph II and Francis were waiting with ox-teams. After loading the wagons with furniture, two bedsteads, one table, and a cookstove, the family headed for their Canadian homesteads.

By 1885, since his homestead was near the Pelly Trail, Mr. Dugan I had established both a store and a Post Office in his yard. His daughters had the privilege of naming the district in which they now resided, "Castleavery".

As in Ireland, so too in Canada, the Dugans were known far and wide for their hospitality and excellent leadership.

Joseph I died March 21, 1889. His wife, Jane, died Dec. 2, 1909.

Joseph I and Jane Dugan had six children, all born in Newtownards, Ireland:

Jane was the first teacher in the Castleavery school. She married George Hunt in 1887. They homesteaded in the district for a short time. Then they moved to England. They had three sons and one daughter.

In 1886, Anna married Sidney White, the first teacher in Shellmouth. They homesteaded on S.E. 1/4 of Sec. 20, 24, 29 (present home quarter of Jim Roe). They had four children. Their oldest son, Ted, who was born in the building the Roes later used as a horse barn, became an Episcopalian minister in Chicago. Ted's son visited the Roes in 1988 and took pictures of the barn. Anna and Sidney White moved to Winnipeg and then to Chicago, USA where Sidney was a news reporter. Frank White, the second son, came to Canada and farmed after World War I. His Aunt Margaret and Uncle Jim helped him purchase the little house which was later the first home of Percy and Jean Jennings. It wasn't long before Frank returned to the USA and finally settled in Arkansas.

Margaret married Captain James Anderson, a veteran of the 1885 Northwest Rebellion, in 1900. They lived in the Assiniboine Valley just a short distance north of Jack and Christian Anderson. Margaret's husband died in 1916. Although she had no children of her own, the young people who knew her, loved her dearly and called her "Aunt Maggie". She took care of her mother until she died. Later when Jack Anderson passed away, Maggie went to live her last years with Christian Anderson.

Joseph II married Isabella Skinner and took over the home place. They had three children: Jean, Isabel and Joseph III.

Francis who had barely established his own 'homestead' was killed instantly in 1889 along with J. Fullerton, who was a friend as well as a hired hand, when a threshing machine boiler exploded during harvest. (The first Castleavery Church was built in memory of J. Fullerton with money sent from England by his mother. A prairie fire destroyed the church.)

John farmed in the Assiniboine Valley until his untimely death from influenza in February, 1906.

Joseph I, his wife Jane, their sons: Francis, John, and Joseph II; and their daughter Margaret, and her husband, James, are all interred in Castleavery Cemetery, Man.

Joseph Dugan II and Joseph Dugan III

by Isabelle Dugan Johnson and Ada Dugan

Joseph Dugan II was born Aug. 3, 1865 at Newtownards, County, Ireland. As a young lad of 17, he worked in the Scrabo Quarry along with his father. He came to Canada in 1883 with his father, two sisters and one brother. As the oldest son, he helped his father and brother, Francis, build their first Canadian home, clear land and help with all the pioneer chores.

Joseph II established his own homestead in the district in 1885. It was he who donated the land on which the Castleavery schools were built.

He ran the Castleavery Post office from April 1898 until it closed in 1910. He was a councillor of the Shellmouth Municipality for 30 years.

Isabella Skinner, daughter of John and Isabella Skinner (Scott - Bernie) was born on June 6, 1968 at Rosehearty, Scotland.

Joseph II and Isabella were married Nov. 11, 1900. They had three children:

Jean Osborne was born Sept. 2, 1901 at Castleavery, Man. She married James Langford in 1925. They farmed in Shellmouth from 1925 to 1969. They then retired and moved to Russell, MB. They had five children: Isabel Margaret, born Mar. 5, 1926, married Frank Welke in 1951. Patrick, born Mar. 17, 1927, married Ruth Collins in 1952. Anne Leslie, born Oct. 27, 1940, married James Petz in 1961. Lawrence James, born April 20, 1942, was married to Judith McCrae. Lynn Norah, born May 5, 1944 married Rodney Welke in 1965 but, is now married to Murray Vandeste.

Allan and Isabelle Johnson

Isabelle, born July 11, 1903, at Castleavery, MB lived on the family farm with her parents, brother and sister until 1924. Then she went to St. Boniface Hospital in Winnipeg to study for her R.N. After graduating, she returned to the Russell area in 1927. Since there were no hospitals, she nursed in private homes, often attending maternity cases, and assisting in numerous "kitchen table" surgeries. When the Russell Hospital opened in 1929, Isabelle worked there as a private nurse for special cases. On Valentine's Day, 1936, she married Alan Johnson. They farmed at Shellmouth for many years. When they retired, they moved to Russell, Man. They had two children: Josephine Lee and Blanche Patricia. Josephine born in 1937 married Murray Russin in July, 1958. Blanche, born in 1940 married Dr. Shig Kuwada in 1967. They live in

Jean and Jim Langford Family
Patrick, Isobel, Jean, Jim, Larry, Anne and Lynn.

The Dugan Farm.

Connecticut, USA. Isabelle now lives in the Elk's Retirement Home in Russell, Man.

Joseph Dugan III was born Oct. 11, 1909 at Castleavery, Man. Ada Kolstad was born May 25, 1914, in Montevideo, Minnesota, USA. They were married in Roblin, Man. Sept. 30, 1937. They had two children: Joseph (Bud) born April 20, 1941 and Richard John born July 22, 1948. Both were born at Russell, Man. Richard married Carol Bergland Dec. 22, 1968. Richard, Carol and family live in Prior Lake, a suburb of Minneapolis, Minn., USA. They have four daughters: Michelle, Kimberly, Heidi and Joy. Richard works as a contractor.

When Joseph (Bud) took over the farm in 1975, he and Ada renovated the 1914 house.

A large family reunion was held in 1983 to mark 100 years of homesteading and farming on the same farm. The Dugans were presented with "The Red River Ox Cart" by Wally McKenzie, M.L.A. and a large plaque to mark the farm site - N.W. 28-24-29.

Bud Dugan (Joseph IV) and his mother, Ada, continue to live in this beautiful home on the farm, which for a hundred and twelve years has seen an ever-changing pageant of history.

Dick and their children.

Richard and Bud, Ada & Joe on their 25th Anniversary.

The Farncombes

by Karen Lynn Dale (Farncombe)

James Thomas Farncombe and Mary Helen Moore - 1900.

James Thomas Farncombe came out west to Portage La Prairie from Ontario. He married Cynthia McCoel, who died in childbirth in 1898, leaving a daughter Hester. He re-married Mary Helen Moore in 1900. James and Mary had 6 children. Allan, James, Melvin and George Henry were born in Portage LaPrairie.

In 1907 they moved to the Castleavery District where they homesteaded SW 1/4-30-24-29. Three more children, Charles, Joseph Alfred and Essie were born on the homeplace.

James was known to be a very hard worker. He was noted for wheat growing and had a threshing crew which moved around the area during harvest time.

Allan moved to LacVert, SK married Elsie in 1931. He had 2 sons, James of Prince Albert, SK and Floyd of Melfort. Two daughters, Shirley in BC and Annette in Saskatoon. Allan passed away in 1970.

Melvin married Violet in 1934. He was a grain buyer in MacNutt until 1942. Moved to Braderwardine, MB to work for the Saskatchewan Wheat Pool, then on to Asquith, SK. He took over a general store in Hughton and was a dealer for Red & White Stores in Sturgis, SK until the late 1950's. He became a dealer for MacLeod's in Outlook, SK, when the Diefenbaker Dam was in the planning stages. There he became well established as a business man in the Outlook area for the next ten years. He retired to Saskatoon where he passed away in 1986. Violet passed away three months later.

George married Margaret in 1935. He was also a grain buyer for some years, later he became a Stationery Engineer working in Regina. He has one daughter, Donna, who lives and works in Ottawa. George died after a lengthy illness in 1977. Margaret lives in a senior citizen,s complex in Regina and is still in good health.

Charles went overseas in W.W. II. He married a nurse in England in 1945. He returned home with his wife, Rose, to live in Yorkton. One daughter, Christine, was born in Yorkton. They returned to England in 1950, where they became parents to twin girls, Doreen and Maureen.

Joseph Alfred was born January 1, 1911 and died in September of that same year.

Jack and Essie Dale.

Essie was born in 1913. Growing up, she became an avid horsewoman. She married Jack Robin Dale in 1935. They had one daughter, Karen Lynn. They farmed and helped James until 1945. James and Mary retired to Yorkton. In the early 50's they returned to live with their daughter, Essie, and Jack, their son-in-law. James died in 1952, Mary in 1958. Essie died in 1964. Jack finally left the farm in 1981. Moved to Virden, MB where he started a game farm. He passed away after a lengthy illness in 1985. He is buried in Castleavery Cemetery beside Essie. He left behind one daughter, Karen Lynn and three grandchildren.

In 1990, Hester, James's first born daughter, passed away quietly in Brandon. Her only son died in W.W.II in 1944. Her husband pre-deceased her in 1976.

In 1993, Charles with his wife Rose, and daughter, Maureen, returned to Canada after 47 years. Their visit included magnet and area, meeting new and old friends and reliving many past experiences. At last report, Charles at 87 years of age, is still in good health.

The House of Ferris

William Ferris, Sr. + Jennie Drake

Henry (Britton)
+ Annie Oaten

Joseph Hugh
+ Tomina "Minnie" Shearer

William George
+ Jessie Roberts

Jack

Myrtle	Arnold	Howard	no descendants
William	Hazel	Alycle	
Florence	Mildred		
Victor	Norman		
Arthur	Laura		
Stanley	Eva		
Mervyn			
Dorothy			
Irene			
Mary			
Violet			

* It is noted, that there exists one brother to the late William Ferris, Sr. His name is recorded as Hugh Ferris born 1860 (circa).

This Genealogical Chart has been created for the Publisher of this book under the direction of R. A. Bauer.

Henry "Britton" Ferris

by Kevin and Kathy Ferris

Henry "Britton" Ferris was born April 11, 1891 in Bruce County, ON. He was the eldest of five sons born to William and Jennie (Drake) Ferris. In 1902 the family moved to McGregor, MB.

In 1904 they moved to Dropmore, MB and lived on the southeast quarter of 34-23-29, now owned by Tom Bauereiss as well.

In addition to farming Britton had a well drilling outfit. He drilled wells in Dropmore and surrounding areas for several years. He also had wood sawing and grain crushing outfits which he used to do custom work.

Annie (Oaten) Ferris was born April 5, 1890 in Tauton, Somerset, England. She came to Canada September 10, 1912 with her close friend Jessie Pope. They sailed from Southhampton, England on the ship "Austonia" and settled in Dropmore upon their arrival. Annie once stated that they came to Canada for the adventure, but they also had jobs waiting for them.

Annie's first job was with the Anderson family. She enjoyed her time with the Andersons. One year latter Britton and Annie married and began a family that numbered eleven children. They moved to Dauphin in 1935.

Britton and Annie Ferris.

The family settled on a quarter of land near the south side of the town. Britton continued his well drilling as well as doing some landscaping. In the early 1950's Britton developed heart trouble and was unable to work. He decided to start up a gas station, which he thought would be easier for him to work at. Britton did not live to see his dream realized. He passed away in 1953. Annie kept the dream alive. With the help of her son Arthur and daughter Joyce, Annie opened a gas station called Parkway Texaco. They kept the station open for 13 years until Annie retired and moved to Happy Haven Home.

Annie lived at the Happy Haven until she could no longer fully care for herself. She spent time with all of her children and finally permanently resided with her daughter Irene. Annie spent her days knitting, quilting, gardening and reading. She lived until 1987 when she passed away at the age of 97. Annie was buried in the Riverside Cemetery in Dauphin.

Children of Britton and Annie

June 28, 1914	Myrtle Jenny
Sept. 17, 1915	William Francis
Apr. 12, 1917	Florence Marion
Nov. 4, 1918	Victor Douglas
Mar. 17, 1920	Arthur Norman
Feb. 4, 1922	Stanley James
Sept. 8, 1923	Mervyn Samuel
Oct. 18, 1926	Dorothy Christina
May 24, 1928	Irene Bessie
June 4, 1931	Mary Joyce
June 4, 1931	Violet Jean

Bill and Eileen Ferris.

William Francis Ferris was born on September 17, 1915 in Shellmouth, MB. He passed away January 15, 1969 in Dauphin, MB and is buried in Dauphin Riverside Cemetery. He was the second eldest in the family of Britton and Annie Ferris.

Upon completion of his education in Dropmore district he worked with his father well drilling.

Bill enjoyed farm animals, especially horses.

In 1941 he enlisted with the Royal Canadian Engineers and served overseas in Europe.

In 1946, in England he married Eileen Jordan. Upon returning to Canada, Bill settled in Dauphin, working as a custodian in Dauphin Whitmore School.

In later years he worked for the Town of Dauphin in the maintenance department. Bill retired early due to ill health.

Bill and Eileen raised a family of three children, Kathleen, Kevin and Brendan and has two grandchildren, Leah and Ryan Ferris (children of Kevin).

Bill's family have fond memories of travelling to Dropmore district.

Art Ferris.

worked at the Flin Flon smelter. He was in the army in 1941 as part of the Little Black Devils. After the war he worked at a lumber camp and helped operate the family service station. he married Sandra Williamson in 1963. They had three children: Margaret, Donna and Glen. Arthur continues to work in Dauphin. He is always busy doing something, likes gardening and flowers and enjoys his four grandchildren.

Victor and Betty Ferris.

Victor Douglas was born on November 4, 1918 in Dropmore, MB He received his education in Dropmore. He went with the family when they moved to Dauphin. While he resided there, he worked for farmers. In 1941 Victor enlisted in the army in the Infantry. In 1943 Vicotr married Gilberre (Betty) Toutant in BC. Only six months later Victor was killed in France. He had been fighting in Bratteville, France and is buried in the country. Victor and Betty did not have any children.

Arthur Norman was born on St. Patrick's Day in 1920. he was born and educated in Dropmore. Arthur has had many occupations over the years. He worked for farmers in Dauphin and

Dorothy and Jack Coles.

Dorothy Christina was born October, 18, 1926 in Dropmore, MB. She began her schooling in Dropmore and completed it in Dauphin. She worked at a laundry and a bake shop prior to her marriage.

She married Clarence "Jack" Cloes in November of 1946. They began their married life in Dauphin but most of the years were spent in various places in Alberta. Dorothy did some work in a seniors' home and hospital. In addition she did a lot of volunteering, including planting flowers at seniors' homes. Dorothy was also a member of the Royal Purple.

Dorothy and Jack raised two children, Clarence and Betty, who now have families of their own.

Dorothy passed away on May 25, 1991 in Calgary, Alberta and is buried in the Hanna Cemetery.

Irene and Melville McLaughlin.

Irene Bessie was born May 25, 1928 in Dropmore, MB. She received her schooling in both Dropmore and Dauphin. Irene worked at bakeries, restaurants and a lodge at Clear Lake, MB.

Irene married Melville McLauglin in Dauphin on March 30, 1949. They farmed a short distance from the Ferris home. There they raised their children, Douglas, Shirley, William and David. They moved off the farm when only David was living at home. The McLaughlin's moved into the north end of Dauphin and are now retired. Irene spends her time knitting, sewing, doing ceramics and enjoying her six grandchildren.

Reg and Joyce Tarrant (L-R) Ken, Don, Debbie and Gordon.

Mary "Joyce" and her twin sister, **Violet "Jean"** were born June 4, 1931 in Dropmore. They were the youngest of eleven children born to Britton and Annie. The twins received all of their education in Dauphin, MB.

Sheldon, son of Ken Tarrant.

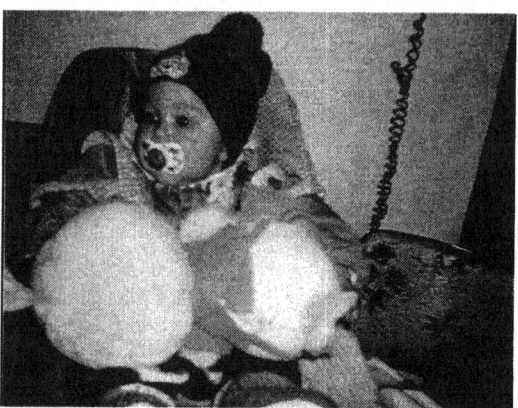
Lindsey Tarrant.

Joyce worked at the family service station until she married Reginald Tarrant in June of 1961. At the gas station Joyce did the books as well as pumping gas and serving confectionery.

Reginald and Joyce moved three miles south of Dauphin where they still reside. Joyce chose to stay home and raise their four children, Ken, Don, Gordon and Debbie.

Jean & Rene Leurquin.

Joyce is involved with several clubs and groups. She spends her days quilting, compiling family history and talking about her children and grandchildren, Sheldon and Lindsey.

Jean chose a path different that of her sister's. She moved to Winnipeg when she was in her 20's. She found work in restaurants and did housekeeping as well.

Jean married Rene Leurquin in 1954. He passed away in the late 1980's. Jean remained in Winnipeg where she met Maurice Heatherington. After several years they married in the early 1990's. Jean did not have any children from these marriages. She thinks of Maurice's children and their dog, as her own family. Jean is now retired, spending her days doing crafts and bowling.

Myrtle Jenny (Ferris) Flett

by Joyce Tarrant

Myrtle Jenny Ferris is the oldest child of Britton and Jennie Ferris. Myrtle was born June 28, 1914 in Dropmore, MB. She went to school there, as well. She worked for Skinner's Nursery.

(Back row L-R) Jack, Cameron and Kay with Myrtle and Jim seated.

While she was working at the nursery she met Jim Flett. Jim and Myrtle were married on October 10, 1934. Jim also worked for several farmers and later settled on a farm of his own in Angusville.

Myrtle and Jim loved the farm. Myrtle liked to raise chickens, and loved her garden and flowers.

They raised 3 children and now they have 4 grandchildren and 10 great grandchildren. Jim passed away on May 31, 1993.

Myrtle is retired and still living on the farm in Angusville. Now she spends much of her time reading, doing crafts and planting her favorite flowers. She still keeps a small garden. She also enjoys her cat and dog.

Florence (Ferris) Kelbert

by Jean Heatherington

Florence was born April 12, 1917. She married Sam Kelbert at Swan River about 1940. They moved to Toronto, ON about 1943. There they ran a rooming house. They moved back to Dauphin around 1946. Then they moved to Winnipeg in 1950.

Florence had her schooling in Dropmore. Our family moved to Dauphin in 1936.

Florence and Sam had 4 boys. They have 4 grandchildren --- 2 girls and 2 boys. Sam passed away 12 years ago. Florence is still living and is in St. Boniface Hospital.

The Ferris sisters - Myrtle, Florence, Dorothy, Irene, (twins) Jean and Joyce taken about the 1930's.

Stanley Ferris

by Stan & Ida Ferris

Stanley James, son of Britton and Annie Ferris, was born February 4, 1922 at Dropmore, MB. He attended school at Dropmore moving to Dauphin with his parents, brothers and sisters in 1935.

In January, 1946 Stan married Ida Pont at Dauphin. He was working at Dauphin at the time, hauling cord wood from the German Prisoner of War Camp at Lake Audy, to the CN yards at Dauphin. The wood was loaded into box cars. Later, Stan was employed by the Dept. of Highways, hauling gravel into many communities. Still later, with his brother Mervyn, they joined partnership in the gravel business purchasing their

Stan and Ida Ferris.

own gravel pit machinery, etc. and were known as Ferris Bros. Gravel Contractors. They continued working together until Stan's death in August, 1966. Mervyn continued on with the business with Ida as his partner. The business closed with the sale of the gravel pit in the fall of 1993.

Stan and Ida raised a family of four in Dauphin, one son and three daughters: Wayne, Beverley, Darlene and Judith. There are eight grandchildren and two great grandchildren as of April, 1995.

A daughter, Beverley and her husband, accidentally drowned at Penticton, BC in 1974, enroute home from a trip to BC leaving two little daughter, aged three and one. They were later adopted by an uncle and aunt in Dauphin.

Mervyn Ferris

by Mervyn Ferris

I, Mervyn Ferris was born at Dropmore, MB on September 8, 1923 to Annie and Britton Ferris. I received my education at the Dropmore School.

When I was twelve years of age, my parents and family moved to Dauphin, MB. I never went back to school, as times were hard and it was the "dirty thirties". I went out working for farmers in the surrounding areas doing chores, etc. A few years later I worked in the bush, cutting cord wood.

Around 1944, I purchased a truck and went out hauling wood from the prison camp to Dauphin. This was a round trip that would be about one mile. This I did for two winters.

In the summer, I would haul grain and gravel and also worked for the Maple Leaf Construction hauling gravel for a couple of years.

Later on, my brother Stan and I purchased a gravel pit about five miles west of Dauphin and we went into partnership. We bought loaders, trucks and conveyors and went under the name of Ferris Construction.

Wood hauling from the prison camp in 1945.

The business carried on for many years. Stan passed away in the summer of 1966. The business was continued on until it was sold in 1993.

On October 10, 1945, I got married to Viola (Vi) Pont at Dauphin. We raised a family of three children, Evelyn of Portage, Victor and Karen, both of Winnipeg. We have five grandchildren and one great granddaughter. We are still living in the same house we had a carpenter build in 1947 at 116-6th Ave., S.E., Dauphin, MB.

Mervyn and Vi Ferris.

Bill, Victor, Stan and Mervyn Ferris. Missing from the picture is Art Ferris. Taken around 1930.

Joseph Hugh Ferris Family

by Mildred Rawlings

Joe and Minnie Ferris.

Joe Ferris was born in Grey County Owen Sound, ON August 2, 1893. He moved with his parents William and Jennie (Drake) Ferris to Beaver in 1901. In 1903 they moved to what is now known as Dropmore to SW 1/4 34-23-29. He attended Grainsby School when able. He had asthma.

He later farmed in the Grainsby District NW 32-23-29. On March 5, 1919 he married Tomina (Minnie) Shearer who was born July 12, 1898 at Cut Arm, North West Territories, now the Province of Saskatchewan. She moved with her parents, George and Barbara Shearer sisters and brothers to the Castleavery District.

At this time, the main means of transportation was with horses; in summer with wagon or buggy and in winter by cutter or sleigh. In later years they owned a Model T Ford car. Some of their entertainment was cards, house parties and visiting with neighbors.

In the early years, Joe could be seen driving Dr. Lee, a doctor from MacNutt with his team Riley and Buster.

Joe was always ready to give his neigbbors and friends a helping hand with sick cattle or horses.

Minnie, his wife, could be found at home, doing house work, farm chores, and many loaves of bread were baked for the family and for the bachelors. Butter was churned. Times were tough in the "dirty thirties". Clothes were washed on the scrub board, or if lucky, a hand washing machine. Land was worked with horses and ploughs until later years with tractors. The crops were seeded with a seed drill, cut with a binder, stooked and threshed until the combines took over. Wood was cut and neighbors got together to saw it into stove lengths.

They raised a family of six, all attended Grainsby School. The younger children attended Dropmore for a few years until Grainsby reopened. It was closed for a few years as there weren't enough students.

Vera and Arnold Ferris.

Arnold George was born January 5, 1923. He helped at home, worked for Jack Ferris for awhile, then farmed in the Grainsby District and then at Dropmore. He drove the school bus for Intermountain School Division from 1954 to 1970. He is caretaker of the Dropmore Cemetery. He married Vera Shearer May 6, 1974. They retired to Russell in 1992.

Hazel and George Bernhard.

Hazel Elizabeth was born November 17, 1927. She worked out for awhile, then married George Bernhard June 21, 1950. They farmed in the Grainsby District on SE 1/4 30-23-29. George was an electrician and played the accordion in the Dropmore Orchestra. One of my favorite tunes was the "Cuckoo Waltz". Some others in the orchestra were Reg Lewis, Jessie Wardle, Cedric and Durward Rowan. Hazel always grew a big garden and helped with harvest and picking roots. They are now retired at their cottage at Madge Lake, SK.

Milly and Jack Rawlings.

Mildred Jean was born March 4, 1929 and married Jack Rawlings January 17, 1970. Jack served in the Army Service Corps overseas. He belongs to the Inglis Legion and is a life member of the Russell Elks Lodge. He worked for farmers and carpenters and for Poole Construction while living at Dropmore. Their daughter Sherry Mildred was born July 21, 1970. She attended Roblin School. She took a secretarial course in Regina, worked for awhile in Winnipeg and married Ronald Koroway from Grandview July 27, 1991. They lived in Winnipeg for awhile and now in Roblin. Their daughter Laurissa Mildred Caroline Koroway was born December 31, 1991. They were unfortunate and lost baby Jordan September 13, 1993. Travis Ronald Rawlings-Koroway was born September 16, 1994.

Sherry, Ron, Travis and Laurissa.

Muriel, Patti and Norman Ferris.

Norman Harold was born February 28, 1931. He drove trucks for Ed Fingas, Harry Toderan, Jack Ferris, Ed Bach for James Transport, Steiners and Gardwine. Then he trucked for Swan River -- The Pas and in 1974 purchased his own Mack truck. He married Muriel Robinson of Roblin, May 31, 1956. They lived on the home farm, Roblin, Grandview and Swan River. They had a family of four. Brian Jeffrey born February 11, 1959 married Marilyn Carriss. They have three boys: Larry Michael, born January 20, 1980, Shale Jeffrey born November 28, 1984 and Brandon Joseph born April 12, 1986. They are living at Creighton, SK and Brian works in Flin Flon, MB. Brenda Jean, born June 15, 1960 married Murray Semeniuk. They have one son Riley, born June 26, 1979. They live in Swan River and have purchased Charlie and Mary Bernhard's house at Dropmore. Patricia Ann, born July 14, 1969 married Lloyd Church, September 14, 1991. They have two children, Dakota Joe-Lynn born May 22, 1990 and Jacob Raymond, born September 5,

1992. They lived at Lloydminister but are at Swan River now. Kevin Wade, born March 10, 1973. He took his schooling at Swan River and now lives and works in Winnipeg.

Norman in the later 80's had reliable men driving his truck and with his love for horses took to racing. He attended races far and near and won a good number of them. On April 1, 1994 family, relatives and friends were saddened to hear of his sudden passing from a massive heart attack at his home.

Laura, Pam and Walter Seidlitz.

Laura Barbara born December 12, 1993 worked for neighbors for awhile then went to Regina. She married Walter Seidlitz February 18, 1968. They both worked for Sears. Their daughter Pamela Laura was born January 29, 1973. After finishing school in Regina she took a Legal Secretarial Course in Winnipeg. She works at a flower shop and also worked at one in Regina. As Pam was growing up, Laura did a lot of baby-sitting. She loves children so it was hard for her to say no to a mother. Walter is retired now due to his health. They are always there, for relatives and friends.

Eva, Reinhold Haas, Bonny, Darlene, Boyd, Garry, Greg and Karen.

Eva Bernice was born March 5, 1937. She married Reinhold Haas March 18, 1955. They enjoyed curling, ball and dancing, along with farm work. Eva was a 4H leader and Reinhold was a councillor. They had six children. Karen Eva was born February 14, 1956. She attended Langenburg School, worked in different places and now she and financé Dennis Hango live in Regina. Darlene Gay, born June 25, 1957 married Terry Pekrul June 27, 1981. They are living at Odessa, SK. They have two children, Bryce Lowell born August 7, 1984 and Breanne Kaelee, born December 19, 1987. Gregory Brent, born August 8, 1981 resides on the home farm and works at various places. Garry Linton, born May 4, 1960 married Lorraine Yates on October 6, 1984. They live on an acreage, the Bud Taylor farm. They both work. They have two girls, Ashley Dawn born December 21, 1986 and Janelle Alynn, born June 20, 1988. Bonny Lee was born March 24, 1963. She lives at Regina and is a registered nurse and works at the General Hospital. She had two boys, Joshua Leo Reinhold Arseneau born October 4, 1986 and Matthew Tomas Arseneau born May 16, 1989. Boyd Carlton, born April 21, 1965, resides at home part time but works at plumbing, pipe fitting or at other jobs.

July 5, 1985 family, relatives and friends were shocked to hear Reinhold had passed away with a massive heart attack. Eva moved to Langenburg and is employed at the Centennial Special Care Home.

Due to ill health, Joe and Minnie retired to the village of Dropmore in 1956. In 1957, Joe passed away after a lengthy illness. Minnie resided in Dropmore until June 1992, when she moved to the Banner Country Court at Russell. In March 1995, Minnie moved to the Russell and District Care Home. At 96 years she still has a great interest in her friends, family, grandchildren and great-grandchildren.

Just before publishing of this book, we learned that on April 30, 1995, Minnie passed away at the Yorkton Hospital and was laid to rest in the Dropmore Cemetery.

William George (Bill) Ferris Family

by Jessie Ferris

Bill Ferris was born in Grey County, Owen Sound, ON April 20, 1895. His parents, William and Jennie Ferris and four brothers moved to Bagot, MB in 1901 and in 1903 moved to Dropmore. He received his education at Grainsby School. In December 1926 he married Jessie Roberts of Shellmouth. they raised a son, Howard and a daughter, Alyce.

Jessie and Bill Ferris.

Howard and Betty Ferris.

In 1933, Alyce married James Johnston of Brandon. In 1971, Howard married Elizabeth Nixon of Brandon.

Bill was a Veteran of the First World War, and a life member of the Inglis Legion. He served 21 years as councillor of Shellmouth Municipality, 20 years on the Roblin Hospital Board and many years on the Roblin Citizens Board. He did a lot of driving for the late Frank Clement, a fur buyer and the soldier's settlement board representative from Winnipeg.

In 1971, Bill and Jessie moved to the village of Dropmore. In 1980, Bill's health was failing and in May 1981, he passed away in Brandon General Hospital. Since 1991 Jessie has made her home in the Banner County Court in Russell.

Howard Ferris

I was born on September 19, 1927 and in 1934 we moved to our present farm in the Grainsby District SW 33-23-29. I attended the Grainsby School and when the school closed, my father bought it and it is still situated on the farm. I farmed with my parents until 1971. Then on July 10, 1971, I married Betty Nixon of Brandon, MB. At that time, my parents retired to Dropmore.

Betty had two children: Valerie born February 13, 1952. She got married in 1973 to Philip Horkey of Brandon. They have three children of their own: David, Shauna and Tanis. Valerie is an R.N. and employed at the Brandon General Hospital.

Howard and Betty Ferris Family (Standing L-R) Matthew, Jim, Howard, David, Philip, Tanis, Shanna. (Sitting L-R) Roberta, Emily, Chelsea, Betty, Jessie, & Valerie.

Jim, the other child, was born October 29, 1954. In 1984, he married Roberta Berry of Vernon, BC. They have three children: Matthew, Chelsea, and Emily. Jim is employed with the Saskatchewan Pool Elevators in Regina.

We are still farming at this time, but we sold our cattle in the fall of 1994, when we decided to retire in Russell for the winter.

Alyce (Ferris) Johnston

I was born on December 1, 1928 at NW 20-23-29. A few years later my parents moved to SE 33-23-29 in the Grainsby District. I received my education at the Grainsby School and finished my education in Russell.

I was employed at the Roblin Hospital and the Roblin Creamery before moving to Brandon in 1952 where I was employed by Canada Safeway for 33 years and retired in 1988.

Alyce and Jim Johnson.

I married Jim Johnston of Brandon on May 10, 1957. He was employed with the CPR. In 1961 Jim secured employment at Brandon Correctional Institution retiring in 1985.

Jim was a widower with a family of four children: Amy, Brenda and twins Kent and Kandy.

Jack Ferris

Jack Ferris was born on September 30, 1897. He farmed and then ranched in the Assiniboine Valley. He also owned his own transfer business for a number years.

He had to leave his home in the valley when the Shellmouth Dam was put in and the valley was flooded. Then he retired in Roblin where he enjoyed his friends' company and his birthday parties.

Jack loved to dance in his younger years and was a member of the Roblin Elks Lodge.

He passed away at his home and was laid to rest in the Dropmore Cemetery in 1975.

Watt, Bill and Jack Ferris.

Watt Ferris

Watt was born on November 3, 1900. He farmed the SW-1/4 34-23-29, the original Ferris farm. In the thirties, he and his brother Jack, took their cattle to Dauphin for a couple of years where feed was more plentiful. The rest of his life was spent on the farm at Dropmore.

John Flynn made his home, and worked for Watt for a number of years, until he passed away and was buried at Moosimen, his original home.

In Watt's younger years, he played football and later curled. he belonged to the Russell Elks Lodge for a number of years.

Watt passed away in 1968 and was laid to rest in the Dropmore Cemetery.

Hugh Ferris

Hugh Ferris.

Hugh Ferris was born in 1860 and he was a brother to William Ferris, Sr. Hugh came from ON to make his home on NE Section 28-23-29 where he farmed for a few years and then, due to ill health, he moved his shack into Dropmore where he made his home. When he couldn't look after himself any longer he lived with his brother, William (Bill) and his wife Jennie, until he died in 1929. He was buried in the Dropmore Cemetery.

W.G. (Bert) Ferriss Family

by Joyce, Gordon and Lyle Ferriss

Please Note: *Two un-related Ferris families moved to the Dropmore area during 1902-1903. The spelling, however, is slightly different in that Bert's family surname had historically ended with double "ss".*

Bert and Ella Ferriss Wedding Picture, November 6, 1899.

W. G. (Bert) Ferriss was born in Bagot, MB in 1879 of Irish descent. He married **Ella Mae Longden** of McGregor in the year 1899. In 1902, with their three month old baby, Hilliard, they joined Bert's father, **Albert Henry Ferris**, (mother deceased in 1898) and brothers, **Harland** and **Guy**, in search of a homestead in the Shell River Municipality. They located in the Castleavery District T24-R29 W. Bert's homestead was the SW quarter of section 16 and Guy homesteaded the NW quarter. Harland and father, Albert Henry, homesteaded the NW quarter of section 10.

Also of interest, W.G. (Bert) Ferriss's in-laws, **Joseph** and **Mary Longden**, homesteaded the NE quarter of 16 --- hence the "Longden Lake". Their family consisted of their son, Bill and their daughters, **Sadie** (Mrs. **Harry Rowan**) and **Annie** (Mrs. **Burnett Ralston**).

The Harland Ferriss Farm.

Bert and Ella's family would grow to eight by 1922 and all these children would go to Castleavery School.

Name	Birthdate	Deceased
Hilliard Lisle	June 8, 1902	July 19, 1974
Vera Selena (Lena)	Dec. 11, 1904	
Oliver Holgate	June 10, 1907	June 1, 1991
Arthur Leonard Guy	May 1, 1909	Aug 4, 1970
Shirley Sadie Mary	Mar. 5, 1912	Sept. 5, 1989
Joyce Eva	June 12, 1914	
Ida Heather	Feb. 23, 1917	Nov. 10, 1982
Percy Gordon Ross	July 24, 1922	

In 1907, Albert Henry is recorded as councillor of Shell River Municipality as well as chairman of Castleavery School Board.

The "Bert" Ferriss home - started in 1906.

The first house on Bert's homestead was built of logs. By 1907 there was a new frame house for Oliver to be born in. It was planned so a parlour and upstairs bedrooms could be added later so it was. Later, Oliver would chop down the transplanted maple outside the front door when it grew faster than he did! This unplanned pruning only served to spread the future growth to three large trunks, providing shade to the house for many years.

By 1909, Hilliard had started school and an interest in the Longden blacksmith shop had a mechanical influence on both Hilliard and Oliver --- after all it was on the road to school! Additionally, the valleys of the Shell and Assiniboine Rivers were a world of trapping and hunting experiences for Bert and his boys.

By 1912 Guy Ferriss and Bill Longden were making cement blocks with a horse powered treadmill on Guy's farm. A building of these blocks still stands on that farm.

In 1913, Bert was a school trustee at Castleavery and in 1916, he was a board member for the new Grain Growers elevator at Dropmore.

An incident which left a mark on Bert for many years occurred along the trapline when he had the misfortune of breaking the stock off his rifle leaving the steel mounting tangs exposed. Later the same day, he came upon a good sized buck deer and, being in need of meat for the "larder" he decided he could withhold the rifle recoil sufficiently to avoid physical damage to himself -- a decision which permanently scarred his upper lip as well as loosened a few front teeth! Bert would wear a "cover up" mustache for many years to come.

By 1918, steam engines were gaining more and more importance and Bert Ferriss would buy one. Threshing crews of 20 men were now common and it was all very inspiring to school boys almost old enough to take a man's place --- most whom already thought they were!

In 1919, Bert purchased a new International thresher of wood construction. It arrived on a flatcar and was left on the Dropmore siding for unloading. Bert and Hilliard Ferriss, with a team of horses and Walter Beals, with a team of mules, took it off. It was powered by steam until 1928, when steam power was replaced with a model "B" Minneapolis tractor with a 4 cylinder motor which ran on distillate. Angle iron cleats provided ground traction for the steel wheels. Little did they know that this tractor would go on to break hundreds of acres of bushland in the Swan River Valley, nor did they know the threshing machine would give way to combines and it would be left in a fence corner. Today it has been refurbished for "antique value" by the "Tall Bros." of Bowsman.

In 1921, Grandfather Albert Henry Ferriss passed away and was buried at Burnside Cemetery.

The mid twenties was a busy time for this family of 4 boys and 4 girls growing up. The piano and violin were an important part of their home life. Three of the four boys would go on to play at dances and Gorden has continued into the 90's.

Lena in 1920, married Sanford (Sandy) Dow. Bert tried to help them start up farming, however they soon moved to Iowa where they raised three children: Ivan, Isobel and Paul.

Hilliard started farming as a bachelor in 1924 when he rented the George Hunt place (NW quarter of section 8). His father supplied four horses with harness to get him started. In 1925, he purchased the SE quarter of 17 across the road from his father. There already was a barn on the farm so he had to build a house. In 1926, he married the Castleavery teacher, (1922-24) Marion Reid. She was a town girl from Virden, MB who learned to be a farmwife. Hilliard and Marion had two sons: Lyle, born in 1928 and Kenneth, born in 1935, both on the farm at Dropmore. Lyle's first years of school were at Castleavery.

By 1930, the Prairies had entered into an economic depression coupled with seven years of drought, that would alter plans dramatically. A bushel of wheat in the granary over winter, fell in price from a $1.33 to 18 cents a bushel and a carload of "feed" barley shipped to the Lakehead would not pay the freight. Compounded with this, was a disease known as "swamp fever" which often depleted the ever necessary horsepower. Income from the trapline equaled that of the farm. Dust blowing in from Saskatchewan, obscured the sun and there were thunderstorms without rain!

After four years with no improvement, the family started looking for a way out and four children would leave over the following four years.

Leonard, in 1934, was first of the family to go to Swan River Valley. He travelled with his uncle and aunt, Burnett and Annie Ralston. They located southwest of Swan River. In 1939 Leonard married Mae Ball of Bowsman. They raised five children: Shirley, Duane, Gaylene, Lance, and Marvin. Leonard operated a sawmill west of Bowsman for a number of winters. He hired out to break land and farmed during summer. His ability to out-produce most people with an axe became his trademark. He passed away in 1970.

Shirley went to visit her sister, Lena, in Iowa and married Ben Dow (brother to Lena's husband). They had three children: Leland, Lawrence, and Loraine. In 1946, Shirley and Ben moved to Bowsman, MB with their children and took up farming. Later, Shirley completed her teaching qualifications and taught school in southern MB. At a later date she retired to Iowa to be near to her sister and her children. Deceased in 1989.

Ida married Keith Smith, the teacher at Dropmore (1931-34). They had two sons: David Wayne and Linton. She served in the Canadian Army during W.W.II. Her second marriage was to Bert Burns. The boys took their new father's surname and two more boys, Greg and Max, were born in Guelph, ON. Ida became a freelance writer and worked as an assistant editor. She also founded an advertising company. After her husband's death, she moved to Vancouver, where two years later, she had a fatal automobile accident in 1982.

Oliver and **Bert**, in 1935, made a trip over the Duck Mountains to see what land was available in the Craigsford District, east of Bowsman. Ironically, Bert took a quarter which proved to be too wet! However, they were able to break land on Oliver's quarter before returning home. Later, Oliver would return to Bowsman, taking with him his cattle and horses. In 1936, he married Keturah (Kay) Watt and he rented an additional quarter of land with a more desirable set of buildings. They had one daughter, Islay, who attended Craigfords School and later married Andrew Giles. Oliver was an ardent fisherman and moosehunter. His competitive spirit and the rapid firing of his "lever-action" long barrel 30-30 will be well remembered by his hunting friends. He died in June, 1991. Kay remained on the farm.

In 1937, both Bert and Hilliard secured land in the Swan River Valley. There was a log house on Bert's quarter and he added the necessary barn. Hilliard's quarter had a barn on it and he built a house. Hilliard's farm was located eight miles east of Bowsman on the Swan River. They returned to Dropmore, and in mid-October, the move north was on. Four horse drawn wagons, loaded with machinery and furniture were driven by Harry Ferris, Jack Shedden, Hank Kester and Bill Hall, followed by 60 head of cattle and a fifteen year old Gorden Ferriss on horseback (with his trusty dog). A few days later, a "low-bed" truck owned by J.J.Lucas of Swan River arrived at Dropmore for the remaining machinery, chickens, pigs, calves, etc. Bert, Ella and Joyce would leave Castleavery, followed by Hilliard and Marion, and their two boys, Lyle and Ken, in a 1927 Touring Chevrolet. Leaving Castleavery after 35 years, was not an easy decision but it really wasn't good-bye to their many friends as communications would be maintained, not the least of which had to be the annual gathering at Madge Lake.

Joyce helped her parents settle in their new home before she went to Winnipeg to take up the profession of nursing. She retired from the Shriner's Hospital after a long career. She has remained a resident of Winnipeg. At eighty, she still boasts "not a gray hair".

Lois Snaith, an eleven year old cousin from Alberta, took her place as #9 of Bert and Ella's children. She attended school, then married George Wilson of Bowsman. They have two boys and reside in Port Alberni, BC.

Bert's move north to Bowsman at fifty-eight years of age, must have revived memories of his father's move to Dropmore at age fifty-four and the uncertainty that goes with being a new settler. However, Gorden was now approaching manhood so he bought the quarter south of Bert's and would farm with his father, which met the needs of both father and son.

The first years in the Swan River Valley were the most trying as the Ferriss families cleared the bush and broke the land in order to accumulate more cultivated acreage. (No bulldozers or chain saw!) However they did use a "scrub cutter" pulled behind the Minneapolis "B" tractor -- that sped up the process. The importance of draft horses for working the land was to diminish rather quickly and to be replaced by modern tractors. In 1939, Hilliard bought the first International tractors. In 1939, Hilliard bought the first International Farmall "H" tractor sold north of #1 Highway --- on steel wheels, no belt pulley, no power take-off, not battery equipped, therefore no lights etc. Price $811. In 1943, Bert and Gorden replaced the Minneapolis "B" with a new Farmall "M". The rewards were evident with this very fertile soil. In fact, Bert always called it "God's country" and it was very good to the Ferriss'.

Gorden, in 1943, married Pauline Beals (another Dropmore family that had moved north). They had three children: a daughter, Darlene, married and resides in Winnipeg, and two boys, Brian, on the farm, and Blake, who has pursued the ministry.

Grandma and **Grandpa Ferriss,** as they had become known, lived on the home farm until their passing --- Grandma in 1957 and Grandpa in 1958.

Gorden continued to farm and accumulate more land. His eldest son, Brian, elected to remain on the farm, so they expanded operations to include a large piggery. Brian and Donna's son, Jason, plans to continue the tradition. These are the only active farmers remaining from the Bert Ferriss family. In 1972, Gorden was an elected delegate to the Manitoba Hog Marketing Board and has served as a Provincial Director for the District since 1985 (nine years).

Hilliard added to his land holdings, served as a municipal councillor for eleven years and was an active organizer in the Manitoba Farmer's Union. He ran for a seat in the Manitoba Legislature to be defeated by 200 votes. He sold the farm in 1967. He and Marion moved to

Langley, BC, but frequently revisited Manitoba. Hilliard's continued enthusiasm for hunting and fishing made him instantly available at the mere mention of such a trip. He took great pleasure from relaying his life's experiences. He passed away suddenly in July, 1974. Marion lived in good health until December 1991.

Lyle, married Ruth Fleming (Craigsford teacher) in 1951. They farmed with Hilliard until 1956 when they moved to Vancouver where Lyle worked for BC Hydro for 33 years and then retired to Kelowna.

Kenneth married Shirley Madill (a local school teacher). When the farm was sold in 1967, Ken followed a future in logging and pulp. He later sold his company and worked for Northern Affairs, Ottawa, after which he returned to logging. Ken and Shirley make their home near Swan River, MB.

The Ferriss Families

by Anne Wishart

Please note: This is a pictorial history of the Ferriss Family; while another family story has also been compiled by Joyce, Gorden and Lyle Ferriss and appears elsewhere in this publication.

Albert Henry Ferriss (1849 - 1921)

Albert Henry Ferriss was born around 1849 and died November 19, 1921 at Dropmore. He was of Irish origin and was married to a Baldwin. My mother (Edith Rowan) related to me that there was a mixture of English, Irish, Scottish and Pennsylvania Dutch or German in his roots. The name of "Schnider" was also found in his family tree.

The marriage of Harland Ferriss and Elizabeth Emma Woods.

Albert Henry had three sons, Harland Vivian (1873-1950), W. G. Ferris (Bert) and Guy Ferriss (1884-1913), who died at the age of 29 from a ruptured appendix. The family migrated west to Bagot in the county of Norfolk, MB.

Harland married Elizabeth Emma Woods, also of Bagot, MB on January 6, 1897, in McGregor, MB. Their wedding attendants were Sarah Woods and Logan McCann.

Harland and Elizabeth had four children born at Bagot, MB. They were: Morley Harland (1897-1973), Olive Fay Ferriss (Roe) (1899-1973), James Gilbert Walter (1900 or 01-1934), Albert Ivan (1902-1972). The remaining children who were born in the Castleavery District are Rodrick Ferriss (1904-1987), Edith Elizabeth Ferriss (Rowan) (1906-1980), Henry (Harry) (1909-), and Jessie (1913) Jessie died of pneumonia a few months after her birth. The Manitoba telephone system was on strike at the time, so they were unable to get the doctor out from Russell in time to save her. She died at the age of 43.

Harland and Elizabeth Ferriss with their family - Morley, Olive, James, Albert, Roderick, Edith and Harry.

Bert and Ella (Longdon) Ferriss with their family. Missing is Gordon, the youngest.

W.G. "Bert" Ferriss married Ella Longdon of the Castleavery District. They lived on SW 16-24-29. They were blessed with four boys and three girls.

Old Castleavery School - all the Harland Ferriss Family attended school here.

Rodrick and Anne (Austin) Ferriss.

Dorothy, Albert Jr. and Edith Elizabeth, the family of Albert Ivan and Katie Ferriss.

James Gilbert Walter Ferriss.

All the Ferriss' attended the old Castleavery School. In 1927, Morley Ferriss went to live with his father in Pavilion, Wyoming. In 1951, he moved to Buffalo, WY where he lived until 1971. He then moved back to Manitoba.

Olive Ferriss was united in marriage to Harry Roe. They were blessed with six children: Eva, Jim, Ilene, Grace, George and Mable. Jim still lives on his Dad's farm.

James Gilbert Walter went to B.C. and worked in the smelter at Trail. He died in 1934 from lead poisoning.

Albert Ivan went to the USA to live. He was united in marriage to Katie and they had three children: Dorothy, Albert Jr. and Edith Elizabeth. They all live in the United States.

Rodrick Ferriss was united in marriage to Anne Austin. They lived in Hamilton, ON until after Anne passed away. Then he moved to BC.

Edith Elizabeth was united in marriage to George Nelson Rowan of MacNutt, SK on December 25, 1928. The were blessed with two

The marriage of Edith Elizabeth Ferriss and George Nelson Rowan.

Great Grandpa Ferris butchering hogs.

children, Elizabeth Anne, August 7, 1930 and Ivan Harland Nelson, December 1, 1934.

Henry (Harry) Ferriss was united in marriage to Loretta Graham of Bowsman, MB. They were blessed with five children: Albert, Vivian, James and twin brothers who died in infancy.

The "Free Press" was Great Grandpa's avenue to catch up on the latest news.

Picking saskatoons L-R) son Timothy Wishart, Uncle Morely, Mom (Edith Rowan) and daughter Linda-Lou Wishart.

"Play ball!" with Great Grandpa Ferriss.

Great Grandpa Ferris (center) and the men folk getting the fields ready for seeding.

An invention by Great Grandpa Ferriss - loading boxcars in Dropmore before there were grain elevators.

The Ferriss Family busy at sawing wood.

Harvesting with Harland Ferriss's tractor and threshing separator.

Union Bank of Canada on Main Street in Dropmore.

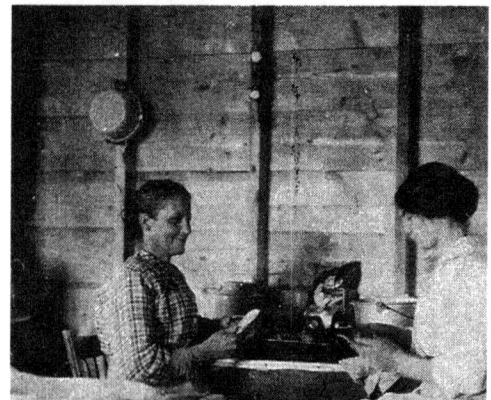

Grandma Ferriss and a neighbor preparing meals for the threshers.

E. T. Lewis General Merchant Store.

Grandpa Ferriss invented this portable grain elevator.

Life in the past in Dropmore Days held many interests. We have many pictorial memories of Great Grandpa and Great Grandma Ferris, from playing ball, reading the latest news in The Free Press, butchering hogs, sawing wood preparing the fields for seeding, inventing and harvesting. Great Grandma Ferriss found herself in meal preparation for all the threshers.

A gathering on the former Dropmore School grounds.

This picture taken from railraod track facing north, shows the house last lived in by Bert and Lillian Hunt. The house to the north-east is the home of Mrs. Beatrice Cameron.

Dropmore in days gone by had many exciting activities.

School house entertainment. Note the "kerosene" lamp on the end of the piano.

Old Pyott Bridge collapsed in 1955.

The Dropmore Ladies' Club in about 1939 or '40.

Assiniboine Valley looking north from the bridge. Meadow used by Jim Craig, then bought by Jack Ferriss.

Dad, Grandpa Ferriss, Anne and brother Ivan (circa) 1948.

And...to finish my family pictorial history, some treasured family photos. Grandpa Ferriss did all of his own photography and developing. He loved to do this and the last picture is appropriate to end the Ferriss History.

Ivan and me (Anne) at our playhouse (1936-37).

My Mom, Dad and me (Anne) in about 1931.

Our humble home taken about 1935, where there was lots of love and care.

My Grandpa and Grandma Ferriss knew their Saviour, our Lord Jesus. Grandpa Ferriss loved to teach Sunday School and loved singing hymns. I'm sure Grandpa prayed for his families to come to know the Lord Jesus as their own personal Lord and Saviour.

II Corinthians 6:2 says, "Now is the accepted time; behold, now is the day of salvation." The whole third chapter of St. John shows us the way. May God bless the reader.

"River Reflections" by Grandpa Ferriss.

Margaret (Robb) Finkbeiner

by Margaret Finkbeiner

Hi! my name is Margaret (Robb) Finkbeiner. My husband and I live in Virden, MB. We both farmed in the Isabella district for many years. I lost my first husband, Jim Ross in 1986 with cancer. We both loved horses. Before we were married Jim showed heavy horses at many summer fairs. After we married we acquired several driving and riding horses and took them around to as many as 14 fairs during the summer. The children were small at the time and friends would take care of them and as they grew older we took them along and taught them how to drive and ride.

John, to whom I am now married, lost his first wife, Dorothy, with cancer in 1984. We farmed close together, so we have known one another for some time. Two years later in 1988 we decided to get married.

My son Bob had bought the home farm and John's son-in-law has John's farm, so we decided we would leave them and move to Virden which is 45 miles from our homes. It is a fairly large town and has everything a person needs.

John is a brother to Sid Finkbeiner who bought grain at the Pool elevator in Dropmore for 2 years and I worked at Roy Robbs who had the Grain Growers at the same time.

My Dad came from Travis, Aberdeen, Scotland and my mother from Rosehearty, Aberdeen, Scotland. After they were married they came to Canada and lived in Winnipeg for some time. My brother Geordie, myself and my sister Dora were born there. Dad worked in the C.N.R. offices then decided he wanted to farm. Geordie started school in Winnipeg. Brother Edward was born on the farm S.E. 30-23-28W. We attended the Rochedale school which was 1-1/2 miles from our home. We lived in a little log cabin for quite some time until Dad could afford to build a house. Our transportation was the horse and buggy, then horse back. We went to the United Church every Sunday for Sunday School which was held in the school house. We had our dances and socials there also. As we grew up Geordie learned to play the accordion, I, the organ, and Jimmy Craig, the guitar and his brother Sandy the violin. We played for many dances and house parties. Practices were always held at our house.

At the time of writing, Geordie is in the Nursing Home at Cardston, AB where he and his wife Pearl live. I also have a daughter Betty who lives in Elkhorn, MB. Who has four of a family. When her youngest one was a year old she lost her husband at age 36 with kidney and lung problems. Her sons, both in their mid-twenties had to have kidney transplants the same night in Winnipeg, December 1989, just before Christmas. We got to visit them Christmas Eve. The oldest one is married and has 2 small boys. The youngest one got a bad kidney so he is waiting for another one. He has to go to Brandon 3 times a week to go on the dialysis machine for 3 hours. The two girls are fine. The oldest, Carol, is married and lives at Hartney, MB. They have 3 little girls. The youngest one, Sandra, is married and lives in Brooks, AB. They have a 3 year old boy. Bob's boy, Jeff, is married and lives not far from us. His wife teaches school in Virden, a block from us. They are planning on living in Virden also. They are expecting their first child May 30th.

John and I enjoy all our grandchildren and great grandchildren. John has 5 grandchildren and I have 5 grandchildren and six great grandchildren plus one more on the way.

Lillian (Lil) Gabrielson
by Lillian Greer

Lil' Gabrielson taken in the spring of '51 at Dugan's.

I came to Castleavery School in the fall of 1950, taking over the teaching position from Mrs. Letz. I boarded with Joe and Ada Dugan. There were nine pupils in grades 2-7.

The Christmas concert, my first, was quite a challenge, but one I thoroughly enjoyed. With a small enrollment, each pupil had to take many parts in the evening's performance but it all seemed to go over rather well.

In 1951-52 I taught at Dropmore school, boarding at Roger Cameron's and Bill Hunter's.

Again I had a small enrollment, starting with eleven pupils - Grades 1-8, three moved away during the year, leaving only eight for the conclusion of the term.

The Christmas concert was shared with Grainsby school pupils and held at the hall.

In July of 1952 I married Jim Greer and I moved to the farm at Grandview, where we still reside. We have four daughters, all married, and five grandchildren.

Lillian and Jim Greer - 1994.

The Archie Goodbun Family
by Alice Goodbun Drever

Archibald Henry (Ike) Goodbun was born in Hayes, England in 1873. He was the first of the three brothers to come to Canada in the mid 1890's. He came to Mr. Dugan of the Castleavery district to learn farming. After a few years he took a homestead and in 1900 married Violet Sheppard who was also born in Hayes, England in 1872. She was the first registered nurse to come to the Russell area. They ranched and farmed near Dropmore. Grannie Goodbun travelled many miles attending the sick. There were seven children: Henry (Chummy), Reg, Archie, Jack, Bill, Nona and Katherine (Nell).

Cora Elizabeth Larsen was born in DeKalk, Illinois to her parents, Christopher Lewis Larsen and Elizabeth Turpin, in 1905. She moved with her parents to Richmond, VA and then to Dropmore in 1911 as a child. She received her schooling and Normal School and then taught at Sunnyslope.

Archie and Cora Goodbun, Betty, Alice and Archie, Jr.

When Grandfather Goodbun passed away in 1928, Archie purchased "The Maze" as his home and it was to that farm he brought Cora as his bride in 1930. Their son, Archie, was born the following years, then Betty in 1942 and Alice in 1943.

Archie loved farm life --- Percheron horses, cattle and stands of hay in the meadow. Some of my favorite memories include mother's piano playing, visits from friends and neighbours, climbing the big hill to catch a ride on the pump car to get to school, hitching the team to a sleigh to get to the dance at the Dropmore hall, trying to get up the slippery hill from "The Maze" to go to town in the Model "A", and being rolled up in a coat and put to sleep behind the piano at the Dropmore Hall.

The Assiniboine Flood of 1945

In 1951 a decision was made to move west where schools were more accessible and on

Alice, Betty Rawlings and Betty - 1947.

December 4, 1951 we arrived in Calgary. Dad's brothers and sisters were already living here so we had a large welcoming crew. Arch Jr. was already on his own, teaching in various Manitoba communities before moving to Alberta. A home was purchased in S.W. Calgary and in the spring of 1952, Dad went to work for the C.P.R. where he stayed until ill health forced early retirement in 1968. Mum fought a five year battle with cancer and passed away in May of 1962. She will be ever remembered for her music, scholastic ability and homemaking.

In 1969 Dad married Irene Sheppard of Calgary and they continued to live in the Calgary home until ill health forced Dad to be admitted to Sarcee Auxiliary Hospital where he passed away in 1988. Irene became a resident of Bow Valley Lodge and remains there in good health.

In 1962 Alice married Leonard Sanderson -- they had 2 children, Greg and Bonnie. Alice was married in 1977 to Harry Drever, owner-auctioneer of the Olds Auction Mart in Olds where they both worked. Greg joined as an auctioneer in 1984 and he and Harry are both very actively involved. Alice retired in 1986 and is a doting Nana to her three grandchildren.

In 1963, Betty married Darrel MacKinnon and had two sons, Grant and Darcy. Betty lives on an acreage west of Calgary and works as an occupational health nurse for Amoco Canada. Betty is very active in fitness related activities and programs and lives to spend time with her five grandchildren.

Archie Jr. married Joan Robert in 1963. They have two girls, Jane and Nancy, both married and living in Red Deer, AB. Archie taught in Red Deer for several years and has now retired. He and Joan enjoy spending part of the winter in Arizona and look forward to coming home to their two granddaughters.

The Hackman Story

by Ed and Claudia Hackman

In the spring of 1900, Petro and Victoria Hackman arrived by ship on the east coast, possibly Halifax. They brought their four children with them: Eugene was 15, John, Olga and Ann. Petro was 47 years old. They came from a small village, Ispas, Bukovinia in the Ukraine. Petro and Victoria Hackman are Ed Hackman's grandparents.

Ed and Ann Hackman.

The land they homesteaded in Manitoba was SW 1/4 sec. 22-23-28W, Asessippi or Shellmouth Municipality, the Shell River runs through the land.

Petro was a Greek Orthodox Priest, the first one in the area and he conducted church services in a field marked by a cross until a church was built in 1903. There were several different nationalities in the area and Petro taught all. The services were generally 2-1/2 hours long with people standing, as there were no chairs. Easter was the biggest event of the year. A plaque is erected at Lennard in the Museum area near the old restored church with Reverend Father Petro Hackman named as the First Parish Priest.

George Palmeruk recalls a white folding comb that his father had bought and used to comb George's hair when George was 2 or 3 years old. When Father Hackman died in 1931 at age 78 they combed his hair with the comb and buried it with him in the church yard. His wife Victoria died in 1941.

Agrapine Gaber recalls the 1918 flu epidemic where people were dying like flies. She was very ill for several weeks and finally was asked if she wanted a doctor to which she replied she wanted the Priest. Reverend Father Hackman came and prayed by her bedside. She went to sleep and the next morning got up and made breakfast for her family. The power of Father Hackman's prayers were awesome.

In February 1928, Eugene aged 43 met and married Sinora Wicheruk age 17, daughter of Nick and Veronia Wicheruk from MacNutt, SK. By this time Eugene's mother and siblings had moved from the farm, to the Mundare area in AB, leaving Eugene, Petro and now Sinora on the homestead. Sinora says she was lucky as she had a treddle sewing machine and thus could sew various clothes for the family which were badly needed.

Petro and Eugene earned $5 per month working on the railroad in the winter and in summer worked to clear the land. Their transportation was on foot or horse and wagon, the closest stores were in Inglis and Lennard.

Sinora and Eugene Hackman and twins John and George.

Eugene and Sinora had eleven children: three sets of twins. Matthew - 1928, twins Tommy and Nelson - 1930, Tommy died 1930, Nelson died 1961, twins John and George -1934, Luke -1937 and died in 1965, Ed - 1940, Ann (Dulc) - 1943, twins Peter and Bill - 1948, Delores (Durant) - 1955.

The first home Ed recalls was two old granaries put together, with a stove sitting in the middle dividing the house in two: the kitchen, and the sitting room by day and bedroom by night.

There were two long barns, and down by the river, a very old barn. Besides the main house they had a "cook house" which was used to cook in the hot summer months so the main house stayed cool for sleeping. There were large gardens and lots of various local berries around: pincherries, cranberries, saskatoons, raspberries, strawberries, etc. Ed recalls there were times when people came to pick raspberries from the farm. One summer the wind came up and blew the roof off the cook house.

The children entertained themselves by playing baseball, football, horseback riding, fishing in the river and in winter playing hockey on the frozen river with frozen cow or horse patties and sledding. The children attended Rochedale School which was a two mile walk. The old school had lots of skunks living under it. The school was also used for Sunday school when someone would volunteer to teach.

Sinora Hackman and twins John and George.

Ed and Luke took an old bicycle and pails to go berry-picking. They were both on the bike and heading down a steep hill when the chain came off (thus no brakes). So they ran the bike into the shrub and didn't lose too many berries at all.

One winter Ed decided to play a trick on his mother. He sat the sled upside down by the cattle drinking hole out in the river, then hid in the snowbank and hollered "Help, Help!". Everyone came running. He came laughing out of the bush after a while and said, "Fooled you". He got a good tongue lashing, but never tried that again.

Victoria Hackman and grandchild.

In 1953 the family sold the farm and moved to Roblin. Eugene died in 1965 after a vehicle struck him down in Winnipeg. Then in 1968, Sinora moved to Consul, SK and is now Mrs. John Dolosky.

Alexander and Mary Ann Hunt

by Betty Johnson

My Grandfather, Alexander Hunt, was born in Bruce County, ON on July 14, 1864. He was the eighth child of a family of six sons and three daughters born to William and Jane Hunt. William was born in Ontario and Jane (Irvine) came from Ireland in the early 1850's.

My Grandmother, Mary Anne, was born in Leeds, Quebec on March 16, 1867, the only daughter of Michael and Ann Henry. She had two older brothers, William and John. Ann Henry (Macitee) came from Ireland in 1864. She had been told that gold could be plucked from the streets of Quebec City. This would have been reason enough to emigrate from the poverty in Ireland. Both my great-grandmothers travelled to Canada in sailing ships, a challenging journey indeed!

When Alex was fourteen, his parents decided to move west to Manitoba. At that time they had to travel through the States and they ended up settling in Pembina, North Dakota. Mary Ann's family moved west in 1874 and lived in Winnipeg for a year. Her father walked to Beaver to secure a homestead. He then returned to Winnipeg and worked at his trade (carpentry), to earn enough money for oxen, plough, wagon, cow and other items for homesteading. Mary Ann was present when the "Countess of Dufferin" steam engine arrived in Winnipeg aboard a boat on the Red River. This famous old engine is still on display at the Museum of Man and Nature in Winnipeg. During their sojourn in Winnipeg, Mary Ann's brother, William, drowned while out with a survey party on Lake Winnipeg.

The Henry's moved to Beaver in the fall of the year in a wagon drawn by oxen. All their worldly possessions were in the wagon and a cow was tied on behind. They spent the first winter and summer in a tent within the four bare walls of a house minus the roof. It was most uncomfortable due to dampness and frost. A creek in the yard was teeming with fish which was a good food source. Eventually they built a nice new house.

Alex and Mary Ann were married on the family farm in the Beaver district on January 1, 1889. They lived for a year in North Dakota and then returned to Beaver where their twin girls were born on January 24, 1890. One baby died at birth and Ann passed away one year later. They moved to

Spokane, Washington where a number of Alex's family had gone to seek work. After a rooming house fire destroyed all their belongings, they moved back to Beaver where their son, Wilfred was born and died at fourteen months of age. They farmed in the Bagot district for several years.

A son Bert, was born on September 6, 1896 and on April 3, 1901, the triplets arrived---Clarence, Edith and Ethel. My Uncle Bert was so excited by this event that he was telling anyone who dropped by that there was "a whole basketful of babies in the house!" Edith died of pneumonia two weeks later. It is truly a miracle that two of them survived.

The Hunts experienced another tragedy while in Bagot. They were practising for a Christmas concert at the school when their house burned to the ground. Once again they had to start over. When homesteading opened up in western Manitoba, they moved to the Grainsby district on N.W. 30-23-29, where they lived for the rest of their lives. Years later, they purchased S.W. 31-23-29 across the road from the homestead. Cousin Robert Hunt and his family lived on the quarter section just east of them. When they moved from Bagot, their household effects, machinery, and livestock were shipped by train to Langenburg, SK and then by wagon to the farm.

Until the elevators were built in Dropmore, grain was hauled by wagon to Langenburg, Russell or Roblin. This made for a lengthy day trip. Mail had to be picked up in Shellmouth and there was no school. Uncle Bert attended a log cabin school in the Castleavery District, until the settlers built the first Grainsby School in 1904. My Grandfather was a trustee of the school district for many years and Uncle Clarence served as secretary-treasurer for twenty-five years. Children walked to school and the older ones drove horses and cutters during the winter months. The school was also used for church with Methodists, Presbyterians, Anglicans, and Evangelists holding services. Picnics and other activities were held on the school grounds. Grainsby had an active baseball team when Uncle Bert was a teenager.

The last Hunt child was born on December 19, 1906. This was my Mother, Violet Elizabeth. She lived her entire life in the Grainsby and Dropmore Districts.

In the early years, people organized their own entertainment visiting friends, holding house parties, dances, concerts, etc. The Hunts enjoyed music and many an evening was spent on the piano and violin. Neighbours relied on each other for friendship and support during good times and bad.

During the First World War, many young men from the Grainsby District served overseas. Uncle Bert joined the Army in March 1916 and returned home safely in July, 1919. Others were less fortunate, and did not return, including cousins Art and Frank Hunt. The Hunts purchased their first car just prior to Bert's return from the war. The Model T Ford proved to be a reliable means of transportation.

Uncle Bert married Lillian Rawlings (my Father's sister) on February 3, 1925. After living a short time in B.C. and the USA, they returned to Dropmore. They celebrated their 50th wedding anniversary in 1975. Uncle Bert passed away in November, 1976 and Aunt Lil in July, 1985. They did not have any children.

Aunt Ethel worked in the bank in Dropmore before returning to complete her high school in Shellmouth and Normal School in Dauphin. She taught school in Lundar, MB where she met and married Kris Myrdal in June 1924. They moved to Chicago and adopted a daughter, Ethel Marie, who was born October 30, 1935. Three years after Kris died, Aunt Ethel married Edgar White (formerly of Deepdale) and moved to Sycamore, Illinois. She worked for many years as an accountant for a large chain of furniture stores.

Both Aunt Ethel and Uncle Ed are gone now. Ethel Marie married and had four children---Michael, Danny, Lynn, and Dawn. She lives with her second husband, George Askins, in Sycamore. Her children and grandchildren are spread across the United States.

Uncle Clarence married Myra Clendenning in Sycamore, Illinois in November, 1953. They lived on the Hunt homestead until 1961 when they moved to Sycamore. They eventually retired to Florida. Uncle Clarence died several years ago and Aunt Myra lives with her daughter in Delray Beach, Florida.

My Mother, Elizabeth, married Walter Rawlings on January 26, 1946 just after he returned from serving four years overseas. They settled in Dropmore where my Father operated a filling station and bulk oil sales. He was in business for some fifty-two years. My Mother was active in the church, both as a Sunday School teacher and organist. She was a faithful member of the women's church club and a correspondent for the Russell Banner for twenty-five years.

Their only daughter, Elizabeth Ann (Betty) was born on April 20, 1947. I completed my nursing education at the Misericordia Hospital in Winnipeg in 1968 and have worked as a Registered Nurse ever since. I was married in the Dropmore United Church on July 1, 1972, to Dean Johnson who is originally from Prince Albert, SK. We met while working up north in Gillam, MB. Our first daughter, Robyn, was born there on September 4, 1974. We left Gillam in 1977 and moved to Ste.

Anne, MB where our daughter, Wendy, was born on January 20, 1978. Our son, Dale, was born in Chilliwack, BC on November 22, 1979.

We have lived in Chilliwack since May, 1979. Dean has worked at the Canadian Forces Base and has just completed a two year college diploma in Graphic Design. I have worked at the MSA Hospital in Abbotsford for almost fifteen years and I am in the midst of completing a degree in Occupational Health Nursing. Robyn has completed her third year in the nursing degree program at UBC. Wendy is in grade eleven and Dale is in grade ten.

My Grandfather, Alex, died on February 15, 1946, and Grandmother, Mary Ann, on November 16, 1950. My Father died on October 3, 1983 and my Mother on January 11, 1984. They are all buried in the Dropmore Cemetery, as are Uncle Bert and Aunt Lil.

My Mother was always interested in the family history and fortunately she recorded all that she knew. I have simply edited her work for this publication.

Hunt Family

by Alice (Hunt) Ardagh (daughter of Robert Hunt Sr.)

Robert Hunt's ancestors from the Parish of Mahill County Leitrim, Ireland, were among the pioneers who settled the township of Fitzroy, Canada over a century and a half ago. They arrived in Montreal in 1832 after a six week voyage on a very rough sea, some baggage being lost. They then travelled via the St. Lawrence and Ottawa Rivers, to Fitzroy Harbour where they faced a trek of seven miles through the forest to the sight of their new home. Many hardships were endured. Some family members developed ship fever (cholera) and even with the best care given, they failed to survive. After living in Fitzroy for many years, Robert's parents and older family members moved to Dunkeld, ON in Bruce County, a short distance from Walkerton, ON where they once more settled in on a homestead. Robert was born at Dunkeld in 1863. The family moved to Western Canada when Robert was about twelve years old. They settled on a homestead near Portage La Prairie, MB. In 1889, Robert married Edith Winona Winter of the Hartney Menteith Area. They homesteaded at Burnside in the Portage La Prairie area. They had five children, all born at Burnside, two died in infancy, Ray Gordon and Ernest Alexander. Frank Earl was born January 1892, Arthur Winter was born in April 1893, and Robert James was born in December 1902. Frank and Arthur served in World War I with the 16th Canadian Battalion. Frank and Arthur were both killed in action in 1917. Frank was killed at Bluely Gennoe, France, while Arthur came to his death at Vimy Ridge, France. Frank and Arthur's names are engraved on the memorial monument of World War I at Dropmore.

Robert, Edith and family moved to Dropmore in the early 1900's, shortly after their youngest son, Robert was born in 1901. They took up residence in the Grainsby area living on the quarter section just east of the Alex Hunt farm. A few years later, Edith Winona became seriously ill with tuberculosis. She was taken by train on the Grand Trunk Railway to Ninette Sanitorium for treatment but she never recovered, and passed away in 1912 at the age of 58. Her remains were transferred by train to MacGregor to be laid to rest with her two sons who had died in infancy. This very sad event was followed by the loss of Frank and Arthur in World War I, leaving Robert (Sr) and Robert (Jr) with much grief and sadness. Time was a great healer as life must go on.

Robert (Jr) lived around Dropmore until the late 20's. In fact, he and Watt Ferris were batching together on Watt's farm. He also worked for Frank Skinner for a time driving a team of horses pulling a wagon and perhaps working around the nursery. About 1927, Robert (Jr) left Dropmore to reside on a farm near Hartney, MB which had been purchased by his father. In 1931, he married Kathleen Dodd, born 1911, who emigrated from Hexham, England in 1928. Robert and Kathleen returned to Dropmore in 1932 and spent some time on the Watt Ferris farm until they found land to settle on. From this point on, they lived at two other locations, one being the Speiss farm in the Dropmore area. Not many gains being made, they decided to move back to farm in the Hartney area in 1936. Robert and Kathleen had five children. Robert Arthur was born in 1932 at Hartney. He lived his early years at Dropmore and Hartney. Bob made his career as a Timekeeper with the Manitoba Hydro for 35 years. He is now retired and living in Brandon.

William John was born at Russell in 1933, and has spent most of his life around Hartney. He and his wife Irene (Perrin) have enjoyed cattle and grain farming for many years and their three sons Neil, Scot and Mark have also joined them in the agricultural field. Mark married Penny (Mills) and they have one son. Albert Francis born in Hartney, trained for a psychiatric nurse in Brandon. He married Mary Haggerty of Brandon. They have two sons, Rodney and Richard. Richard is married and has one son and one daughter. Bert and Mary now reside in Victoria, B.C. where Bert is a director of Nurses at Glendale Hospital. Mary also works in a hospital.

Brian David was born in 1951 and raised and educated in Hartney. He now lives in Winnipeg and has a government position.

Doreen Winona was born in, raised and educated in Hartney. She is married to James Logeot of Deleau, MB and they own and operate a cattle farm. They have four sons: Andrew, Albert, Gary, and Joseph. Doreen is very talented at drawing, making signs and very clever at doing crafts.

Robert and Kathleen retired to the town of Hartney in 1968. Robert passed away on Dec. 9, 1981 and was laid to rest in Riverside Hartney Cemetery. Kathleen, as of 1994, is a resident of the Hartney Care Home.

The widowed Robert Hunt remarried, his bride being Jessie Ellen Pope from Faunton Somerset, England. They were married in 1919 in the home of William and Edith Wardle, very dear friends of the bride and groom.

Jessie Pope emigrated from England along with her close friend Annie Oatem (who became Mrs. Britton Ferris) in 1911. Mr. and Mrs. Joe Duggan sponsored Jessie. She worked in their home for a number of years. Mrs. Duggan's maiden name was Isabella Skinner (a sister to Frank Skinner). Through this relationship, Jessie was well acquainted with the Skinners and through the years was always interested in the progress of the Dr. Frank Skinner Nursery.

Jessie worked in the Wardle home prior to her marriage to Robert. The first part of their married life was spent at Dropmore, MB on the NE 1/4 27-23-29 W, Shellmouth Municipality (in 1992 part of the house and barn were still standing). Robert operated an Esso Gas Station for Imperial Oil until 1927 besides doing some farming (perhaps on his Grainsby farm).

In 1928, Robert, Jessie and their five young children who had all been born in their Dropmore home, set out for Hartney Area to the farm which Robert had purchased earlier. They bade farewell to the Dropmore folks with many happy memories never to be forgotten. It was a great neighbourly community. Names which were very often mentioned were the Wardles, Duggans, Skinners, all the Ferris families, Rawlings, Goodbuns, Larsons, Leives, Speiss, Victor and Frank Bird families, Alex and Mary Hunt family who were our cousins.

Alex and Robert spent much time together being like brothers. Alex and Mary were always known to us children as aunt and uncle, even though we were cousins. In later years we returned to Dropmore for a few good visits. We will always remember Lizzie (daughter) playing the piano and Bert (son) on the violin. It was great old time music and fun to dance to. These good times we'll always remember. Some of our family attended the baptism of Betty Ann Rawlings. The baptism service was held in the Dropmore Community Hall. This event took place in 1947. Dropmore will always have a special place in our hearts.

Robert and Jessie Hunt spent the rest of their lives farming in the Hartney area. Robert passed away in June, 1947, and Jessie in November, 1959. They were laid to rest in the Riverside Cemetery, Hartney. They both took a wealth of memories with them, many of which we cannot remember.

Jessie Hunt has a brother, Ernest Pope who is interred in Dropmore Cemetery. He served in World War I as a stretcher bearer with the British Army. He was presented with a medal for bravery in the field. He came to Canada after the war was over. He settled in Dropmore, expecting his bride-to-be to arrive the following spring, but death came to him around Christmas time. His health wasn't the best as he had been gassed during the war. I believe this took place close to the 1920's. Ernest Pope's name is inscribed on the World War I Memorial Monument at Shellmouth.

Robert and Jessie Hunt's family were all born in their Dropmore home on the N.E. 1/4 27 - 23 - 29 W Shellmouth Municipality. I remember mother saying that Mrs. Goodbun and Mrs. Fry both of Dropmore were the midwives at the birth of their children and that Doctor Lee of MacNutt, SK was the attending doctor. George Arthur Francis was the first born in 1920, Ernest Ralph born in 1921, Alice June born in 1923, Gwendolyn Matilda born in 1925 and Irene Mae born in 1927.

George and Ernie both attended Dropmore School for several years and one of their teachers was Miss Jean Harlow. Church services and Sunday School were held in Dropmore School during this period of time. George and Ernie were baptised during one of these services. Upon moving to Hartney Menteith area we all lived our younger years on the home farm. As we grew older we shared in the farm chores. About 1950, George left the farm to reside and work in Brandon. Here he met his bride-to-be, Elva Green, who was a hairdresser. She was born in Tisdale, SK. They were married in May 1952 at Benito, MB. Later they moved to Hartney where their four sons were born: Ralph, Kenneth, Douglas (deceased in

1966) and Dale. George operated a road grader in Cameron Municipality for a number of years, later moving to Brookdale where he was employed by the Department of Highways. Now retired, George and Elva continue to live in Brookdale, MB and do a lot of travelling to visit with their family.

The family of George and Elva Hunt - Ralph was born in August 1953. He was first employed by Hudson Bay Mining Company, Flin Flon doing office work, and later moved to Yellowknife, N.W.T. continuing in an office position and still resides there. He and Wendy Ko of Burnaby, BC were married in May 1990. They have two sons, Alexander and Edward.

Kenneth was born in July 1954. He and Sharon Jasper were married in 1972. They have two children, Francis and Kenneth. Kenneth now lives in Saskatoon doing carpenter work, and helping to install refrigeration systems.

Dale was born in October 1958. He and Connie Davis of Decker, MB were married in 1981. Dale is employed in Northern BC. Dale and Connie have three children.

Ernie joined the Army in 1943. He served overseas with the Winnipeg Rifles. Upon his discharge he farmed the home place. In 1959, Ernie sold the home place and was then employed by the Department of Highways. In the late 1960's, he moved to Flin Flon and adapted very readily to the northern country. He was an employee of the Imperial Oil Company until retirement and still makes Flin Flon his home.

Alice was employed at No.7 AOS Air Base at Portage La Prairie for a time, then joined the C.W.A.C. in 1943 serving in Montreal. In 1946, Alice and William Ardagh were married at the farm home of her parents. William joined the Army and served overseas in World War II and upon his return, he worked 23 years for C.P.R. Railway. He then worked at Hartney Hospital from 1966 - 1988. William and Alice raised four children, all born in Hartney. Roberta June was born in 1948, John Gregory born in 1949, Ian Patrick born in 1958, and Janice Lee born in 1962.

June worked for the Civil Service at River's Air Force Base, where she met Robert Egdell of Glace Bay, Nova Scotia who was in the Armed Forces. They both transferred to Edmonton where they were married in 1969. During the years they have had many postings, the latest being at Air Command in Winnipeg. They had one daughter, Allison Merrilee, born August 1974 in Lahr, Germany. They have since adopted two nieces, Jasmine Alicia, born in 1984, and Jamie Eva Lee, born in 1986.

Greg drove a semi-truck at a young age, later doing mechanic work in Flin Flon. He now lives in Saskatoon. He has worked for sometime with Indall Metals, now known as Cardadon Metals. He is now the coordinator of the building products. Greg married and divorced. He helped to raise three step children, namely Richard, Barry and Wendy.

Ian, upon leaving school, worked for the Department of Highways and later on, the Oil Rigs, and then moved to Saskatoon where he now makes his home. He works part time for Caradon Metal Company and has a full time job at the Travelodge Hotel working the bar and off sales.

Janice, after completing her education, first worked in a grocery, then a hardware store in Hartney. Later she moved to Saskatoon where she now resides, working in the Travelodge Hotel and waitressing in a bar. Janice's hobby is painting ceramics in her spare time. Janice is a single mother having two daughters, Jasmine Alicia, and Jamie Eva Lee. The girls are being raised by their Auntie and Uncle in Winnipeg.

Gwen joined the C.W.A.C. and served in Canada from 1943 to 1946. She married William Crawford of Erinview, MB who had served in World War II. They were married at the home farm of Gwen's parents. They built their home in St. Vital, Winnipeg, where they still reside. William retired early due to ill health. Gwen worked 25 years or more as a nurses' aide at the St. Amant Centre (a home for our special people). Bill and Gwen have two children, Reginald William was born July 1953, at Winnipeg. He worked for MacLeods for quite sometime, and is now employed by a building construction company. Reg is married and has one daughter. Darlene Ellen was born January 1958. Darlene's husband Brian, works for Air Canada in Winnipeg. Darlene works at the St. Amant Centre. They have two children, David and Jordan.

Irene chose her career as a hair dresser and was employed in Brandon. She and Stewart Powell of West Ealing Middlesex, England, were married in December 1952. Stewart served in World War II. Stewart and Irene resided on a farm near Hartney. In later years, Stewart worked for several lumber companies. He worked last in North Battleford, SK, where they built a house and now make this city their home.

Stewart and Irene have two adopted daughters, Kathe Leigh, born March 1958 at Winnipeg, and Wendy Ann, born in October 1960.

Kathe trained to be a registered nurse and is now employed at the University Hospital,

Saskatoon. She married Ron Driedger, a plumber. They have two daughters, Stephanie and Marissa.

Wendy Ann still lives in North Battleford. She trained as a life guard and worked at a pool in the city. Wendy has a daughter, Cindy attending school in North Battleford, and like her mother, is an excellent swimmer.

I was only five years old when we said farewell to Dropmore, but have always held a special place in my heart for Dropmore due to special memories Dad and Mom related to us and through visits from Dropmore friends. I have also occasionally visited Dropmore.

I don't know if this story holds true, but we were always told that a group of men were having a social drink, and discussing a name for their little village. One fellow said, "Let's have little drop more." Suddenly one said, "That's it! Our village has a name, Dropmore".

Things I Remember

Robert Hunt Sr. and Robert Hunt Jr. were always known as great horse traders. Since horses were used for working the fields, for all chores around the farm and for travel, many good horses were needed. I heard they made many good deals but there were always the deals where they got stung on a tricky trade.

Even though I was quite young, I remember the "Russell Banner" coming to our home weekly. That was some 68 years ago and to my knowledge, this local weekly paper still serves the communities.

I will always remember the day we left Dropmore for our new home. We had dinner at Bill Ferris' Sr. (seemed like he lived in the village of Dropmore, where we boarded the train). It was a mixed train, so our livestock rode along with us in the stock car. Never having ridden on a train before, I was very frightened of the hills along the way and thought at any minute we might crash into them. Thus the journey ended safely with my head down on the seat many times.

I will always remember the Ralston kids and us taking a drink to Leonard Ferris, who was working a field with a plough and horses, one early spring day. Masses of beautiful crocuses lined the edge of the road.

I was young, but will never forget the gasoline lamp we had hanging from the ceiling of the living room which had mantles for light, and a pump to pump gas into the gas tank. Sam Erickson, a neighbour was visiting us. He was putting on his jacket to leave.

Holding his arm in the air he hit and knocked the lamp flying, bending the main stem. Our father was very upset.

Robert Hunt and Family

by George A. Hunt

Robert Hunt (1863-1947) was born at Dunkeld, Ontario on November 14, 1863 to John and Elizabeth (Body) Hunt. He was the ninth child of a family of five boys and six girls. Robert came to Manitoba at the age of ten with his parents, brothers and sisters in 1873. They came from Walkerton, Ontario, settling near Rat Creek in the Burnside-MacGregor area. They arrived by horse drawn wagon with chickens and one or two cows. The first house that they lived in was known as a stopping house, for people coming through Winnipeg on their way west. Winnipeg was just a cart trail and the Hudson Bay Company was the only store at that time. Their first barn was made of poles and sod.

The first association between the Hunt family and Hartney occurred in the summer of 1885 as Robert drove through Hartney and met the person who would become his first wife - **Edith Winona Winter** (1864-1912). The Winter family had moved from Listowel, Ontario to the now forgotten hamlet of Malta, situated one mile west of Menteith in 1880. Malta's history was short and now only the cellars can be seen. The would-be community of ten families, including a blacksmith, general store and stopping house, was founded in the hope that the Canadian Pacific Railway would follow the west side of the Souris River rather than the crossing at Menteith and again at Melita.

Robert Hunt and Edith Winter were married on January 7, 1889 and returned to the MacGregor area. They had five sons, Roy Gordon, Frank Earlby, Arthur Winter, Ernest Alexander and Robert James, all born at Burnside. The family moved to the Shellmouth at Dropmore to homestead, sometime before 1903. Edith died in 1912.

Roy Gordon (1890-1890) died at three days of age.

Frank Earlby (1892-1917) was a Private in the 16th Canadian Scottish. He enlisted in 1914 and died in France during World War I in March of 1917 at Buely Gennoe. Frank is buried in France. He was survived by a wife and two daughters.

Arthur Winter (1893-1917) was a Private in the 16th Canadian Scottish. He enlisted in 1914 and died in France during World War I in April of 1917 at Vimy. Arthur is buried in France.

Ernest Alexander (1895-1895) died at two months of age.

Family of George & Elva Hunt.(L-R) Michael, youngest son of Ken; Ralph, George's oldest son; Connie, Dale's wife; Dale, George's youngest son; Elva, George's wife; George, George Hunt; Ken, George's second son; Karen, Ken's friend; Francis, Ken's oldest son.(Front Row)is Shawn, Dale's son.

Robert James (1901-1981) was the only remaining son after the war. In 1931 Robert James married Kathleen Dodd (1911), who emigrated from Hexham, England in 1928. They farmed on rented farms in the Dropmore area until 1936, when they moved to the Hartney-Menteith area. They have four sons and one daughter, Robert Arthur, William John, Albert Francis, Brian David and Doreen Winona, all of whom were born at Hartney.

Robert Arthur (1932), retired from Manitoba Hydro and now resides in Brandon, MB.

William John (1933), farms at Hartney with his wife Irene (Perrin) and sons Neil Thomas (1967), Scott Malcolm (1969) and Mark Leslie (1970).

Albert Francis (1938), lives near Victoria, BC with his wife Mary (Haggerty) and sons Rodney James and Richard Allan. Bert is a hospital supervisor.

Brian David (1951), resides in Winnipeg, Manitoba.

Doreen Winona (1956), farming at Deleau, Manitoba, with her husband James Logeot and their children: Andrew Robert and Albert James.

The widowed Robert Hunt returned to Dropmore-Shellmouth and there met his second wife, **Jessie Ellen Pope** (1892-1959) who had emigrated from Trull, near Sommerset, England in 1911. They were married in 1919. Robert and Jessie Hunt had five children, George Arthur Frances, Ernest Ralph, Alice June, Gwendolyn Matilda and Irene May, all born at Dropmore, Manitoba. In the spring of 1927, the family left Dropmore and returned to the Menteith district. Robert was a member of the first board of directors of Menteith Elevator. George and Ernie received their education in the Menteith district, attending Forbes School. Alice, Gwen and Irene also went to the Forbes School and completed their education at Deleau Consolidated School.

George Arthur Frances (1920). Upon leaving the farm, George was employed in Brandon, Manitoba. He met Elva Elizabeth Green (1922) who was a hairdresser at the Nu-Fashion Shop. Elva was born at Tisdale, Saskatchewan. They were married May 31, 1952 at Benito, Manitoba. Later, they moved to Hartney and built a home. Their four sons, George Ralph, Kenneth Arthur, Douglas Raymond and Robert Dale were all born in Hartney. George worked as a grader operator for the Rural Municipality of Cameron and later as a grader operator for the Manitoba Department of Highways. He and Elva now reside in Brookdale, Manitoba and are retired.

George Ralph (1953) has a Technical Support position in the computer department of the Government of the Northwest Territories in Yellowknife, Northwest Territories. Ralph met Wendy Ko, who was a Computer Programmer, in Yellowknife. They were married on May 5, 1990 in Vancouver, BC. Their two sons, Alexander Jeffrey (1992) and Edward Christopher (1993) were born in Yellowknife.

Douglas Raymond (1955-1966)

Kenneth Arthur (1954) married Sharon Eileen Jasper in 1972 in Hartney. They have two children, Francis Edward (1973) and Kenneth Michael (1974). Ken is a construction worker at Saskatoon Saskatchewan. Francis was born at Souris, MB and Michael was born at Flin Flon, MB.

Robert Dale (1958) married Shirley Corrine (Connie) Davis in April, 1981 at Decker, MB. They reside in Prince George, BC where Dale is employed in a motor rewind shop. They have three sons, Shawn Robert (1983), Ryan Douglas (1987) and Daniel Jonathon (1989). Shawn and Ryan were born at Winnipeg and Daniel was born at Prince George.

Ernest Ralph (1921). Ernie worked on the home farm prior to joining the Army in 1943. He served overseas with the Winnipeg Rifles. Upon his discharge from the Army he once more farmed the home place. In 1959, he sold the farm, and was then employed by the Department of Highways and made his home in Hartney. During 1963, he and Mary McPhee were married in Souris. In the late sixties, Ernie moved to Flin Flon, MB and adapted very readily to the North Country. He was a faithful employee of the Imperial Oil Company there and has since retired.

Alice June (1923), after leaving school, worked in several homes in the Deleau District and also in Hartney. In 1942 Alice was employed at No. 7 A.O.S. Air Base at Portage La Prairie, Manitoba servicing airplanes. In 1943, she joined the C.A.A.C. serving in Montreal for a short period of time. Alice returned to the home farm in 1944 to help with the farm duties. Later she taught school (on permit) in the Cavell School District from April 1945 to June 1946. She married William Aradagh in June of 1946 and raised four children, Roberta June (1948), John Gregory (1949), Ian Patrick (1958) and Janice Lee (1962).

Gwendolyn Matilda (1925) joined the C.W.A.C. on November, 1943 and served until March 1946. Gwen and William Crawford of Erinview, Manitoba were married at Hartney in September, 1946. He served in England and Northwest Europe. He built their home in St. Vital, MB where they reside. Gwen worked in the St. Amant Centre as a Nurses' Aide for eighteen years. The St. Amant Centre is a home for mentally handicapped children. Bill was employed by Breen Motors. Bill's uncle, William Crawford, owned a jewellry store in Hartney and also owned and operated the theatre in Hartney, called the "Lyceum". They have two children, Reginald and Darlene.

Reginald (1953) married Doreen Sopiwnyk at Vita, MB in May of 1975. Reg is presently employed by McLeods in Winnipeg as an assistant buyer.

Darlene (1958) works as an Aide at the St. Amant Centre.

Irene May (1927) chose her career as a hairdresser, employed at the Nu-Fashion Shop in Brandon. Irene worked with Elva Green, who was to be Irene's sister-in-law. She and Stewart Powell, who was born in West Ealing, Middlesex, England were married December 11, 1952. They resided on a farm near Hartney. In later years, Stewart was employed by several different lumber companies and at Hartney Co-op Lumber yard for several years. Since then, he has worked in the western provinces. They reside in North Battleford, Saskatchewan. They have two children, Kathe Leigh, born at Winnipeg, Manitoba and Wendy Ann born at Calgary, Alberta.

Kathe Leigh (1958) is a Registered Nurse and is presently working in the University Hospital in Saskatoon, SK. Wendy Ann (1961) is employed as a Life Guard at a swimming pool in North Battleford.

James C. Hunter Family

by David Hunter

James Hunter was born November 24, 1880 in Kirkmichael, Scotland. Here he attended school and went on to train as a druggist. However his wish to immigrate to Canada was stronger than his desire to dispense drugs. He sailed from Glasgow, Scotland, March 21, 1901, arriving in Halifax, Canada, April 2, and in Winnipeg shortly after.

For a year he worked for Johnny Allan at Franklin, MB. He then moved to Castleavery and homesteaded the NW 1/4 of 28-24-29. He batched with a fellow homesteader, Leonard Gysin. I think porridge was their main source of food. (Mr. Gysin rose to the rank of Major in World War I. He lost his life September 1916, in France.

In 1908, James Hunter purchased the SW 1/4 of 28-24-29 from Walter Robertson. Next he purchased the SE 1/4 of 29-24-29. A few years later he purchased the NE 1/4 of 29-24-29.

James Hunter's first neighbours were Andersons, Dugans, Robertson, Birnies, Shearers and G. Mitchells.

Marion Lang Mitchell was born April 2, 1887 on the Mitchell Farm (now under Lake of the Prairies). At first she was tutored at home by her aunt because there weren't any country schools. Later she attended Sterling, a new country school. She took Normal School training at Winnipeg, went to Scotland for more education, and then returned to Canada to teach in Cromarty five miles from Roblin. Later she taught in Castleavery.

James Hunter and Marion Mitchell married in 1911 and began their lives together as farmers.

Horse power was the first means of power on the farm. Then, a steel-wheeled Case tractor was used, followed later by a rubber-tired one. Next came the threshing machine, and let's not forget the big threshing crews that kept Mom hopping to feed. Finally, along came the best machine of all --- the combine!

We had milk cows, pigs, chickens and turkeys. Work was hard! With the coming of Hydro electricity in 1952, things started to get better. I also remember the big garden Mom planted and all the potatoes that took hours to hoe.

Later neighbours of ours were the Comforts, Rowans, Roes, Nichols, Farncombes, Ferrisses and Langleys to name a few.

Dad, Mr. Comfort, Mr. Dugan and Mr. W. Robertson were early trustees of Castleavery School. Later trustees were James and Albert Shearer, Arthur Nichols, Harry Rowan and Harry Roe.

We attended church in the summer in the school house for many years. The ministers were mostly Presbyterian and United Church.

In 1953, Dad and Mom travelled to Scotland. They enjoyed their trip; but, Dad said he wasn't sorry he had come to Canada.

Jim Hunter.

David in England.

Dad and Mom had seven children: Margaret, William, George, James, David, John and Colin.

James served in the RCAF during World War II. His plane was lost over the Mediterranean Sea. It was never found.

I served in the Canadian army from 1942 to 1946 with the Queen's Own Camerons.

Mum, Dad, Margaret, William, George, John and Colin are at rest in the Castleavery Cemetery.

Peggy, George, Dave, John, Jim, Bill and Collin Hunter.

Hunter Family

William James Hunter, the eldest son of James C. Hunter and Marion Lang Mitchell, was born on Sept. 15, 1913. He received his education in the Castleavery School. In June 1941 he was united in marriage to Irma Agnes Shearer, the eldest daughter of Mr. and Mrs. Albert Shearer.

They moved to a farm south of Dropmore, 23-23-29, where they farmed until Bill's sudden death in November 1958. Bill was active in community affairs, having spent many hours in the construction of the United Church in Dropmore, and serving as a member and as a steward on the church board since its inception. He was a member of the Co-op elevator association, serving on the board for a number of years. He was an active worker in the building of the curling rink and enjoyed curling. Bill was also interested in the 4-H Club, especially with his sons. He served on the Dropmore School Board for many years, being a trustee and chairman at the time of his death.

Bill and Irma had a family of three children: Douglas, Terry, and Isabel.

William Douglas was born on June 19, 1943. He attended school in Dropmore and high school in Tummell and then took the Diploma Course in Agriculture in Winnipeg. Douglas was a member of the 4-H Club and between the years of 1958 and 1966, he had a herd of purebred Shorthorn cattle, which he sold before going to university.

After graduation from the University of Manitoba in 1968, Doug was employed by Manitoba Agriculture. He worked out of Winnipeg for six years as a Swine Technician. He was the first to probe pigs using an ultrasonic machine. In 1974, Doug moved back to Roblin where he continues to work for Manitoba Agriculture as a Livestock and Forage Technician out of the Roblin District Agriculture Office.

After returning to Roblin, Doug also began farming again. In 1980, Doug and Reg Robertson formed R and H Cattle Company and began raising purebred Charolais cattle. They later dispersed this herd in 1985.

On November 9, 1985, Doug married Marianne Gancher, daughter of Felix and Nell Gancher of Sifton, Man. Marianne was a graduate of the Western College of Veterinary Medicine at Saskatoon and is currently employed as a veterinarian at the Roblin Veterinary Clinic.

Doug and Marianne started Hunter Charolais the year after they were married. They purchased an acreage just west of Roblin where they built a home and continue to raise their purebred stock. They also still own and operate the home farm south of Dropmore.

Doug and Marianne have three children:

William James "Jimmy" born February 7, 1987;
Kristi Marie born Jan. 23, 1989;
Michael Douglas born Oct. 12, 1991.

Terrence James was born November 27, 1945. Terry attended primary school in Dropmore and high school in Tummelll and Roblin. He was also a member of the 4-H Golf Club. After completing high school, he went to Winnipeg to the "Manitoba Institute of Technology" and graduated with a Civil Technology Diploma in 1966. He worked for Manitoba Highways, AIM Engineering, Defregrov Consultants and Public Works Canada.

On June 20, 1969 he was united in marriage to Emily Mae Brown of Roland, Manitoba. Emily graduated from the U. of M with a Diploma in Physiotherapy. She worked at the Shriners Hospital, the Rehab Center and Community Therapy Services at Steinbach. She presently owns Hunter Physiotherapy.

Emily and Terry have lived in Winnipeg since they were married and celebrated their 25th wedding anniversary in 1994. They have two daughters, Tracy Ann, born Dec. 21, 1969 and Dawn Leah born June 16, 1971. Tracy married John Einarson on July 23, 1994 in Winnipeg. Tracy is studying at U of M to become a teacher. John is a CBC cameraman. They have two daughters: Ashlee Marie and Kristen Taylor. Dawn graduated as a Massage Therapist from the "Atlanta School of Massage" in 1993 and is presently working at Hunter Physiotherapy. Dawn is very active in sports, especially rugby and team handball.

Margaret Isabel was born November 8, 1947. She attended school in Dropmore and high school in Roblin, MB. She was very active in sports, curling, softball, basketball, volleyball, track and field and also with the Student Council. She was very active in 4-H work, being a member of the Sewing Club and the Golf Club. She took piano lessons and completed grade eight music. June 1965 was high school graduation.

During my final days at the Roblin Collegiate Institute, I spent most of my time planning for a move to the "BIG CITY", Winnipeg, and day-dreaming about a career in physiotherapy. That summer, I lived in Winnipeg Beach with a family named Wald, and at the end of August moved back to Winnipeg with them. I thought I was prepared for my first year at the University of Manitoba, but the following eight months were the most intense and dedicated time I had ever spent.

May 1968 - University of Manitoba Graduation. Three gruelling, educational and fun years of physiotherapy school had come to an end and I prepared for my first professional job with the Canadian Arthritis and Rheumatism Society. After two months of training I was relocated to Flin Flon and The Pas area with my room-mate and best friend through physiotherapy school, Jane Keating.

August 1968 - Flin Flon, Manitoba. We settled into a residence in the Flin Flon Company Hospital and within the first week, I met a young hockey player, Reg Leach, who played the Flin Flon Bomber Junior Team. This young man became my husband and one year later we prepared for a move to Boston, Massachusetts and the beginning of his national hockey league career with the Boston Bruins.

August 1970 - Boston, Mass. We had been blessed with a wonderful son, Jamie, who was the joy of our life. The one and a half years we all spent in Boston included trips to the historical sites, the famous Universities, the ocean, some great shopping and a very exciting hockey team. My son, at two years of age was Bobby Orr's biggest fan.

March 1972 - Oakland, California. Before we were ready, a phone call changed our lives, and we had been traded to the California Golden Seals Hockey Team. For two very enjoyable years we lived by the San Francisco Bay in a small town, Newark.

A second addition to our family, a beautiful daughter, Brandie Lynn, was born April 1973. We all enjoyed the ocean, the weather, the wineries and the California lifestyle. But California is not a hockey state so the news of an upcoming trade was exciting.

August 1974 - Philadelphia, Pennsylvania. Reg was looking forward to playing again with his old Flin Flon team mate, Bobby Clarke, and the Philadelphia, Flyers. We didn't realize then, but this was to be our last big move, except for one short season with the Detroit Red Wings. Philadelphia was the area my two children would grow up in and call home and the area where I would continue to live.

Our years in Philadelphia, as a family were very exciting and included the team winning their second Stanley Cup. My son grew into an outstanding young hockey player and my daughter also became an All-Star field hockey and lacrosse player.

Each spring we loaded the motor home and travelled back to our summer cottage in Arnes, MB. This beautiful site just north of Gimili on Lake Winnipeg was the place where we spent many wonderful hours with our children, our families and our friends. The "cottage" still remains in our family and we all find precious time to spend there each summer.

Unfortunately in 1984, Reg and I were divorced, but we remain good friends and share the responsibilities of parenting.

My life on my own, as single parent had begun so I went back to school to upgrade my courses and became licensed as a physical therapist in New Jersey and Pennsylvania. I have worked very hard on developing a career and today I am the New Jersey Physical Therapy Director for a company that staffs forty departments in the State.

My two children have both grown into wonderful adults and are off following their dreams. Jamie plays hockey professionally and has played for the Pittsburgh Penguins, The Hartford Whalers and the Florida Panthers. This past year he travelled with the Canadian National Team to England, Norway, Sweden, USA, and Switzerland.

After high school, Brandie tried out and made the Canadian National Lacrosse Team. Following two years of dedication and hard work she went to Scotland and played in the World Lacrosse Championship with Canada. She now resides in Florida and is practising to become a golf professional.

My life includes restoring an old house, collecting antiques, playing tennis and racquetball and spending time with my fiancé, Mark Stevens. Our plans include purchasing a Victorian house in the country and running a "Bed and Breakfast Inn". You're all welcome!!

Percy Jennings Family

by Rene Merrick (nee Jennings)

In 1922 at the young age of twenty two, Percy Jennings boarded a ship in Southhampton, England to venture to Dropmore, Manitoba. He wished to visit an old acquaintance, Basil Bradley-Hunt. On this visit, he became friends with the Goodbuns and the Comforts in Castleavery. Sunday sports were participated in, with great enthusiasm.

After returning to England, he decided to move to Canada permanently. He married Jean Morrison in 1937 and built a new home in the Assiniboine Valley. Here, on Section 27-24-29, Jean and Percy raised four children: Rene, Lesley, Alan and Janet.

In 1963, with the building of the Lake of the Prairies Dam, Percy moved his family to Brandon. Percy was employed at the Brandon Clinic until 1980. When he retired he moved to Winnipeg. Percy and Jean lived in Charleswood until Percy's passing in 1987. Jean moved to an apartment for seniors. In 1992, she moved to Medicine Hat, Alberta.

Rene and George Merrick reside in Winnipeg and raised four daughters: Sheila, Leanne, Carol and Gwen.

Leslie and Janice Jennings reside in Sidney, BC.

Alan and June Jennings reside in Vernon, BC with their children Ryan and Jill.

Janet and Bruce van Mulligan reside in Medicine Hat, Alberta with their children Tyler and Calvin.

There was no lack of entertainment. Since babysitters were unheard of, one had to involve the whole family. At whist drives, bridge games, dances, curling, tobogganing, visiting, movies, fishing, picnics and ladies' meetings, children were accepted as part of the event.

The feeling of belonging to a great community, made education possible in very trying times. A classroom of eight or nine grades with twenty students, was instructed by a young person who had a mere six weeks training. It might have been a nightmare, but the teacher soon felt the support of the students and parents. These one room schools produced independent students.

Life in small communities was not easy by today's standards, but it had qualities such as pride: everyone dressed-up, to go to any social event. Trust: no one locked their house doors. Some didn't even own a key! Support: sawing wood was a yearly event when neighbors helped one another. Enthusiasm: if there was a party, everyone came. Hope: each year that the crops didn't turn out as expected, everyone thought that next year would be better.

Albert Jones

by Beth Bowley

Albert Edward Jones, son of William John Jones and the former Elizabeth Mabel Tribe, was born in London, England in 1884 and received his education there.

He came to Canada in the early 1900's and worked for various farmers in Manitoba and also at Hanbury's lumber camp in the Boggy Creek area. He also trapped for many years in the Porcupine and Duck Mountains and in the Shell and Assiniboine Valleys.

It was during this time, he learned to play the violin and having a good singing voice he entertained at many gatherings and dances.

Eventually he settled on the south-west quarter of section 22-22-29 about 1915, where he built a frame house and 40 foot hip-roofed barn. In later years he rented section 15-24-29 from Mr. Luther Johnson who lived on the north-west

Albert and Ruth Jones on their Wedding Day in 1917, at Roblin.

Ruth (Atkinson) Jones (right) and her brother William (Bill) Atkinson and Bill's wife Hilda Temple and their daughter Ruth taken in Russell about 1916.

quarter. Luther and his wife retired to Lincoln, Nebraska.

In 1917 Albert married Ruth Mary Atkinson of the Cromarty District. The Atkinsons, James and Ruth Mary originally came from the Bagot, Manitoba area, farmed there and around the Shellmouth, Roblin and Dropmore Districts. Mrs. Atkinson passed away in the 30's and James in the 40's. They are buried in the Dropmore cemetery beside our mother, brother Edward, and our father.

The Atkinson's had a family of five. They are - James, Ruth, Gordon, Arthur and Faye.

The Jones family consisted of five children too, and were educated in the Castleavery School. They were -

Edward, born in 1918, deceased in 1929. He was very musical, learning to play the violin and organ in his early school years.

Harold and Dorothy Jones - 1962,

Harold, born in 1919 helped his father farm and after spending some time in the Army, he married Georgina (Pat) Souter from Roblin.

They farmed in the Castleavery District for a few years, then moved to Russell where Harold started an Auto Wrecking business. About 1978 he sold that business to his eldest son Gordon and moved to Birch River where he operated a small used - car and auto wrecking business. He sold that business about five years later and now has a used - car and auto wrecking business 15 miles north of Canora, SK. Harold and Pat have a family of seven children; Gordon, Beverly, Lloyd, Darcy, Penny, Pamela and Danny. Of the seven children, Gordon was the only one who lived for a short time in the Castleavery District.

Dorothy and Beth (twins) were born in 1923.

Dorothy left home at age 17 years and worked in Yorkton and Winnipeg. She managed, during this time, to take correspondence courses and attended night school to become a teacher, after taking teacher's training in Winnipeg. She taught school in Manitoba for several years, then moved to Calgary, AB where she taught for almost another 20 years, retiring in 1982. Then she moved to British Columbia. When she was only 17 years old she played her guitar and sang over the radio from C.J.G.X. Yorkton, SK. When she was 16 years old she composed an ode or poem to our youngest brother Ivan which I am including in this write-up.

Beth Bowley's four boys. (L-R) Jerry, Kevin, Guy and Barry Prokopetz, in 1969.

Beth has 4 sons from a previous marriage. They are Jerry, Barry, Guy and Kevin. In 1962 Beth married Leonard Bowley who farms near Binscarth, Manitoba. In 1985 we built a home in Russell where we reside in the winter, and lived for some summers on the farm. We have a daughter,

Bernice Bowley daughter of Len and Beth Bowley.

Bernice Ruth, born in 1963. She is presently a lawyer in Winnipeg and is married to Joseph Paraskevas of Winnipeg.

Ivan and Maxine Jones (McArthy) on their Wedding Day, in 1953.

Ivan born in 1927, farmed with his father for awhile, then worked in Winnipeg and Calgary, mostly driving cross country semi-trucks. Then he bought his own semi-truck, but after a near fatal accident, he sold it and bought a farm near Rocky Mtn. House, Alberta. He is married to the former Maxine McArthy and they have three children: Wendyle, Colleen and Sheldon. They all live in Alberta, but Ivan and Maxine spend most winters in Arizona.

The home of the Albert Jones family in the Castleavery District, in 1940's.

Besides the barn and our house which had lean-to's on them, there were several granaries, a chicken house, blacksmith shop garage and a well-house where we kept our cream separator. This really was only a granary with a large opening in the centre and a pit dug underneath. This was partly filled with blocks of ice and covered with sawdust. We kept our cream and other perishable food items down there.

For a few years I remember we had to lower the cream can down into our deep well by ropes, to keep it cool.

In the 30's and 40's most farm families milked several cows and sold the cream to the creamery in MacNutt, SK. This bought our groceries and other needed items.

Of course in those days, we had no hydro. Our homes were heated by wood burning stoves, which of course the fires would go out during the night. In the wintertime the water in the house would freeze, and we would wake up to quite a cold house, until the fires were made. On school days, we walked a mile to school on a road that was seldom used. Some winters, this created quite a problem when there was alot of snow. Then, when we arrived at the school it was usually cold until the teacher got the fire going. Sometimes we gathered around the stove.

The highlights of the year were the picnics and school Christmas concerts. We could hardly wait for spring to arrive when we pupils could play soft ball at school. Some winters we played broomball but not having brooms we used green sticks which could really hurt if we got hit with one. We also had checker tournaments, spelling bees, Halloween parties and Valentine exchanges. We also played out-door games like stealing sticks, pom-pom pullaway, fox and geese, and still-water.

In early years, horses were used both for farming and our mode of transportation. Later on we had a model T Ford in the early 30's and better cars toward the 40's. In the winter time when the roads were blown in with snow, it was back to the horses, cutters, sleigh boxes and later on, vans.

Albert Jones, about 1946.

It was during this time that Albert began writing on his book "Lure of the North" which was mostly about his life as a trapper and hunter of wild animals. He had this book published in Tulsa, Oklahoma and sold several copies.

Dorothy and Beth Jones and housekeeper, Lena Nahirney, on the Jones farm, about 1931.

Our mother and brother Edward, passed away in 1929 and our father was left to raise 4 children during the depression years. No easy task! But with several house keepers and hired men we managed. One of our hired men who I think deserves to be mentioned is Henry Schneider who worked for us for almost 7 years when we were young children. He was always kind to us and sometimes when we didn't have a housekeeper he even made the bread. I can still see him kneeding it. He later married Polly Germain who worked in the Dropmore area and for awhile they lived in the Castleavery District on the North-west quarter of section 31-24-29.

Harold & Pat Jones, Len & Beth Bowley, Ivan & Maxine Jones, our step mother & father.

Henry's oldest son lives in Russell and is a maintenance man at the hospital. Henry passed away in Leamington, ON in 1993. Polly still lives there.

We children, carried on the musical tradition of our parents' singing at school Christmas concerts. Later on, we had an orchestra and played for dances.

Albert spent several years in Tulsa, Oklahoma but returned to Canada with his 2nd wife in 1952 and lived in Roblin until about 1972. After spending several years in the Roblin Personal Care Home. He passed away in 1981 at 97 years old.

We children are scattered in 4 provinces, Beth in MB, Harold in SK, Ivan in AB, and Dorothy in BC.

To a Kid Brother
by Dorothy Jones

Who has a face still smudged and small,
Who waits to hear each luncheon call.
Who has a lanky frame and tall,
But plays a riotous game of ball,
My brother, who's "the kid".

Who laughs with carefree easiness,
Who has ties, shirts and suits to press.
Who teases me and makes me "guess" -
But fills my days with friendliness,
My brother, just "the kid".

Who robs the sparrow's nests and crow's,
Despite the tears to self and clothes;
Who tells me all his schoolboy woes
But for the cattle yodelling, goes
My brother, what a kid!

Who takes my tall boots on a hike
Who rides and rides his best pal's bike
Who tags along when I'm with Mike
But if I've fanned, says "one more strike".
My brother, still a kid.

Richard and Margaret Keay

by A. Keay

Richard, better known as Dick, was born in 1873 at Copenhurst, Cheshire, England. He came to Canada in 1892 to Millwood District, which is south-west of Russell in the Assiniboine Valley. Here he worked as a farm hand and at other odd jobs, such as cutting ice on the river and loading it in R.R. box cars which were shipped by train loads to Winnipeg. He also hauled poles into Saskatchewan to be used for telephone lines.

He moved to Rochedale District in 1898. This was the district which Maggie Lougheed called "home".

Maggie was born in 1876 at Bracebridge, ON and had come to Manitoba with her parents in 1880 and settled in Rochedale District.

She gained her knowledge of the 3 "R's" by walking across country and through the Shell River Valley to Asessippi School.

This, was at the time of the Riél Rebellion and there were plans being made to evacuate the settlers in this area if hostilities came closer.

After her school years, Maggie worked at the Barnardo Home (a home for children from England) which was south of Russell.

Dick and Maggie were married in 1903 and settled on Sec. 19-23-28 in Rochedale and started a mixed farming operation. They gradually acquired more land and raised a fairly large herd of beef cattle, which were wintered at the foot of the hills of the Assiniboine Valley just west of their buildings. Growing grain and feeding cattle required alot of horse power. So, there were a number of horses kept, which also meant hiring extra men.

Dick was always interested in the lumber business and eventually had sawmills of his own at Madge Lake, then Boggy Creek, in the Duck Mountains. The last winter in the bush, his men hauled logs to Sandy Doering's mill in the Riding Mountains, then hauled the lumber home.

Bill Keay, Lulu & Frank Fulbrook, Tug & Rudy Lowenberger, Mr. Bassil, Freddie Keay, Marilyn, Doreen, Bernice Lowenberger.

Maggie stayed on the farm with the chore men and the children, which she and Dick had been blest with over the years.

Lucile (Lulu) married Frank Fulbrook. They had three daughters and one son (deceased in infancy). Lu and Frank reside in Calgary. The three daughters all married and have families and reside in southern USA. Beatrice (Tug) married Rudy Lowenberger. They had four daughters and one son. They all married and have families scattered across Canada. Rudy and Tug lived in Yorkton, SK, where Tug still lives, Rudy having past away a number of years ago. Richard was deceased in infancy.

Harold (Bill) married Alice Patterson. They were blessed with two children, a son and a daughter. They lived in Rochedale then retired to Russell.

Jack married Evelyn Haberstock. They had a son, deceased in infancy and a daughter. They lived in Brandon at the time of Jack's death in 1951.

Fred married Eva Folina and they reside in Ontario.

Then the depression came in the thirties; the cattle had to be sold and Dick worked as a foreman with the construction crews, building roads and highways.

In 1936 he was moved to The Pas and worked for the Manitoba Government under Public Works. They built that part of Highway 83 known as "The Bog".

Maggie passed away in May, 1937 and Dick, in January of 1945.

They had both been good community workers and everyone was made welcome in their home.

Harold (Bill) and Alice Keay

by A. Keay

Bill and Alice Keay - 1943.

Harold, better known as Bill, with brother Jack, took over their father's farm in the 1930's and farmed it until 1943.

Bill married Alice Patterson in March 1943, then later that spring sold his share of farm equipment and cattle. Then enlisted in the Canadian Army and went overseas that same summer where he served in active service until 1946. During this time he was wounded and hospitalized twice.

When he returned to Manitoba late spring of 1946, we came back to the Rochedale area and settled on E 1/2 of 29-23-28 which Bill purchased in the early 1930's, but due to the Depression he was unable to pay for it. The owner volunteered to hold it for him until he came back, which he did through a Veteran's Allowance Plan. Highway 83 now borders the East side.

There were no buildings so we lived in two portable granaries that summer until November 22 when we nearly froze. We then moved into an old house we had purchased and moved onto the site on which we had planned to set up our farm yard. Starting from scratch, those were hard years. Not only was money short, but building supplies and machinery, which had all been put into War Effort. To compound our hardships, the small crop we had the first year, was lost to an early frost in the fall and the second year it was wiped out by hail. Through determination and hard work, we gradually acquired more land and a sizeable herd of Black Angus cattle. We milked a number of cows and sold cream, raised chickens and turkeys which were sold, also crates of eggs.

Keay Farm gate sign.

Bill and Alice were blessed with a daughter and a son over these years.

Bonnie attended Rochedale and Inglis schools, then went to Brandon University and received her Bachelor of Arts. She then volunteered for two years teaching service with C.U.S.O. in Tanzania, Africa. On returning to Manitoba she went to University of Manitoba, taking Education. When she completed this, she went to The Pas, where she taught for three years. There she met and married Arnold Young. He worked for C.N. Telecommunications and the next year he was moved to Edmonton. Bonnie taught for one year out there, then worked for Alberta Government Man Power Dept. in Career Counselling for a few years. Then she went to Concordia College where she worked with Native students in up-grading their education and career counselling for five years. Then she decided to take her Masters in Psychology and was successful. At this time she is working at NAIT College and a private counselling company. She enjoys her work.

Arnie took early retirement from C.N. a few years ago and is dabbling in real estate and carpentry. Arnie had three daughters, two of them are married. Bonnie & Arnie have four grandchildren. Their other daughter is a nurse.

The Barn raising at Keay Farm - 1949.

During this time we had made the old house liveable and built a barn and a few other buildings. Then in 1960, we built a new home as we needed more room. In the following years other buildings were built to complete the farmstead which was known as "Keay's Knoll".

Rick Keay hauling hay stacks home from Shellmouth with Allen Johnson's two grandsons.

Rick & Donna Wedding - (L-R) Bill, Alice, Rick, Donna, Bonnie & Arnie Young - 1984.

"Keay's Knoll" - Keay Farms.

Britni and Reece Keay.

Rick took his education at Rochedale and Inglis, then went to Assiniboine College in Brandon and took a welding course. After working on construction for a couple of years at Gillam and in Ontario, he decided to come home to the farm. In 1984, he married Donna McDuffe and they lived in a trailer on the 1/4 Sec. just north of the home farm. They have a daughter, Britni and a son, Reece, who are just getting into school at Roblin. Rick is a councillor of the Rural Municipality of Shellmouth and both he and Donna take an active part in community affairs.

In 1961 we were honored by the Roblin Chamber of Commerce with their Roblin and District Award for good farming practices and family home making and citizenship.

Feeling we have had a very rewarding and blessed life, we left the farm the fall of 1991 and moved into Russell.

Rick and Donna took over the farm and have expanded and diversified in many ways. The past year, 1994, they built a lovely new home and are all very happy.

Kerry and Erla Klein

by Erla Klein

I, Erla, was born to Jean and Earl Morrison, September 1, 1944, and raised on 8-24-29.

One very vivid memory I have was getting electricity in 1950. I also started school in Grainsby that fall. The school had been closed for four years. But with us Baby Boomers, we opened it up again. There were six of us to start, Verna Piwniuk, Dennis Seebach, the twins, Larry and Lorraine Kruger, Vernon Nerbas and myself. Margaret Dillabough was our teacher.

In the spring and fall, my dad drove me to school but often my Mom picked me up on horseback. She would put my tin lunch kit in an army bag and put the strap over the horn of the saddle and that was my seat. In the early years, the roads weren't plowed so my Dad took me with a team and cutter. The roads would blow in so badly we would have to travel through the field. When it was very cold I remember crawling right underneath the cowhide robe to keep warm. I also rode horseback a couple of Falls. And the last few years I was fortunate enough to be able to get a ride with the teachers that drove past our house.

In 1959-60 the school closed again due to low enrollment. There were still three originals, Larry, Lorraine and I in Grade IX. In 1960 was the first year of the school bus (van). Arnold Ferris drove the Grade IX and X's to TummelII and the XI and XII's went to Roblin. Many a time we heard "To the back", so we all piled to the back of the van so we could make it to the top of the Pyott Hill. I attended both TummelII and Roblin schools and in 1962 went to Winnipeg and took a secretarial course later working for MTS.

In 1964 I moved to Yorkton and worked at the UI office and then the Bank of Nova Scotia. In 1965, Kerry Klein and I were married in Roblin.

Kerry was born in Saskatoon to Deed and Laura Klein. He spent his first winters in the USA, where his Dad played professional hockey. Kerry received his education in Saskatoon and went through the ranks of the Minor and Junior Hockey there. He spent a couple winters playing in the USA, also. He played Senior Hockey in Yorkton for three years.

We spent a year in Yorkton after we were married, then moved to Hythe, AB, where Kerry bought grain and played hockey. Tracy was born in Hythe in 1967. In 1968 we moved to Beaverlodge and then to Dawson Creek, BC. In 1969 we transferred up to Fort Nelson, BC (Mile 300, Alaska Highway). Brad was born in 1970. We remained there until 1977, when the company Kerry was working for, ran into financial trouble. It was off to Prince Rupert for a year and a half and back to Yorkton (living about three blocks from our first place) in 1979. Kerry worked for Leons and then Morris, until their big layoff in 1984. Kerry decided to venture into the hotel business in Grande Prairie, AB. In July 1985, the kids and I moved up there only to return in 1986, less one kid. Tracy stayed up there working. We are still in Yorkton and expect it will be our last major move.

Tracy married Dave McLennan in 1989, in Saskatoon. They have twin boys, Mark and Michael, born in 1989 and Megan born in 1992. They are presently living in Langham, SK.

Brad took the university route, spending three years in Regina obtaining his Bachelor of Business Administration. Presently he is articling for his Chartered Accountant designation at Skilnick and Partners in Melville, SK.

Walter Henry Kurtenbach

by Charlotte Kitz

Walter and Gen Kurtenbach.

Walter Henry Kurtenbach was born on Dec. 25, 1926 at Cudworth, SK. Genevieve Mary Medernach was born on Mar. 30, 1931 at Cudworth, SK. They were married on July 26, 1950. They farmed at Cudworth until they moved to Dropmore on April 29, 1966. They bought a farm from J. B. Andrews. The home quarter is SW 2-24-29 W of 1st. They had a large family of ten children. The youngest one, Mag, was known as "The Manitoba Kid" by the rest of her siblings!

A few years after we moved to Dropmore, Dad and Mom added to the farm with two quarters purchased from Ed Ziebach and 1 1/2 quarters from Connie Hertlein.

The day we moved to Dropmore, we came through Shellmouth. We had to take the bikes off the top of the big truck to get under the Shellmouth bridge.

When we drove into our new yard, we were all very excited. The house was a big white 2 1/2 storey (which our family sure needed). We named it "The Ponderosa". We have many happy memories of our house. In the spring of 1990 it burnt to the ground.

Everyone must remember all the chickens we had. We must have picked, washed and candled millions of eggs. You know that not one of us have chickens now.

Dad loved fishing and hunting. He always used to take time every Sunday to take all of us for a drive somewhere special. Dad and Mom bought us our first two horses, Gypsy and Topsy. Dad used to call them "hayburners" but he always had peppermints in his pockets to feed them. Dad passed away on Nov. 9, 1983. He was 56 years old.

Mom loved horses and the outdoors. In the last ten years she spent a lot of time going on trail rides and enlarging her "extended" family (There is always room for one more!). One of Mom's greatest joys was teaching her grandchildren to ride and love horses like she did. Mom passed away on Sept. 1, 1994. She was 63 years old.

Mom and Dad always took time to spend with their grandchildren. They will be remembered dearly by their children, their outlaws (Dad's nickname for the in-laws), their grandchildren and all their many friends.

Kurtenbach Farm at Dropmore - 1966.

Gen Kurtenbach funeral - September,1994 in Langenburg, SK. Horse drawn hearse.

Children of Walter and Genevieve Kurtenbach

Adrian Walter was born on Nov. 3, 1952. He passed away on Nov. 4, 1964.

Adrian Kurtenbach.

Janielle, Roy, Cathy, Tyler, Megan, Justin Kurtenbach.

Royden Louis was born on March 22, 1955. He married Debra Bot on Oct. 21, 1978. They had three children: Janielle Theresa born Nov. 25, 1979, Justin Walter born Apr. 11, 1981, and Tyler Andrew born May 3, 1983. They live in Langenburg, SK. Roy married Cathy Shepherd on Mar. 16, 1992. They have one child, Megan Ashley born June 25, 1991. Roy and Cathy live in Swift Current, SK. A *memory* is picking all them stones and stumps.

Noreen, Lawrence (holding Kirstin), Monty (friend) Jennifer, Angie, Crystal Fatteicher.

Rose, Ron, Amos, Wade Eftoda.

Noreen Genevieve was born on June 19, 1956. She married Lawrence Fatteicher on Mar. 1, 1976. They have three children: Crystal Eve born June 16, 1976, Angeilque Grace born Jan. 19, 1979, and Jennifer Lynne born Jan. 14, 1984. Noreen and Lawrence live in Moose Jaw, SK. A *memory:* After our work was done on the weekends, we got to go riding. We rode all over the Dropmore Area.

Rosalyn Elaine was born on Dec. 15, 1958. She married Ron Eftoda on May 30, 1981. They have two children: Amos John born Nov. 11, 1981 and Wade Ronald born Sept. 28, 1983. Rose and Ron live on the homequarter at Dropmore. A *memory:* Riding all over the Dropmore Area (especially the valley) with Pam Dietrich, or when we brought home our first cow from John and Violet Robertson. She was such a quiet cow that we walked her from their place to ours.

Carissa, Alvin, Cardell, Wendy & Nathan Holinaty.

Lisa, Char, Dale, Rebecca, Rachael, Suzanne Kitz.

Wendy Edna was born on Dec. 6, 1957. She married Alvin Holinaty on Sept. 1, 1979. They have three children: Nathan William born Oct. 10, 1981, Carissa Margaret born Sept. 20, 1984, and Cardell Alvin born Apr. 8, 1991. Wendy and Al live on an acreage at Esterhazy, SK. A *memory:* When we had to walk to school in Dropmore. The girls had to walk and the boys got the bikes because we only had two bikes.

Charlotte Mary-Ann was born on Apr. 30, 1960. She married Dale Kitz on Apr. 26, 1980. They have four children: Rachel Charlotte born Sept. 23, 1982, Suzanne Joan born Aug. 29, 1985, Rebecca Anne born Sept. 10, 1988 and Lisa Cheryl born Dec. 17, 1991. Charlotte and Dale live on a farm by MacNutt. A *memory:* My first day of school in Dropmore. Riding horses all over the Dropmore Area.

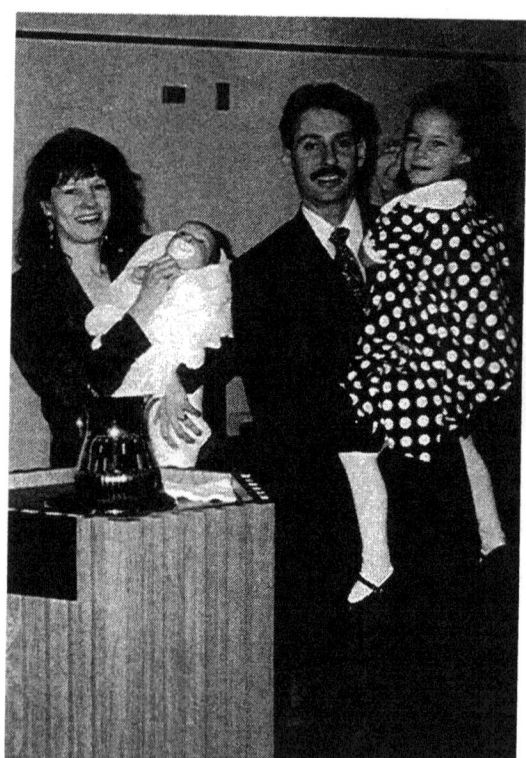

Joan, Tim, Brady, Kirsten Kendel.

Joan Adeline was born on April 30, 1961. She married Tim Kendel on March 13, 1982. They have two children: Kirstin Joan born July 5, 1990 and Brady Tim born Sept. 8, 1994. Joan and Tim live in Saskatoon, SK. A *memory*: When we used to visit Bill and Wilma Neilson and I used to get to sit in their rocking chair and rock my doll.

Randy, Marg, Jessica, Tyrel Poier.

Margaret Agatha was born on July 12, 1965. She married Randy Poier on May 3, 1986. They have two children: Tyrel Phillip born Jan. 23, 1987, and Jessica Paige born Sept. 20, 1991. Marg and Randy live on what used to be Fred Mann's farm. A *memory*: Riding down to Jack's and Ole's Hole in the valley for weiner roasts with the whole family.

Shelly, Doug, Joshua, Zachary Kurtenbach.

Douglas Earl was born on Feb. 5, 1963. He married Shelly Adams on June 13, 1987. They have two children: Joshua Douglas born Feb. 8, 1990 and Zachary Adrian born Jan. 25, 1993. Doug and Shelly live in Inglis, MB. A *memory*: Farming with Dad.

Mag, Neil, Tiffany, Courtney Kotzer.

Magdalena Elsie was born on Aug. 24, 1966. She married Neil Kotzer on July 20, 1985. They have two children: Tiffany Megan born May 27, 1985 and Courtney Desiree born Nov. 11, 1990. Mag and Neil live on a farm by Langenburg. A *memory*: Picking crocuses by the elevators and the Rabbit Path. Also riding our horses to Petz's Store and Mr. Petz used to give us a bubblegum.

The Lewis Family

by Don Lewis

Lewis Home.

Edward T. (Barney) Lewis married my mother, Clementina Skinner, September 24, 1906. They came to live in Dropmore from Winnipeg in 1912. My mother came from Scotland with the Skinner family in 1895. My Dad built a large home in town, opened a general store and settled down. Six boys and one girl were born: Edward Francis in 1907, William Russell (Buzz) in 1909, Reginald John in 1912. At two years old, Reg contracted polio (then called infantile paralysis). It was a struggle to keep him alive and he remained crippled. My sister Violet May (Gale) was born in 1913, then James Douglas in 1915. I came along in May of 1917 and Mervyn (babe) in 1919.

We all grew up in Dropmore and attended school in the little one room school, since replaced and now retired as a school. Living in Dropmore was carefree and fun. We had to make our own entertainment. Life was quite different in those days, especially in winter when travel was restricted and temperatures around 30 below. No automatic heating, just the old wood stove in the center of the schoolroom. By about 10 a.m. it was tolerable. One morning someone placed their ink bottle on the stove to thaw but it exploded and spattered ink all over the ceiling. Years later, the spots were still there.

As we boys grew up, sports dominated most of our spare time. Ed and Buzz played soccer for the Rochedale team, competing at Birtle, July 1st and at sports days in Russell, Dauphin and Minnedosa. For a small village, the Dropmore softball team won its share of tournament games. The field in front of our store was the practise field. Many hours were spent there during the 30's when customers were few and far between. During those days, Buzz was the storekeeper and Reg, Postmaster. When Buzz and Ed moved on to Trail, BC. I took over operating the store. Monday, Wednesday and Friday the train came in the afternoon, the days when people came to town.

Winter was hockey under Harry Gilhooley's direction. We built a rink, no need for artificial ice. I suppose we spent more time shovelling snow than skating. Rivalry with Shellmouth was intense. In tournaments in Russell and Roblin where sometimes we would come close. Playing outside in -30 degree weather was considered fun.

My father died in 1934 and in time we all went farther afield. Ed and Buzz first went to Trail, BC, followed by Jim. When Reg and Frances

(L-R) Eddie, Don, Buzz, Jim & Grannie Lewis

Bloomfield were married in 1941, I also went west to BC and they took over the post office and store.

Ed married Evelyn Gray in 1940, they have one daughter, Lynn. Ed died in 1982. Evelyn still lives in Chilliwack, BC. Buzz married Betty Senior in 1940. They divorced and Buzz married Brenda Tucker. They have one daughter, Judy. Brenda died in 1960 and Buzz in 1988.

Reg died while he and Frances were visiting Gale in England and Frances died at Abbotsford in 1993.

Gale married Jim Alston in 1942; they live in England. They have two daughters and two sons. Jim married Lorna Harrison in 1940; they have a daughter, Patty, and three sons, Ronnie, Tyrell and Kim (adopted). Jim died in 1968.

I married Beatrice Wood in 1942. We have two daughters, Lillian and Diane and two sons, Don Jr. and David. Lillian lives in Australia, the others still in BC. Diane's husband, Bill, died in 1993 and Diane and her son and daughter are in Vancouver while Diane is studying for the United Church ministry. David lives in Port Coquitlam with his family and Don and Margaret in Sechelt, BC. Babe married Anita Davidson in 1943; they have one daughter, Wendy. They divorced in 1948 and Babe married Pat Simpson in 1954. They have three children, Erin, Troy and Tamma. Babe died in 1975.

In 1958 I was ordained as minister in the United Church of Canada and retired to Courtenay, BC in 1981. We now live in Sechelt, BC. My mother moved to BC and was living with Beatrice and me until her death in 1966. Both Mum and Dad are buried in the Dropmore cemetery.

My parents were very active in the life of the Dropmore community. Dad was interested in music and drama. He shared the music of many operas played on Edison records by the gramophone. Winters were taken up with the preparation and production of three act plays with the local talent. Much of that local talent would be bedded down in our home when storms prevented people from going home after practise. My mother, being a Skinner, was a gardener. Our grounds were a showpiece of flowers and shrubs. The vegetable garden kept us in vegetables all year round. Hospitality was the norm and no one was ever turned away from our home when a meal or a bed was needed.

Reg and Frances

Reg was a part of the Dropmore scene longer than any of us. He and Frances built a small home beside the store and post office, and the old home was sold.

In spite of his handicap, Reg participated, along with Frances, in community activities. The Dropmore orchestra produced much danceable

Reg and Frances.

music. Jessie Wardle, violin, Reg, the drums and saxophone, Cedric Rowan, clarinet and piano along with Beatrice Wood, while she was a teacher. The dances helped the long winters pass and built the community spirit.

From his workshop, Reg built the pulpit for the new church and many other projects. Frances worked the store in spite of terrible arthritis, was always an inspiration with her friendliness and smile. A real companion for Reg.

Life in the world today makes us appreciate the quiet, sane and peaceful life we lived in those early days. Our parents, along with those pioneers, made a good life for us all and we learned to survive under harsh conditions. Those experiences enabled us to cope in our later lives.

John Russell MacFarlane
by Joan Collie

Our family moved to Dropmore in May 1946 and lived on the Jack Ferris farm east of Dropmore. At the same time, our grandparents, Sam & Emily Furneaux also moved to Dropmore, and lived in a house of Fred Brown's just across the field from us and right beside the track. We were happy in Dropmore and names are still very familiar to us. Dad did custom work, hauled grain, did stooking and harvesting, or what ever else there was to do to, make a dollar. That winter, Dad and Jim went to Ontario to work in the bush camps. In February we had a terrible snow storm, everything was blocked, the train wasn't even running. Mom was expecting Harvey anytime, so Dad came home. The only way to travel from Russell was by Clement's airplane. They got to

Dropmore fine and took Mom back to Russell. Mom stayed with a friend till time to go to the hospital, which was only a day or two. Dad came back to see us kids before returning to Ontario, but just as they were taking off, the plane crashed. Dad was badly hurt and spent months in Winnipeg having treatment for back and neck injuries. We left Dropmore in June 1947. Dad and Mom farmed in the Millwood and Harrowby districts until they moved to Regina in 1961. In 1962 they bought a service station and cafe in Pense, 20 miles west of Regina.

Dad had a heart attack and passed away very suddenly, in July 1963. Mom and the two youngest boys, Harvey and Donald, along with guidance from Ken and Vernon, ran the business till 1965. At that time they sold to the Department of Highways, as the new double lanes would go through their property, and moved back to Regina.

After Grandpa Furneaux passed away in 1959, Grandma lived with the family until 1970, then she resided at the Blind Institute till her death in May 1971.

Mom worked at The Bay in Regina until she retired in 1977. Then she bought a house in Virden and was very happy there. Vern and Dessie were close by and she enjoyed the church and senior activities. She went on my trips with different family members and she was always a joy to have along. We were all devastated by her sudden death in March 1992.

Over the years, our family has scattered and grown. At the time of writing, this is our whereabouts:

Gerald married Eleanor Keebaum from Endcliffe, they are retired and live in Nelson, BC. They have 4 children and 9 grandchildren.

Ken is married to Helen and they have retired to Kamsask. He has 2 children and 2 grandchildren.

Jim married Rexine. They live in Dundee Oregon and they have 1 daughter.

Joan married Bill Collie from Hamiota, MB. They farmed there till 1968 then moved to Regina. They have 2 children and 5 grandchildren.

Vernon married Dessie Cranwell from Roblin. They live near Virden, semi retired raiseing race horses in Winnipeg. They have 3 children and 8 grandchildren.

Marion married Garry Robinson from Binscarth, and they live in Winnipeg. They have 3 children and 3 grandchildren.

Dave married Leona and they live in Qu'Appelle, SK. Dave is a truck driver. They have 3 children and 7 grandchildren.

Betty married Stewart and he has retired from the City Police force. They have a trailer and are travelling at present. They have 3 children.

Harvey is married to June. They farm at Rimby, AB. He has 2 children and 1 grandchild.

Donald is married to Shirley. He is an insurance salesman and they live in Saskatoon, SK. He has 2 children.

We are looking forward to the reunion, meeting old friends and hopefully some new ones.

John Graham (Jack) MacLeod Family

by the Family

Jack was born at Inverness, Scotland, a son of John and Jessie (nee Graham) MacLeod. He received his education in Scotland and served with the Seaforth Highlanders (a Scottish Regiment).

In 1925, the family came to Canada and settled in the Bield District. Jack worked on farms in Saskatchewan and in the Tummell District. He also worked on the building of and gravelling of #83 Highway. He was then employed with Skinners Nursery from 1932 to 1977.

In October 9, 1936 he was united in marriage to Gladys Irene Mary Cooper, a daughter of William and Maude (nee Allingham) Cooper. Jack and Gladys were blessed with six children, all of whom are married. There are 13 grandchildren and 6 great grandchildren.

Eileen married Tom Linton of Deepdale on June 30, 1956 in the Dropmore United Church. They have 2 children, Joanne married Terry Marteniuk of Calder, Saskatchewan and they have three boys, Kelly, Kyle and Kraig. Robert works and lives in Roblin.

Noreen married David Bailes of Bield on June 1, 1957 in the Dropmore United Church. They have 3 children - Terry married Kim Matskiw and they have 3 children, Ryan, Adam and Dreya and they live in Stonewall. Douglas lives in Winnipeg and Willa lives in Calgary.

Graham married Barbara Braitcher of Bield and they have one daughter, Laura Lee and they live in Winnipeg.

Bryne married Sylvia Waage of Watrous, Saskatchewan. They have two daughters, Melissa and Sasha and they live in Roblin.

Wayne married Leticia Jimenez Garcia of C.D. Valles, Mexico, on April 28, 1979. They have 3 children, Christopher, Myles and Jessica. They live on an acreage west of Roblin.

Jacqueline married Donald Klemetski of Roblin on July 21, 1975. They have two daughters, Karisa and Karmyn. They live on a farm several miles north of Roblin.

All six of us attended school at Rochedale as long as possible and completed our education in either Bield or Tummell and Inglis, or Roblin or Russell School picnics, Christmas Concerts,

Jack and Gladys McLeod Family.

dances and card parties were always exciting events as nearly everyone in the neighbourhood attended.

The first house we lived in at the Nursery had the greenhouse attached to it and sometimes we were allowed to accompany dad to water the plants etc. We all learned to appreciate the beauty of the trees and the flowers. In the early 1940's we moved to a bigger house with indoor plumbing. We were all so excited. It was just like Christmas.

Gardening and picking fruit were always summer holiday chores. There were always lots of trees to climb, paths to explore and lots of people to visit. We made many friends among the people who worked at the Nursery over the years.

Dad loved sports, especially football and soccer. He played on the Rochedale Rangers Soccer team which won the Pratt Cup in 1930 -31 -32. Mom was a member of the Rochedale Ladies Club and the Dropmore United Church Ladies group. Dad and Mom were both members of the Dropmore Curling Club and from the stories we have heard, had some great times.

Dad retired from Skinner's in 1977 and in 1978, they moved to Roblin. They were both active members of the Roblin Horticultural Society and received Life Memberships. Dad also received recognition for his contribution to the Roblin Agricultural Society.

In October, 1986 they celebrated their Fiftieth Wedding Anniversary. A "Come and Go Tea" was held at the "50 and Over Club" with their family and many relatives and friends present. They were pleasantly surprised by the attendance of several members of the Dauphin Pipe Band whom we had hired to entertain. Dad and Mom both loved the bagpipes and the good old Scottish tunes.

Dad passed away on October 27, 1992 after a brief illness.

Mom lives in an apartment and keeps busy with the Horticultural Society and the Ladies Legion Auxiliary. She is a member of the United Church and of one of the ladies groups, and she is a member of the "50 and Over Club".

Daniel Martel

by Marilyn Liske

(Front Row) Daniel and Emily Martel.

Daniel Martel immigrated from Guernsey in the Channel Island to Asessippi in 1903 at the age of twenty-eight. He worked for various farmers for several years. He finally homesteaded on 488 acres of land, the home quarter being NW 4-23-28. In 1915, he built a house on his property, in which his great niece and her family still live today, Larry and Marilyn Liske and family.

Daniel Martel with prize Aberdeen Angus Bull - 1945.

At one time Dan purchased the top Aberdeen Angus cow in all of Canada. From this he was able to build a large, very expensive herd of cattle. Many a prize was won by Dan in the local summer fairs.

Dan was a good Christian man. He loved children and always liked to be involved with them. Since he married later in life to his housekeeper of many years, Mrs. Emily McDonald, he never had any family of his own. His land was inherited by his nephew Fred Parmentier, who had lived with him from the age of 12 years. Of his uncle, Fred said, "He was a very good man, kind, but very firm."

Dan passed away on August 12, 1946 at his home.

James Edward Miller

by Hazel McLean

Jim was born on a farm south of Fork River, in the Mowat, SD on October, 1912. He was one of nine children born to Willis and Hannah Miller.

He attended school at the Mowat School. He enjoyed sports. At about 19 years he went to work at Skinner's Nursury in the Dropmore area.

In 1940 of December, he met and married Hazel Patterson of Shellmouth. In December 1942, a son, Garry Laing, was born, and in April of 1945, a daughter, Gwennth Adele.

We moved to a farm east of Fork River in 1943, where Garry and Adele attended school in Fork River.

We resided there till May 1956, when Jim passed away, after which we moved to Shellmouth and then moved to Winnipeg.

Garry and I worked, while Adele finished school and went to business college, and then to work.

They both married in 1963 and they, and their families, reside in Winnipeg.

I retired in 1980 in Shellmouth and in 1982, I married Emmett McLean of Dauphin and we reside in Dauphin.

Earl Morrison Family

by Jean & Earl Morrison

Earl Morrison was born in 1918 on 6-23-29. In June 1921, they moved to 9-24-29 (Glen Young's). He started school in 1923, at the age of five, in Grainsby, and continued there except for one year, 1927, when Ronnie, Jean and Earl attended Castleavery so Ronnie could take his Grade IX. They went to school by horse and buggy in summer and team and cutter in winter, or on horseback.

After leaving school, he worked on the family farm until June 1941 when he joined the Royal Canadian Artillery. He trained in Shilo, MB and Debert, NS. Due to physical disability, he returned to Winnipeg and worked at the Fort Osborne Hospital, for a short time, and then was discharged.

On November 11, 1943, Earl married Jean Birnie at the Birnie farm.

Jean was born in 1921 and raised on 2-24-29 (Kurtenbach's). She attended school in Dropmore. The first couple of years she didn't go to school during the winter as there was no one available to take her. She walked until she was old enough to ride horseback. This also involved taking feed for her pony in a gunny sack. Jean loved her horses and spent many hours riding.

Jean and Earl started farming on 8-24-29 with six horses and Jean's pony, sixteen head of cattle, thirteen chickens and three turkey hens. Since they were married during the war and sugar was rationed, Mrs. Lewis (Auntie Clem) held a Fruit and Pickle Bridal Shower, which they appreciated and ended up with a well stocked fruit cellar.

In 1947 they spent the winter in the valley, in a two roomed log house and wintered 60 head of cattle.

Their farming began with horses and slowly progressed to powered equipment. They raised cattle and pigs, as well as grain.

Earl loved Auction Sales and could be found around the junk boxes searching for treasures. Seldom did he come home without some antique and its story. He took great pride in displaying his collection and sharing the history with anyone who was interested. Jean also became very interested in the collection.

In 1966, they sold the farm and moved to Brandon, taking their antiques with them. Earl worked for the Lindenberg Seed Co. on their farms and in the seed depot. He had eye surgery in 1969. Then he worked at the Prince Edward Hotel until it closed, and the Red Oak Inn until he retired in 1984.

Jean started helping some elderly and arthritic ladies with household tasks, making wonderful friendships over the years. The few that are left still look forward to her cheerful visits at their homes or in the hospital.

Jean and Earl still live in their house in Brandon, MB.

Jean and Earl have one daughter, Janet Erla, born in 1944. She attended school in Grainsby, Tummelll and Roblin, then took a business course in Winnipeg. She worked at MTS for awhile and then moved to Yorkton where she married Kerry Klein in 1965.

The Earl Morrison Family and How It Grew!!! (Back row L-R) Kerry Klein, Tracy, Dave McLennan (holding Megan) and Brad Klein. (Middle row) Erla Klein, Jean and Earl Morrison. (Front row) Mark and Micheal McLennan. Photo taken on Jean and Earl's 50th Anniversary 1943-93.

The Wilbert Morrison Family

by Judy (Morrison) Becker

Wilbert Morrison was born September 10, 1911 at Shellmouth, MB. He moved with his family to the Grainsby district. He attended school at Shellmouth and Grainsby and then started farming. On October 18, 1939 he married Laura Anne Shearer of the Castleavery district. Anne was born December 9, 1913. She attended school at Castleavery and Shellmouth and took a hairdressing course at Winnipeg. Wilbert and Anne farmed on the west half of section 16-24-29 in the rural municipality of Shellmouth. They had three children: Garry, born in 1941, Elaine born in 1943 and Judy born in 1944. In 1947 they purchased a general store in MacNutt, SK.

Besides working long hours in the store, Wilbert and Anne were actively involved their community and church. Wilbert was a member of the Board of Trade, the Curling Club, the Recreation Board, and the Dropmore United Church Board. He was among those involved with the building of the curling rink and the Recreation Centre in MacNutt, the Dropmore United Church and the establishment of the MacNutt Credit Union. Anne volunteered many hours with the Community Workers, the MacNutt Curling Club, the Red Cross and other charities.

They enjoyed camping, fishing gardening, curling and visiting. Their family now includes Garry and Phyllis Morrison and Bob and Elaine Digby of Dropmore, and Frank and Judy Becker of MacNutt, thirteen grandchildren and seventeen great-grandchildren.

They retired in 1974 and moved to Roblin in 1978. Wilbert is a resident at the Crocus Court Care home and Anne lives in her own home. She is a member of the UCW and the United Church Quilters and spends many hours gardening, crocheting, knitting, quilting and baking for her family and friends.

Judith Anne Morrison was born October 11, 1994. She received her education in MacNutt and after graduating, she attended Teacher's College in Regina. She taught at Rocanville, Calder and MacNutt until 1968. She married Franklin Becker in 1965 and they farm near MacNutt. They have three children: Brenda born in 1968, Laurel in 1971 and Warren in 1974. Since 1987, Judy has been teaching adult education at Langenburg (part-time). Frank and Judy are active in community and church activities and they enjoy time with their family.

Brenda has a diploma in micro-computer management and is employed by the Royal Bank in Langenburg. She is married to Leslie Adams and they farm in the MacNutt area. They have two children, Jonathan born in 1992 and Brittany in 1993.

Laurel has a degree in Education and is employed by the Potashville School Division. She is married to Elden Kentel and they farm south of MacNutt.

Warren has a diploma in Mechanical Engineering from the technical institute. He is attending university to get his degree in engineering.

Garry Morrison

by Phyllis Morrison

Garry Morrison, only son of Wilbert and Anne Morrison, born June 19, 1941 while his parents lived on SW16-24-29 W. They moved to MacNutt, SK in 1947.

Garry completed school in MacNutt and worked for Murray Shearer, Peppler's Garage, and Dropmore Transfer. In 1963, Garry moved to Regina and worked for Refrigeration Installation until March 1974.

Married Phyllis Hamblin (Berner) in 1966 - widow with three children whom Garry adopted in 1967 - Raymond (1955), Daniel (1958), Susan (1962). To this family we added two more children, Donald (1968) and Gwen (1969).

Garry always enjoyed the farm and thought it was a great place to raise a family. In 1974, we purchased the George and Hazel Bernhard farm NE 30-23-22 W in the Dropmore area, where we still reside.

Garry drove the feeder school bus from 1978-1983 until the route was discontinued. Garry also drove the road patrol from 1978-1985.

Ray and Cindy (Dean) have two daughters - Katherine (1989) and Ellen (1992) and they reside in Saskatoon, SK.

Danny and Terri McDuffe live in Longview, AB.

Susan and Jake Robak have four children - Michael (1980), Jonathan (1984), Jennifer (1988), Matthew (1992) and they live in Grandview, MB.

Donald and Sheryl (Lindemann) have one son, Kyle (1994) and they reside in Regina, SK. Gwen and Wayne Weber live in Roblin, MB.

We have both enjoyed living and raising our family in this community. We have been active in the Dropmore Community since our arrival in 1974 with many fond memories and many good times. We were both active in the Dropmore United Church until its closure in 1985 and we still enjoy going to the Church since Margaret and Martin Neufhofer bought and moved it to their Shellmouth Strawberry Farm. With some renovations they turned it into "The Church Caffee" and serve great food!

Harvey Munro Family

by Bessie (Patterson) Munro

The Munro Family in 1976 (L-R) Myles, David, Bessie, Marlene, Harvey and Terry.

My father William Patterson born in 1877 came west from North Easthope, ON in 1882 via CPR and then to Birtle by ox-cart. After 9 years they came to the Shellmouth district and took up a homestead 4 miles south of Shellmouth where they built a log house.

In 1909, he married May Wise who came from England at the age of 8 with her grandfather. On the homestead they raised a family of six children of whom I am the youngest, born in 1921.

I received my schooling, grades 1 - XI, in Shellmouth, Grade XII in Russell and attended Winnipeg Normal School where I received my teaching certificate.

My first school in 1939 was at Castleavery teaching 21 pupils, grades 1-VIII. I was also the caretaker, lighting the fire, thawing out the ink wells, and water cooler, sweeping etc. Many cold morning we sat around with our backs to the stove until the schoolhouse warmed up.

I stayed at this school for 2 years. The first year, I boarded at Joe and Ada Dugans, the year Bud was born, I rode my bike or went on horseback to school. The second year, I boarded at Edgar and Effie Comforts. That year, Edwin & Jack Rowan started school 7 & 6 years old. They drove with a cutter or buggy as far as Comforts. Then I would drive the rest of the way to school, and back at four o'clock as far as Comforts and see them safely on their way home.

My salary was $500 a year and board was $18 a month. While at Comforts, being a farm girl, I would bring the cows home and help them milk. Some weekends I did it all myself so they could have a free weekend, so I seldom paid the full $18.00.

On weekends when I wanted to go home, I would bike. It was a long ride. My brother Walter would bring me back part way on Sunday and I would bike the rest of the way.

After teaching at Oak Ridge, near Killarney and Russell, I came to teach in Dropmore in 1944-45 with 29 pupils attending in grades 1 - X. The grade X's started taking correspondence courses but were having difficulty, so we decided I would teach them, too.

On weekends I would catch the train at 3:45, (we shortened the noon hour by 15 min.) so I was able to catch the train and the conductor would let me off right near the farm. My salary was then $2000.00 a year and board was $50.00 a month.

It was in 1944 that my brother David was killed in action in France.

While teaching in Dropmore, I met Harvey Munro, son of George and Laura Munro who were of Scotish and Irish decent. Harvey was born in 1912 in Wood Bay, MB where his parents farmed. He was an elevator agent in Dropmore and was boarding at Bradley-Hunts where I also boarded. We were married in 1915 and lived in the former Bert Hunt house.

In 1946, I was asked by 3 families if I would teach 5 of their children who were in Grade X and they would pay my salary. So we started a private school in the former Andy Francis store. The pupils were Bob and Jessie Pyott, Ivan and Anne Rowan and Evelyn Brown. We were under the supervision of the Department of Education. I was the caretaker, too. This was quite a unique experience.

In 1948 we moved to Inglis where we raised 4 children. Harvey operated the municipal grader and later operated a "cat" on different roads in southern Manitoba. I went with him and cooked for 12 men when our oldest son was 9 months old. He later drove a school bus, worked in a garage, and fixed typewriters for Pelly Trail School Division. I went back teaching after 11 years off and taught in Inglis for 21 years, making a total of 28 years of teaching.

Harvey passed away in 1981.

I still live in Inglis, in my own home and have done considerable travelling in the past several years.

Our children:

Terry was born in 1948 married Angela Setter of Russell in 1972. He is manager of Midas Muffler. They live in Winnipeg with their 2 children, Ryan 15 and Dawn 11.

David born in 1952 married Kimberly Tibbatts of Foxwarren in 1975. He is a heavy duty mechanic for George Smith Trucking Co. They live in Winnipeg with their 2 children, Krista 13 and Michael 6.

Marlene born in 1954 married Anthony Dziad of Arbor in 1976. She nurses at the Health Science Centre. They live in Winnipeg and have 2 children, Jesse 8 and Ashley 3.

Mylis born in 1959 married Wendy Pringle of Tuelon in 1987. Has his own semi truck and works for Arnold Brothers. They live in Tuelon and have a child, Brett, 5 years.

Philip and Margaret Nerbas Family

by Margaret Kozak

Philip and Margaret Nerbas.

Philip and Margaret (Kitsch) Nerbas emigrated from Austria to the Hoffental District (the North West Territories) in 1899 and lived with Mr. and Mrs. Valentine Mack, while Philip worked for farmers in the area. He also worked for Mr. Tuelon of Shellmouth, MB. Philip took up his homestead (the Albert Geres farm). They built a barn Sec.4-23-30-W1 and lived in the barn while the house was being built. Rudolph was born in the new barn. Frank, Margaret, Laura and Minnie were born on the homestead and some time later moved to the Dropmore area and on April 26, 1922, Laura passed away. Mrs. Harry Peppler (Minnie Nerbas) describes the tragic death of her twin sister Laura.

Minnie, Rudolph, Dad, Philip Jr., Mom, Frank and Laura.

The Philip Nerbas Family in 1911 - (Back row) August, Adam, Fred (holding daughter Elizabeth), Fred's wife Dora, Jacob (Middle row) Lena Catherine, Philip Sr., John, Margaret, Dorothea. (Front row) Philip Jr. and Rudolf.

Laura was born June 24, 1915. Laura took ill Sunday afternoon shortly after she and her sister Dorothea returned home from a walk to the creek. She complained of a pain in her side and was getting worse. Her parents called Mrs. Chris Stevenson, a nurse who lived nearby. Upon examining Laura, she advised the parents to call Dr. Lee. Brother Jake went on horse back to MacNutt to seek help from the doctor. Jake had to cross Blackbird Creek which was overflowing as a result of a flash flood, which came along with the spring breakup. In crossing he had to lie flat on the horse's back to prevent his feet from getting wet. The doctor arrived on Monday noon and advised my parents to bring Laura to MacNutt in order to have an operation done. Horses and wagon were the only means of transportation available. Laura was placed on a cot (donated by Mrs. Stevenson), and placed in the wagon box for the journey to MacNutt. When they reached the creek, crossing became difficult, as water was now running into the wagon box and the trip was slowed down. Laura was operated on Tuesday. When a nurse from Yorkton who was to assist Dr. Lee, didn't arrive, Mrs. Lee, also a nurse, and Nurse Sleeker had to assist instead. Mr. and Mrs. McFadyn offered the front room table on which to perform surgery. By this time the appendix had ruptured. In the early

August and Margaret Nerbas.

hours of the morning, our mother noticed that Laura's condition was deteriorating. She called Dr. Lee and Nurse Selkirk. It was now evident that nothing could be done to save Laura's life. Laura passed away at 6 am, Wednesday morning.

Laura's casket was made by Peter Rathgeber and her sister, Katherine Dietrich, lined

Minnie and Laura Nerbas.

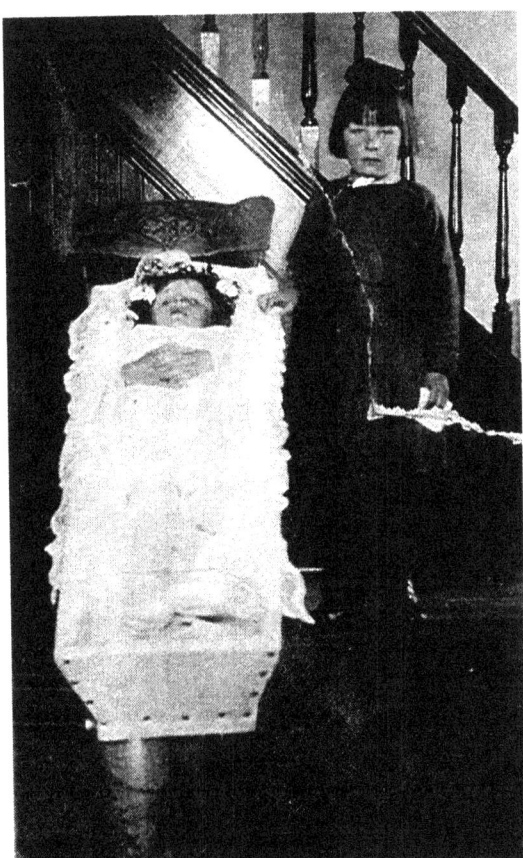

Laura Nerbas in coffin with Minnie Peppler standing beside.

the casket. Many people attended the funeral which was a sad one indeed.

Laura was missed not only by the family, but also by a pet lamb which was given to us by our neighbor, Chris Stevenson. Whenever the lamb was allowed to come in the house it would search every room and look under the beds for Laura. After searching both up stairs and down, the lamb continued its never ending vigil hoping that someday Laura would return.

August and Margaret Nerbas lived on a farm near Dropmore. They had 9 sons. The youngest died in infancy and Henry died in a tragic death when his truck stalled on a railway crossing and he was hit by a train.

Jake and Bena had 3 sons and 1 daughter. John and Lena had 1 son. Philip and Ethel had 1 son and 1 daughter. Rudolph and Louise had 1 son and 1 daughter. Frank and Margaret had 2 daughters and 1 son. Margaret and Forrest Patterson had 1 son and 5 daughters. Margaret was divorced from Patterson and got re-married to Harry Kozak. Harry owned and operated his lumber yard and in 1985 they retired to Yorkton. In 1987 Harry suffered a stroke which left him paralyzed and was in a wheelchair. He entered the nursing home March 16th 1988. He passed away March 13, 1995. His funeral was held March 16, 1995. I live in Queen Elizabeth Court. Margaret has 21 grandchildren and 33 great grandchildren. We are expecting 2 more great grandchildren this year.

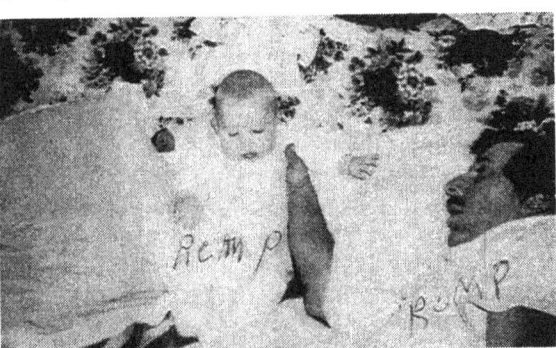

Robin Christopher Manley Patterson and Royce Clifford Manley Patterson.

Minnie and Harry Peppler had 1 daughter and 2 sons. They have 6 grandchildren. We were a family of 17 children and only 3 of us left. Frank in Winnipeg, MB, Margaret Kozak and Minnie Peppler of Yorkton, SK. Harry Peppler passed away June 1994. He suffered a stroke. Philip and Margaret Nerbas celebrated their 69th wedding anniversary January 18th, 1956. Margaret Nerbas passed away August 9, 1956 and Philip Nerbas passed away June 23, 1957. They had 53 grandchildren and 52 great grandchildren. Philip and Margaret Nerbas attended the Evangelical

Jean Lawrence, Fern Miller, Margaret Kozak, Arla Harde, Pam Wiley, Heather Kowalchuk.

Lutheran Church in MacNutt, Hoffental and Landestreu Church.

Philip and Margaret Nerbas moved to the Castleavery District in the fall of 1929 and lived on the Farncomb farm and rented the McNair farm. Rudolph, Frank, Margaret and Minnie attended Grainsby School.

Margaret Kozak, Pam, Beth and Royce Patterson and Beth's two sons.

I lost my only son in 1991. He took his life and his 2 children, Kimberly 8 years and son Robin of 15 months. They died of asphyxiation caused by carbon monoxide poisoning from exhaust fumes. They died at Fort Nelson, BC.

My sister Katherine married in 1919 and she took me home to her place to live with them. I was 5 years of age. At the age of 6 years I was left in charge of a 5 month old baby while my sister, Katherine and her husband, John went stooking after supper. I had dishes to do and wash the baby and put her to bed. I had to get up in the night to change the baby and warm her bottle over the lamp, feed her and put her back to bed, while they went to visit the neighbors for a game of cards after it was too dark to stook.

Margaret Kozak.

I am 81 years old and I am getting very slow. Hope to see you at the homecoming.

Rudolf and Louise Nerbas

by Louise Nerbas

When Rudolf's father, Philip, retired in 1934, Rudolf stayed on and farmed the land which was known as the "Farncombe farm" in the MacNutt/Castleavery district. On October 29,

Wedding of Rudolph Nerbas and Louise Schaan October 29, 1934.

1934, Rudolf and I (Louise Schaan) were married and on July 16, 1936, our son, Roderick, was born. We farmed on the Farncombe farm until the fall of 1940 when we moved to the Blackstone district in Grandview. Our daughter Carol, was born February 13, 1945, in the Grandview Hospital.

I recall that gypsies camped east of the farm on the prairie and peddled their wares. We bought a wicker clothes basket from them which I still have and use occasionally.

Wicker clothes basket made by the Gypsies.

When Roderick was a young baby, I would take him with me once, and sometimes twice a week, to MacNutt in a one-horse buggy to sell cream, while Rudolf was busy working in the field.

We raised pigs, cows, horses, chickens and turkeys, grew our own food, and made our living off the land.

Neighbors of ours were Sam and Fred Moskalyk, Jim Shearers, Hunters, Dugans, Fred Schaans, John Wagners, Art Rowans, Jim Christies, the Comforts, Johnny Shearer and his two sisters.

During the time we lived on the Farncombe farm, Rudolf's brother, Frank, lived with us off and on until 1940, and until 1944 with us in Grandview. Elizabeth Puritch (now Nykyforak, of Roblin) also worked for us for awhile. A midwife delivered Roderick at home on the farm and the one time I needed to be hospitalized, the doctor came from Roblin by snowplane and I had to be taken to the Roblin Hospital.

Rudolf passed away March 29, 1974, at the age of 64. I still live in Grandview and have just celebrated my 82nd birthday. Our son, Roderick, is married and he and his wife, Dianne, have two sons, Scott and Michael. Roderick is a retired teacher and lives in Selkirk, MB with his family. Our daughter, Carol, is married to Wayne Densmore (also a retired teacher) and they live in Roblin, MB.

Memories-The Sadie Nerbas Story

by Sadie Nerbas

Sadie and Rudy Nerbas.

Rudy and I, and our son Vernon, came to the Grainsby District in 1944. We lived on Rudy's father's farm 1-1/2 miles from Grainsby School. We were both raised on a farm so we were familiar with farm work and the chores such as hauling water, picking stones and chopping wood. We had very good neighbours and got to know a lot of new friends.

Rudy Nerbas getting ready for the field.

Sharon, Vernon, and Gene Nerbas in go-cart.

In 1945 our daughter, Sharon, was born. In 1949 we had our second son, Gene. Both Vernon and Sharon went to school at Grainsby for a short time. We farmed there for seven years and then moved to Shellmouth and lived and farmed there for 21 years. We added 3 more sons to our family, Kelvin, Ivan and Armin.

All of our children have married. Vernon and his wife live in Langley, BC. Vernon is a hydraulic technician. They have 3 children and 3 grandchildren. Sharon and her husband farm north of Langenburg. They have 4 children and 2 grandchildren. Gene and his wife farm at Shellmouth with his brother Kelvin and his family. Gene has 3 children and Kelvin had 4 children. Ivan and his wife live in William's Lake, BC with their 2 boys. Armin and his wife have 3 girls and live in Sardis, BC.

In 1973 we moved to Chilliwack, BC where Rudy worked for the District of Chilliwack for 12 years. We have since retired and remain in Chilliwack.

Memories of My Time in Grainsby District

by Vernon Nerbas

I came to Grainsby as an infant with my parents and lived there until I was 8. I took grade one and part of the second grade in the Grainsby School before moving to Shellmouth. My first grade fellow students were Larry and Lorraine Kruger, Dennis Seeback, Earla Morrison and Verna Piwniuk.

The things I remember from that time: How deep the snow was. At the Grainsby school we dug a tunnel across the road with the "big" boys, Freddie Piwniuk, Frankie Petz and Ronnie Kruger.

The time George Petz put his Austin panel van on a hayrack and brought it to the main road with a team of horses.

Walking to school with the Kruger, Seaback, Petz, and Piwniuk kids or all of the kids piling onto Freddie's two-wheeled horse cart.

How Dennis Seeback and I would go to the yard fences and yell at each other across the field because we had no telephone.

Going from Grainsby School to the Dropmore Hall for the Christmas concert practices in vans and going to dances in the Dropmore Hall with my parents and later on as a teenager.

I am married to Karen and we have 3 children and 3 grandchildren. I worked at IMC in Esterhazy for 13 years and then moved to Chilliwack, BC and presently live in Langley, BC. I have my own hydraulic installation business.

The Bill Nerbus Story

by Bill Nerbus

My Grandma and Grandpa Nerbas, Philip and Margaret, arrived from Austria in the late 1800's (to the best of my knowledge) and settled in Saskatchewan, half way between MacNutt and Langenberg, SK. Their family consisted of eight boys and six girls.

August Nerbas had a homestead in that part of the country and married Margaret Kitch in 1913. My mother's parents, Adolph and Margaret Kitch, also came form Austria. My mother and father had nine sons: enough for a baseball team. Bill Nerbus:

Born on the farm. My family consists of three daughters - Geraldine, Terry and Ivy, and one son Shawn. The daughters all live in and around Vancouver and my son lives on Vancouver Island. I have fourteen grandchildren and eleven great-grandchildren.

Henry, August and Rudy Nerbas.

Henry Nerbus:
Born on the farm. His family consists of one son and two daughters, grandchildren and great-grandchildren. Henry was killed in a train/truck accident in 1947.

Art Nerbus:
Born on the farm. He had one son and one daughter. He has grandchildren and great-grandchildren and lives in Osoyoos, BC.

Art Nerbas and Rudy Nerbas.

Rudy Nerbas:
Lives in Chilliwack, BC and has five sons and one daughter, grandchildren and great-grandchildren.

Rupert Nerbas:
Lives in Sicamous, BC. He had three daughters and one son, grandchildren and great-grandchildren.

Merv Nerbus:
Lives in Vancouver and had one son and one daughter, grandchildren.

Wilbert Nerbus:
Lives in Kelowna and had one son.

Harvey Nerbas:
Lives in Winnipeg, MB. He had three daughters and grandchildren.

Vernon Nerbas:
Passed away in infancy.

My dad bought a place one mile south of Grainsby School where Rudy was born. My dad then sold out and moved back to Saskatchewan near MacNutt where Rupert, Merv and Wilbert were

The Nerbas Brothers - (Back row L-R) Bill, Merv, Harvey, Art (Front row L-R) Rupert, Rudy, Wilbert in 1981).

born. We then moved back to Dropmore, MB, the old Bradley-Hunt place where Harvey and Vernon were born.

My mother passed away in 1934 and we moved back to the old Dunne place, one mile south of Grainsby School where I started school along with Henry and Art. My other brothers went to school in Saskatewan and Dropmore, MB.

I left that part of the country in 1938 and moved to Flin Flon, MB for a short time when I left there and moved to Vancouver, BC, where I made my home until I retired and moved to Parksville, on Vancouver Island where camping and fishing is fantastic. My dad passed away in July of 1944.

I went to school with Jessie, Lucy and Mary Wardell, Archie MacPhaden, Wilbert, Ronnie Morrison and Jean Morrison, Konrad Koch, Bill and Lena Koch and Gus Koch, Albert Bieber, some of the Ferris family, my uncles and aunts, Frank, Margaret, Minnie and Laura Nerbas.

Those were the horse and buggy days and we attended the Lutheran Church.

If God is willing, we will be attending the Dropmore Homecoming but do not know how many of my children will be able to attend. I am looking forward to meeting everyone once again.

History of the Nichols Family

by Cliff Nichols

William Henry and Louise Nichols immigrated from Michigan, USA to Roblin, MB in 1908. In 1909, William and Louise moved to the Castleavery district, having obtained homestead rights to the north west quarter of Section 21-24-29. Jim Nichols resided with William and Louise for a few years before returning to the USA.

Nichol's old house.

In 1919, their son Arthur married Margaret Shearer. This was the start of the second generation of Nichols to live in the district. Arthur and Margaret (Aunt Maggie) were blessed with six children who are still living. In 1968, Arthur and Maggie moved to Roblin and in 1969, celebrated their fiftieth wedding anniversary. Arthur passed away in February, 1977 and Maggie in February, 1987.

Maggie Nichols and family.(L-R) Dorothy (Dot) Talbot, Cliff Nichols, Arthur Jr. Nichols, John (Jack) Nichols, Robert (Pat) Nichols, Margaret (Marge) Gerrard.

The eldest child, Dorothy (Dot) was born in 1920. Dorothy married Edward (Red) Talbot. Dot spent her working years in the food services business as an employee, manager and restaurant owner. She is now retired and continues to reside in Regina, SK. Red passed away in 1981. Their daughter, Arva and husband, Glen Traynor reside in Lethbridge, Alberta. Glen is a pilot for Time Air and Arva is self employed as a Realtor and computer consultant. They have two very busy children, Michael and Erica. Their son Donald is married and resides in Calgary, AB. Don, like his father, is employed in the construction business and Donna, his wife, is employed by the Toronto Dominion Bank as an executive secretary. They have two children, William (Billy) and Kelley.

John (Jack), the eldest son was born in 1923. Jack served in the Canadian Army, returning from overseas in 1946. Jack has remained on the family farm which grew considerably since 1909, in both acreage and livestock production. Jack, along with his brother Arthur (Junior), continue to farm a considerable acreage.

Robert (Pat) was born on March 17, 1927. Pat and his wife Marlene (nee Kendal), have one son Brian, born November 6, 1975. Pat and Marlene also reside on the family farm. Unfortunately, Brian is the only child from the third generation to continue the family name.

Arthur Nichols, Junior, was born on June 15, 1928. In addition to being involved with the community and also the Roblin and District Hospital Board, Junior is kept busy operating the family farm.

The youngest son, Clifford (Cliff), born in 1934, married Ruth Matchett in 1962. Both Ruth and Cliff spent their working years in education until they retired in June, 1994. They continue to live in The Pas but are in the process of looking for a warmer climate. The eldest of their three daughters graduated from the University of Manitoba and is presently employed as a real estate appraiser. Her husband Thorsten is a mechanical engineer employed by the local pulp mill. Their two younger daughters, Shelley and Lori will be graduating from the University of Manitoba in 1995.

The youngest of Arthur and Maggie's children, Margaret (Marge) is married and resides in Winnipeg. Marge was once in the teaching profession but has been employed as a librarian by the University of Winnipeg for many years. Her husband, Garry Gerrard in employed in the electronics (radar) industry. Marge and Garry have two sons. David, stationed is Comox, BC. Brian and his wife Karyn reside in Yorkton, SK. Brian has an agricultural degree and is employed by a major chemical company. Brian and Karen have two children, Karli and Parker.

Maggie Nichols, grandchildren and great grandchildren.

The local outdoor skating rink and the curling rink for the District of Castleavery, were built on land belonging to Arthur Nichols, Sr. Thus, the Nichols home was often filled with skaters and curlers of all ages, coming and going. Aunt Maggie was truly an aunt to all the children in the neighborhood. People would often stop for water which was considered the best for many miles. This tradition of friendship and community involvement, has been continued by the third generation of Nichols, who continue to reside on the much expanded homestead of 1909.

The Nichols new home.

William Nielson
by Wilma Nielson

Wilma and Bill Nielson.

In August, 1955 the Nielson's arrived from Langruth, MB. Eldon was a year old, Linda nine, and Bill a grain buyer for Manitoba Pool. Since Langruth had been an extremely bustling community.

There were many apprehensions of loneliness, as the close ties with family and friends of their home community, would be lost by coming to a small community at Dropmore. They were hopeful for the future as the two elevators and new school looked promising. Dropmore had a store, church, hall, curling rink, municipal office, post office and a station providing the basic essentials of any community. The beautiful valley with all-weather roads, hunting and fishing was attractive. When Walter Rawlings unloaded a girl's bike, Linda knew she had at least one close friend to play with, as Betty had a bike too. Needless to say, many country drives were taken.

A special memory of the humorous side, was when Eldon went fishing at Reg Lewis'. Eldon was about 4 years old. One day Eldon caught his first fish down by the river. When he went about town showing it off, Reg Lewis said, "There is only one thing wrong with your fish. The head is too close to the tail." It was a frog.

Hermann enjoyed his start of teaching at Dropmore, recalling the excitement of Dropmore Christmas Concerts with a dance to follow in the community hall. I remember the barrel stove when it got red hot. Taking the school children to a Friday afternoon curling game with Jack Kruger who the caretaker, is remembered. The preparation for the Field Day at Inglis was an exciting way to enjoy the coming summer. While at home Linda taught Sunday School and also sang for several weddings.

On July 30, 1966, Herman and Linda were married at Inglis with the reception at the Roblin Community Hall. The Dropmore community was in full attendance.

The Bill and Wilma Nielson Family.

Bill and Wilma's grandchildren.

In early January, 1970 the Nielsons were transferred to Swan Lake. At a farewell party and dance held at the Dropmore Hall, the many feelings of apprehension felt in first moving to the community, were unequalled by the fond memories and loss of community spirit when leaving. We had worked closely with the community. Bill belonged to the Inglis Legion, Dropmore Board of Trade, and the Curling Club. Wilma retained her Ladies Auxiliary to the Legion at Langruth now at Cypress River, also with Dropmore United Church Club and Ladies Curling Club. Also took part in all local activities. The Nielsons and Wagners have rekindled their attachment to community ties on an annual return trip. The "Glory Years" of living in Dropmore will always hold our fondest memories.

We will be returning to the homecoming with Linda and Hermann and their daughter Lindsay Wagner, Eldon and Connie with their three children Crystal, Riley and Chelsea Nielson.

Fredrick and Flo Parmentier

by Marilyn Liske

Fred and Flo Parmentier Wedding December 9, 1950.

Fred Parmentier immigrated to Asessippi from Guernsey in the Channel Islands in 1917 at the age of 12. He arrived in Inglis at the train station on December 24, 1917 late in the evening. He was met by his Uncle Dan Martel. The five mile trip to Dan's home was made in an open cutter. It was -40 degrees below zero. Fred was dressed in his school uniform from Guernsey, which was shorts, knee high socks, and light jacket. Needless to say it was one of the coldest trips he ever made from Inglis to his home. Fred's mother had made arrangements with her brother, Dan, for Fred to come to Canada to live and work with him, as there was a large family, Fred being the oldest boy. So the next morning December 25, Christmas morning Fred was taken out and shown how to do the chores. Fred lived and worked with his uncle until his uncle's death in August

1946. Of his uncle, Fred said, "He was a good man, kind, but very firm." He loved and respected his uncle.

After his uncle's death, Fred lived alone for several years. On December 9, 1950, Fred married Flo Hammond, daughter of Robert and Maggie Hammond, of the Rochedale District. She was born August 19, 1915. They continued to live on the same farm which had expanded to 1760 acres. The cattle herd numbered 150 head. Fred had many different fellows work as farm hands over the years. After their marriage, Flo's brother, Forrest Hammond, came to live with them and help with the farm labor.

Both Fred and Flo were active members of the United Church. They both belonged to the choir, taught Sunday School and helped in any way they could. As lay minister of the United Church, Fred conducted many of the church services in Inglis, Dropmore, and Shellmouth churches. Flo was a member of the U.C.W. and the W.I. Fred held many different positions on the church council. Flo was also a member of the Rochedale Women's Group. Flo always had a large garden, milked cows, raised chickens and pigs. She was a great cook and prepared many large meals for wood cutting crews and threshing gangs. She made her own bread and churned her own butter. As a child, I remember sitting with a little jar, shaking the cream to make butter. There was no running water in the house. All the drinking water was hauled from the well, which was at the top of a steep hill. Snow was melted to get water to do the washing and laundry.

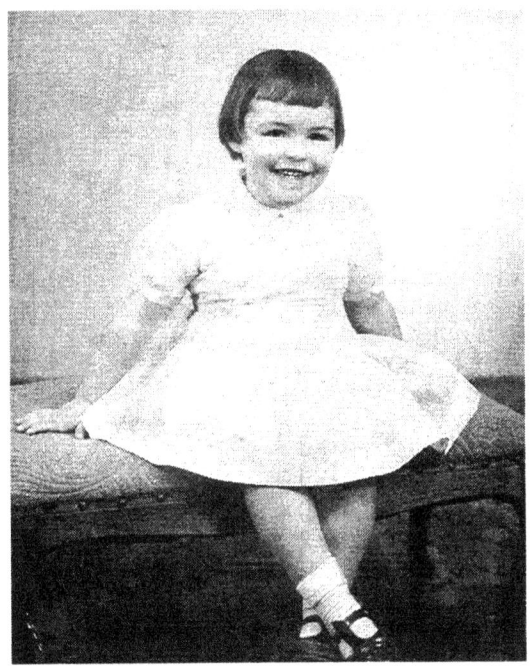

Marilyn Parmentier.

Fred loved to sing. He entertained at many concerts, harvest homes, weddings and funerals.

Fred and Flo were blest with one child, a daughter, Marilyn Mae, born September 17, 1954. Unfortunately, their happy family life was short lived. In 1960 Flo was diagnosed with cancer. After a courageous battle she passed away on February 6, 1963. Fred was a devoted husband and father. Fred cared for her and his young daughter plus all the farm work, with Forrest's help. The last three months of Flo's illness were spent in a hospital bed and at home. Fred never went to bed during those months. He spent the nights, after a long days work by his wife's side. He only slept a few winks when her pain was eased enough that she dozed off. Several other relatives came and helped out when they could. After Flo's passing, Fred continued to farm and look after his wee daughter. He was a wonderful father and did everything possible to make a happy home for the two of them.

Fred loved to travel and passed this on to his daughter. In June 1963, Marilyn and Fred visited his native Guernsey to reunite with his family whom he had not seen since the 1940's.

In the early 1960's the government decided there was a need to construct the Shellmouth Dam to help relieve the people of Brandon, Portage and Winnipeg from severe flooding which occurred in spring. With this many changes came to the area, many lost not only their land, but also their homes. As the government set about buying up land from the farmers for the dam, Fred was not spared. The government purchased approximately 700 acres of prime hay and pasture land for the creation of Shellmouth Dam and Asessippi Provincial Park from Fred. The farming operation changed at this point from mixed farming to strictly grain operation. Over the years, Fred won many awards for his crops of barley and flax. One year he won 9th place at the Royal Canadian Winter Fair for his sample of flax. That sample had to be all hand-picked, examining each kernel separately.

Fred's love of travelling took him to numerous destinations across Canada and the United States. As well as China, Japan, Australia, New Zealand, South America, and England. He always returned to Asessippi and he'd say, "There is no place more beautiful than right here in this peaceful valley". Fred loved people. No matter where he went, he'd always make friends. His generous gentle nature and twinkling blue eyes drew people to him. He was a hard working person, but he always had time to lend a helping hand. One observation he made was that people, no matter what color their skin, what language they spoke, rich or poor, are all the same. "They are all God's children." Fred sponsored several foster children through Foster Parent's Plan. He had the privilege of meeting some of them on his travels. He experienced first hand the handing over of his support cheques directly to the child and its family. In China he was actually able to hand pick a foster child and accompanied the Foster Parent's Plan worker to the little boy's tar paper shanty. He watched the faces of the little one and his family light up as they were told that Fred was to be their child's foster parent.

In December of 1973, Fred left his peaceful valley in Canada and made the trek once again to his beloved Guernsey and his family. He spent two months with them. On February 14, one of his sister's birthday, he gathered some forty-one relatives together at a restaurant for a meal. During the meal, Fred moved from table to table visiting each one. Little did they know that would be their final visit. On February 20th, in the church Fred had attended as a child, while he was speaking to an audience about his many travels, his Lord called him home. Fred's final trip was the air flight back to Canada and the Asessippi Cemetery over looking his peaceful valley, where he had grown up, lived, worked and prospered.

Marilyn (Parmentier) Liske

by Marilyn Liske

Marilyn Parmentier, the only daughter of Fred and Flo (Hammond) Parmentier, was born on September 17, 1954. Marilyn attended the Rochedale school from grade 1 to the end of grade 7 in 1967. At that time our school closed because of the amalgamation of the country schools. Grade 8 and 9, I attended Inglis Elementary and Junior High schools. My high school education was taken at Major Pratt School in Russell.

Because my Mom became ill when I was six years old in 1960 and passed away in 1963 when I was eight, I spent much time in the homes of kind neighbours. Some of these families were Mr. and Mrs. Skinner, Mr. and Mrs. McNeil, Mr. and Mrs. Pete Galatiuk, Mrs. Elsie Zetaruik, and Mr. and Mrs. Bill Fisher to name a few. These people opened their homes and their lives to me, for which I am grateful.

During my youth I was a member of the Assiniboine Sonnets 4-H club in Dropmore. I belonged to the Explorers group and Inglis United Church Youth Group. I attended Sunday School and belonged to the church choir. I was able to take up skating and swimming lessons. Some of my summers were spent at church camp at Clear Lake.

In February 1971 I met the man I was to marry, Larry Liske, son of Lily and Adolph Liske, of the Freefield District. In June of 1972, I graduated from grade twelve. On December 9, 1972 Larry and I were married in Inglis United Church, twenty-two years to the day of my mother and father's wedding. Larry and I resided on Larry's farm six miles east and one mile north of Inglis. Larry had purchased the farm from his mother after his father's death in June of 1970. On February 20, 1974, my father, Fred Parmentier, passed away. That summer Larry and I started farming my father's land as well as Larry's farm. Today we still operate both farms, being a mixed farming operation. However, we moved to the Parmentier home in November, 1975 on the NW quarter of 4-23-28 in Shellmouth municipality, near the old Asessippi town site. We still reside in the house my great Uncle Dan Martel built there in 1915.

Larry spent five winters working in the Thompson mines in the late 1960's and early 1970's, three winters at the 1400 foot level and, two winters at the 2200 level, voming home to farm, in the summer.

In one way or another, Larry and I have been employees of Pelly Trail S.D.#37 for most of our twenty-two years together. Larry was a school bus driver, with a perfect driving record, for seven years. I was secretary/paraprofessional at Inglis Elementary and Junior High for three and half years. Larry was trustee for Ward 1 for six years. For the past seven years, Larry and I, along with our two children, have been the custodians of the Inglis School.

Our family was made complete with the blessed gifts from God of two healthy happy children, Shawnovan Lawrence arrived on September 22, 1977 and Jodine Nicole on January 5, 1979.

Larry and I, and our children have been a very active family. We attend Trinity Lutheran Church in Inglis. The children attended Sunday School and youth group. I taught Sunday School and am presently a youth leader. Larry served two, three year terms as elder and has recently taken on the position for another three years. Jodine and I sing in the choir. Shawn has taken part in services from time to time and is an usher.

4-H was a big part of our lives for years. Each of the children and myself received our five year membership certificates. Shawn was always in the Woodworking projects and it helped influence him in the career he is pursuing. Jodine took a wide variety of projects, but the baby-sitting course is the one which influenced her the most. She has been a busy baby-sitter since she turned 12. I was assistant head leader for three years, and taught different project groups.

Larry, Marilyn, Shaun and Jodine Liske.

The children both took skating, swimming, and music lessons as well as various other activities.

Larry has been a volunteer fireman with the Inglis Fire Dept. since August 1, 1984. He was on the Inglis Skating Rink committee and the Inglis Beach committee for a number of years.

I served as vice president and president of the Inglis Figure Skating Club for several years.

Shawn will graduate from grade twelve in June of this year. He will be attending ACC in Brandon this fall in the Carpentry/Woodworking. Jodine is presently in grade 10 at Major Pratt School in Russell.

On April 15, 1987 after several years of bad luck in the way of drought, losing half our calf crop to scours, huge vet bills, and several very expensive repair bills, we found it necessary to make a very hard decision. We had a farm sale, selling the machinery, the purebred and the commercial cattleherd. By doing this and renting out the land for several years, we were able to save the land. Larry went to work for Earl Jackson & Sons. Marilyn went to work at Saan's in Roblin. After three years, Larry was able to start working the land by renting equipment and working with Jacksons. At this point in time, Larry is back farming the land. He still works at the Jackson's. Marilyn and Larry and our children caretake the Inglis School.

Larry's hobbies are hunting, fishing, ski-dooing. Marilyn enjoys cooking, sewing, and knitting. Our family enjoys camping and fishing trips. We have led a busy and fulfilled life.

Richard and Sylvia Peats

by Sylvia Peats

Richard, Eric, Tim, Sylvia, Trina, Colby & Bryce.

On October 14, 1977 the Peats' family moved from Roblin to the west 1/2 -27-23-29 the former George Rowan farm.

Richard (1947), Sylvia (1946), Trina (1969) and Eric(1972). Richard worked for Wellings Construction and then on the oil fields in Alberta for the winter months so he could farm during the summer. The children graduated from Roblin Goose Lake High School.

Trina went on to college in Brandon taking Business Accounting and found a job at an accounting firm in Winnipeg. In 1992 Trina married Tim Hoeppner from Winnipeg. They have a daughter Colby Chantel born May 16, 1992 and a son Bryce Bradley June 4, 1994.

Eric is working with Danton Construction out of Redwater, AB. In the fall of 1994 Richard, Sylvia and Eric moved to Redwater, AB.

George and Anne Petz Family

George was the eldest of fourteen children born to Alex and Rose Petz. His father, Alex was born March 3, 1893 in Drachintsi, Cheronetz in the Russian Ukraine. In 1900 he moved with his parents, George and Kerri Petz to the MacNutt area in SK. His mother, Rose was born in Austria on October 16, 1900. At age eleven she moved with her parents to Calder, SK. Alex and Rose were married June 27, 1918 in Calder. Their son George was born July 19, 1920. In 1923 they moved to the Tummelll area in Manitoba. From Tummell, his parents moved to the Rochedale District and then to Shellmouth. Rose passed away in May 1969 and Alex in July 1976.

George attended Tummell School and then he worked at Skinner's Nursery until he was called to serve in the army. During the Second World War, he served in Italy, France and North Africa. He returned to Canada in the Fall of 1945. On January 12, 1946 he married Anne Piwniuk and they farmed in the Grainsby area. Anne was the daughter of Mike and Teenie Piwniuk. She was born on December 25, 1923. Anne attended Grainsby School and worked at home until she got married. They farmed in the Grainsby area until 1965 at which time they moved to Dropmore. George was the Postmaster in Dropmore until his death. George also drove the feeder bus for the Intermountain School Division for many years. George and Anne also opened up a convenience store in Dropmore for a number of years.

George passed away May 31, 1978. Anne continued to operate the Post office until she retired in 1992. She now lives at the Maple Manor in Roblin.

George and Anne had six children: Frank, Phyllis, Nancy, Gary, Brenda and Angela.

Frank George Petz
Frank was born on March 19, 1942. He attended Dropmore School for grades one, two and three. Grainsby school opened so he finished the remainder of his schooling there.

In 1959 he left home to go to work in Regina. There he met Darlene M. Klatt and they were married June 29, 1963. Darlene was born May 11, 1942.

In June of 1966 they moved from Regina to Langenburg, SK. They both worked at International Minerals and Chemical Corp., a potash plant in Esterhazy, SK.

Danica Wyss.

On October 11, 1971 they were blessed with a daughter "Carmen Lee". Carmen completed her education in Langenburg. She then took four years of university in Saskatoon and got her degree in Biology, and has a job with a firm there. Carmen married Dale Johnson July 23, 1994 and they reside in Saskatoon.

Darlene passed away on March 29, 1994 with a brain tumor. Frank still is employed at I.M.C. and lives in Langenburg.

Phyllis Petz
Phyllis was born on November 1, 1946. She married Wayne Digby and they have two children, Shauna and Todd. Phyllis and Wayne live in Brandon. Phyllis works for the Brandon School Division (See Wayne Digby History for more details).

Nancy Petz
Nancy came into this world on May 16, 1951 at home in the Grainsby District. She attended Grainsby, Dropmore and Roblin Collegiate Schools. After graduating in 1969, she went to work at the University of Manitoba Animal Science Department, until she married.

She was married September 4, 1971 to Gerald Adam of MacNutt. Their marriage was blessed with three daughters and a son. Nicole,

The family of George and Anne Petz.

born February 15, 1972, is working as a chemical technician with Agriculture Canada in Lacombe, AB. Nadine, born January 14, 1974, is in her third year of Business Administration at the University of Regina. Garett, born January 1, 1979 is in grade 10 at Langenburg High School. Their children first attended MacNutt school until grade nine after which they went to Langenburg High School. Gerald and Nancy farm in the MacNutt area.

Gary Petz

Gary was born on September 16, 1952. He attended Dropmore and Roblin Schools. After graduating from Roblin Collegiate in 1971, Gary attended Red River Community College in Winnipeg and received a diploma in Business Administration.

After working a brief time in Winnipeg, he accepted an accounting position at International Minerals and Chemicals in Esterhazy, SK. Gary met and married his wife Nicole on June 29, 1974. Nicole was born in Ste. Rose on August 27, 1954. They were blessed with a daughter Colette, born January 6, 1976 and a son Dion, born January 2, 1979. Colette attended Rivier Academy in Prince Albert, SK for grades 10, 11, and 12. She is finishing her first year of University at Waterloo, ON. Dion is in grade 10 at Major Pratt in Russell.

In 1988, after years of study, Gary graduated as a CMA (Certified Management Accountant) and continues to work at IMC. They reside in Russell where Gary spends most of his spare time managing Dion's hockey team.

Brenda Petz

Brenda was born March 7, 1957. She attended school at Dropmore until 1968 when it closed. She completed elementary and high school at Roblin. She married Brad Robin of Rochedale, July 26, 1975 where they farm today. They were blessed with a son, Kiley, born March 20, 1975 and a daughter, Kristy, born November 27, 1979. They both attended school at Inglis and then they transferred to Roblin in 1990. Kiley has enjoyed 4-H beef, Cubs and Scouts and is now member of Parkland Special Olympics. He graduates this year then he will be going to Brandon with Career Connections. Kristy is in Grade 9 at Goose Lake High in Roblin. She enjoys the Inglis 4-H beef Club and her piano. Brenda was part owner of a children's clothing store in Russell for five years and continues to work at the store under new management.

Angela Petz

Angela was born on December 28, 1957 in Russell. She attended school in Dropmore until

Grade 5, then went to Roblin Schools. After graduating in 1975 she went to Winnipeg to take Cosmetology at Red River Community College. Here first hairdressing job was in Yorkton, SK. for one year then moved to Brandon where she worked for two and half years. In 1979 she moved to Roblin and worked at Lee's Beauty Salon till she took over the business in 1985. She still runs Shear Creations and works part time.

On September 12, 1992 she married Peter Wyss. He was born May 30, 1960 in Bern, Switzerland. Peter moved to Roblin in 1982 and owns and operates Parkland Landscaping. They were blessed with a daughter, Danica Ann who was born November 12, 1993.

Mike and Teenie Piwniuk

by Piwniuk Family

Mike, Teenie and Fred Piwniuk.

Mike was born in the western Ukraine on May 6, 1895. At the age of 17 (in 1912) he came to Canada. Ending up in Roblin, MB.

He worked for the CNR for two years. During that time he met Teenie Boyanski and they were married on November 21, 1914 at St. Michael's Church which is 9 miles north of Roblin.

Their first homestead was in Merridale. By 1919 they moved to MacNutt, SK by horse and wagon. In 1922, they moved to the Marchwell district, where they rented a farm for seven years. In 1929, they bought their present farm from "Julius Peter", five miles southwest of Dropmore.

Mike and Teenie raised up seven children. Their names are Pete, Bill, Kay, Mary, Anne, Johnny, Joe, Steve, Fred, Julie, and Verna.

Sadly, Mike Piwniuk passed away in 1965 at the age of 70 years. His wife, Teenie passed away in 1984 at the age of 85 years. In either case, they left behind their children, grandchildren and great grandchildren.

Steve and Cathie Piwniuk

by Steve Piwniuk

My Mom (Teenie Boyanski) and Dad (Mike Piwniuk) moved onto the farm that my brother Fred now lives on (17-23-29) in 1929, the year I was born. Of course I don't remember that, but I do remember the first day I attended school in Grainsby (believe it or not). I think the reason I remember that is because I had a fight (skirmish) with Garner Bolton that day over the football. Usually children start school after the summer holidays. I started after Easter because my late Mother (bless her soul) said I was too much for her to handle being the only one home while the rest were in school. Besides, being sports-minded, I did enjoy learning and studying even though it was three miles to walk to the Grainsby school. Occasionally we got a ride. When I was ten years old on March 15th, early in the morning, my Mom showed me a little baby that was just born. Minutes later I found out "it" was a boy. We all thought he was really cute so we all agreed he should be named Freddie. I don't know how we connected a nice baby with the nice name "Freddie" however the rest is history now. Everything went fine except I was usually chosen to baby-sit. It wasn't too bad baby-sitting one, but then two more sisters arrived. In those days you didn't ask for a raise, you just did as you were told.

In those early days of my life, I remember we did a lot more socializing. Of course in the winter it was by horse drawn sleighs, like in a grain box or "cutter" or in a heated van. If a grain box was used, we used to put hay in first then cover with blankets or quilts. When guests arrived, their horses were always put in the barn and the host always made room, even if he had to let some of his cattle or horses outside. In most cases the visitations took place without an invitation. We either played cards, various games, told jokes or unbelievable horror stories. We also used to have many house dances with a live 2 piece band orchestra usually. In the summer months visitations were also made by some horse drawn type of 'buggy' like "Bennett Wagon" or "Democrat" or a regular farm wagon. As economic times improved, more and more people were able to afford a car or a Model T truck. However these were only used in the summer time as the roads were impassable in the winter time. My brother Joe and I made some money in the spring time or after a heavy rain, by pulling "stuck-in-the-mud" motorists with a team of horses. I recall a couple of guys (this was when they had a couple too many) getting stuck. They got out to see what their next move would be. When they looked at the back wheels they noticed they were in the mud almost up to the axle. They both agreed that the only way out was by getting a pull. When they got pulled out, they noticed one of their rear tires was missing. They never did find it. Only God knows how far they drove that way before getting stuck. The 'Black-bird Hill' was something else after a rain also. We used to have to take the lower road to Dropmore. This was the long way around but a sure way. Our neighbor, Sid Beach, had a Model-T truck. Quite often he took me with him, to Shellmouth for the ride. If his truck ran short of power up the Black-bird Hill he would glide the truck down, turn it around and back up the hill without any trouble. On one occasion when I was with him he got a rear flat tire just as we were topping the Black-bird Hill. He didn't stop till we got to the very top where he took the tire off the rim, threw it in the back saying, "I'll fix it when I get home." In those days the rims were so thick the stone, etc. didn't even dent them without the tire on. On another occasion, Sid Beach was with me in our buggy drawn by one horse called, "Scotty". I think I was about 9 or 10 years old then. As we came to go up the ravine hill I made him and myself get off and walk up because I felt sorry that little Scotty would have to pull us up this "steep" hill. Of course he had to tell my Dad about this and they both had a big laugh which I didn't think was funny at all. Harvesting season was the most enjoyable of all. Although it was hard work, everyone pitched in. Threshing time was most memorable. The long hours didn't deter on pulling a joke one another. As we took turns getting up early to feed the horses, someone changed the alarm to go off at 2:00 am instead of 5:00 am. This fellow whose turn it was, promptly got up, dressed and fed the horses. When he finished he wondered how come no one else was up yet. That's when he decided to check his watch. A favorite pastime was horse racing with the hay racks. My brother Joe and someone else were both sure one could beat the other through this single gate coming into our yard. As it turned out, they were both dead even. Needless to say this gate was made double the width it once was. Our socializing didn't diminish just because it was harvest time either. On more then one Monday I rushed Joe to the farmer whose crop was being threshed to be in time for breakfast and I went straight out to till our land at home. We slept good the following night.

After my school days at Grainsby I went to St. Vlad's College in Roblin and then to St. Joseph's college in Yorkton where I completed Grade XII. My summer holidays were used up working on a farm.

After high school, I took a bookkeeping course for one year in Winnipeg. I enjoyed office and bookkeeping work in Roblin, but my heart was in farming. During several years of farming we, (the younger folk) really had some enjoyable times. Practically every week-end we attended dance socials, car games (penny-anti poker) and anything else that we could afford. Halloween night was exceptionally exciting. (A whole book could be written on what happened on those nights - especially about the 'out houses'.) When I was still in grade school, us kids used to go to the Assiniboine River to swim just below Mr. Henry Dietrich's farm. In those days, none of us boys could afford swimming suits, but that didn't deter us from staying out of the water. On one of those sunny Sunday afternoons, a bunch of us in our birthday suits were surprized by about a dozen Dropmore school kids (boys and girls). Needless to say we all scrambled for our clothes to cover. All would have been OK if it hadn't been for two boys trying to get into the same pair of pants.

One of my most memorable events was my late sister Mary's wedding. Of course I remember all weddings that I attended, but this one stands out a little more than others. Maybe it was because it was a three day event. On that wedding day, in our yard, a total of nine gallons of whiskey was consumed and one keg of beer. The Ukrainian tradition in those days was to have a gathering the following Sunday for relatives and close friends who stayed sober during the wedding, to help with wedding chores. That following Sunday my Dad said we only drank seven gallons. I believe the crowd was a bit smaller.

One of the saddest moments in my life was the passing of my brother Johnny. Although all funerals are sad, especially if it's one of your family members, this one stands out much more so than others. Maybe it's because he was the first in the family to leave us; maybe it's because I was still quite young (18 years); or maybe because he was only 22 years old. Whatever the cause, I still vividly remember, even today, how horrible it was when he became unconscious on a Tuesday in our presence during lunch time and how sad I was to learn he passed away the following Sunday in a Winnipeg hospital.

As the years went by and although I enjoyed farming, I slowly but surely was realizing

Steve Piwniuk about 1945..

that farming was not for me. I felt that if I was going to succeed in anything, it wouldn't be in farming. I truly hated even the thoughts of leaving but I knew down deep I had no other choice. On July 7th, 1956 I hopped on a Greyhound bus and headed for BC with two hundred dollars in my pocket. I headed for Kelowna where I knew I had a cousin (and still do), I began job hunting. My first five years were not satisfactory with the jobs I held, which were various. On June 30th, 1961 I got a job with the P.G.E. railway - now BC Rail. This was the first job I not only enjoyed but I also felt I had a future in. After four or five years I was promoted to a supervisory position which I held until my retirement on December 31, 1989.

The Steve Piwniuk Family.

I stayed single as long as I could (enjoying the freedom and all that goes with being single). I finally met a young lady, Cathie Tiley, in the spring of 1963 that changed my mind. On May 9th, 1964 we said our "I do's" in a Roblin church (where I once went to school) and the "Knot" was tied by a priest, Fr. Bzdel, with whom I went to school. (Fr. Bzdel has since been elevated to Archbishop now residing in Winnipeg.) For one reason or another the family doctor told my wife that having children was out of the question. We didn't hesitate to adopt a girl (Tina) and a boy (Jimmie) within the first three years of marriage, when lo and behold my wife got pregnant somehow and on May 16th, 1969 we received a beautiful daughter and named her Tara. Actually this all didn't occur without the help of pills, etc, etc., prescribed by a doctor. Oh well, we thought now that we have three, it'll have to do even though we planned for four children before we got married. Then after five years we were surprised with another child. On August 9th, 1974, Kevin was born and all our dreams were fulfilled. All our children are living in Prince George, BC. The two daughters are married and both boys are still single. We are grandparents to five children. I'd like to see them all more often than we do, but as I stated earlier, people do not socialize as much now as we once did.

Cathy, Ryan and Steve.

Bill Piwniuk

by Love Carefoot

Bill Piwniuk is the second child born to Mike and Teenie Piwniuk. Bill got married to Blanche Yaworksi. The couple moved to Kelowna, BC in 1956. Since then Bill died on May 3, 1977 and Blanche deceased on May 5, 1988.

The couple had 5 children:
Love married Gary Carefoot and they live in Coquitlam, BC. They have 2 sons, Darren and Brent.

Laura married Vic Tockar (deceased 1994). They lived in Kelowna, BC. They also had 2 children, Lee and Tracy.

Johnny lives in Kelowna, BC. He has a son named, Neil.

Shirley married Gord Omeis and they live in Kelowna, BC. They have a daughter, Stephanie and a son, Tyler.

David lives in Kelowna, BC and has a daughter.

Bobbi has a son named Bill.

Catherine (Kay Piwniuk) Carefoot

Catherine and Al Carefoot.

Catherine (Kay) is the third oldest child born to Mike and Teenie Piwniuk. Kay was married to Al Carefoot and they lived in Burnaby, BC. Kay is now deceased as of May 5, 1993.

Together, Kay and Al had 1 son named Lance. Lance is married to Cindy. They live in Calgary, AB. Lance and Cindy have two children, Leonard and Collinda.

Fred and Janet Piwniuk

by Janet Piwniuk

Fred was born to Mike and Teenie Piwniuk. He is also a younger brother to Steve Piwniuk.

Fred attended Grainsby and Dropmore Schools. After leaving school, he helped his father and brothers on the family farm (SE-17-23-29). He took over the family farm in 1960.

In 1962 he married Janet Thickett from Binscarth, MB.

Fred worked on construction from 1965 - 1971 at the I.M.C. mine in Esterhazy, SK. He also worked on the Shellmouth Dam, bridge and school construction.

Fred played in a band called, "The Parklanders" for a few years. He also attended parades all over with his team of horses.

In 1972 he started a dairy, which he maintained with the help of his sons. They continued to raise beef cattle and horses. Fred presently drives a school bus in the Roblin area.

Janet likes to attend to her gardening and working with the animals. At least once a year, Fred and Janet like to organize a trail ride with the use of their horses.

The Fred Piwniuk Family - (Back row L-R) Randy, Michelle, Doyle, Janet, Fred. (Front row L-R) Darren, Alice, Laurel, Kelly.

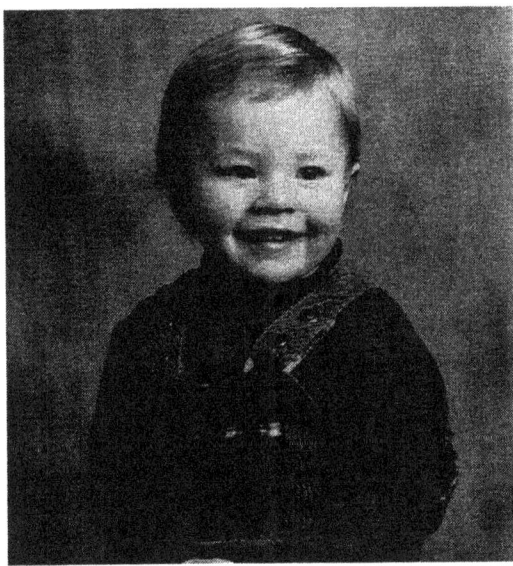
Brandon Piwniuk, son of Darren Piwniuk.

Together, Fred and Janet, have raised a family of four boys, the oldest being Darren who was born in 1963. Darren attended Goose Lake High School in Roblin and graduated in 1981. After graduating from high school he took an electrical course at Keewatin Community College in The Pas, MB. Darren has enjoyed playing hockey. He worked at Dee's Electric in Roblin for three years. he moved to Winnipeg and was employed at NorTec Electric and then onto Manitoba Hydro. He then left Manitoba Hydro in 1994 and is presently working for Allied Aluminum.

He is married to Alice Arnason. They were married in 1992 in Winnipeg. They have a son Brandon Dale who is now two years.

The second oldest is Kelly (see Kelly Piwniuk story for details).

Doyle was born in 1967. He graduated from Goose Lake High in 1985. He graduated from Red River Community College with an accounting degree. He went to work at Investor Group in Winnipeg. He worked for an insurance company in Winnipeg for two years. Then in 1994 he bought into his own insurance business in Virden, MB. In August of 1994, he married Michelle (Jerrard) in Winnipeg.

The youngest of the boys is Randy. He was born in 1976. He graduated from Goose lake High in 1994. He is presently taking a year off from schooling to assist on the family farm. In the fall of 1995, he is hoping to attend ACC in Brandon, MB.

Kelly and Laurel Piwniuk

by Laurel Piwniuk

The Wedding of Kelly and Laurel Piwniuk
August 14, 1993.

Kelly was born on March 25, 1966 to Fred and Janet Piwniuk in Russell, MB. He attended school in Roblin and graduated from Goose Lake High in 1984.

His first place of employment was at Asessippi Park as labor operator. In 1988 Kelly ventured from home for a few months to work in the mine in Snow Lake. He helps out on the family farm, and he has cattle of his own. He still works at Asessippi Park and he has been there now for eleven years.

Kelly married Laurel (Bell) on August 14, 1993 at the Holy Redeemer Church in Roblin, MB.

Kelly Piwniuk Family - Lindy and Blake.

Laurel was born in Regina, SK on June 2, 1971. Her family resided in the Roblin area later. She spent her childhood racing harness horses with her parents. Laurel stays home with their two children, Blake who is four years old and Lindy is one year old. Laurel enjoys it. She also likes gardening and helping out with community projects.

Kelly and Laurel have purchased their house in August of 1993. Their house is located in Dropmore where the old post office and general store used to be.

Robert and Jessie Pyott Family

by Jessie Shearer

The Pyott family emigrated from Perthshire, Scotland. The first members to arrive were brother and sister, William and Marjory in 1905. They worked for a relative, William Anderson, in the Clova district in Saskatchewan. Marjory married John Birnie in 1910. William took a homestead in the Lintlaw, SK area.

Back in Scotland, their father and mother, Robert and Jessie Pyott, were making arrangements to come to Canada with the remaining unattached members of their family, to farm the James Anderson land in the Clova District. This they did

Robert and Jessie Pyott

in 1914. Sister and brother, Margaret and Robert (Bob), came in the spring, and in the fall the senior Pyotts came with Charles and Winnifred.

In Scotland the oldest daughter, Jane, had married Robert Crerar and lived out her life there. Son, Alexander, was also married but moved to British Columbia a few years later. He died at a young age as a result of a logging accident. Another son, James, had joined the army and lost his life in the Great War. Charles served in both World Wars.

In 1918, the family moved to the Assiniboine Valley (SW 1/4 of 2-25-29) in the Shell River Municipality. The buildings were approximately one quarter mile east of where Pyott's Campground is now located.

Bob Pyott and family.

In 1930 the senior Pyotts, with Margaret, moved to Armstrong, BC. Winnifred had married John Hayhurst and moved to Vernon, BC sometime before 1930.

Bob married Agnes M. Case in 1930 and took over the farm. They had a family of four, Robert, Jessie, James and Marjorie. These, of course were the Depression years; however the children of this couple remember lovely, growing-up years with the Assiniboine River and Valley being their private playground - swimming as soon as it was warm, until Fall, skating in Winter, river banks for sliding, lovely hills for horseback riding and just plain adventure.

Raising black Angus cattle was the main source of income for the family. Haymaking took up most of the summer and fall. In those days, rather than auction-marts, we had cattle buyers. Those whom Dad dealt with, were Spigelman and Lichter, who either called at the farm and bought cattle, or shipped them on consignment. In the early years, the cattle to be shipped to Winnipeg were driven to the Roblin stockyards by men on horseback. Usually these cattle drives took place in the spring.

With the building of the dam at Shellmouth, land owners were forced to sell to the Government their land which was required for the reservoir. With all the hayland gone, cattle ranching was no longer possible and Mom and Dad reluctantly left the lovely valley and moved to Swan River in the spring of 1968. Dad passed away in June, 1974 and Mom in June 1981.

Bob and Agnes Pyott.

Robert Pyott had moved to The Pas in 1961 and passed away in 1932 as the result of a stroke.

Jessie married Murray Shearer and lives at Swan River, their family:

Kathryn worked for several years as a Civil Engineering Technologist for A.G. Pratt and

Associates, Engineering Consultants in Winnipeg until October 1994, when her husband John Charowsky, an Engineer with Reid Crowther was transferred to their office in Vancouver, BC. They now live on Mayne Island, one of the Gulf Islands.

Grant and his wife Dawne live on Vancouver Island. Grant is a mechanic at Nanaimo, searching for a business of his own. Dawne works with the Ministry of Finance, Revenue Division in Victoria.

David graduated from Red River College with a Diploma in Communications Engineering Technology and is a Network Administrator with the Consulting Firm INSI, in Winnipeg.

James (Jim) Pyott married Edith Davis and lives at Swan River. Their family:

Patrick is attending the University of Manitoba, completing his degree in Commerce.

Shelagh is attending the Brandon University, taking Education.

Marjorie married Lorne Jamieson and they live in Saskatoon, Saskatchewan. Their family:

Corinne has her Law Degree and is articling at her father's law firm.

Blair is completing his degree in Education at the University of Saskatoon.

Charles Pyott lives in a Nursing Home in Victoria. He will celebrate his 99th birthday in June 1995. He is in good health, still smoking his pipe, and determined to be around for the turn of the century.

Burnett and Annie Ralston

by Reta Draper

Annie Longden with her parents Mr. and Mrs. Joseph Longden.

Joseph and Mary Langden moved from MacGregor to Castleavery in 1902. They settled on a farm beside a small lake which was later known as Longden Lake. Joseph Longden was a butcher by trade. He also enjoyed fishing and hunting on the lake. Mrs. Longden was a lovely singer, trained in England. She helped support the family by being a midwife. Her suitcase was always packed ready to leave at a moment's notice. She was often paid for her services in bags of vegetables and meat.

Sadie Longden Rowan and her sister Annie Longden Ralston with their cousin Edith Snaith Rossiter.

The Longdens had four children, William Longden, Ella, (Mrs. Bert Ferriss) Sadie, (Mrs. Harry Rowan) and Annie (Mrs. Burnett Ralston).

Annie, their youngest daughter, left early each morning for school in Castleavery. She was responsible for sweeping the schoolroom and lighting the fire. As she walked along, alone, sometimes on snowshoes, she was often afraid. Her route to school took her past range cattle and distant howling wolves. It is interesting to note that for a time her sister Sadie (Miss Longden) was also her teacher.

Burnett Ralston married Annie Longden in 1918. He had met Annie Longden in 1918. He had met Annie at a dance when he was fifteen and she was twelve. They had never forgotten each other.

The Ralstons settled on a farm in Castleavery and had two children, Dorris and Orvis.

Castleavery School and pupils about 1912.

This is the house the Ralstons rented in Dropmore in about 1926. It is still there today.

Mr. and Mrs. Burnett Ralston, formerly Annie Longden.

After farming a few years, they moved to Dropmore and rented a house until Burnett built their home and barn. They had three more children in Dropmore, Murza, Ralph and Reta.

The family lived in Dropmore for eight yaears. Burnett farmed and did construction work, his brother Alex ran the blacksmith shop. Burnett and Annie joined in the life of the community and even played for some dances. Due to the drought and the depression, they moved to Swan River.

The Ralston family lived in Swan River for six years. These were very difficult years because of the Great Depression and the lack of work opportunities. Finally, Burnett left his family in Swan River and went to work in construction in Hamilton, Ontario.

In 1942, the family sold out and moved to New Westminster, B.C. They purchased a very small home with two lots. Burnett went to work in the Mohawk Lumber Mill. Each night, after working all day, he walked two miles home, carrying lumber on his back. At night he used that lumber to build a home on the extra lot. This home was sold and this was the beginning of his career in house construction. He built many homes in the area and some for the veterans after the war, under the V.L.A.. Veterans Land Act.

Dorris Ralston, the oldest child, married Hilton Bertram (1914-1983) in Flin Flon, Manitoba. Hilton worked in the mines and later joined the Canadian Army. He was promoted to the rank of a Sergeant and became an instructor in the Armoured Corps at Camp Borden, Ontario. After the war, Dorris and Hilton moved to Coquitlam, B.C. Hilton was a millwright and also worked in the plywood department in the Fraser Mills until his retirement.

Dorris was a section head in Woodward's Department Store and later worked part-time in Fields Department Store. She was, and is a faithful member of the Calvary Baptist Church.

The Bertrams had two children. Marilyn (1943 - 1962) was tragically killed in a car accident when she was eighteen. Blaine and his wife Patricia Badger own and operate Bertram Excavating Ltd. They live in Maple Ridge with their two adult children, Jarrod and Kari.

Orvis Ralston moved to Hamilton, Ontario when he was nineteen. He joined the Royal Canadian Navy, and later the Commandos. He served with distinction with the Allied Invasion

Forces in the Italian landing campaign and received a medal for his valor. After the war, he married Mildred Fife, a telephone operator in the B.C. Telephone Company. Orvis and Mil own and operate their own business, Ralston Excavating. They have three sons, Russell, Lyle and Brian, who also own and operate excavating companies.

Russell Ralston lives in Coquitlam with his wife, the former Barbara Bewley, and his two children, Jason and Jenna. Ryan (1977-1992) their oldest child was tragically killed in an accident when he was fourteen.

Lyle Ralston married Kathy Waslewsky and lives in Matsqui with his two sons, Daniel and Jonathan. Lyle completed his B.A. in psychology and is planning a career in Massage Therapy.

Brian Ralston and his wife Dorothy Bristow live in Mission. Along with their bulldozing business, they have interest in the movie industry in Vancouver, B.C.

Murza Ralston (1929-1992) was a telephone operator and supervisor for the B.C. Telephone Co. Later, she and her husband, Gordon Millhouse (1932-1984) owned and managed a construction company. Murza managed the office and did the interior decorating for the various apartment complexes. After her husband's passing, and before her untimely death at age sixty-three, she worked for Canada Mortgage and Housing Company and was very active in her church.

Ralph Ralston completed his Bachelor of Education and his Master of Education degrees. He taught high school in Trail and Vancouver and later became a supervisor for the Vancouver School Board. He married his high school sweetheart, Marion Smith. Dr. Marion Ralston was a teacher, a Professor of Education at the University of British Columbia and an international speaker. After retirement, Ralph opened a boat building company called Seair Marine.

Reta Ralston completed her Bachelor of Education degree and taught elementary school for thirty-six years. She married Richard (Dick) Draper, a high school teacher who advanced to be an Administrative Officer in the Richmond High Schools. After retirement, Reta and Dick enjoyed the good life, trailering and cruising.

On a personal note: British Columbia was a very good move for our parents; they never looked back. When our father (Burnett Ralston) stopped working, we would ask him, "Should we tell people you are retired?"

He always answered, "No, just say I am too tired."

Although our mother (Annie Ralston who preferred to be known as Mary Ann) never really worked outside the home, she was a pillar of strength to our father and the Rock of Gibraltar to her family.

The Ralston Family - (Back row L-R) Murza Millhouse, Reta Draper, Orvis Ralston, Dorris Bertram, Ralph Ralston. (Seated) Mr. and Mrs. Burnett Ralston upon the occasion of their 60th Wedding Anniversary.

George Walter and Fanny May Rawlings Family

by Sherry Rawlings-Koroway

George was born May 28, 1874 in Somerset, England. He came to Canada to Strathclair, MB, in the late 1890's.

He met and married Fanny May Wilson. She was born on July 11, 1884 and they were married on Dec. 25, 1901 in Newdale, MB.

Their first home was in Rossland, BC. George worked in a gold mine. Fanny had poor health so they moved back to Strathclair. During the spring of 1905 they came north to the Municipality of Shell River and took up homestead in the Grainsby District.

Their social life consisted of playing cards, dancing and house parties. The nearest town was Shellmouth. They attended the United Church which was held in homes or the school house.

George and May Rawlings December 25, 1901.

After a few years they moved to a farm near MacNutt, SK. They farmed there for quite a few years.

In 1916 they returned to the farm of Mr. John Bernie. In 1920 they moved to a farm one mile west of the village of Dropmore. George passed away Jan. 15, 1927 at 52 years.

Fanny and family moved into Dropmore in the late 1920's. She kept boarders and the student ministers for a number of years.

Walter Melville born Nov. 9, 1902, served in World War II for four years. He married Elizabeth Hunt on Jan. 26, 1946. He worked for Imperial Oil for fifty years. They had one daughter, Elizabeth Ann (Betty) born Apr. 20, 1947. She married Dean Johnson on July 1, 1972. Betty and Dean have three children: Robyn, Wendy and Dale. They live in Chilliwack, BC. Walter passed away Oct. 3, 1983 and Elizabeth passed away Jan. 11, 1984.

Lillian Edna born Feb. 13, 1905 married Bertram Hunt on Feb. 3, 1925. They moved to Vancouver, BC and the USA for awhile and then came back to Grainsby District to farm for a number of years. They retired in Dropmore. Bertram passed away Nov. 29, 1976 and Lillian passed away July 22, 1985.

Beatrice Matilda born Mar. 24, 1908 married Roger Cameron on Nov. 16, 1932. They farmed in the Rochedale District for three years. They moved to the Grainsby District and then to the village of Dropmore. They had three sons; Roger, Burke and Garry. Roger Blake born Sept. 5, 1933, married Shirley Williams Aug. 27, 1957. They have two daughters: Cheryl and Marie. Cheryl married Len Bennett and they have a daughter, Shannon and live in Saskatoon, SK. Marie married Greg Thomas and they have a son, Benjamin, and a daughter, Nysa, and live in Winnipeg. Roger and Shirley also live in Winnipeg.

Walter Burke born Oct. 1, 1934, married Delores Sanders on July 20, 1956. They have two children, Curtis and Corinne. Curtis married Lillian and they live in Smithers, BC. Corinne married Robert McLellan. They have a daughter Jasmine and two sons Daman and Quaya, and live in Coal Lake, BC. Burke and Delores live in Comox, BC.

Garry Dennis born Oct. 10, 1937, married Thelma Yerma on Sept. 10, 1955. They have five daughters: Beatrice, Debbie, Beverly, Patricia and Maureen. Beatrice married Gerrard Devenny. They have a son Cameron and a daughter Kelly. They live in Biggar, SK. Debbie married Doug Goldstrand. They have a daughter Bobbi-Jo and a son Garry and live in The Pas. Beverly married Mark Marin and they have two daughters, Nicole and Renee and they live in The Pas. Patricia married Jim Kerwin and they have a daughter, Giselle and two sons, Patrick and Clinton and they live in Warren, MB. Maureen lives in Kelowna, BC. Garry and Thelma live in The Pas. Roger passed away Dec. 31, 1971. Beatrice moved to Roblin in 1992.

Gladys May born Sept. 30, 1911 married William Craig Sept. 22, 1934. They had a son William Roy born Mar. 14, 1935. He married Doris Edwards Nov. 3, 1962. They have three children: Valarie, Kevin and Colyn. Valarie lives in Vancouver, BC. Kevin married Allison Shearer and they live in Shoal Lake, MB. Colyn lives in Alberta. Roy lives in Roblin. Doris passed away Nov. 13, 1991. William passed away May 18, 1986. Gladys moved to Roblin in Jan. 1994.

Dorothy Hazel born July 22, 1913 married Joseph Herbert on Nov. 4, 1938. Joe served in the Navy during World War II. They have a daughter Maxine who married Charles Thomas on Dec. 5, 1959. They live in Victoria, BC. Maxine and Charles have two daughters: Meagan and Jody. Meagan lives in Victoria, BC. Jody married Curtis Coates and they have a daughter Samantha and a son Andrew and live in Victoria, BC. Joe passed away Nov. 1962. Hazel lives in Victoria, BC.

William (Jack) John born Nov. 13, 1916 married Mildred Ferris on Jan. 17, 1970. He served in World War II. They have a daughter Sherry Mildred born July 21, 1970. She married Ronald Koroway on July 27, 1991. They have a daughter Laurissa and a son Travis. They were unfortunate and lost baby Jordan in Sept. 1993. Sherry and Ronald and family reside in Roblin. Jack and Mildred moved to Russell in June of 1992.

Fanny moved into the Russell Personal Care Home, as she was in poor health. She passed away April 22, 1980 at the age of 95 years.

May (Richardson) Kelly

by Mervyn Kelly

Mervyn & Barb Kelly

Granddaughters Kimberly & Michelle Kelly

May Richardson was born in 1899 in the Rochedale District, married Ray Kelly from the Roblin area in 1894. Three children arrived from this marriage: Mervyn born in 1924, Harold born in 1926 and Allison born in 1931. Roy passed away in 1936 and May passed away in 1964.

Mervyn married Barbara Sneesby and together they operated a dairy farm in the Gladstone Area until 1984. They were blessed with four children. Lyle born in 1942, has a refrigeration shop in The Pas, MB. He is married to Shirley Major and they have two children, Rhonda and Trevor.

Roy, born in 1946, is in sales in Brandon, MB and is married to Linda Whitwell. They have two children, Chad and Kimberly.

Valerie, born in 1957, works in a trophy shop in Abbotsford, BC.

Cheryle, born in 1958, works with Family Courts in Burnaby, BC. She lives in Abbotsford, BC and has a daughter, Michelle.

In 1986 we started the Pyott's West Campground, offering seasonal and daily camping. We are open from the middle of May to the end of September. This is our home now.

(Back row L-R) Shirley & Lyle (Front row L-R) Cheryle, Roy and Valerie.

(Back row L-R) Lyle, Shirley, Rhonda, Lynda and Roy (Front row L-R) Trevor, Mervyn, Barb and Chad.

Roy Robb Family

by Irene Pete

Mom and Dad Robb.

Lawrence and Clarence Robb.

Dad came West in the early 1900's to the Russell area. He met Mom there and they married on Christmas Day in 1918, settling in Cracknell, MB as a grain buyer for United Grain Growers. They transferred to Stornoway, then Endcliffe before moving to Dropmore in 1930 with a son and daughter, Alvin and Kay. They moved into the only house south of the tracks and lived there for 25 years. As the family grew with twin sons, Laurence and Clarence in 1933 and Irene in 1936, Dad kept adding to the house. It eventually became a house with three porches. The yard consisted of the house, a barn of sorts, chicken coop and a large garden. Our garage housed a '28 Chevy which was the only car we had until the early 1950's when we acquired a '40 Chevy. That made the Saturday night trips to Russell a little more comfortable. We always had a cow, pigs and chickens and a garden which provided most of our food. The rest came from the General Store on monthly credit. Dad always seemed to be able to meet the bills, so we didn't lack anything. The only thing we never seemed to have enough of, was heat in the winter. Our house was heated by the cook stove so the kitchen was warm until the wood burned down, and by morning, inside and outside temperatures were almost the same. Later on, we had an oil space heater.

What I remembered most about our home was the company we had. We always seemed to have the room for everyone and there was plenty of food for all. Mom and Dad liked to have people over for cards (bridge or canasta) and relatives came for days at a time. Special holidays were marked with big dinners, including what, at that time, appeared to be half the town.

Church was an important part of Dad's life. He served as Treasurer for many years. Mom always made sure we attended as well. Kay played the piano for most of the services, which were held in the Community Hall.

During the war years, Dad was a member of the Manitoba Reserve Army. I don't remember much of that era, but I do recall many ladies coming to our house to pack parcels to send to the men overseas. Mom always had a quilt on the frame, which covered the whole dining room area. We still have one of those quilts in our family, as well as many crocheted items as well. One of Mom's tablecloths covered the table when her twin grand daughters signed the register at their weddings in 1990.

Mom and Dad retired in 1955 and moved to Winnipeg, Dad took a part time job looking after the local community club skating rink.

Mom got to know only one of her grandchildren, as she passed away in 1958, but Dad enjoyed all eleven of his grandchildren before he died in 1973.

We all have a lot of great memories of our life in Dropmore. Community dances, barn dances, spring walks to the flooding Assiniboine, skating on ice in the ditches, sledding on the hills, snow forts down the road by the school, travelling by horse and van to winter dances in Shellmouth and many more happy times.

Now for a short history of the family:

Alvin married Bernice Beeleart. Bernice later had a baby and both died in childbirth. Al later married Opal in Regina where he worked for Eatons for 25 years. Opal gave him a ready made family of two daughters and one son. Al passed away in May of 1994. They have three grandchildren and one great grandchild.

Lawrence, Kay, Alvin, Irene and Clarence Robb.

Kay worked in Winnipeg for a time before returning home to look after the family during Mom's illness. She moved to Winnipeg in 1955 when Dad retired, working part time at the local grocery store. Kay and Steve retired in Winnipeg. Steve passed away in March, 1993.

Laurence worked for the Royal Bank after high school in Russell. His position took him from Jamaica to Churchill, where he left the bank to take a position for the Federal Government at the Harbour's Board. He retired from the Harbour's Board in 1992 and came to Winnipeg. Knowing he wasn't ready for the easy life, he is presently working for the Canadian Corps of Commissionaires.

Clarence retired after 25 years in the RCAF. He spent three years in Germany, his last posting being in Moose Jaw where he retired. He and his wife, Edith have three children and three grandchildren. Clarence passed away in January, 1995.

Irene attended high school in Russell and was a school teacher at Gamblers School District for one year before moving to Winnipeg with the family in 1955. She married Bill Peters in 1956, and they are still living in Winnipeg. They have five children and eight grandchildren.

Hugh A. Roberts Story

by David Robers

My father was born at Shellmouth, MB on July 10, 1891. My mother was born at Langenburg, NWT on April 8, 1904. They grew up in their respective areas, attending school and working. It seems that in those days, heavy emphasis was placed on work, work and more work and sometimes there was precious little time to attend school.

Dad started working for Canadian National Railways in 1922. It was then known as the Grand Trunk Railroad.

In July 1925, Dad and Mom were married in the United Church in Shellmouth. Three sons were born to them while living there; David (Bud), Reg, and Nelson. Another son, Bryan was born at Demaine, SK.

Presently Reg (married to Norma) is manager of the T.D. Bank at Vernon, BC, Nelson (married to Claire) is a C.N. agent at Three Hills, AB, (expecting a move), Bryan (married to Helen) is secretary to the board of a Worker's Compensation Board, at Yellowknife, NWT, and I, David (married to Ethel) am retired from the Federal Department of Communications and living in Grande Prairie, AB.

In 1934 we moved to Dropmore, MB and lived there until December of 1942. It was during this period that I spent my formative years (growing up years) - from 8 1/2 to 16 1/2 (one's youth)! I have many, many fond memories from this period, of which I'll try and list a few.

While attending school there, I had the following teachers: Mr. Clifford Wood, Mr. Douglas Pomeroy, Miss Beatrice Wood and Miss Belle Patterson. Clearly the teacher I remember the best of all the teachers I had was Miss Wood. I still remember some of her teachings - especially in the grammar department, such as 'do not use double negatives' and 'watch the syntax'. I've tried to hand this down as I was raising my family and now, even to the grandchildren.

I still have my grades 2, 3, 4, 5, 6 and 7 Dropmore school report cards.

As kids, during the summer months, I remember: playing ball in front of Lewis' store; playing hide and seek; horseshoes at Alex's blacksmith shop; rolling our tires around town; riding stick horses; playing cowboys and Indians; and in the fall, travelling around the country with Walter Rawlings, hauling grain and even having a trip to Gilbert Plains or Grandview with Walter. I think a Pool elevator agent moved there from Dropmore. We used to go to the swimming hole at Goodbuns on the weekends. Other incidents recalled were: going for the town cattle each evening; Jean Birnie riding to school on her spirited horse; taking long walks along the railroad tracks. Once or twice a year we would see a movie in the hall, sponsored by the Pool and if our luck held, we would see one or two movies in Russell. There were occasional trips to Roblin, Inglis and MacNutt as well as Shellmouth, and when we went we had big money to spend (a big 5 cent piece). I remember going to school picnics at Grainsby and Castleavery. (In those days we were a little older and the spending allotment went up to 25 cents.)

When the summer holidays came we spent more time at the swimming hole at Goodbun, (one

Swimming fun at Goodbuns: (L-R) Florence Gilhooley, Margaret Gilhooley and Nelson Roberts.

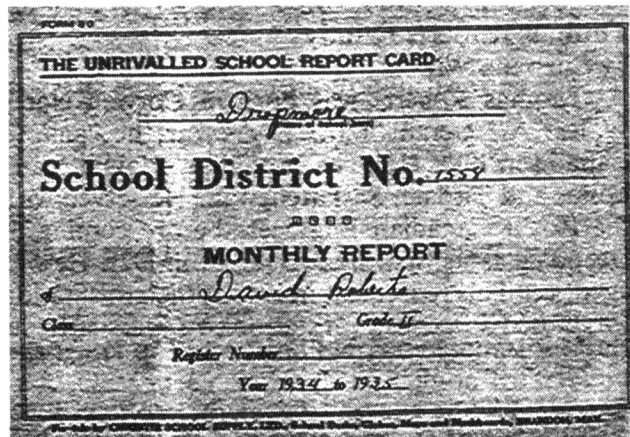
School report card for David Roberts Grade II in Dropmore School 1934-35.

The Goodbun's swimming hole attracted many young people in the summer.

of our favorite haunts) and they were so good to all of us.

In the winter I remember spending most of the leisure time on the open air rink and some tobogganing on the hill north of two, on the way to Birnies. I remember the excitement of the Christmas season with old fashioned Christmas concerts, and the country kids driving to school in their heated vans.

Some of the events that happened in those days were fairly earthshaking: the death of King George V in 1936; the abdication of Edward VIII; and the eventual crowning of George VI, were a few. I also remember those strange sounding overseas broadcasts, covering these events and rarely, the deranged screaming of Adolph. In 1938, I remember the gravel trains, a very exciting time for a young boy. The rides we had on those trains to the pit in Shellmouth on the empty train and the hop onto a fully loaded train again was fun. The train crews were very nice and very tolerant. In 1939, the King and Queen came to Canada and we went to Brandon to see them (again a ride in Walter's truck). Then in September came the War. I was 13 then, and its full implications were not fully absorbed nor fully understood at the time.

On December 7, 1941, some of us had gone skating that day. We had started off at the Red Bridge and skated down river to where Dietrichs watered their cattle (a long, long skate!). After reaching this point we hurriedly removed our skates, donned our boots and scampered up the hill to Dietrichs, to warm up and catch our breath before going the last lap home. It was through this period that they told us the Japs had bombed Pearl Harbour - something I still remember each December.

Some other recollections were of the distant radio stations we could pick up, such as WLW - Cincinnati, Ohio; WLS - Chicago, Illinois (Bam Scotty); WHO - Des Moines, Iowa; KOA - Denver, Colorado; KSTP - Minneapolis/St. Paul, Minnesota; and I think there was a station from Oshkosh - either Nebraska or Wisconsin but I cannot recall the call letters, and XERF - Reynosa, Mexico at the high end of the dial. This was a powerful station with high powered advertising that in part went something like this - tear off the carton top and mail it to Peruna (or Purina) care of XERF Reynosa, Mexico.

Locally we listened to Lux Radio Theatre, Jack Benny, Fred Allen, George and Gracie Burns, Fibber McGee and Molly, Henry Aldrich to name a few. The adventurous programs that fascinated kids (and adults) were: The Lone Ranger, The Shadow, Tarzan, The Green Hornet and others.

In July of 1942, Bryan was born and by Christmas time we were in Demaine, SK. I finished school there and during that period I learned the morse code at the railway station.

In September, 1944, I left for Grande Prairie, AB where I had my first job as an operator/agent for the Government Telegraph Service.

In November of 1944, my folks moved to Hoosier, SK and remained there until Dad's retirement in 1956. In July, 1956, the folks moved to Manning, AB. From 1957-61 Dad worked as towerman for the Alberta Forest Service at Naylor Hills Tower.

In September of 1972, Dad and Mom sold their home in Manning and purchased a home in Rosetown, SK and lived there until Dad's death in July 1981. In 1982, Mom came to Grande Prairie to live in a senior citizen's apartment.

I worked for the Government Telegraph Service from 1944-58 at various places in Northern Alberta and N.E.B.C.

In December, 1947 Ethel Cook and I were married. We lost our first born D'Arcy David, and have Wendy, who is Mrs. Gordon McLean. She lives in Beaverlodge, AB, with her two children, David 12 1/2, Shellie almost 10 and her husband, Gordon.

From 1958-66 I was with the Department of Transport Air Services at many northern postings. From 1966-82 I was with the Department of Communications for two years at Fort Smith, NWT, and from 1968-82 I was in Grande Prairie. I retired on December 30, 1982.

Ethel is still working as Matron of a senior citizen's lodge and I spend a lot of time with Wendy and her family and do some amateur radio work, I got back into it after I retired.

The Robertson Family
by The Family

John & Ann Robertson Family - about 1915 (Back row) Jim Robertson and John Robertson (Front row L-R) John Robertson, Sr., Clementine Robertson and Ann Robertson.

Jim and Florence Robertson Family - 1981 (Back row L-R) Shirley Radford, Murray Robertson, Reginald Robertson, Bill Robertson, Elaine Laycock. (Front row L-R) Jim Robertson, Florence Robertson.

John Robertson Sr. (1856 - 1943) came to Canada from Edinburgh, Scotland. After a brief stopover in Rossburn, he homesteaded on the NW 1/4 of 18-25-29 in 1883 (patent issued 1887). In 1884 he travelled by ox team to Brandon to meet his mother, brother Walter, and his sister Mary. They came to live with him now that he had the house ready. In 1893 he sold the homestead and bought the NE 1/4 of 1-24-29 in the Assiniboine Valley. In June 1900, John married Ann Skinner (1864 - 1957). In 1902, they homesteaded a second time, this being the SE 1/4 of 2-24-29 (patent issued in 1906). However, they continued to live in the Assiniboine Valley; home was a log house, 16 x 20, with two log stables, and a frame granary. They worked hard, fencing for thirty head of cattle and seven horses, and breaking and cropping a few acres of land each year on the new homestead. The railway came through Dropmore in 1910; the school was built a year later. John was Secretary-Treasurer of the School Board for many years. John's mother lived with the family until she died in 1911. In 1912, John, Ann and family of three, James M., John S. and Clementina moved from the valley to their new home on the second homestead. John's sister Mary married Harry Albright from Shellmouth. His brother Walter married Ellen McIntyre from Scotland, and they farmed in the Castleavery district. After Walter's death, Ellen moved to Roblin. One other brother, Jim, lived in Toronto. John and Ann continued to farm until 1941, at which time they went to live with William Skinner, Ann's brother, as their daughter Clementina was already working there. Ann needed help to get around with her bad knee. James M. wed Florence Bassil, and John S. wed Violet Bassil. They raised families and worked together, farming on adjacent lands to each other. They later retired to Roblin and Russell. The homestead remains under the Robertson name.

James Murray (Jim) was born on May 9, 1901. He enjoyed sports as a young man, and was a member of the winning Rochedale Ranger's Football Club in the 1930's. Jim worked for his uncle, Frank Skinner, at the well-known Dropmore Nursery for many years, before buying his own homestead. On October 28, 1936 he married Florence Mary Bassil of the Rochedale district, and they settled on the NE of 11-24-29 where they farmed and raised their family of five children.

John Murray (Murray) was born November 16, 1937. He attended school in Dropmore, and was an active boy who helped his parents with the many farm chores. He was a member of the Assiniboine 4-H Beef Club, winning a trip to the USA and a gold watch. Murray married Winona (Nonie) Keating, a school teacher from Silverton, in 1959, and they lived on the family farm for a short period. They have three children. Deborah Ann was born in Russell. Murray and his family moved to Glenboro, MB where Murray was employed with Dr. Robson D.V.M. Brian Murray was born there. Murray, Nonie and family returned to live on the Keating farm near Silverton. Their family was complete with the birth of Cathleen Louise in 1965. They sold the farm in 1967, and moved to Alberta where Murray worked with cattle for several years. Debbie married Tom Brennan of Calgary in 1982, and they reside in Comanche, OK, USA. Debbie works at the airport there. Brian married Shirley Odger of Calgary in 1987, and they currently live in Red Deer, AB with their two daughters, Cassandra and Kimberly. Brian is employed with an oil company. Cathy resides and works in Airdrie, AB. Murray and Nonie also reside in Airdrie, and Murray is co-owner of a pallet repair company in Calgary, while Nonie is employed by an accounting firm.

William Edward (Bill) was born October 1, 1940. Bill received his early schooling at Dropmore, and completed his education at Tummell High School while boarding with the Clarence Robin family. He worked at Skinner's Nursery for a few years before going to Winnipeg where he was employed with Eaton's for many years. Bill married Beryl Bauming of the Castleavery District, and they resided in Winnipeg for several years before moving to Toronto where their only child, Meredith Sue was born in 1973. Beryl resides in Mississauga, and is employed in Medical Records at the Mississauga General Hospital. Bill remarried in 1981. His wife Elaine (Toni) formerly of Australia has two sons from previous marriages. Meredith lives in Toronto, and has completed Business Administration at the University of Toronto. Bill and Toni reside in Scarborough, and Bill is President of his own company, Classic Products, with which Toni assists him. Bill travels frequently to other countries promoting the business.

Reginald James was born on May 27, 1942. He brought a lot of joy as it was very dry that spring, and the day he was born it started to rain. Reg was a happy youngster helping on the farm and attending school in Dropmore. His high school years were spent in Tummell and Roblin, where he also boarded with the Clarence Robin family. He was also active in the Assiniboine 4-H Beef Club for several years. Reg married Ellen Jan Mortemore, a telephone operator from Roblin, in 1964. They resided on the former Wm. Skinner farm for a few years before moving into Roblin where their two children were born. Kevin Dwayne, a surviving twin, was born in June 1966. Karen Dawn was born in February 1972. Reg was a salesman for International Harvestor for several years. Reg and Ellen continue to reside in Roblin, and keep very busy farming near Dropmore, so they spend each summer at Pyott's West Campground, their second home. Reg also manages the North West Bull Test Station near Roblin, and is a distributor for Pearson Livestock Equipment and International Stock Food. Ellen very ably assists Reg in these ventures. Kevin obtained his B.Sc. at Brandon University, and is currently completing a Medical Lab Technologist Course in Regina. Karen has taken various courses at Brandon University and in Winnipeg, and is currently employed in the dental office in Roblin.

Florence Elaine was born on August 28, 1948. She had lots of fun trying to keep up to three big brothers and has many fond memories of her grade school days spent at Dropmore. Elaine was very active in the 4-H program for nine years, and enjoyed its various activities. Upon graduating from the Roblin Collegiate in 1967, she moved to Russell, where she was employed as a legal secretary at the law office for many years. Elaine married James Roderick Wright (Rod) Laycock, a carpenter from Russell, in July 1976, and is very happy with her family of two stepsons and three stepdaughters, children of Rod's previous marriages. Rod and Elaine live in Russell just a block from where she was born. They are involved in various community organizations.

Shirley Ann was born October 6, 1950. Shirley and Elaine had a wonderful time playing

Shirley & Bob Radford, Nonie & Murray Robertson, Ellen & Reg Robertson, Toni & Bill Robertson, Elaine & Rod Laycock, Jim & Florence Robertson.

and going to school together in Dropmore, and Shirley was also very active in the 4-H program for many years. After finishing her high school education at the Roblin Collegiate, she took her nurse's training at the Misericordia Hospital in Winnipeg, and graduated as an R.N. in 1970. She married Robert Radford of Roblin, in 1971, and they lived in Winnipeg and Lockport. Their daughter, Sheri Lynne was born in Winnipeg, and they moved to Leaf Rapids, MB in 1974. Son, Christopher Robert was born in Leaf Rapids in 1975, and both children graduated from the Leaf Rapids Education Centre. Sheri received her B.A. from the University of Ontario, and currently resides in Toronto having recently graduated as a Child and Youth Counsellor. She and her fiance Tim Wasik are planning an October 1995 wedding. Chris has taken heavy duty electronics and mechanics courses at A.C.C. in Brandon. Bob and Shirley still reside in Leaf Rapids, where Bob has been employed at the mine since its earliest days, and Shirley continues her nursing career at the Health Centre. Bob and Shirley recently purchased three quarters of land overlooking the Shell River Valley, and are also owners of Purebred Red Angus.

It was a good life growing up on the farm, and there were many happy times as it was not all hard work. We were very fortunate to live only two miles from the John S. Robertson farm, and a lot of wonderful times were spent together. Jim raised Black Angus cattle, and we always had pigs, chickens and a garden so there was lots of fresh milk, cream, eggs and vegetables to enjoy. We also picked wild berries to make jelly, and spent many hours haying in the valley. We were members of the Dropmore United Church, and Sunday was also a special day for entertaining friends and neighbours. Florence was an elder of the Church and a member of the R.C.D.G. Church Club. She was also a 4-H Leader for many years. Easter and Christmas were memorable times of the year, and over the Easter holidays it was fun to colour eggs and roll them down the hills. There were many great dances throughout the years in the Dropmore Hall, where we all learned how to dance. The Field Days consisted of various sport's events and were highlights of the school years, attended by students from the surrounding areas. The two main events of the year at Dropmore which everyone attended, were the annual school picnic at the end of June, and the Christmas concert in the Dropmore Hall. There was real community spirit as everyone gathered together for these events, as well as for fowl suppers, curling and numerous other functions held in Dropmore.

Jim and Florence retired to Roblin in 1978 after selling the farm to Garry Digby. They spent their time travelling to visit family and friends, playing cards, and returning to Dropmore frequently for various activities. Jim passed away on September 11, 1987, and is resting in the peaceful Castleavery Cemetery beside his parents and sister. Florence continues to reside in Roblin, and remains very active in many organizations and activities.

John S. & Violet Robertson Family - 1983 (Front row L-R) John & Violet Robertson, (Back row L-R) Ann Donorer, Irene MacMillan, Allan Robertson & Joan Jenkins.

John S. was born on October 24, 1902 at home. He helped his Dad on the farm and went to both Dropmore and Rochedale Schools. While attending Rochedale, he lived with his Aunt Nell (the school teacher) and Uncle Fred Richardson. He married Violet Bassil July 7, 1942, and they had a family of four children, Ann, Irene, Joan and Allan. They lived in the old Robertson farm house on Sec. 2-24-29 until 1950, when they built and moved to a new home which stands today. The children were raised on the farm, and went to school in Dropmore, Tummell and then Roblin. Ann was a spelling whiz, in contests in Dropmore, Russell and Birtle (1956). All three girls belonged to the 4-H Club. Allan took up skiing at the Roblin Ski Hill. The four children all curled and loved tobogganing on the hills. The family all attended the Dropmore United Church. John was active with the church, school, elevator, curling, and the building of the Dropmore Hall. He enjoyed his yearly activity of being the Chairman for the Dropmore Christmas Concert, keeping things on track and welcoming jolly old St. Nick. He was a Councillor for the R.M. of Shellmouth for eight years from 1969 to 1976, Chairman of the Roblin Veterinary Clinic, and member of the Roblin Hospital Board. Violet kept busy with the home and family, church ladies group, helping with baking and activities within the community. Although retired from farming, they continued to live on the farm until 1984 when they moved to the Town of Russell. John passed away October 22, 1987; Violet currently lives in Russell.

We hayed in the Assiniboine Valley along the river, cropped the fields on the top West side, and sustained herd of Black Angus cattle. Though there were many, Violet remembers one story in particular. One of the cows, about to calf, decided to go back to the summer pasture in the valley. There were piles of snow then, so they followed the cow tracks to the valley and found the cow and a very cold calf. John stayed with them, and Violet walked home to get the children's sleigh and some blankets. Upon returning to the valley, they picked up the new calf, and pulled it home, with the cow keeping a close watch. Luckily it only lost the tip of its ears and tail.

Ann went to Winnipeg and married Jim Denorer. They have four children, Cheryl, Sheila, and twins Jamie and Judy. Cheryl married Brent Masters (three children). Sheila married Richard Bauer (two children). Jamie and Judy still live at home. All of the families reside in Winnipeg.

Irene also went to Winnipeg and married Gordon MacMillan. They have two children, Lori and Lisa. The MacMillan family reside in Stony Mountain, MB.

(Back row L-R) Violet Robertson, Allan Robertson & Ann Donorer (Robertson) (Center) John S. Robertson, (Front row L-R) Irene MacMillan (Robertson) and Joan Jenkins (Robertson).

Joan followed her sisters to Winnipeg, met and married Ted Jenkins. They have three children, Aron, Teresa and Shannon who all live at home. The Jenkins family reside in Oak Lake, MB.

Allan followed the path to Winnipeg and currently lives there; he returns to the farm at Dropmore regularly. All the families enjoy spending some holidays and weekends at the home on the farm.

Clementina was born September 12, 1904. She received her education in Dropmore, Roblin and Foxwarren. After finishing at Foxwarren, she returned home to the farm. In 1940 she moved to work for her uncle, William Skinner. She lived in the Wm. Skinner house until he passed away, and then went to Winnipeg where she cared for elderly people in their homes. She enjoyed travelling; making a trip to England and Scotland with her niece Elaine. She never married, and returned to Roblin in 1981 to live with, and be a companion for her cousin, Allan Anderson. She passed away March 20, 1988.

Mr. and Mrs. Walter Robertson

The Walter Robertsons were homesteaders on the NE quarter of 20-24-29 on the farm where Grant Pope now resides. Walter had a brother John,

Home of Mr. and Mrs. Walter Robertson.

(father of Jim and John Robertson) who homesteaded in the Dropmore area.

Walter was Secretary-Treasurer of the school board from 1913 - 1928 and for many years they boarded the school teachers at Castleavery School. They had no family.

They are both buried in Castleavery Cemetery.

Mr. and Mrs. Wally Robertson.

The Clarence Robin History

by Mary H. Hull

Dad built a new house on his homestead in the spring of 1919. We moved in when I was two months old. It was a one and one-half storey frame house with a lean-to kitchen and a large pantry. There was a cement basement with an earthen floor under the main house. I remember its lovely etched glass deer and fawn on the window of the front door and its polished newel post and banister where we hung our stockings on Christmas Eve.

There was a new frame stable east of the house and a log chicken house. We were three hundred yards from the Shell River where Dad taught us all including Mum, to swim. Our nearest neighbor on the west side of the river was

Frank Skinner's Nursery about 2-1/2 miles. The Joe Stefflers and Peter Montenkos were closer but we saw them only in the winter when they crossed the frozen river.

We travelled by buggy or democrat in summer and sleigh in winter. Dropmore was our nearest town and Dad hauled grain up and down and up hill the 7 miles to the elevator and got our mail and groceries. As a family we travelled to Inglis more often because Dad's brother, Amice Robin lived at Asessippi and Mum's father, Grandpa William Berrington lived just above Inglis and he supplied the town with milk for over 20 years. In winter we crossed the ice near Montenko's. This shortened the trip by about three miles and we went to Grandpa's nearly every year for Christmas. We never had a tree at home because after breakfast and chores we set off for Inglis. Grandpa always had a large tree with real candles clipped on little trays to the branches.

After a huge midday dinner, starting with turkey and finishing with plum pudding and lots of talk, about four o'clock Grandpa would announce that it was time to milk. A few minutes later we'd hear bells and stomping at the front door and Father Christmas would arrive to distribute gifts from his bag and the tree. We were quite at ease with Santa Claus at school and Father Christmas at Grandpa's as both were being the same "Jolly Old Fellow". Some child would tell Grandpa when he came in from milking that it was too bad that he'd missed Santa. Later in the evening every child had to repeat the part played in the local Christmas school concert and adults participated, too. One year, Grandpa had Dill Bassett who later farmed at Grandview, working for him and we had John Hannon with us. John sang Scottish songs and with Miss Smart, Grandpa's housekeeper, sang the duet, *"Madam will you walk and talk with me"*. Miss Smart played carols on the organ and everyone joined in. Dill Bassett sang, *"God Bless the Prince of Wales"* in Welsh and Dad was prevailed upon to sing *"Joan of Arc"* in French. One uncle showed us and talked about the wonderful new invention "cellophane" and how it would revolutionize packaging and food preservation. My mother recited the tragic *"Curfew shall not ring tonight"* which I always thought too sad and bloody for the Christmas season. One uncle, who could not carry a tune, sang, *"Where do all the flies go in the wintertime"* and a small cousin, equally tuneless, sang, *"Sunbonnet Sally and Overall Jim"*. Our youngest aunt and uncle demonstrated the latest dance craze, "The Charleston".

Education was a problem in the valley. We were in Tummell School District but it was eleven miles away. It was planned that we would stay at Grandma and Grandpa Berrington's and go to Inglis, but Grandma died when I was five. I did not start until I was nearly 7-1/2 years of age. I stayed with Mr. and Mrs. Chester Cook and went to Rochedale School with Frank, Muriel Cook and Peter Craig in a patched red buggy pulled by Whitey in summer. In dry weather the buggy had to be pushed into a slough every night to tighten up the tires. In winter we went in a huge grain tank, half-filled with straw, pulled by little Whitey and a big roan horse named Sandy. My sister Muriel (born 1921) joined me when she started and Doris (born 1922) the next year. By this time, Peter Craig and Frank Cook had finished school so we still fitted into the red buggy. The last year at Rochedale we stayed with Mr. and Mrs. Fred Richardson and walked the mile to school joining Winnie and Violet Bassil halfway along.

The teachers at Rochedale were Mr. Privat, Mrs. Anderson, and Miss Eunice Bullard. Mr. Privat introduced us to MacLean's magazine, tried to teach us cricket, which we didn't catch on to, and settled for football(soccer) and softball. We went to a sports day in Inglis. For a small rural school there was an excellent library established by Miss Skinner (later Mrs. Fred Richardson), when she taught there. I remember several series --- Highroads to History - to Geography - To Greek, Roman and Norse mythology; L. M. Montgomery's books: Black Beauty, Beautiful Joe, and The Secret Garden (which has recently become a play and a movie).

Grades Seven and Eight studied music, a squeaky wind-up gramophone played one opera and one oratorio and other classics each year; by the time one reached Grade VIII in a one-roomed school one had heard IL Travatore, the Messiah, Aida and the Elijah at least four times. We learned patriotic songs, English, Irish and Scottish songs. Mrs. Anderson taught us "The British Grenadiers" and when we went home for the week-end, Muriel, told Mum that we'd learned a lovely song about dogs. She went around singing, "The Bow Wow, Wow of the British Grenadiers".

Miss Bullard taught us the Highland Fling and other dances. When Archie Lloyd dislocated his shoulder at recess she gave his arm a sharp pull and reset it. Teachers had to be resourceful and courageous in the 1920's with doctor and other help so far away. Doris says this is about the only incident she remembers. She was only eight when we left Rochedale.

There was no church in the area so services were held in Rochedale School. When we were very small we had an Anglican clergyman one Sunday and a Presbyterian the next. If we missed church, as we often did because of bad weather and distance, we lost track of which service would be conducted. I remember Rev. Selkirk and Rev. Carefoot. Later we had Mr. Riggs and a United Church service.

One summer Muriel had a pet crow. Dad found it as a slightly injured fledgling but it soon recovered under Mum's and Muriel's care and "Jim" the crow became attached to Muriel, perching on her shoulder and following her about. He loved teasing the dog. When the dog was asleep Jim would fly down, peck him and resume his place on the fence, innocently looking the other way. Of course, when Muriel went anywhere in the democrat, Jim came too, and attended church regularly, flying from fence post to tree, the five and a half miles. If Jim decided that the service was too long, he'd sit in a tree by the gate and "Caw" continuously until he heard the final hymn. Children, restless, would titter and whisper, "There's Robin's crow". Mr. Jack Bassil once remarked to Dad, "I was thankful for your crow. He was getting a bit long-winded."

During our residence in the Rochedale District, a Women's Institute was organized and Mum became a member. The W.I. started a hot, school lunch program in the school. Families took turns supplying soup, cocoa or a hot dish every day in the winter months, a welcome addition to cold lunches. One day, cocoa was sent in half-gallon syrup pails. At recess, the older boys put the cocoa on the barrel-shaped heater which had level ledges on each side. They were told to loosen the lids but one was overlooked. About a quarter to twelve there was tremendous bang and an explosion of cocoa hit the ceiling. Small children screamed and ran to the teacher. Hair, faces and clothing were spattered with descending cocoa. Fortunately, no one suffered serious scalds, but after repeated coats of paint, cocoa stains were still visible on the ceiling when we moved away in 1930.

The W.I. organized house parties in the winter months and one winter put on a three-act play. I was the only one in school at the time and Muriel and Doris accompanied Mum to the many rehearsals. Mum's part included fainting in one scene and both girls saw this repeatedly. On the night of the big performance in Dropmore Hall with the stage setting, bright lights and costumes when the fainting scene occurred Muriel starting howling and Doris wept uncontrollably. Dad had to take them outside. The whispers of the other children --- "She's dead - she's dead", as they made their way out of the crowded hall didn't help. The play went on and I, the older sister, was thoroughly embarrassed. Later Mum demonstrated, "You've seen the play time and time again. You knew I had to faint" - "But", insisted Muriel, "it was so real."

Our brother Michael was born while we lived in the valley in 1928. As a toddler he developed a mastoid following whooping cough which had swept through the school. Mum's sister, Mrs. J.H. Gillies, R.N. and brother Leonard Berrington came from Inglis and Margaret Robb came to help with the housework. Dr. Drach made frequent visits and stayed all night at times. With round the clock nursing, Michael recovered without an operation. He had to learn to walk and talk again. His ear was bandaged all summer.

In the fall of 1930 Mrs. Cook's health was poor. Mrs. Richardson was getting older and three lively girls were a handful to board; we could not find a place to stay. Dad rented a farm and we went to Tummell where we had the van pick us up and deliver us home at night. For the three oldest girls this enabled them to attend high school from home. I was finished with child care forever, although it was a long time before I ceased to miss the friends I'd made at Rochedale. We had an excellent basis for learning and although delayed for many years by the Depression and the war years we all went on to university; I, Mary, graduated from the University of Manitoba and the University of London, England; Muriel took her training in St. Boniface Hospital and a nursing degree from McGill, and Doris went to the Winnipeg Normal School (Teacher's College) and the University of Toronto where she graduated in Occupational Therapy. Doris served the CWAC in the war and later in RAMC. Mary spent 4 years in RCAF (WD).

During the years we lived in the Shell Valley, we had no telephone, no radio, no electricity, no car and for many years a very bad road. We did have good vegetable gardens, a lovely flower garden with lilac bushes, hops climbing along the fence and in an arch over the gate, plenty of fuel and wonderful spring water. There was a raspberry patch on the hill, saskatoons just outside the garden, wild strawberries. We had the river for swimming, hills for sleigh-riding and skiing in winter. There was plenty of fish in the summer and game in the fall. We had our own milk, butter, eggs, poultry, beef and pork. Mum made all of our clothes, she had studied dressmaking in Russell before she married, and she had an auto-knitter and made our winter stockings and sweaters. In the coldest weather we wore two or three pairs over our long underwear and under our felt boots or moccasins. We had an organ in the front room and Dad had brought a large chest of books from Guernsey when he emigrated. From the time we were little, we were read to every night very short stories in summer and lovely long ones in winter. Later when we went to bed in winter Dad read to Mum as she knitted or sewed. We had two weekly newspapers, the Free Press Weekly and the Family

Herald and Weekly Star, and Grandma Robin sent us the Guernsey Weekly Press until July 1st, 1940 when the occupation began.

I remember seeing my first plane - biplane with an open cockpit flying over Skinner's field. Dad said, "You'll never get me up in one of those. I've seen too many shot down." We never did. The first radio I heard was one Sunday when we were visiting the George Robbs. It was a headphone set and they divided each in two so more people could hear. Yorkton was celebrating its incorporation as a city so must have been 1928 as it celebrated its 50th Anniversary with the Queen and Prince Philip in attendance just before the Commonwealth games in Edmonton in 1978. Later, the Craigs had a radio with a horn loudspeaker and "Abdullah Bulbul Amir" came through loud and clear, all nineteen verses!

There have been so many changes in the world that the days in Rochedale seem very remote to-day... Mary, Muriel and Doris all married eventually; Doris at 31, Mary at 41 and Muriel in her 50's, thus fulfilling a prophecy of a principal in Tummell to Mum; that her girls were not academically inclined, very domesticated and would probably marry very early!

Dad died in 1961 and Mum in 1980. They are buried in Tummell Cemetery. Mary and Doris are widowed now, Doris lives in Ottawa near her two daughters. Muriel and her husband Douglas Dale live in Kingston when they are not travelling. Michael married Elizabeth (Betty) Hardy of Inglis. They have two sons and a daughter and still live in Shellmouth Municipality. Betty, who wasn't born when we moved, married Walter Ritchie of Roblin and they live near all their family in Neepawa, MB.

Don and Freda Robin Family

Don is the son of the late Amice and late Sadie Robin. He was born in Asessippi, took his schooling there and at Inglis. He lived at home on the farm until he joined the Army in 1941. He served overseas in the European Theatre until he returned home in December of 1945. In the spring of 1947, he bought a farm in the Rochedale District.

He met Freda Bradley-Hunt of Dropmore, the youngest daughter of the late Basil and Dorothy Bradley-Hunt. She took her schooling at Dropmore, Grainsby, Russell and attended Normal School in Winnipeg. After teaching at Asessippi, Beautiful Valley (Oakville) and Grainsby, they were married in 1952.

Their three children, Brad, Lori and Sally were raised on the family farm. They all took their

The Robin Farm sign.

schooling at Rochedale, Inglis and Russell. They all participated in most school sports.

Brad, after graduating, took up farming with his Dad. He married Brenda Petz, daughter of the late George and Anne Petz of Dropmore, who took her schooling at Dropmore and Roblin. Brad bought the farm belonging to Ben Cameron and they lived there until he took over the home farm, now known as "The Robin Farms". Brenda was a partner in a store, "Junior Edition", in Russell for a few years and now works part time there.

They have two children, Kiley and Kristy, who are attending Goose Lake High in Roblin. Kiley is taking his Grade 12. He has been employed at "Gaber's Implements" the last two summers as well as working on the farm. Kristy is taking her Grade 9. Her interests are music, riding her horse and 4-H Beef Club.

Our second child, Lori, attended Assiniboine College for two years, taking Business Administration. She then moved to Calgary and was employed by Norcen Energy Resources.

Sally, our third child attended University in Winnipeg for four years and received her Bachelor of Education. She taught school up North at Nelson House for five years. She returned to Winnipeg and took one more year of University. She married Charlie Linski of Winnipeg, son of John and the late Marie Linski. Both teach in Winnipeg. They have two children, Alice in kindergarten and Gabriel at part-time day care.

Mr. and Mrs. Harry George Roe

by Liz Roe

Mr. and Mrs. Harry Roe.

Harry G. Roe, was born July 1, 1887 and was raised and educated in Andover, Hampshire, England. As a young man, he worked as a draftsman at Taskers, a company which produced threshing machines, trailers and steam engines. He worked around Toronto and later worked for a threshing crew near Portage la Prairie, MB and later Russell, MB to raise enough money to buy land. He walked from Russell to the land he had purchased in the Castleavery District, the SE 1/4 of 20-24-29 in 1915. Here he farmed and batched for seven years.

Olive Ferriss was born April 7, 1899 in Baggot, MB. With her parents and brothers she moved to the NW 1/4 of 10-24-29 about 1904. Olive attended Castleavery School when she could. As an older child in a large family and her mother not well, she too often was needed at home.

Harry and Olive were married Oct. 18, 1922. They worked very hard paying their debts and adding more land and livestock to their farm.

Harry and Olive raised a family of six children: Eva, Jim, Ilene, Grace, George and Mabel.

The dry years of the thirties were rough for the Roes. To add to their troubles, Harry was diagnosed as having diabetes. But with the help of Eva and Jim, they managed to carry on.

For many years, Harry was one of the trustees of the Castleavery School.

In the winter of 1928-29, he managed to make his one and only return visit to England to see his mother, sisters and brothers.

Harry remained on the farm until he passed away, Sept. 25, 1959.

Olive continued living in her own little house on the farm until 1965. Then she bought a small house in Roblin. Here she spent many happy hours tending her garden flowers and house plants and visiting her neighbours, especially Mrs. Alexander. Olive passed away April 3, 1973.

Eva, the eldest child was born July 25, 1923. She attended Castleavery School and later helped on the farm.

She joined the Airforce in 1943, where she trained as a cook. After the war, she continued her trade as a cook until she moved to Sarnia, ON. Here she worked in the Prestolite Factory until her death in 1972.

Eva had one son, Jeffery. Jeffery and his wife live in Campbell River, BC.

James and Elizabeth Roe

by Elizabeth Dorothy Roe

James Alford Roe, first son, second child of Harry Roe, from Andover, Hampshire, England and Olive (Ferriss) Roe of Castleavery, MB was born on SE 1/4 of 20-24-29 on Aug. 21, 1924. The midwife was Mrs. Archie Morrison. He went to Castleavery School shortcutting across Nichol's field by horse and sleigh in winter and horse and buggy when the snow was gone. When his father was diagnosed with diabetes, Jim just 13, left school to help run the farm.

I, Elizabeth Dorothy Taylor, youngest child and only daughter of Allan Taylor from Glasgow, Scotland and Elizabeth (Burkart) Taylor from the Hoffenthal District, south of MacNutt, SK. was born July 30, 1930 in Roblin, MB.

I attended MacNutt School and Yorkton, Y.C.I. Then I went on to Saskatoon Normal School to become a teacher. Later I took correspondence classes from, and summer school classes at the University of Saskatchewan, to improve my qualifications. I taught school for 35 years. Two of those years were spent happily teaching in Castleavery School.

Jim and I were married Aug. 17, 1956 in Roblin United Church. We began our married life on SE 1/4 of 20-24-29. Before long we were blessed with three children: Marilyn, Leyton, and Murray.

At first, things were often hectic on the Roe farm. What with Liz teaching school, planning lessons, and attending school functions, not to mention having to do the myriad of chores expected of every farm wife. I loved gardening, liked cooking, didn't mind housework, or even milking cows. But I hated operating the cream separator and having to wash and clean it twice a day! It wasn't a hard chore, it just seemed to take so long to do.

I remember thinking "picking stones" was a lark because it didn't require any great amount of thinking. Then Jim worked the field with a cultivator. My visiting Aunt Emelia, whose eyesight was failing, thought we had sheep - the field was covered with stones.

When I became Vice-Principal of the MacNutt School, I smartened up and hired first, Mrs. Basso, then Mrs. MacLean, and when Murray was five, Mrs. Helen Robertus, as housekeepers. These ladies were absolute gems. They were more mothers to all of us than hired help!

Our children were involved in 4-H, music lessons, sports and various extra-curricular school activities which kept our lives interesting.

Jim and Liz Roe with their children: Leyton, Marilyn and Murray.

(Back row L-R) Leyton Roe, Karen Roe, Murray Roe, Jim Roe, Randal Trussler. (Front row L-R) Carley Roe, Liz Roe, Sarah Roe, Marilyn Roe.

Murray and Karen Roe on their Wedding Day, December 29, 1984.

Jim and Liz Roe.

I fondly remember the many evenings we spent around the kitchen table doing school work and sharing anecdotes about the day's happenings. Jim would be watching television, but he'd be listening to us with one ear so he could add his comments.

Preparing for 4-H Achievement Days when everybody got into the act, stirs my memory. Pushing, prodding, and dragging calves to get them to lead and, then being dragged across the barnyard when the calf took off like greased lightning. Feverishly washing calves and brushing them until their hair shone on the morning of the Big Day, when one's eyes were still heavy with sleep and her only desire was to crawl back into bed, was a hectic time; but, I miss it now!

Marilyn is a Counsellor, running her own business "Parkland Family Counselling Services" in Dauphin, MB. She specializes in Group, Family, Individual and Children's Counselling. She and Randall Trussler, who is a teacher in Gilbert Plains, were married July 30, 1994. They make their home in Gilbert Plains, MB.

Harry Leyton is a chemical technologist working for the Whiteshell Nuclear Research Station at Pinawa, MB. Leyton enjoys travelling to different countries, playing baseball and cheering for the hockey team - the Montreal Canadiens!

Murray is a member of the Regina Police Service. He married Karen Rubletz from Wroxton, MB, Dec. 29, 1984. Karen works part time as an employee of the various branches of the Bank of Montreal in Regina. They have two daughters: Carley Marie and Sarah Ashley, who at present love school, all their friends, and their dancing lessons.

Jim and I have been blessed, not only with a loving family, but also with many friends and good neighbours. Castleavery is a great place to live and we hope to continue living here for sometime.

Ilene (Roe) McFadyen

by Ilene McFadyen

Ilene Roe is the 3rd child of Harry George Roe and Olive Ferriss. Ilene was born in the Castleavery District. She married Albert McFadyen on November 5th, 1948. They farmed in the Tummell District from 1948-1979. They then rented their land and moved into Roblin 1982 where they still live. Ilene worked as a nurse's aide in the Roblin Personal Care home from 1976 until she retired. They have 3 children Rodney, Lynn and Shelly. Rodney graduated form the University of Manitoba with his B.Sc. He trained and worked as a park ranger for several years. He is now a park manager in the Parkland Region. He married Jacqueline Precourt from St. Francis Xavier in September 1974. She works as a Telecoms Operator for the RCMP. They have 4 children.

Marc, Shawn, Kyle and Reneé. They now live in Dauphin, MB. Lynn married Lynnet Perrin of Brandon on August 1, 1987. They have 3 children: Christopher, Vincent and Cherilyn. Lynn is power electrician and works for Manitoba Hydro in Brandon. Lynnet was a hair dresser beautician, but now stays home with her family.

Shelly trained as a Registered Nurse. She graduated from the Grace Hospital School of Nursing in 1981. She has continued to study while working as a nurse. She is presently studying law. She works at the Victoria Hospital, Winnipeg. She starts her final year of law this fall.

Mabel (Roe) Cranwell
by Mabel Cranwell

Mabel was the youngest daughter of Harry and Olive Roe. Mabel met and married William Cranwell in 1956.

In 1961 they purchased a farm in the Tummell district. For several years they operated a dairy farm. In 1981, they sold the dairy cows and purchased some beef cattle, instead. Today, they still operate the beef farming business in addition to the mixed grain.

They were blessed with five children, three girls and two boys. Donna was born in 1957, David in 1959, Denise in 1961, Douglas in 1962 and Danette in 1965. The children now have families of their own. Bill and Mabel are now the proud grandparents of seven girls and five boys.

I Remember
by Elizabeth Roe

No matter where you go in this world of ours, you will not find better people than those living in the Castleavery District of Manitoba. They personify what "good neighbour" means. I'd like to tell you about a few of these people and share a few experiences I've had with them.

The first year I taught in Castleavery, I boarded with the Maurice Digbys. What wonderful people they were! I remember well, my first evening with them. Wayne tried so hard to get his young sister to tell me the dog's name. Poor, innocent Faye couldn't pronounce her l's; but, was good at the a's and s's.

I also remember the wild horseback ride on the horse, "Jack", when he was frightened by an engine starting up suddenly on Maudsley's farm. Bobby Digby said, "Hang on", and I sure did! Bob had a dickens of a time getting hold of Jack's halter to slow him down because Jack liked to win races! I just hung on for dear life, shouting, "Whoa! Whoa!" and prayed I wouldn't be scraped off Jack's back when he entered the barn door. You'd think we were taking part in a movie production because Bobby stopped Jack mere feet from the barn door.

I also remember how ambitious Garry Digby always was. It was not unusual for him to be up and out helping his dad while I was still snuggled under the bed covers: that is, until Olive pounded the ceiling with the broom!

During my first week in Castleavery, I was invited to the Simair home. The evening before, they had put their potatoes into the basement via the basement window and left the window open. During the night an inquisitive skunk happened along and fell into the basement. There was a bit of excitement next morning when Maggie went for potatoes! They lured the little sucker out by placing a plank up to the window. Then Joe shot the invader. That, Joe informed me with a twinkle in his eye, was the reason, they invited me over - to eat roasted skunk!

I also visited, and occasionally stayed overnight with the George Hunters. I enjoyed the lively discussions we had on everything from teaching techniques, and federal politics, to farming problems.

I'll never forget my first concert in the Castleavery School. The children practised for weeks. Everything was going well at the concert. I was behind the curtains dressing one little girl for some act when the curtain suddenly fell down. I made a frantic grab for it and hauled it up in front of me. The little girl who was just in her knickers, darted behind me and hung onto the back of my skirt like a little monkey to make sure no one saw her.

The second year, I taught in Castleavery, I lived with my mother in MacNutt and drove to school. The spring of '54 there were three potholes on the school road, and I believe my car got stuck in every one of them. Either George, or Dave Hunter pulled my car out.

My second Christmas concert in Castleavery had one play in it in which the actors, portraying Joe and Ada Dugan, were looking through an album of pictures of friends they'd left behind in Castleavery. Then other actors would perform some fun thing: curling, dancing, partying, etc. that the Dugans were supposed to have done with these friends. You see, the Joe Dugans were leaving the District in the New Year for Benson, Minnesota, USA. I remember the play well because Ada cried through most of it and I was wishing I'd never created it.

Miss Elizabeth Taylor's Class in Castleavery taken in the Autumn of '53. (Top row L-R) Ross Rowan, Donavon Baumung, Terry Simair, Betty Rowan (Third row) Billy Case, Wayne Digby, Richard Hunter, Marion Hunter, Ellen Maudsley, Garry Digby (Second row) Sharon Rowan, Robert Hunter (Bottom row) Ellen Rowan, Robert Digby, Bud Dugan, Beryle Baumung, Rene Jennings.

Castleavery pupils under Elizabeth Taylor's charge. (Bottom row L-R) Ross Rowan, Donovan Baumung, Betty Rowan, Terry Simair, Garry Digby (Middle row) Richard Hunter, Wayne Digby, Robert Hunter, Ellen Maudsley, Marion Hunter, Billy Case (Top row) Sharon Rowan, Frank Case, Janice Maudsley.

I'll never forget the day Buryle Doole, Cheryl Digby, Murray and I created the 4-H Calf. Peter Glogoski and Jim Roe made the basic frame and stand. Our job was to mix up enough paper maché to slather on the frame to make it look like a real calf. We had paper maché coming out of our ears! In fact, with Murray and Cheryl diligently mixing the gook, they almost plugged the sink. Cheryl, Murray, and I slapped on the gook. It was Buryle's job, as architect, to tell us where to add more gook, or remove it. "A little more on the brisket", or "No, that's too much on the rump!" she'd caution.

At noon we were all finished. We went in for dinner. When we ventured out after dinner, most of the paper maché was lying on the garage floor! Paper maché should be put on, a thin layer at a time and allowed to partially dry before another thin layer is added. Well, we defied the law of gravity and the law of gravity kept defying us! The ears, constantly fell off even though the little suckers were thin. By the time they finally remained in place, they were more Elmer's Glue-All, than paper maché. But, after four coats of red spray paint and a dash of white enamel for the ears, that calf looked mighty good and it's still on display at the museum.

Remember the Family Socials that were held in the Castleavery School? We always had contests. One contest, I remember well, involved the tossing of eggs. Who could continue to toss an egg back and forth the longest without breaking the egg? In this particular contest, Irv and Vi Young and Bus and Caroline Hunter were the last of the competitors. Bus wound up and heaved the egg to Caroline. She neatly side-stepped and the egg smacked the floor. Irv and Vi were the winning couple! Now it was down to who the winning single would be. Everyone watching, would hold their breath while the egg was in the air. When it was caught safely, there was a sigh of relief. Of course Irv was clowning throughout, keeping the rest of us in stitches. He lobbed it to Vi. She caught it, but the egg broke in her hands!

Remember the Castleavery Family Ball Game and Picnic we used to hold every year? I well remember the last one. Murray Roe was pitching, Marilyn Roe was batting, Lloyd Shearer was on first. Leyton Roe was on second, John Hunter played shortstop and others were on third and in the field. Then, of course, there were the spectators! Murray wound up and pitched and Marilyn missed hitting the ball. Everyone turned to see where the ball had gone. Under an old table about 15 feet behind home base, lay Bus Hunter, face down, with his catcher's mitted hand firmly holding the ball above his head, and his other hand clutching his head to protect his bald spot. Oh! how we all laughed. He passed away that year and we never had another annual district picnic. It wouldn't have been fun without Bus.

Who can forget the fun we had at the Castleavery Curling Rink. Everyone took the final games very serious. The whole district would be sitting behind the glass in the waiting room playing the game verbally: "No. I don't think he should try a draw shot from there!" "I never thought it would pull in like that" or, "There must be a run in the ice." The truth of the matter was, the whole rink was a mass of runs. To make a decent shot you usually played against the run. This worked to our advantage until the visiting rinks caught on.

The two years I taught in Castleavery, I played on Bob Pyott's rink which also included Arthur Nichols and Ivan Shewchuk. Bob and Arthur would take forever to decide their shots. It was all strategy, of course and it must have almost driven the opposition nuts. Arthur would saunter slowly down the ice humming to himself as he went to make his shot. If my rock even came within five feet of the front ring, Bob Pyott would shout, "Grr-ate Shot, Gurrly!" Bob Pyott never remembered the score or what end we were playing. It wasn't important to him. It was playing the game that counted. But I have to admit he and Arthur were tricky old codgers.

I remember sitting on the hill with Mr. Arthur Rowan on his farm looking north-east over the valley. He was explaining to me how he brought water from a creek up to his farmyard, by means of a machine called a "Ram". Mr. Rowan was a reticent, hardworking gentleman who possessed many skills.

Jessie, Allan, and Gilbert Anderson were such nice people to visit. Although much older than I, they were young in mind and so caring. In the summer of 1954, Jessie went with me to Vancouver. On our way there we stayed at one motel that had cups and plates, but no pans, pots, or cutlery. The next motel had one small cooking pot and no dishes or cutlery, and the third just had two bowls, two spoons and a can opener. Jessie kept saying,"The next motel will have everything. You just wait and see." We never did see anything of the kind!

I remember a day during the first week of school in '54. I had explained what 'imagination' was and how to use it to tell a story. The children closed their eyes and put their heads down on their desks. I then proceeded to orate the beginning of a story. Each pupil was to give a story ending. To keep the story simple, all the children had to do was describe some imaginary creature that they supposedly saw. Even the big boys and girls got into the act. The story endings got better and better until we came to Frank.

I'd forgotten that Frank had missed school the previous day when I'd started the imagining game. I asked, "And what did you see, Frank?" He looked at me with such a bewildered look on his face and replied, "I didn't see nothing. Miss Taylor! It was all dark."

I remember the day one of the little ones took sick in school. She made it as far as the girl's cloak room before she threw up. I can clean up almost any kind of mess without flinching: except, vomit! I grabbed a handful of paper towels, covered my mouth and nose with one towel and with towels clutched in my other hand, valiantly tackled the cleanup. I tried my best to keep from breathing and gagged convulsively when I had to come up for air. At the same time I was trying to be quiet so as not to embarrass the sick child. It wasn't easy! Suddenly, this dainty, little lady, named Rene Jennings appeared at my side with paper towels in her hands and asked, "May I help?" Both the little child and the floor were cleaned up in no time. While I quickly drove the little girl home, Rene and the Grade Eight class looked after the other children.

I remember the day I left school as soon as the last team was hitched up and ready to go. Assuming everything would be okay, I never looked back. For some reason, Donavon lost control of the horses. He fell and was dragged. Then the sleigh runner slewed and cut a deep gash in his thigh. The horses were gone! With his sister's help he managed to walk home, a distance of almost two miles. Fortunately neither a vein nor an artery had been severed. I still shudder when I envisage him trudging through the deep snow suffering such awful pain.

I remember the day I forgot my lunch. While the children were eating their lunches and talking a mile a minute, I quietly corrected papers. Marion Hunter suddenly looked at me and asked, "Don't you have any lunch?" I had to admit that I didn't. You should have seen those children. They were convinced I'd starve. Many felt remorse because they had already eaten most of their lunch. Buddy Dugan, came up to my desk and offered to ride home and get some lunch for me. I remember saying, "No. It's my fault. I forgot my lunch and it won't hurt me to fast for a few hours." Bobby Hunter was horrified. His two favourite occupations were talking and eating! And because he had been talking a fair amount, he had eaten the least lunch. He wanted to give most of it to me, but I convinced him, half a sandwich would do. It didn't end there! Most of those children, wanted to share with me a little bit of whatever they still had left. I realized they'd be hurt if I didn't accept their generosity. At the time, their thoughtfulness almost overwhelmed me and tears were close. I've taught many wonderful children in my life: but, none who were better than the Castleavery children.

All of the people in the district were very hospitable. To stop in for lunch after school at one of the homes was to my way of thinking like having "High Tea at the Manor!"

John Nelson Rowan

by Mrs. E.C. Rowan

Ivan and Dad.

John Nelson Rowan was raised in Glamis, Ontario and came to the Castleavery district in 1902, and homesteaded on Sec. 14-24-30.

The land was broke with a plow and his team of horses, "Mike and Skip".

Christmas Day, only two days after his marriage to Elsie Barry, was spent papering their log cabin with newspapers to keep out the cold winter winds of the prairies. Their log cabin was along the Old Pelly Trail and many a weary traveller would stop for the night to feed the horses and rest. No one was ever turned away.

Their sons: David Arthur, George Nelson, William Edward, and Harold Henry were all born in this little log cabin.

In about 1912 the family moved to the S.E. quarter of section 22-24-30 W. I so that the boys would be near a school. Dad was named to the committee to organize a school district, and the boys attended the first school that opened in 1913.

More land was needed to feed the family so more land was purchased from the C.N.R. (S.W. 1/4 of sec. 22-24-30 W. 1) along the Assiniboine

River, seven miles from the home place. Mom would pack enough food for a week and Dad and Art would work and batch on the C.N. land and come home weekends for clean clothes and more food. Mom, George, Ed and Harold looked after the home place. Mom was up at 4 AM making pies, cakes, etc. for a the threshing crew. She, with the younger boys did the chores on the home place which included milking six or seven cows. She packed the food and kids in the buggy and drove seven miles to make dinner for twelve to fifteen men. At three or four in the afternoon she brought lunch into the field. Then she set the table and readied supper for the men to serve themselves. At 5 PM she would be on the road home, only to repeat the day until harvest season was over. A day was from daylight to darkness.

Dad used to pick up cream from the neighbours and take it to the Russell Creamery which was about twenty to thirty miles round trip. Many a time the cream was so sour that the lids of the cream cans would pop off.

Mail was picked up at the Dugan farm in Castleavery; shopping was done in Shellmouth, Langenburg, SK, Roblin and Russell. Those trips generally took days, and of course, there was always the Eaton's catalogue.

Grain was taken in before Christmas to the grist mill in Roblin to made into flour. This was a yearly trip. Dad used to dress up as Santa Claus every Christmas and go around to the different schools in the district. It was years before some of his own children knew their father was Santa Claus.

Mom and Dad settled in the MacNutt district where they worked and raised their family of four boys and one girl. Their descendants are scattered from Ontario, through the Prairies, and right to the British Columbia Coast.

Dad passed away in 1940; the farm was sold a few years later and Mom and Mary Elizabeth (Betty Waite) moved to Roblin. Mom passed away in 1946.

As to the remaining members of this family, David Arthur and his wife Gladys passed away; George who farmed in Dropmore and operated the road grader passed away also his wife Edith. They are all buried in the Castleavery Cemetery. William Edie is in a nursing home in Edmonton, his wife Cora resides in Edmonton. Harold was killed in Sicily during the Second World War. There are lots of descendants of the three boys living some around your district, others in Ontario, Alberta, Saskatchewan, and British Columbia.

The only daughter, Mary Elizabeth, is a widow living in Ottawa and has one son recently retired from the RCMP and has two grandsons.

I am Ed's wife. We visited the farm every year with the children. Ed's father died suddenly. They had finally got the windmill up and going. Ed took a leave of absence from his job an we moved in with his mother. Ed sold some of the stock and cleared up things. Then we left and went back to our home.

Ed and Betty are the only ones remaining in the family. Ed is 87 years old and Betty is 79.

The Rowan Family

by Anne Wishart

Please Note: *This is a pictorial history of the Rowan Family. Another family history of John Nelson Rowan by Mrs. E.C. Rowan also appears in this publication.*

David Henry Rowan came from Glammis, ON. He was of Irish origin and was born in the early 1800's. He would be my Great Grandfather, my son Tim's Great Great Grandfather and Great Great Great Grandfather to Tim's children. From David Henry to Johnathan Wishart would have been six generations.

From what I heard from my mother and father, there was a mixture of Irish, Scottish, English and Pennsylvania Dutch on both sides of George and Edith Rowan's families.

All I know about David Henry was that he had three sons, John Nelson Rowan, Harry Rowan and a Valentine Rowan.

Nelson and Esther Rowan.

The sons of Nelson and Esther Rowan: Rowan, Arthur, Edward, George and Harold (in highchair).

Harry Rowan was united in marriage to Sadie Longdon. They lived in the Castleavery district on Sec.22-24-29 until the family moved to BC in the Fall of 1946 or 47. From this marriage there were four children, Cedric, Derward, Orland and Marrice.

Nelson Rowan was united in marriage to Elsie Esther Anne (Barry), also from ON. They migrated West and took up a homestead in the Castleavery District. This marriage was blessed with six children, David Arthur 1904-1967, George Nelson, May 18, 1906-1975, William Edward 1908, Henry Harold, September 15, 1909-1943, when he was killed in action in World War II, Mary Elizabeth, January 6, 1913, and a baby girl, Mary Elenea who passed away in infancy. The four boys were born in the Castleavery district, while the girls were born at MacNutt, SK.

Arthur was united in marriage to Gladys Curle of Calder, SK. They lived on Sec. 5-25-29 in the Castleavery district. This marriage was blessed with eight children. Edwin was born 1931-1922, Jack, Ellen, Ross, Betty, Sharon, Donald and a baby which passed away in the Roblin Hospital.

Edward Rowan was united in marriage to Cora O'Meara. They were blessed with four children, Marian, Donald, Irving and Harold. They raised their family at Port Arthur, now called Thunder Bay. They now reside in Edmonton, AB where their son, Irving and family reside.

George Rowan was united in marriage to Edith Elizabeth Ferriss on December 25, 1928. They knew each other from the time they were children. The families would visit back and forth and the children played together. Mom's bridesmaid was Beatrice Rawlings (Cameron) and the bestman was my Dad's brother, Arthur Rowan. This marriage was blessed with two children, Elizabeth Anne born August 7, 1930 and Ivan Harland Nelson born December 1, 1934. Both of us were born at MacNutt, Sk.

Marriage of George Rowan and Edith Elizabeth Ferriss on December 25, 1928.

The Rowan Family - (Back row) George and Edith, (Front row) Elizabeth Anne, Ivan Harland.

In 1935 George and Edith moved to the Dropmore district and secured the west half of Sec. 27-33-29. They lived here until George passed away on June 1, 1975. Edith continued to live there until she had a sale in the fall of that year. The following year, in 1976 she sold the land to Richard Peats.

In the thirties there were hard times, but I never remember going to bed hungry. Our home wasn't much to look at, but there was lots of love and happy memories. I remember the gramophone that Mom and Dad bought from

Foullaird's at St. Lazar, Manitoba. They bought records from the T.E. Eaton Catalogue.

My first set of toy dishes were made of tin. I lost most of them, but I still have all my china toy dishes which I got in the thirties.

I recall in the thirties travelling with a team of horses and a wagon and box, later we had a buggy. In the winter, we travelled by team and sleigh with box. Whenever we would go to MacNutt in the winter, Dad and Mom would heat up a couple of large stones in the old wood stove oven before we left for this ten mile trip. We also had blankets and a big roan coloured cowhide which my Dad had tanned.

Sometimes my Dad would take the train from Dropmore to MacNutt to get whatever we may have been in need of. Then he would walk back home by the railroad track which was a seven mile walk, instead of the road which was ten miles.

The CNR Train going west by our farm.

My Dad did most of his farming with horses. At one time he used an old Fordson Major tractor. It was on steel wheels with logs about 1939-40. He also used a Case tractor some. In 1946 he bought his first new Ford tractor.

Dad had to pick it up at Langenburg, SK. He bought this tractor through Albert Rathgaber of MacNutt. Dad walked to Langenburg to pick it up.

About 1944-45, Dad bought a Model A Ford Coupe. We were able to go places now. We would go to Roblin to shop and take in the afternoon matinee at the theatre.

About 1947-48, my Dad invented a hay stacker from a couple of old car frames, some cable, the teeth and back from 2 x 4's and whatever else.

Ivan - 2 yrs and Elizabeth - 6 yrs with Flossie, our dog, in the Spring of 1936.

Travelling with a team of horses and wagon, Dad Rowan, Ivan and Elizabeth along with their horses "Pat and Mike". Taken in 1935.

George Rowan's 1948 hay stacker invention.

Case tractor and separator at Uncle Art's farmyard.

Class of '40 - (Back row L-R) Margaret Gillhoolie, Fred Hunt, Miss Beatrice Wood (teacher for 3 yrs.) Reg Roberts and Wilfred Brown. (2nd Row L-R) Evelyn Brown, Marjorie Bird, Ray Bird, Robert Gillhoolie (hidden, just can see the top of his head), Harold Smith and Harold Dietrich. (3rd Row L-R) Mervin Dietrich covering face, Nelson Roberts, Olive Bird, Anne Anne Rowan and Archie Goodbun. (4th row L-R) Joan Bird, Lawrence Robb, Clarence Robb, Jean Bird, Mary Bird and Ivan Rowan.

My Dad had a Cockshut binder which he used to take the crop off. Then, the sheaves had to be stooked. In the later thirties, my Grandpa (Nels Rowan) did the threshing for my Dad. He had a Case tractor and a threshing machine.

When Dad's threshing separator wore out, he had Clive Leflar do the threshing with his big old Rumbly tractor and separator. Clive lived about a mile west of our farm on the south side of the road, across from the old Grainsby schoolyard. In this threshing gang there was Sid Beech, Lloyd Leflar, Jack Kruger, Frank Bird, others I don't recall and of course, Dad (George) Nerbras.

There was great excitement in about 1943 when my Dad bought our first radio from Reg. Lewis who ran the Dropmore Post Office and the Lewis General Merchant Store. Now we had our own radio! It was run by an A battery which had to be charged up regularly and two big B batteries. We used this radio until about 1949 or 50. Then we got this electric radio. Mom's cat would sit contentedly beside it.

My brother Ivan and I attended the Dropmore School. My first teacher was Mr. Pamroy in the later thirties. Our next teacher was Beatrice Wood, who later married Don Lewis. Don ran Lewis General Merchant Store, also.

I took my Grade Ten at Roblin Goose Lake Collegiate in 1947-48. We had lots of snow that winter and in the spring of 1948 the Assiniboine River flooded its banks.

Dad would test the water depth of the old Dropmore bridge before driving across it with our old Model A Ford Coupe.

During the summer of 1948, I got a job at Smellie Bros. Creamery in Roblin. I worked there until the end of November. While I was in

Class of '44 - (Back row L-R) Archie Goodbun, Andy Turta, somebody hidden, Mervin Dietrich, Harvey Nerbas. (2nd row L-R) Leona Kruger, Anne Rowan, Evelyn Brown, Alice Ferris, Milly Ferris. (3rd row L-R) Blake Cameron, Ivan Rowan, Lawrence Robb, Johnny Ziebart and Melford Dietrich (4th row L-R) Rose Bird, Marie Barnett, Irene Robb, ? , Rublets and Donnie Turta. Missing were Clarence Robb and Burke Cameron.

Roblin, I boarded at Mr. & Mrs. William Cranwell's.

In the spring of 1949, I got a job with the Manitoba Telephone System at Russell, as a telephone operator. "Number Please....".

On November 15, 1952, Albert Wilfred Wishart and I were united in marriage with Dr.

School bought by George Rowan in about 1957.

Mom and Dad Rowan's Silver Wedding Anniversary, 1953.

The old Dropmore School turned into a home.

Linda Wishart   Tim Wishart

Rothwell of Inglis United Church officiating. Bridesmaid was my cousin, Mabel Roe and bestman was my brother, Ivan. In this marriage we were blessed with two healthy children,

Wedding of Albert Wishart and Anne Rowan on November 15, 1952.

Linda-Lou Darlene born July 30, 1959 and Timothy Albert Nelson born July 12, 1964.

In 1963 I was born again through gospel meetings held at the portable Gospel Hall at Russell, MB. The scripture verse was John 3:16. "For God so loved the world that He gave His only begotten Son, that whosoever believeth in Him should not perish, but have everlasting life." And I thank God for saving me, for we had our happy times and our sad times, but God was with me through it all. Praise God!

On December 25, 1953 Mom and Dad celebrated their 25th Wedding Anniversary. There were friends and neighbours there to celebrate with them.

Well, as the years went on, Dad bought the old Dropmore school, about 1957. It was moved by Wm Waggoner of Roblin. It was renovated and it took on a new look.

Linda-Lou, our daughter met with an untimely death in a car accident on November 11,

1978. She was 19 years of age. Linda also accepted the Lord Jesus into her heart at the age of 13 years. The scripture she was saved on was from Romans 10:9 & 10: "That if thou shalt confess with thy mouth the Lord Jesus, and shalt believe in thine heart that God has raised Him (Jesus) from the dead, thou shalt be saved. For with the heart man believeth unto righteousness, and with the mouth confession is made unto salvation." The believer's hope is found in I Thessalonians, Chapter 4, verses 13-18.

(Back row L-R) Ivan, Dorothy, Bev, Linda and Anne (Front row L-R) George (holding Barry), Edith, Tim and Albert.

Marriage of Tim Wishart and Wanda Gail Boire, January 5, 1984.

held at Shellmouth by Brother Boyle, Brother Norris and Brother Earle Ritchie.

My son Tim Wishart was united in marriage to Wanda Gail Boire on January 5, 1984. They have been blessed with three beautiful children, Natasha Anne, Vanessa Wanda and Johnathon Timothy. I love my grandchildren. They are special to me. Tim and his family have all accepted the Lord Jesus into their hearts and are serving the Lord at Grace Community Church in Estevan, SK.

That pretty well covers my family tree from my Dad's side. May God bless you that read the history of the Rowan Family.

Tim, Johnathan, Vanessa and Natasha Wishart Family picture taken in 1990.

My Mom was saved, born again as it says in John 3:3 "Except a man be born again, he cannot see the Kingdom of God." She accepted the Lord Jesus into her heart in 1964, and my Dad was saved in 1965, through the nightly meetings

The final resting place for George and Edith Rowan.

John and Barbara Shearer

by The Family

John George and Barbara Jane Shearer.

The Shearer families emigrated from the Orkney Islands in Scotland between 1888 and 1890, and settled in the Cut Arm District near Bredenbury, SK. Saltcoats was the closest town at that time. Our parents, John George and Barbara Jane Shearer were married there and the five eldest of their family were born there. In 1901 they moved to the Castleavery district to a farm south of the present Pyott picnic area. Later, they moved to section 22, now the Maurice Digby farm, and then to the west half of section 20-24-29, just one mile from the Saskatchewan boundary.

The first Castleavery School was located on the farm where we grew up, but was no longer in use when our family moved to that farm. We drove two and a half miles to section 28 where the school is now. This school was closed in 1965 when the children of the area were bussed to Roblin. Our family all remained in the area. All were married except for John and Barbara who lived on the home place until 1984.

Our neighbors were Mr. and Mrs. Walter Robertson and Mr. and Mrs. Harry Roe who both lived on the same section as us. Other residents of the Castleavery District at that time were: Mr. and Mrs. W. Nichols and Arthur, Mr. and Mrs. Harry Rowan and family, Mr. and Mrs. Bert Ferriss and family, Mr. and Mrs. Harland Ferriss and family, Mr. and Mrs. James Farncomb and family, Mr. and Mrs. Joseph Dugan and family, Mr. and Mrs. Jack Anderson and family, Mr. and Mrs. William Case and family, Mr. and Mrs. James Hunter and family, and to the west of us, the Langley and Peppler families.

Our mother's parents had come to Canada also and are buried at Saltcoats. Mother had one sister who married Joe Horner and lived in the district for a while before moving to MacLeod, AB. She also had a brother who farmed near Bredenbury, SK. Our father's family remained in the Orkneys except for one brother, Robert, who came to Canada and was killed in 1916 in the First World War.

Our family consisted of four boys and six girls.

Albert, born April 10, 1892, married Dagmar Lauritson; James, born April 11, 1894, married Isabel McFadyen; Margaret, born April 19, 1896, married Arthur Nichols; Tomina, born July 12, 1898, married Joseph Ferris; Robert, born April 199, 1901, married Vera Gorlick; Elizabeth, born 1905, died June 1914 of a ruptured appendix; Mary Isabella, born April 6, 1908, married John McFadyen; John Ernest, born December 11, 1911, never married; Laura Anne, born December 9, 1913, married Wilbert Morrison; Barbara Jane, born November 7, 1915, never married.

Robert died March 1973 and is buried in Castleavery Cemetery. His widow, Vera married Arnold George Ferris on May 6, 1974.

John and Barbara remained single and stayed on the home farm. Barbara passed away in September, 1984; while in the meantime John also passed away.

Albert Shearer and Dagmar Lauritsen

by Irma McFadyen

Albert Shearer, the eldest son of John George and Barbara Jane Shearer, was born April 10, 1892 at Bredenbury, Saskatchewan. In 1902, the family moved to the Castleavery District, to the Birnie Bridge, later called the Pyott Bridge and is now known as Pyott's Wayside Park on the west side of the water.

In 1914, Albert moved to MacNutt, SK. taking over and operating the livery barn business for a couple of years. Here, he met Dagmar

Lauritsen, who had come with her brother, Louis Lauritsen, from Clinton, Iowa, USA, to a farm east of MacNutt, SK.

In 1916, Albert bought the N. E. 1/4 22-24-29 and started farming on Dec. 9, 1916 Albert and Dagmar were married in Clinton, Iowa, USA. They farmed there until 1946, when they sold this farm and bought the W 1/2 of 16-24-29 and farmed there until 1946, when they sold this farm and bought the W 1/2 of 16-24-29 and farmed there until they retired to Roblin in the fall of 1962.

Albert was always the handy-man and did a lot of work repairing broken windows, or whatever needed fixing for the Castleavery School. He was a member of the Manitoba Pool Elevators in Dropmore, MB and as a senior member, received a scroll commemorating the Pool's 50th Anniversary, April 1975.

Albert and Dagmar had two daughters, Irma Agnes born July 25, 1918 and Isabel Marie born October 29, 1922.

Irma married Archie McFadyen and lives in Roblin, MB and Isabel married John Todd and lives in Vancouver, BC.

Albert passed away in the Grandview Personal Care Home, November 24, 1975, after a lengthy illness.

Dagmar moved into the Roblin Residence where she lived for nearly three years, when failing health forced her to move to the Roblin Personal Care Home. She passed away in the Roblin Hospital, September 5, 1983.

James Shearer Family

Jim and Isabel Shearer.

James Shearer was born April 11, 1894 at Bredenbury, N.W.T. He married Isabel McFayden, born August 8, 1903 in Shellmouth. James and Isabel were married at the bride's home in Shellmouth on November 19, 1924. They settled on Jim's farm in the Castleavery District on S.W. 1/4 of 29-24-29 where they raised their family of three boys - Donald, Murray and Lloyd.

James and Isabel were active in community activities, Jim acting as trustee on the school board for many years. They enjoyed curling in the local rink, and Isabel, an active member of the ladies club, loved to quilt and sew. Each June, the annual school picnic was held on their farm, complete with ice cream, ball games and races for the younger folk. Supper was served in the implement shed which with neighbourly help, was emptied out for use prior to the big event.

Jim and Isabel's farming years took place during the transition from horses to tractors and later from threshing machines to combines. For many years, Jim travelled around the area and neighbouring districts, sawing wood with the sawing outfit he had built. The original 6-horse Fairbanks-Morse motor, that he used to run this outfit, is on display in the Roblin Museum. He also built and operated one of the first small sawmills in the district and often helped a neighbour out by sawing the lumber for whatever building the neighbour was constructing. Fall months found him again travelling the area with his threshing machine and Titan tractor and a crew of threshers.

In later years, with three sons starting their farming careers at home, newer methods were quickly adopted by the family, but the older ways were still appreciated as necessary steps in progress.

His sons took their places in the community in their younger years, operating the first snowplows when winter car roads came into being, doing welding, grain cleaning, spraying and custom grain hauling for neighbours who welcomed the help in their expanding farm operations. Cattle were always an important part of the farm operation, the hay from the valley being harvested to winter the cattle, without taking acres out of grain production. The boys used the knowledge they had gained in Agricultural School, introducing new ideas into the farming practice to make the farm more productive. All of them, encouraged by their father to be inventive, used their hands and tools to fix, repair, build and modify equipment and facilities to suit their needs.

Donald Allan Shearer (Son of James Shearer)

Donald Allan was born May 8, 1927, attended school in Castleavery and Tummell, and earned a diploma in Agriculture at the University of

Manitoba. He bought the W 1/2 10-24-29 and NE 3-24-29 from John McFadyen in 1951. Previous owners were A.H. Ferriss and Mary Cash W 1/2 10, and Earl Morrison and Wm. Ferris Sr. and sons Britton and Joe NE 3. They sold the land to Lloyd and Marlene Shearer. He married Gladys Mickelson, a secretary. In 1963 they moved to the Tummell District and bought N 1/2 8-24-28 from Joe Wolowetz where their two daughters Allison and Brenda were born. They bought SW 1/4 21-24-28 from Eugene and Edie Brumwell and SE 1/4 21-24-28 from Keith Alexander. For a number of years they rented three quarters from Oliver Mickelson and a half section from Ruby and Keith Alexander. Allison graduated as an R.N. from Brandon General Hospital. She worked at Russell Hospital for three years. She married Kevin Craig in 1991. They lived in Swan River for three years where Kevin worked at the T.D. Bank and Allison worked at Halliday's Ambulance, Swan River Hospital and taught piano lessons. They are presently living in Shoal Lake. Kevin works for M.A.C.C. and Allison works at Russell District Hospital. Both are active with the Shoal Lake Ambulance. Brenda graduated from the University of Manitoba with a Bachelor of Education Degree in 1992. She lives in Hartney where she teaches Kindergarten and piano lessons.

Murray George Shearer (son of James Shearer)

Murray George was born March 27, 1930 and attended school in Castleavery and Tummell. He then attended the University of Manitoba, earning a diploma in Agriculture. He married Jessie Pyott, a secretary, and they farmed in the Castleavaery District NW 1/4 14-24-29, the Bill Case farm, where their three children - Kathryn, Grant and David were born. In 1968 they moved to Swan River where they continued to farm until 1990. Murray works for Manitoba Housing and Jessie is a Homecare Attendant.

Kathryn worked for several years as a Civil Engineering Technologist for G.A. Pratt and Associates, Engineering Consultants in Winnipeg, until October 1994, when her husband, John Charowsky, an engineer with Reid Crowther, was transferred to their office in Vancouver, BC. They now live on Mayne Island, one of the Gulf Islands.

Grant and his wife Dawne, live on Vancouver Island. Grant is a mechanic at Nanaimo, searching for a business of his own. Dawne works with the Ministry of Finance, Revenue Division in Victoria.

David graduated from Red River College with a Diploma in Communications Engineering Technology, and is a Network Administrator with the Consulting Firm INSI in Winnipeg.

Lloyd Shearer Family (son of James Shearer)

Lloyd Alvin was born October 9, 1934, attended school in Castleavery and MacNutt, and remained in the Castleavery District to farm, first on the NW 32-23-29, previously farmed by Joe and Minnie Ferris, and presently on the SW 29-24-29, the home farm of Jim and Isabel. He married Marlene Laliberte, a teacher at Castleavery School. Marlene is a daughter of Paul and Verna Laliberte of Roblin.

Lloyd and Marlene married in 1957 and together raised a family of five children. After the children were in school, Marlene worked for fourteen years as an adjustor for Manitoba Crop Insurance, retiring in 1994. Lloyd worked at Route 83 Service Station and Roblin Forest Products in the early 1960's while continuing to farm.

Lloyd and Marlene Shearer.

Terry Lynn Shearer - Laindsay, Kris and Brady Andres.

Isabel and Jim retired to Roblin in 1966 at which time Lloyd and Marlene took over the home place. Jim died in 1978 and Isabel lived in the Senior Citizen's Home in Roblin for a few years prior to her death in 1985. Both are buried in the Castleavery Cemetery.

All five children attained their early schooling at Roblin Schools and their secondary degrees at the University of Manitoba during the years of 1976 to 1994.

The oldest daughter Terry Lynn, born in 1958, attended the University of Manitoba and Brandon University, attaining her degrees in Home Economics and Education in 1979 and 1980 respectively. She married Lee Andres, son of Oswald and Louise Andres. They had three children and are now divorced. The children are Lindsay Dyan, daughter, born in 1984, Kristian Lee, son, born in 1986 and Brady Jonathan, son, born in 1989. Terry teaches at Goose Lake High in Roblin and the children attend Roblin Elementary School.

Diane Michelle, born in 1959, graduated with her degree in Social Work in 1981. She married Brian Titanich, son of Muriel and Doyick Titanich, of Roblin and they live in Calgary where Diane is employed by the Province of Alberta as a supervisor in Mediation in Family Court. Brian is employed as a supervisor for GST with Revenue Canada. They have one daughter, Carly Lauren, who was born in 1990.

Const. Kevin and Const. Michelle Shearer.

Brian Titanich, Diane Shearer and Carly Titanich.

Garry Roloff, Erin Roloff and Tannis Shearer.

Bruce Shearer.

Tannis Dawn, born in 1962, graduated with her degree in Social Work in 1984 and has been a Case Coordinator with the Provincial Government Continuing Care Program since 1985. She married Garry Roloff, son of Freda and Bruno Roloff, a journeyman carpenter from Dauphin. They reside in Dauphin and have one daughter, Erin Dawn, born in 1992.

Kevin Lloyd James, born in 1968, graduated from the University of Manitoba in 1989 with a degree in Arts, majoring in Criminology. He was accepted into the RCMP during his last year of University and continued on with French Immersion in Montreal and basic training in Regina in 1990. He graduated from the RCMP Depot in 1991 and was posted to Craik, SK. Here he met Michelle Bishop, also a member of the Force, and they were married in 1993. They are presently stationed at Broadview and Kipling, SK and live at Kipling, SK.

Bruce Robert, born in 1971, attended Roblin Schools and earned his degree in Agricultural Engineering in 1994. He is employed as a design engineer with MacDon Industries based in Winnipeg.

Lloyd and Marlene continue to farm, raising Simmental cattle and grain.

The Mike Shewchuk Family

by Daniel Shewchuk

Nonie in our first home in 1939.

The Mike Shewchuk family came to the Castleavery District in 1957, the homequarter was SE Sect. 4 ____. Mike and Nonie (previously from the Clova District) came with family: Teeny (age 14 and already moved to The Pas) Ivan 13, Daniel 10, and Elias 5. Though rustic and secluded, Daniel at least thrived in the protection of the tall trees.

In our home north of MacNutt, SK in 1954.

Our neighbors to the east was the Bob Pyott family and to the west Sam Maskalyk, then Art Rowan. One-half mile southwest was the Joe Simair farm.

During these years, we were associated with the Romanian Orthodox Church west of MacNutt and this was where much of our activities were centered, and therefore competed for our time in the community. The curling rink, well established 4-H and other programs offered in the school were appreciated. Of course the Assiniboine River was one of the major attractions with its rugged beauty.

Our total tenure here was only about seven years due to the Shellmouth Dam and eventual flood. In 1964 the move was made.

Ivan, six weeks after the accident in Regina, SK hospital.

The seven years were a difficult period for the family, a time of great emotional hardship with Ivan's accident in 1960, and eventual crisis' of various origins, made each day a new challenge. The neighbours were very helpful to us on many occasions.

Mike and Nonie, Ivan, Teen and Elias presently reside in the town of The Pas with their respective families and Daniel and his family at Lethbridge, Alberta.

On the 24th of June 1937 Mike and Nonie got married and settled 4 1/2 miles north of MacNutt, SK on a farm for seven years, and found it inconvenient with cattle, we moved to the 1/2 section we owned along the Assiniboine River where it was good with cattle and lumbering, as well as farming.

Assiniboine Valley home after Ivan's accident.

Our fourth home in The Pas, MB.

Teen Rose in rock garden in the valley.

Ivan and Daniel at home.

Teen was out of school and went working Art Morrison and others in the district.

Ivan, Daniel and Elias went to Castleavery School with their favorite teacher being Holly Andrew and Michael Kozensky. They had a strong 4-H Club there, where the boys had entered their calves and swine, Harold Boughton being the Agricultural Representative.

We lived there until 1964, when the Government bought us out to flood the valley to build the Shellmouth Dam, and were relocated in The Pas where we have 10 more frost free days than the south, and 14 feet of top soil that grows almost anything, especially strawberries and potatoes.

Teen Rose married Ted Hlady who worked at the Post Office, and she worked at the Hospital. They got 4 children, Teresa married Eric Yeo from Roblin, MB. They got 3 children: Kathy, Michael, and Christopher, and live in Flin Flon, MB. Greg a single parent with Jordan.

Adele married Greg Baschak they have 3 children: Ryan, Andrew and Laisha who live in Russell, MB.

David left University, travelled Australia for a year, and is working at the mill now.

Mike with foster children in the back yard at our home in The Pas.

Ivan with his 4-H calf and Daniel with his 4-H calf.

In 1962 Teen and Ted Hlady back home in the valley from their honeymoon.

Ivan who is handicap lives at Pine View Manor, on his own, with a little help, he works at the museum two days a week, and wherever necessary, and does well.

Daniel married Deanna Easton, they have 5 children. He is a male nurse and she is with home care.

Amber married David Johanson, he works in Lethbridge.

Glenn, Karmen and Lance are working, and Leah is going to school.

Elias married Nancy Newstead. He works at the Repap Mill, and she is working with the Mental Health Association. They have 3 children: Joel who is working at the mill, Tim is going to school and Debbie is in school.

Holly Andrew taught her first class at the age of 18. Her parents, Earl and Edith settled on the farm on Young's Point Road in The Pas, MB and we became very good friends ever since. Earl since passed away, but Edith lives in Winnipeg on 52 Flye, phone 204-632-8862, also Holly is there, as far as I know.

J.T. Shipp, Memories of Dropmore

by Dorothy Simms

My memories of Dropmore are many. I started school there in 1920 when our family moved to the Clark farm some three miles south of the town. I had three brothers and one sister. Tom, the eldest, went to work for Mr. Hunter, and sister Annie, for the Beals family. We had wonderful neighbours, the Goodbuns, Coopers, Bradley-Hunts, and Mr. Lefler, a bachelor, close by. Winona Goodbun and I became quite good friends.

Father got a buggy for Jack, Joe and I to go to school and we managed to wreck the wheels driving across the many stoned road on section fifteen. Often when joining the Goodbun buggy we would race, and on one occasion locked wheels, a frightening experience. Much of the summer we walked to school. The road curved around a bush near Dropmore where gypsies once camped. Needless to say, we were too frightened to walk home.

Mrs. Goodbun was a trained nurse and a very kind, loving person to have in our midst. Being that we were many miles from a doctor, she would be called to attend the sick at any hour of day or night. When I was twelve years old, I became very ill the day after Christmas and she came to see me. She told my parents to get me to a hospital right away. Her son, Chummy, had a very fast team of hackney horses and a sleigh democrat in which a bed was made for me and we set off for

Langenburg where I would see Dr. Denmark, and with Dad take the train to Portage la Prairie for an operation. Lucy Wardle had just come home from having the same operation (appendix).

A short distance from home, there was a gully which we could run down to the Shellmouth road that passed the Martin Bell place. Mrs. Bell sewed white dresses and veils for Annie and me to wear to confirmation in the Anglican church in Shellmouth. We would go down the gully, cross the road and trail back to Mrs. Bell's house to be fitted.

The Dropmore hill was not far away from our farm and in the summertime, a gentleman named E.F. Miller would come from the United States to live in a small house at the top of the hill. He was a clever man in many ways. Water was hard to find in our area and when a well was dug he would crib it with stones. He was also a very talented musician and wrote many songs which he sang beautifully. I have a book of songs that he wrote and put to music. This book of songs was given to me by Mr. Lefler who had kept it these many years and seemed to know that I would very much appreciate having it.

Mr. Miller, living quite near to our home, came often to visit and during one visit when he had dinner with us, mother cooked mushrooms. He enjoyed them so much he later picked some to cook. They were the wrong kind and he became violently ill. He walked over to our house with a newspaper in his pocket on which he had written "I ate mushrooms". Mother quickly induced vomiting which I do suppose saved his life. This man was a devoted Christian as many of his songs told.

I remember another time when my mother helped in an emergency. Mr. Frank Reich was bindering somewhere near and while trying to fix a canvas with his jackknife, pierced an eye. He came to our house where mother did what she could for him and quickly called help to get him to a doctor. Unfortunately he lost the eye.

The people in the Dropmore area were all kind, friendly people. Mr. Ferris Sr. was a good friend of Dad's and during harvest time he would let Dad have a horse when he needed it the most and probably did not have money to buy one. The late Bill Ferris Jr. had the smartest team and buggy and a pretty girlfriend to court whom he later married. Jessie now lives in the Banner Court. My mother was a close friend of Mrs. Britton Ferris and was called many times to help when a new baby was to arrive. Some of the Rawlings family who were always good to be with, are now living in the town of Roblin and the Bradley-Hunt daughters live near their dear old mother in Russell, and on a farm at Rochedale.

Due to much rain and a sudden drop in grain prices, Dad decided to give up trying to pay for the farm, so we moved to Asessippi and went back to renting arrangements. It was from there that I finished high school by riding horseback to Inglis to get on the 7 a.m. train to Russell, after leaving my horse in the De Lamare livery barn. Most of my years were given to helping on the farm and in 1945 I married George Simms, moving to the Russell area where I am still living on the farm.

The Simair Family

by Brenda Kerswell

The original wood frame house for Joe and Maggie Simair.

Original round-roofed barn.

Joseph and Margaret Simair moved their family from Springside, SK to the Castleavery District in MB in November of 1951. They purchased the Edgar Comfort farm and settled on to Sect 33-24-29. The family had rented land in SK but this was the first home they had owned.

The Comfort farm consisted of a section and a quarter of mixed farm land bordering the Assiniboine River Valley. The original house was

Joe and Maggie Simair taken approximately a year after moving to Castleavery. (L-R) Maggie (holding Brenda), Cecil, Terry, Joe holding Florette..

Joe and Maggie Simair on their 50th Anniversary in July, 1987. (Back row L-R) Cecil Simair, Maureen Simair, Terry Simair, Ray Borejsza, Brenda and Vernon Kerswell. (Front row L-R) Florette and Diane Borejsza, Maggie and Joe Simair, Paul Borejsza..

a two storey four bedroom frame house. The outbuildings consisted of a huge round roofed barn (that exists to this day), and a number of smaller buildings.

The original farm house and round roofed barn (photo taken in the early 1950's) are included.

Joe and Maggie, and their four children entered the small social circle of the Castleavery District, and participated in whist drives, bingos, bonspiels, 4-H activities, fall suppers, picnics, turkey shoots, and all the activities that centered around a one room schoolhouse and a one sheet curling rink.

At the time of the printing of this book, Joe (now 84) and Maggie (79), still live on, and actively farm, their originally purchased land. They celebrated their 50th wedding anniversary in March of 1987.

They have raised four children: Cecil Simair, who currently farms with Joe and Maggie. Terry Simair, married to Maureen, is a pilot with Air Canada and lives in Grimsby, Ontario. Florette Borejsza and her husband Ray own an import business, and also live in Grimsby. They have two children: Paul (14), and Diane (9). Brenda Kerswell, a nurse, currently works and lives in Dauphin, MB. She has a daughter, Whitney, who is 6.

Frank Leith Skinner Family

by Helen Skinner

Frank Leith Skinner was born in Rosehearty Aberdeenshire in 1882, on the rocky, north-east coast of Scotland. His father, John Skinner, was a fish merchant in the nearby town of Fraserburgh.

A very good herring season brought a glut on the fish markets with shiploads of fish in European ports remaining unsold. The family's livelihood disappeared and they began to work and save to come to Canada.

Frank's mother's family were gardeners and Frank showed a very early love of growing things. When he was five years old he was given a geranium slip in a pot. He proceeded to turn it out of the pot, check it, put it back again and then announced, "It will grow". In the eighty-five years of his life he never lost that love of growing plants.

He was thirteen years old when he came to Canada in 1895. His family first settled in the Castleavery district near Pyott's bridge. John Birnie, a half-brother lived in this area at that time. He had been in Canada since 1883.

Granny Skinner.

A short time later they moved into an area west of the Shell River. Then Frank, his father, and his brother, William took up homesteads in the Rochedale district (SE 1/4 of 4-24-28 and NW 1/4 of 32-23-28). Eventually they had a large herd of cattle and several sections of land in grain.

Frank kept his interest in growing perennials, shrubs and trees, but to his sorrow, he found that the roses, etc. which he had seen and loved in Scotland would not survive the severe winters in Western Canada. Thus began his search for hardy material. It led him to correspond and visit with plantsmen all over the northern hemisphere, to plant-hunt over the prairies and in the mountains of British Columbia, to travel to Ottawa, Boston, Washington, Dc and to Europe. He never managed to reach Asia, but it wasn't because he didn't want to look for hardy material in the North Islands of Japan, Manchuria and Mongolia. He did receive many interesting introductions from the area - the Manchurian Elm, Korean lilac, Siberian pine and Fruiticosa cherry from Mongolia, to mention a few.

Besides being a plant collector he was a plant breeder. he used hardy species with less hardy, more spectacular species in his plant breeding experiments. His success in many, generally led to his recognition as an outstanding plant breeder among his colleagues in Canada, United States and around the world.

The Skinner sisters - 1944: Chris Anderson, Clem Lewis, Nan Robertson, Nell Richardson and Bell Dugan.

The Skinner brothers - 1944: William, Frank and Alex.

He received many honors. In 1933 he was awarded the Cory Cup by the Royal Horticultural Society for his Maxwell Lily. In 1932 he was the first recipient of the Stevenson Memorial Gold Medal for "Conspicuous achievement in Horticulture". In 1937 he was awarded a bronze medal by the Minnesota Horticulture Society. In 1943 he was made a member of the British Empire in King George VI's birthday honors. In 1947 he received an Honorary Doctor of Laws Degree from the University of Manitoba. In 1960 he was given a special citation by the Roblin Chamber of Commerce. In 1963 he was awarded a silver medal from the International Horticulture Exhibition in Hamburg, Germany for a display of lilies. He was also given the E.H. Wilson Award by the American Lily Society for his work with lilies. In 1964 he received a citation from the American Horticulture Society. In the same year he was present with the golden Boy Good Citizen Award in Manitoba and in December, Shellmouth Municipality awarded him a plaque.

In 1967 he was presented with the "Order of the Buffalo" by the Manitoba Government.

After his death on August 27, 1967, the Manitoba Horticulture Association established a Memorial Library in the Agriculture Library of the University of Manitoba to perpetuate his memory.

His picture hangs in the Canadian Agricultural Hall of Fame at the C.N.E. in Toronto and in the Manitoba Agriculture Hall of Fame in the Keystone Centre in Brandon.

Frank and I were married in 1947. The difference in our ages was bridged by common interests. I had been raised in a family of naturalists and horticulturists. My father, Hugh Duncan Cumming, a teacher, was an ardent naturalist and my brother, Dr. W. A. Cumming was head of ornamentals at Morden, MB research station.

We had five children:
F. Leith is with the RCMP in British Columbia married to Gladys Klimack. They have three children: Heather, Colleen and Brian.

Hugh William, B.Sc. in Agriculture and runs Skinner's Nursery.

Helen Isabel is a piano teacher whose husband Tim Wendell is a bee keeper in our area. They have three children: Jeremy, Keely and Nathan.

Heather Ann, B. Sc. in Agriculture, M. Sc. with her husband Tim Loeppky, works at the C.D.A. Research Station at Melfort, SK. They have two children: Jessica and John.

John Cumming, B.A. (Hons), B. Ed., A.D. is the principal of the Roblin Goose Lake High School and is married to Joanne Hamilton. They have two children: Sarah and Michael.

Cal Stauffer

Calvin Stauffer about 1965.

Cal moved to Dropmore from Roblin in January of 1964 to train under Mrs. D.A. Bradley-Hunt as Secretary-Treasurer for the Rural Municipality of Shellmouth. He boarded with his sister Buryle and brother-in-law Bill Doole.

His term with the municipality was for four years and during that time (through his job) became acquainted with most of the residents and many other people in the surrounding areas. He also collected telephone bills, hydro bills and hospitalization - even issued birth and death certificates. One of his less popular duties was when he signed the certificates to expropriate land from the people who had to make way for the Shellmouth Dam project which later created "The Lake of the Prairies".

For a few years, Cal was called upon to be the emcee at the annual Christmas Carol. He thoroughly enjoyed that because he was able to poke fun at some people and actually get away with it.

Another event which sticks in his memory was when a calf on the farm at the Doole's contracted rabies in 1967. The family dog had been playing with the calf before it got sick, so everybody in the family had to get rabies shots. And the dirty work of disposing of the dog fell upon Cal. As he called the dog away from the house and around the back of the buildings to do his dirty deed with the 22-rifle, unbeknownst to him, Hazel was peeking around the corner to see what was going on. Following that, and for fourteen days in a row, everyone went to Roblin early in the morning to get a needle in their stomach. After a few days, there wasn't a spot on the stomach which wasn't sore, so when the doctor asked where you wanted it next, you just closed your eyes and said, "Take you pick." Hazel who was only three years at the time, was very brave about it all and hardly made a fuss.

Another time, Cal got a panicked call from Buryle while he was at the office. Hazel had fallen into a scalding hot pail of water that Buryle had just put on the floor. Needless to say, there was a fast trip to the hospital in Russell, breaking all speed limits. Luckily she had been snatched out of the water quickly enough so that she didn't suffer from really serious burns.

One time, when the auditor (J. K. Barnes) was working on the books of the municipality, Cal went home for supper. The auditor, who had been given the key to the municipal office, came back from his supper early and heard noises in the office. He called out Cal's name because he thought he could be let in without having to use the keys. But when he got no answer, he tried the door and found it was not locked. He opened it a crack and what he saw, caused him to run in panic. Someone was poised to the side of the door with a claw bar raised, ready to whack him on the head. While he ran to call the police from the phone at Dave Bushko's store, the crooks made their escape. Luckily, Mr. Barnes had noticed that the lower left headlight of the car parked to the side of the office was burned out. With this knowledge, the police rushed from Russell to get to Dropmore and on their way, spotted the burned out headlight as they met the crooks who were on their way to Russell. It had been tax collection time and the vault was found open with $6,000 in cash in it, but the crooks had been scared off and did not get a cent.

Near the end of his four year term, he was cleaning out the storage area at the back of the municipal office and came across a case of dynamite. It had baked in the heat for so many years while being stored, that beads of nitroglycerine were coated on the surface of the sticks. When you flicked a drop of it off your finger and it hit the floor, it exploded like a firecracker. Needless to say, it was disposed of in the safest way possible, sank to the bottom of the old outdoor toilet.

When Cal left Dropmore he began working as assistant Secretary-Treasurer for the Rural Municipality of North Cypress and the Town of Carberry. While living there, he married Katie Louise Klassen from Winnipeg and they had two sons, Sean and Mark and a daughter, Heather. In 1974, he moved to Leaf Rapids, near Thompson, and was Secretary-Treasurer of Leaf Rapids School District. In 1976 he moved to Vancouver and worked in the office of a courier company and in an insurance office. In 1981, he came to Toronto and started a printing brokerage. In a few years the companies that he did business with, began getting their own computer equipment and printed their own forms, so he closed the company and went to work for Cigna Insurance of Canada for eight years. Then, when they downsized, he went to work for Sears Canada in their catalogue department. He is still working there as of this writing.

One of the most recent highlights in his life was the marriage of his daughter (Heather) in Clearbrook, B.C. in November of 1994. His two boys (older than Heather) are currently living there and are still single.

Edward and Katherine (Adam) Threinen

by Edward and Katherine Threinen

The Threinen Family 1948 - Ed, Katie, Ninite, Norman, Jeanette, Dennis in our Saskatchewan home.

Edward and Katherine were both born in Saskatchewan. Ed's ancestors originated in Luxembourg. His grandfather had emigrated to the United States. His father was raised at Mazeppa, Minnesota. As a young man he farmed a homestead twelve miles south of Langenburg, SK. At the age of 25, he married Maria Dietrich. Maria and Katherine's parents, John and Minnie Adam, came to Canada as young children with their parents and grandparents who came from Bukowina in eastern Europe. At that time, it was part of the Austrian Empire. The area is now a part of Romania. They were German-speaking farmers who came to Canada in the 1890's. Edward was born in 1906 and attended Landestreu School when it first opened. Katherine, born in 1914 attended the Zorn School. They both attended the Landestreu Lutheran Church, six miles south-west of MacNutt. Katherine's parents who were John and Minnie Adam. Katherine tell their story:

"Immanuel Lutheran Church at Landestreu, SK was the centre of our social and religious life. We were baptized and confirmed there, and we attended regular Sunday services with our parents. As young people, we had Bible Class, choir practice, and social activities. As a result, most of us got married to someone we knew from the church."

Ed and I were married on October 4, 1931. It was an early fall and harvest was all done. It was time to settle in for a long, cold winter. The custom was that when a son got married he would move his bride into his parents' home. Ed's sister, Elsie had been married a month earlier and moved to her husband's family home at Rhein, while I moved into the Threinen home with my new husband.

We lived with the folks for about one and a half years. It was right near the Landestreu Church. After that, we were able to rent an old farm yard and land in Manitoba, about thirteen miles away. Dad Threinen had bought one-half section there. He was trying to farm it with the idea of perhaps moving there some day. We found out that there was a farm yard available on the same section: Section 9. It was known as the Mustard place, close to Wm Morrison's place. It was located about 4 miles north of Shellmouth and 4 miles south-west of Dropmore. In the spring of the year we moved there and started our own home.

The farm had a nice, big barn, but just a little old log house. We tried to fix it up as it was very cold in the winter. While we were cleaning and fixing it, we lived in a granary. When we moved into our first home, we had only a few meager belongings such as homemade furniture, a wood stove, coal oil lamps. We had an old wagon, four horses, a few cattle, a pig and some chickens. It wasn't much, but we were happy to be together in our own home.

When we bought groceries, it was only the essentials like sugar, salt, flour and coal oil. We milked about six cows by hand, then used a cream separator which was hand-operated, and separated the cream from the milk.
The skim milk was used for drinking, feeding the calves and for making cottage cheese. Some cream was made into butter for our own use. The rest was taken to Dropmore by wagon or sleigh and then shipped to Russell by train. The average price for a five gallon can of cream was $1.25. This doesn't seem like a lot of money, but I could also order a dress from the Eaton's catalogue for $1.25. You could actually buy something with a nickel or a quarter in those days. For extra income, Ed would cut a load of wood and take it to Shellmouth where he would sell it for $2.00 a load.

At that time it was decided to have church services in an old building in Dropmore. There were quite a few of us Lutherans there, so the pastor from Landestreu came and served us. At least it was only about four miles instead of thirteen. We travelled by horse and buggy in summer and by sleigh in winter.

Compared to what we have today, we were poor, but we didn't know any better and so we were happy with what we had. Everyone was in the same boat. We had no telephone, no power (except horse and man power), no TV or radio, but we got along just fine.

Our first baby, a darling daughter, was born in February, 1934. Ninita Doris was baptized at home by Rev. T. Kaufeld who was serving the small flock of Lutherans in Dropmore. Her godparents were Uncle Philip Dietrich and his wife Aunt Margaret. They were such a big help to us when we moved to Manitoba. They were always ready and willing to help us when we were in need...real Christian love.

In May of 1936, Ed's wish came true. We had a fair-haired, blue-eyed son. Norman John was his dad's pride and joy. Our dark-haired daughter was now two years old. Norman was baptized in our church in Dropmore. My brother Rudolph and sister Elizabeth Adam were godparents. We still had only a horse and buggy, so Rudolph took us to church with his car. What a treat it was to ride in a car!

By now we were thinking of renting another farm. The one we had wasn't too good. There were too many stones, and not enough rain. Our crops didn't turn out too good. We were able to rent a place closer to Saskatchewan: the Bieber farm.

Before we moved, Ed went to make summerfallow on the new farm. It being about 4 miles away, he would stay there all week. I had a hired girl staying with me, to help with the milking and care of the children. One morning we thought we would hitch up old Dan and drive out to the new farm. The girl went to the yard, caught the horse and hitched him up. Then away we went. When we got to the farm, Ed was surprised. He looked and said, "Whose horse do you have?" Dan was white, and so was this horse, so somehow we didn't see the difference. But Dan was a male and this horse was a female. What a shock for us, and what a good laugh we had. We never forgot our old Dan. When we got home, there was Dan, as big as can be. We put the other horse out where we found her. We found out that she was Henry Dietrich's horse. He had come to visit us and we had put her to work.

We now had three quarters of land, which we hoped would produce better crops. We had a nice house with one big room upstairs, but it was quite cold and we had lots of those dreaded chimney fires.

We still had no phone or car, just horse and buggy. By now we had quite a few horses, so we had lots of horsepower. We also milked quite a few cows, and our chickens laid lots of eggs, so things looked a bit brighter. The only running water we had was when we ran to the well with an empty pail. I also had to melt snow to do the washing. We had lots of exercise and fresh air; no need to go on a diet.

In February, 1939 we were blessed with another darling blond daughter. We called her Jeanette Elizabeth. Because it was winter, we had the baptism at home. It was too far to take a baby to church in the cold. Her godparents were George and Elsie Threinen.

Now with five of us, the buggy was getting a bit crowded. So we looked around and were able to buy a Model T Ford for about $50 from Albert Rathgeber of MacNutt. Now we were really travelling in style. It took very little gas. I even learned to drive it. The bike was another means of transportation in the summer. Ed would take two cans of cream on the bike four miles to my brother Rudolph's farm, and then catch a ride with him to deliver the cream to the MacNutt Creamery. Quite a trip with a bike!

For winter driving, my brothers, the Adams boys, made us a closed-in cutter with a stove in it, so we wouldn't freeze while driving in the winter. Later they made us a van which was like a little house with a wood-burning heater. Everyone was using them in those days. By then we were going to Landestreu church again, as it was only five miles west of us. We were even able to get a radio run by batteries which was nice to listen to in the winter.

This new farm was a bit more profitable than the first one. We got a bit more rain. In 1939 Mom and Dad Threinen decided it was time to give both us and George and Elsie each a quarter section of land. We would have to build a house on our quarter-section. We had no money, so Ed sold ten head of cattle for a total of $100 and we went to the sawmill and bought lumber to start our own home at last. We built just around the corner, west of Landestreu church. We didn't move until spring of 1940, as we had no barn on the new place. Now in our new home we at last had a telephone. We felt we were in a civilized country again.

In October, 1942, we were again blessed with a sweet little dark-haired baby boy. Now we had a perfect family: two boys and two girls. Our children all went to the Landestreu School two miles west, the same school that their dad had attended. Our last baby we called Dennis Barry. Dennis' godparents were Elsie and Alex Propp, Ed's sister and husband. He was the only one baptized in the Landestreu church where I was baptized about 28 years earlier. All of our four children were confirmed in the Landestreu church, so this church played a big part in our lives.

We went through hard times, but we learned from our experiences. We know that you can't spend money you haven't got, so we do with little if we have to. Now it's nice to have money to spend and to spend it wisely.

Our home in Yorkton, Saskatchewan since 1971.

The years went by and our children grew up. Our eldest daughter Ninita taught school for a couple of years. She married Howard Hautz. They live in Regina and have two sons, one daughter and six grandchildren. Norman, our first son became a Lutheran pastor, and is now a professor at Concordia Lutheran Seminary in Edmonton. He is married to Muriel Ertman. They have a son and daughter who are both married. Jeanette, our second daughter is also a teacher. She married Elmer Haberstock. They have two daughters and a married son. Dennis, our youngest son, married Sandra Schmidt. He took over the family farm. They have two sons and a daughter. Dennis died in March of 1994 at the age of 51.

We moved from the farm to Yorkton in the fall of 1971, just after our 40th wedding anniversary. We have been active in the New Horizon's Senior Club and Zion Lutheran Church. Up to now we have been enjoying good health. Praise and thanks to God for the many blessings bestowed on us and our family throughout the years of our lives on this earth.

How We Did Our Laundry
by Katherine Threinen

When we first moved to our own place in Manitoba, my only way to do laundry was to heat some water on the wood-burning kitchen stove and pour it into the big round wash tub. Then I would take the wash board and some home-made soap and go "rub-a-dub-dub" on the wash board. It wasn't much fun rubbing each piece, but it was good exercise and my hands would get as ripply as the washboard from being in the soapy water so long. At least they were clean. After the clothes were washed I would hang them out on the long clothesline and let them flutter and sparkle in the sun. Big bed sheets were especially hard to wash and to wring out by hand. In the winter I dried the dark clothes inside, but still hung out the bedsheets, tea towels and other whites. The thinner fabrics would freeze and gradually dry out. The long underwear would freeze so stiff that you could stand them up when you brought them in. When clothes were brought in they had to be hung up on makeshift clotheslines strung around the house. Later I got a clothes "horse" - a wooden rack on which I could hang smaller items. The whole rack could be put outside to freeze-dry and then brought in to complete the drying process. The sunshine on the white snow also acted as a bleaching agent for white clothes.

After a while I got a manual washing machine and wringer. It was easier, but I still had to stand and turn the handle for about 15 minutes for each load, and then crank the wringer. What a relief when I got a gasoline motor washing machine.

When we were in Landestreu we got a 32-volt electric power plant. It had a set of batteries which had to be charged regularly with a very noisy motor. Now, all I had to do was heat up the water, put the soap and water into the machine, switch it on, and it did my laundry. Then I fed the clothes through the electric wringer, put them through the rinse water, through the wringer and hung them out to dry. The 32-volt power ran our lights, radio and washing machine, but more convenience came a few years later when the Hydro line finally came through. Now we could have a refrigerator, freezer and even a black and white television, and, of course a new washing machine.

And so the laundry became easier as the children grew older. It would have been nice to have all those conveniences when I had to wash diapers. Now that we are alone and the children are grown, I have an automatic washer and dryer. It's no work washing clothes now, rather fun.

Tony and Stella Turta
by Andy Turta

Stella and Tony Turta.

Tony and Stella arrived in Dropmore in 1942. Tony had bid on the section foreman's job. Barring a short period of time he worked in Barbour SK. They remained in Dropmore until he retired in 1963 and moved to Saskatoon.

They lived in the railway station during their stay. This building consisted of a waiting room, freight shed and office with living quarters in the rear. There were two bedrooms, kitchen and livingroom.

They had five children: three boys and two girls: Pauline, Elsie, Micheal, Andrew and Donald.

Pauline married Phillip Grosse and they had seven children, four girls and three boys, Judith, Barry, Lynne, Leslee, Melville, Cheryl and Rodney.

Elsie married Wilf Corregan and they had three children: Maureen, Pam and Douglas.

Micheal married Sophie Zaporoski and they had five children: Lynda, Jayne, Timothy, Zoria and Nadine.

Andrew married Leafa Wismer and they had five children: Valerie, Gerald, Kathleen, Marilyn (deceased) and David.

Donald married Ann Kowal and they had five children, Dwayne, Dale, Terry, Deborah and Sherry.

Tony passed away in 1980, a few months before his 80th birthday.

Working for the C.N.R., they had a pass to ride the train. Stella took many trips to Ontario, B.C. and other places. They did not have a car so did not get around much in the Dropmore area. Tony used the track motor car for more than his daily work. He used to take the children and grandchildren for rides and sometimes go to MacNutt for groceries, etc.

Stella lives in an apartment in Saskatoon. She is in her 90th year and enjoying good health.

She still has fond memories of Dropmore and district and loves to come back for a visit whenever possible.

Raymond Ungarian

Dad, Mom (John and Dora), brother Rod and myself moved to the Rochedale area in the summer of 1945. Dad bought a parcel of land from John F. Keay for $1000.00 (NW 7-23-28W) in the R. M. of Shellmouth. Mom and Dad were born and raised in the Lennard area before moving to the Rochedale area.

They brought with them to the Rochedale farm 4 horses, 4 or 5 cows, 50 chickens, an old model T car which was green with yellow wooden spokes, and a dog named Bingo (I called him Beegee because I couldn't say Bingo).

The soil was a sort of blackish sand. If you got enough rain, barley would grow very good. The land wasn't all broken because I remember Dad clearing and breaking more land on that quarter. Part of it ran into the Shell Valley and the Assiniboine Valley. The buildings were situated on top of the hill where the Shell and Assiniboine Rivers meet. The area was good to raise cattle because there was lots of water and rolling hills for pasture.

Dad used to rent a half section in the Assiniboine Valley. One quarter was cultivated and the other quarter was hay meadow. You could have counted hundreds of stacks of hay in the Assiniboine Valley at that time. Now it is covered with water and known as the Lake of the Prairies.

Boys taking off for school - Feb. 16, 1956.

Rod and I started school in the Rochedale school in the late 40s or early 50s. I'm not sure exactly what year. The number of the school was 1268. Our first teacher we had was Miss Irene Lovas. Other teachers we had were Miss Ruby Kolstad (taught us for a couple of years); Mrs. Freda Robin who taught us in 1954-55; Mrs. Mack Cameron taught us in 1955-56 and 1956-57. I was in grade 8 then. Wynona Keating was the last teacher to teach us. We took Grade 9 by correspondence and she helped us with French during the noon hours. We then went to high school in Inglis.

I remember all the field days we had in Inglis and the many ball games between Dropmore, and Castleavery and Tummell. The first curling rock that I threw was in the Dropmore Curling Rink. It is still in use today.

Ken Chaboyer, Rod and Raymond Ungarian and Milton Chaboyer - 1950's.

In the summer, we had to travel to school in a buggy pulled by a big brown horse. In the winter this big brown horse pulled a cutter or van. When it got too cold he would go part way and then turn around and go back home. We couldn't do anything with that horse because we weren't strong enough. After we grew a little bigger, Dad bought us a grey pony from Bill MacDougall. This pony was young and fast. The pony was a male but we called him "Darling". We used to upset the cutter a lot of times. The box would break off and the horse would run home alone. Rod and I would walk behind - both of us crying!!!

The winters were very rough in the 50's. The snow was piled up so high that we could walk over the telephone wires.

In the spring we couldn't go with the cutter because it was melting and too wet for the buggy. So we used to ride horseback. That was all right for a while until our buns got blisters and sore. Then it was very hard to walk. We had to walk three miles to school.

As time went by, we invested in two bicycles which we used to ride to school when the weather was nice.

In the 50's, two boys, Kenneth and Milton Chaboyer, came to stay with us for four years. Milton, who was the oldest, was in the area two years ago and said he was coming back to meet the rest of his Rochedale school pals. They both live in Thompson.

Our closest neighbors in the Rochedale area were two bachelors - Nick and Charlie Harrick.

We moved out of the Rochedale area in 1960 and went back to the Lennard area.

My sister Cathy was born in 1960. She is currently living in Winnipeg where she is a legal secretary.

I married Dianne Hume from Saltcoats, SK in 1974. We live in Inglis. I am still farming and drive a school bus. In the summer I do some carpentry work.

Dianne works for the R. M.'s of Boulton and Shellmouth as the assistant administrator. We have two daughters - Rayanne and Jillian.

Rayanne was born on April 26, 1975 and is finished her second year of university at Brandon. Her sights are set on becoming an accountant. Jillian was born on January 1, 1979 and is finishing Grade X at Major Pratt School in Russell. She is a ball player like her dad and also enjoys other sports such as hockey, ringette and volleyball.

Even though we moved out of the area, I still enjoy going back to look things over and talk with the people. The Rochedale area is very special to me because this is where I grew up and I have a lot of boyhood memories which I will always cherish.

The Winter of 1956.

Raymond, Dianne, Rayanne and Jillian - 1990.

Ron and Kim Walter

by Kim Walter

Ron and Kim Walter Family.

Ron was born in 1969 in the Lestock, SK hospital. He attended school in Yorkton, then decided to farm with his father in the Jedburgh, SK area.

In 1986 his family moved to Russell and farmed in the Russell area. Ron still continues to farm with his dad.

Kim was born in 1971 in Russell, MB. She attended school in Russell.

Kim and Ron met in 1987 and later met up again in 1990. Ron and Kim were married December 31, 1993. They have three children, one girl and two boys. Shawnica who is five years old, goes to school in Roblin. The oldest of the boys is Shaun who is three years old, and the youngest is Shane and he is 19 months.

Ron and Kim moved to the Dropmore area with their family in 1992, taking over the Phil and Barb Zimmer farm (SE 22-23-29.

Kim is staying home with the kids, helping Ron farm, and she also sells Tupperware on the side.

The Wardle Family

by Sandra M. Wardle

Billy (William) Wardale, the sixth child and second son of Jesse and Jemima Wardale was born in Grimsby, Lincolnshire, England on 5 February, 1866. He contacted measles when he was 8 years old and developed ear trouble which left him hard of hearing for the rest of his life. Billy had a grade 4 education. His father would keep him out of school to work until the truant officer came around; send him back for a few days and then keep him out again. Mary Jolliffe had one of her father's Copy Books, dated November, 1879.

Just outside of Grimsby is a place called Grainsby. The chief landowners at the time Billy lived in Grimsby were William and George Henry Haigh. Samuel Harrison (Billy's grandfather) used his threshing machine on Haigh's land. It is extremely possible Billy worked there as well. It is also possible that the Haighs arranged his passage to Canada on a bulk grain carrier returning to Canada. When Billy left Grimsby, it is highly likely that he took the train from Grimsby to Liverpool, where he would have boarded a boat for Canada.

The William and Edith Wardle Family (circa)1912. (L-R) Edith (holding Mary), Jesse and William (holding Lucy).

Billy immigrated to Canada in the spring of 1889, at which time it appears he changed his name to William Wardle. He lived in Ontario for a short time before moving to Melita, MB and then to Bagot. In 1903, he moved to the Grainsby District where he homesteaded. He built a log house on the farm and called it "Poplar Grove Farm". (I do not know if my grandfather named Grainsby District, but it is possible.)

On 14 June, 1909, William married Edith Grace Goss in Russell. Edith was the daughter of John and Pollie (nee Sanders) Goss of Barnstaple, Devonshire, England. She was born in Coombs Cottages in Goodleigh, Devonshire on 14 June, 1885. Edith came to Canada with her family when

The first home of William and Edith Wardle - Grainsby, Manitoba.

she was in her teens. They lived in Portage la Prairie. Pollie Goss could not take the climate in Manitoba, so they moved back to England. While in Manitoba, Edith met William Wardle and they corresponded for some time.

On her return to England, Edith worked as a cook for Lady Clark at Willsleigh House in Goodleigh. In early June, 1909, Edith returned to Canada. She came by ship via Newfoundland. Just before they got to the shores of Newfoundland, they struck an iceberg. It made quite a hole in the side of the ship and they had to dock for about five days while it was repaired. The ship then sailed on to Montreal. From there, Edith caught a train to Shellmouth, where she was met by William Wardle and the Hunt family. Edith stayed with the Hunt's

The Wardle Sisters - 1933 (L-R) Lucy, Elizabeth and Mary.

(Alex, I think) (who were neighbours on the farm) until 14 June, 1909, when she married William Wardle on her 25 birthday. In 1914 or 15, William and Edith built a new house. In 1916, the Grainsby School burned to the ground. The only thing saved was the school bell. School was then held in the old log house on the Wardle farm until a new school was built.

William and Edith had three children:

Name	Born	Died
Jesse John	14/07/1994	16/04/1910
Mary Eunice	03/06/1989	08/06/1911
Lucy Edith		08/06/1911

In 1914, Edith contacted Tuberculosis. She had several operations in Winnipeg General Hospital, performed by a Dr. Galloway. He said she would never walk again, but with William's perseverance, she did.

In November, 1927, Edith returned to England to visit her family. Mary Jolliffe remembered that harvest was very late that year and Jesse was still threshing when his mother left for England. He had to build a fire under the old Hart Parr engine to keep it going and he had to shake the snow off the stooks.

William and Edith farmed in the Grainsby District until William's death on the 9th of October, 1941, at which time Jesse took over the farm. In 1958, Edith married Tom Garnett of Inglis. They lived in Carberry for a short time after their marriage and then separated. Edith then moved to Roblin where she remained until her death on 2 July, 1964. William and Edith are both buried in the Dropmore Cemetery.

Jesse John and Lucie Wardle

Jesse John Wardle, the eldest of the three children worked on the farm. He took an electrical course by correspondence and also learned to play the fiddle at the age of 9, under the watchful eye of Garnett Leflar, a neighbouring farmer. Jesse got his first fiddle from the T. Eaton catalogue for $4.95. Jesse and his friends, Reg Lewis on saxophone and drums, Cedric Rowan on the piano and Durward Rowan on the fiddle - played for many dances in the area. During World War II, Jesse worked in Dauphin and Transcona on war time construction, until his father's death, when he took over the farm. (Over the next few years, Dad added three more quarter sections to the original homestead - the adjoining quarter section to the north, which gave him the east half of 32-23-29. Then he bought the quarter section across the road - where Grainsby School was located - we didn't own those four acres, and finally another quarter - we called it "3" - take main road east from Grainsby corner, turn north at the corner just east of Howard Ferris's and go one mile and it was the south east quarter. Unfortunately, I do not know the legal description of these other two quarter sections.)

On 25 November, 1943, at the home of his sister and brother-in-law, Lucy and Mac Gillies of Transcona, Jesse married **Ellen Lucie Brooks**, (born 18 April, 1908) the only daughter of William and Catherine (nee Cuthill) Brooks of Glenboro. William Brooks was the son of Maria Brooks of Lincoln, England. Catherine was the daughter of John and Christine Cuthill of Glasgow, Scotland.

Jesse Wardle about 1938.

Catherine died on 7 August, 1909. William died on or about 23 January, 1917. Both are buried in the Glenboro Cemetery.

When Catherine died, Lucie was placed in a foster home. She lived in many foster homes and attended school in Patricia and Glenboro. Upon graduating from high school, she attended Normal School (Teacher's College) in Brandon. She taught school for several years in southern Manitoba. In 1941, she accepted a teaching position in Grainsby, where she boarded at the Wardle's.

Jesse and Lucie had one child, Sandra Mae, born 16 July, 1945 in Russell.

Jesse was an avid fisherman and hunter. He and his friends made many trips to Northern Manitoba to fish for Pickerel. When the Shellmouth Dam was built and the Lake of the Prairies stocked with pickerel, good fishing was available closer to home. Jesse, along with the Nichols boys, Allan Anderson and a couple of others had a cabin in the Duck Mountains that they used as a home base for hunting moose and elk. Deer, ducks and geese were other things Jesse liked to hunt. Another of Jesse's hobbies for many years was photography and he had his own dark room for developing.

In the spring of 1960, Jesse and Lucie sold the farm and moved to Roblin where Jesse did electrical work until he retired. Lucie sang in the United Church Choir and was a member of the U.C.W. Jesse and Lucie wintered in Weslaco, Texas for several years during their retirement. During this time, Jesse took up his fiddle playing again and has won over 120 trophies in old time fiddling contests in Manitoba and Saskatchewan - most of them on the fiddle he purchased for $4.95.

Jesse also developed an interest in Indian Artifacts and had an extensive collection, which is now on display in the Dauphin Museum.

Jesse passed away on 14 July, 1994 in the Roblin Hospital after a short battle with cancer. His body was cremated and the remains are buried in the Dropmore Cemetery beside his parents.

After Jesse's death, Lucie sold the house and now resides in the Roblin Residence.

Sandra Mae Wardle

Sandra, the only child of Jesse and Lucie Wardle attended Grainsby School from 1951-59 and was a member of the Assiniboine 4-H Sewing Club. Grainsby School closed in the spring of 1959 and all students were bused to Tummell where Sandra took her Grade 9. She attended High School in Roblin. In the fall of 1963, Sandra moved to Winnipeg where she took a secretarial course at the Angus School of Commerce, graduating in June, 1964. She then worked for the Canada Manpower Centre at the University of Manitoba, Student Placement Office Branch and then the Main Branch, downtown for five years. In December, 1969 she moved to The Pas where she obtained secretarial work with Churchill Forest Industries. In May, 1973, Sandra moved to Vancouver and obtained employment with Kaman Industrial Technologies, where she remained for 20 years, in various positions. She was laid off in April, 1993, due to restructuring. She is now employed as Payroll and Benefits Administrator with The Buy and Press Ltd. Her main hobby is genealogy. She is also Secretary-Treasurer of a slow pitch softball Beer League, and does volunteer work for the Salvation Army and the March of Dimes. She has recently become involved with the organizing committee of a Manitoba Reunion which is being held in the B.C. Lower Mainland in September of 1995. Sandra lives in Burnaby, remains single and has no family.

Lucy and Mac Gillies

Lucy, twin daughter of William and Edith Wardle was born at Grainsby on 8 June, 1911. She remained at home until her marriage to Mac Gillies, the eldest son of Dan and Ellen Gillies of Lenore, MB.

Mac attended Normal School (Teacher's College) in Brandon in 1928-29. He taught school in Grainsby from 1930 - 1933 and boarded at the Wardles. Lucy and Mac were married on the lawn of the family farm on 13 August, 1938. They resided in Transcona for 19 years, where Mac taught school. In August, 1957, Mac was appointed to the Inspector Staff and they moved to The Pas. In 1961 they moved to Carman where Mac continued as an Inspector until his retirement in 1980. Since their retirement they reside in Winnipeg. They too, resided in Weslaco, Texas for several winters during their retirement.

Lucy is to be complimented on the fine knitting she has done throughout the years. She is a beautiful knitter and has made herself many lovely suits, dresses and sweaters as well as sweaters and dresses for her grandchildren. Until recently, Lucy and Mac enjoyed golfing, ten pin bowling, dancing and attending live theatre productions.

Lucy and Mac had two sons, Kenneth Malcolm, born 27 August, 1941 and Donald Boyd born 12 January, 1946.

Kenneth Malcolm Gillies

Kenny, the first born of Lucy and Mac Gillies, was born in Transcona. He attended school there until his death on 13 January, 1953, from a malignant brain tumor.

Boyd and Emily Gillies

Boyd, the second son of Lucy and Mac Gillies was born in St. Boniface Hospital on 19 January, 1946. He attended primary grades in Transcona before moving to The Pas in 1957 where he completed grades 5 - 8. In 1960 the family moved to Carman, where Boyd completed his high school education. In 1964 he enrolled in the School of Pharmacy at the University of MB, graduating in May, 1968. From 1968 to 1974 Boyd was employed in several Pharmacy positions in the Brandon General Hospital and Assiniboine Hospital.

While in Brandon, Boyd met Emily Ferguson, who was a Practical Nurse at the Brandon General Hospital. Emily was born on 23 May, 1947, at Russell, the second daughter of Grace and Victor Ferguson. Boyd and Emily were married in Russell on 9 October, 1971.

In November, 1974, Boyd and Emily moved to Swan River (for a couple of years!) where Boyd was employed as Chief Pharmacist of Swan River Valley Hospital. Emily worked as a Practical Nurse for the Swan River Valley Health unit for two years. In 1976, they adopted a son, David Andrew, born 8 July, 1976, and in 1979 they adopted a daughter, Erin Marie, born 22 July, 1979.

Boyd and Emily still make their home in Swan River where Boyd is now Director of Pharmacy of the Swan River Valley Hospital, including the Swan River Valley Lodge and Personal Care Home. Emily works part time in a doctor's office.

Boyd and Emily enjoy golf and curling. Boyd and David are computer "nuts", and Boyd is a member of the Swan River Lion's Club. Emily does a great deal of volunteer service work for the Cancer Society and has been highly recognized and honoured for her work.

David is in first year university at University of Manitoba. Erin is in Grade 11 in Swan River.

Mary and Leon Jolliffe

Mary, twin daughter of William and Edith Wardle, was born at Grainsby on 8 June, 1911. She also remained at home until her marriage. On 24 September, 1938, on the lawn of the Wardle farm, Mary married Leon Ross Jolliffe, only son of Lorenzo and Minnie Jolliffe of Deepdale. Leon was born in Rolla, North Dakota and moved to Deepdale in 1902. He attended school in Wyndham School in Deepdale and High School in Roblin. Leon then attended Normal School (Teacher's College) in Regina, before going overseas during World War I. Upon his return, he furthered his education at the University of Manitoba. He later settled on the Jolliffe farm and married Mary, whom he had met while visiting his sister and brother-in-law, Dorothy and Allan Grundy, the grain-buyer in Dropmore. Mary and Leon farmed in the Deepdale District until their retirement in 1967, when they moved to Roblin. Leon passed away on 13 March, 1972.

Mary was always very active in the United Church, singing in the Choir, and as a member of the U.C.W. for approximately 50 years. She was also very involved in the Ladies Quilting Club. Mary was a member of the Agricultural Society for 20 years and while on the farm, she entered her

Leon and Mary Jolliffe   Lucy and Mac Gillies

fancy work, sewing and canning in many fairs in the province and won many prizes. Mary passed away very suddenly on Saturday, June, 1989. Eunice and Jim Ferguson were with her at the time. Eunice and Mary were doing dishes after lunch when Mary had a heart attack. She was pronounced dead shortly after arrival at the hospital. Her body was cremated and the remains are buried in the Roblin District Cemetery beside Leon.

Mary and Leon had two daughters, Marney Edith, born 11 June, 1940 and Eunice Lynn, born 14 October, 1953.

Marney and Ed Scribner

Marney, the eldest daughter of Mary and Leon Jolliffe was born in Grace Hospital in Winnipeg on 11 June, 1940 and attended school in Deepdale and Roblin. She worked in Winnipeg for two and a half years before training at Brandon General Hospital as a Registered Nurse. She graduated in 1966. She nurses at Brandon General for six months and then at Rockyview Hospital in Calgary for a year. She then moved back to Winnipeg where she nursed in the Manitoba Rehabilitation Hospital for five years and for another three at the St. Boniface Hospital.

Marney met Ed Scribner at the University of Winnipeg while he was working on his Bachelor of Arts degree and she was taking a Nursing Administration Course. Marney and Ed were married in Roblin on 29 August, 1971. Ed is the son of Dr. Frank and Margaret Scribner of Gimili (now residing in Winnipeg). Marney and Ed live in Winnipeg and have two daughters, Lisa Marie born 5 June, 1976 and Karen Irene, born 6 November, 1978.

Ed enjoys sports, reading, church work, carpentry and mechanics. Marney is active in church and school volunteer work, enjoys reading, sewing and family upkeep. The whole family enjoys travelling. Marney and Ed have a Good Roads Auto System franchise in Winnipeg.

Lisa is enrolled in first year at the University of Manitoba. She teaches piano and swimming in her "spare time". Karen is in grade 10 and is active in various school activities, drama, swimming, dancing and piano lessons.

Eunice and Jim Ferguson

Eunice, the second daughter of Mary and Leon Jolliffe, was born in Roblin and attended school in Deepdale and Roblin. Eunice remained at home after high school and worked at the Gulf Restaurant for two and a half years. In 1974 she moved to Regina where she worked for Wheatland Restaurant, the Regina Curling Club, Robert Simpson Co., and King Size Photo.

In the spring of 1983, Eunice met Jim Ferguson at a Singles Dance. They were engaged on 14 October, 1983, Eunice's 30th birthday. They were married in Roblin on 19 May, 1984. Jim is the youngest of a family of five. His parents, Doug and Elva Ferguson, are retired farmers from Melfort, SK. Until recently, they wintered in Arizona.

Jim worked for Inter City Gas Corporation from 1977-85. Just prior to their marriage, Jim was transferred to Winnipeg. Jim and Eunice lived in Winnipeg for one year before returning to Regina, where they both worked for Bi-Rite Drugs, a

Saskatchewan Drug Store Chain. In the fall of 1991, Jim changed jobs and is now General Manager of Cosmopolitan Recycling. Eunice continues to work for Bi-Rite Drugs as well as working part time as a Sales Representative for Uniglobe Travel. They have no family.

The Wiesner Family
by Dave Wiesner

The Dave Wiesner Family - 1993.

Dave was born at Morris, MB, the son of German immigrants who came from the Ukrainian Province of Volynia. Mary Jane was born at Gravelbourg, SK and is the daugther of basically French-Canadian parents whose background can be traced via North Dakota to Trois Riviere, Quebec. Their meeting can be attributed to a burnt out headlight on the Trans-Canada Highway near Broadview, SK where Dave was employed on Highway Patrol duties with the RCMP. They were married 25 September, 1965 at Esterhazy, SK. Three great snow storms occurred that month, the last one being the day before the wedding. In 1967, the 4th of September their first child, Troy, was born at Broadview. Following further transfers to Lumsden and Regina Beach, SK, the decision was made to change their lifestyle, and a farm was purchased in the Castleavery District from Mrs. Theresa Pope. They moved to this location at SW16-24-29 on Hallowe'en night in 1968.

Shortly after moving to the district, they discovered that a normal sized family seemed to be comprised of five children. They earnestly set out to follow this pattern and in 1969, Wanda was born on October 23rd. Scott was born the 18th of September 1971. Grant came along the 22nd of December 1974 and lastly, Ryan was born on the 6th of February, 1978. In order to make sort of a living, they began to milk cows and shipped cream. Available cows were bred to Brown Swiss until a satisfactory herd of 15 milk cows was established. However, with distant funerals and weddings to attend, it was determined that milking was too time consuming an occupation. Thus, in May of 1977, David obtained employment at Asessippi Provincial Park, where he has been seasonally employed ever since. The position as Park Patrol Officer has proven to be a meaningful occupation. The same year Dave also began the leadership of a brass band at the Evangelical Mission Church at Roblin, MB, which has also proven to be very meaningful to the entire family. All of the children were taught to play brass instruments, and through the years they played together at various functions from Alberta to Quebec City. Being on a farm also gave Dave the opportunity to work with horses, to the point of being considered a candidate for the mental institution. With a family of this particular size, Mary Jane has had the opportunity to practise her most beloved skill, that of cooking. She also has a large productive garden and flock of Cornish Giant hens, which some years are not too decimated by the foxes. Mary Jane also thoroughly enjoyed the time spent with the "Dropmore Chicks". Through this experience she learned to play the ukulele and kazoo. A few years ago she became a charter member of the Castleavery Walking Association, and has worn out numerous pairs of athletic walking shoes.

Dave and Mary Jane Wiesner.

As of 1995, the children are grown up. Troy is a Pastor at an Alliance Church at Burlington, ON. In 1990 he married Lorilee Jespersen at Quebec City. This year she will be graduating with her Masters Degree in Social Work. Troy has obtained his Masters degree in Missiology, and their goal is to become foreign missionaries. Wanda will be graduating this May as a Medical Doctor, having obtained a resident position in Chilliwack, BC with the Family Medicine Program. In May she is also marrying Dave Marlatt who is a pastor at an Alliance Church at Coquitlam, BC. Scott obtained his Bachelor of Theology degree and is presently interning as a pastor at an Alliance Church at Windsor, ON. It is probable that he will continue as pastor at that point upon completion of his internship. Grant has just completed his third year at Brandon University, where he is working toward a Bachelor of Education degree. The youngest child, Ryan, is presently in Grade 11, and has a passion for sports, especially basketball.

The Wiesner family feel exceptionally fortunate to be able to live in this district, and feel that they are in the place where the dear Lord has placed them. Lord willing, they hope to continue residing here and continue to enjoy the life they have been given.

The Wright Family

by Grandson Rod Laycock

Mr. and Mrs. Fred Wright farmed and bought grain in Dropmore from 1911 to 1921. In 1921 they moved to Endcliff, where Fred was an elevator agent for thirteen years. From there they moved to McKim, SK in 1934. Here they operated a General Store and a gas station.

Fred and Mary had three daughters, Violet, Myrtle and Freda and one son, Gordon. Rod Laycock (Russell) is the son of Oscar and Myrtle Laycock.

Nick Yaworski

by Adam Yaworski

Nick Yaworski came to Canada from Poland in 1906 at the age of 18 years. He lived in Merrydale, MB and then moved to MacNutt, SK in 1915. Later, he married his wife Nellie and raised 10 children. Nick and his family lived in MacNutt and farmed 3 miles south and 2 miles east on Sec 36-24-30. Adam Yaworski went out to work for farmers for $10.00 a month and that amounted to 35 cents a day. Also, there were no coffee breaks. This was in 1933. The government paid a laborer $7.00 a month and it also paid the farmer, $5.00 a month for keeping the hired man.

Their main travel was done by horse and buggy, or walking from to place to place.

Farming was done by horses and small machinery and a lot of hard work was done by hand.

Later their son Adam was married to Mary on October 22, 1944 and they farmed south of the home place near MacNutt until 1960. Adam and Mary raised three children of their own.
Bob born September 16, 1951, Judy born December 26, 1953 and Susan born December 9, 1958. The children had attended Zorn and MacNutt Schools and later attended Roblin Public School.

In 1961 we bought Mr. Clarence Hunt's farm and moved there. Later in the year our home was moved from MacNutt to the farm and finished off, ready to live in.

We farmed there until 1978 and later that fall, we moved to Roblin and our son Bob and his wife Joyce took the farm over and started farming and raising their favorite cattle. They are still living there. They have a family of three children, two of whom are now gone from home.

Ervin and Viola Young

by Viola Young

We arrived in the Dropmore area in September of 1965. We purchased the farm from Harry Wosney but it was known as the Archie McFadyen Farm as Harry had only had it for a few years.

We had sold our dairy farm at Caron, SK in the spring of 1965.

After travelling to B.C. and Alberta looking for a farm, we arrived in Roblin. After looking at a few in the area, we decided on the McFadyen farm.

We arrived at the farm on a wet and snowy day around the middle of September, 1965. The Wosneys were moving out and we were trying to move in.

Our oldest son, Brent, was in Alberta, working. He and his wife Bea still reside at Medicine Hat with their two daughters, Tannis and Colleen.

So we had Leah and Glenn to start school. As Leah was in Grade 8, we thought we should send both her and Glenn on the bus to Tummell. Arnold Ferris drove the bus. The first day, Leah wasn't on the bus. Glenn got left at school, so Mr. Dinsmore attempted to drive him home. Glenn hadn't a clue to where home was, neither had Mr. Dinsmore. We met them coming across the valley. I don't know who was more relieved.

Our neighbours across the road, Jean and Earl Morrison, made our move into a new district so much easier. They took us to Roblin and introduced us to our neighbours. One of the nicest Christmases we ever had was at George and Flo Hunters. As strangers, and not able to go home for Christmas, they asked us to come to their place. What a jolly crowd. It was a Christmas we haven't forgotten.

Looking back over the years we spent in Dropmore and area, we realize they were filled with good friends and good times. Our small Dropmore Church, the Dropmore Chicks, the showers and weddings, all made for wonderful memories.

Our son, Glenn is now on the farm. Leah now resides in Saskatchewan. Her two daughters, April and Rebecca reside there as well.

We retired to Moose Jaw, Saskatchewan on August, 1989. Ervin passed away June 18, 1995.

The Ziebart Family

by Anna (Ziebart) Harding

In April 1944, the Ziebarts bought the Ike Goodman farm located 1-1/2 miles south of Dropmore at S1/2 23-23-29 (the big brick house) and moved from the White Beach District of Arran, SK. They arrived by horse and wagon and a 1928 International 1-ton truck. The family consists of Gottlieb and Emily with sons Henry, Ernest, Rudolf, John and daughter Anna. Their other daughter, Wanda (Kitz), was already living in the Landestreu District by MacNutt.

The farm buildings were a big three-story brick house, a barn with a hay loft, a chicken coop, granaries, and of course an outhouse. This one, befitting the large house, was a three-holer --- 2 large and one small in the middle. The brick house built by the Goodman's had been empty for 8 years and was in poor condition. The fields had begun to return to their natural state. The farm had a very deep punched well but no working pump. A shallow well was dug for water.

The farm was worked with horses until 1946 when they purchased a steel wheeled tractor. Horses, however, continued to work on the farm for many years.

Social life consisted of attending the Lutheran Church in Landestreu, dances and Christmas concerts in the Dropmore Hall, and visiting neighbours for Sunday dinner or, on cold winter nights, to play cards. The popular card games were whist, hearts, and King Petro (King Peter). In summer they would enjoy swimming in the Assiniboine River.

Where were they and where are they?

Gottlieb Ziebart

Born July 19, 1889 Wolinian (Wolinske) Russia. He immigrated to Canada April 10, 1912 and homesteaded at Fox Valley in south west Saskatchewan. On April 9, 1918 he married Emily Wuschke and a few years later moved to Mossbank and then Arran, SK. In April 1944 he moved his family to Dropmore. He joined the Wheat Pool in Saskatchewan in 1924 and remained an active member until he retired in 1962. He took an interest in political matters and his practice was to never accept a ride to the polling booth with a

Gottlieb and Emily Ziebart

member of the party he was going to vote for. He and Emily retired to Roblin where he died on May 10, 1978. He is buried beside Emily in the Roblin Cemetery.

Emily (Wuschke) Ziebart

She was born on June 10, 1901 in Cholm Lublin, Poland. Immigrated to Canada 1910. Married Gottlieb and had four sons and two daughters. She and Gottlieb moved from Dropmore to Roblin in 1962 where she dedicated many hours of sewing and care giving with the ladies of the Lutheran Church. She died February 9, 1970 and is buried in Roblin, MB.

Henry George Ziebart

He was born on June 13, 1919 at Bateman in the Municipality of Seward, SK. He moved to Dropmore in 1944 and shortly thereafter, having already had a ship torpedoed out from under him in the Merchant Marine, he joined the army until the end of W.W.II in 1945. Then he worked as a mechanic for Harold Jones Auto Wrecking, the Ford Dealership in Roblin and MacNutt. He moved SW 23-23-29 from 1963 until 1968 when he sold it to his nephew Larry Ziebart. In 1964 he married Fia and moved to Vermilion Bay, ON and BC. He died in Abbotsford, BC in February of 1992.

Louie Ernest Ziebart

Louie was born on January 30, 1921 at Rostad PO, (Fox Valley) SK. He moved to Dropmore from Arran, SK with the rest of the family in April, 1944 and farmed S 1/2-23-29-29. He married Lillian Clara Dietrich, the daughter of Henry Dietrich, November 10, 1946 at the Landestreu Lutheran Church. Their son, Larry Ziebart, was born at Gray Nuns Hospital in Russell on June 3, 1947. Their daughter Loretta Clara Ziebart was born 22 September, 1951 in Roblin Hospital. Ernest and Clara owned and lived on the Henry Dietrich farm from 1957 to the Fall of 1963 when they moved to the Gottlieb Ziebart farm. In 1966 they rented Douglas Hunter's farm and the family moved there because it had a better water supply.

On August 11, 1974, Clara died from a stroke. Her funeral was held in the Dropmore Church and she is buried in the Dropmore Cemetery.

Ernie and Marj Ziebart - 1982.

Ernest helped build the Dropmore church and the curling rink. For several years he was the ice maker in the rink. He also worked for the district's road maintenance. On October 23, 1982 Ernest married Marge Stephen. They live in Moosomin, SK where they are active in Old-time pattern dancing.

Larry Ziebart

Larry attended the Dropmore School. On August 14, 1971 he married Shirley Olm. They have 3 children: Craig, Kimberly, and Colin.

Ernest Ziebart and Clara Dietrich - Married November 10, 1946.

They have moved a house onto the Gottlieb Ziebart place and are farming the Ziebart and Dietrich farms.

Loretta Ziebart

She attended Dropmore School. In 1969 she graduated from Roblin Collegiate and took up residence in Brandon. On 19th of April 1975, she married Brian Bridgeman in Oak River. They have two children, Russell and Susan. They now live in Brandon, MB.

Rudolf Albert Ziebart

He was born on June 18, 1926 at Bateman, SK. He now lives in Brandon, MB.

Anna Ziebart

Anna was born on November 29, 1928 in Gravelbourg, SK. She married Charles Harding on 24th of January, 1951. She had 5 sons, Donald, Harry, Wade, Herb, and Ted and 4 daughters, Linda, Joyce, Helen, and Carol. Chuck died on April 4, 1984. Anna is now retired and lives in Victoria on Vancouver Island, BC.

John Ziebart

John was born January 3, 1934 at Mossbank, SK and he was the only one of Gottlieb's children to attend the Dropmore Elementary School. He completed his grade 8 in 1948. On August 2, 1951 he joined the RCAF. Shortly thereafter, his Dropmore School classmates, Blake Cameron, Clarence Robb, Burke Cameron, Melford Dietrich also joined the RCAF.

While stationed in Whitehorse, Yukon he met Frances Renouf. They were married on February 6, 1955 in the Dropmore church. (The wedding had to be delayed for a week because there was a curling bon spiel in town and the wedding guests were curling.)

John served in the Canadian Arctic, Europe, and the Middle East. When he retired from the Armed Forces, he was the Commanding Officer of 748 Communications Troop in Nanaimo. John and Fran are now retired and live in Nanaimo on Vancouver Island, BC.

John Ziebart and Francis Renouf - Married in Dropmore Church, February 6, 1955.

Captain John Ziebart and Fran Ziebart..

Phil and Barb Zimmer

Some members of the Zimmer family moved from Strathclair to Sec. 22-23-29 in Dropmore district in 1946. They had originated from Grayson, SK. Phil remained on the farm and in 1951 married Barbara Bradley-Hunt who was born and raised at Dropmore. She had previously taught school at Rivers, Rapid City and Dropmore. They farmed until 1992 when they sold the farm and retired to Russell, Man.

Their hobbies have been camping and fishing. They have travelled to all the provinces and various places in the United States. They curled a lot in the winter months and now enjoy bowling and cards for winter activities.

This picture shows (L-R) Phil and Barbara Zimmer, Charlie and Mary Bernhard, Ernie and Pauline Sudbury, Kay Dietrich and Frank Zimmer.

Some of the Early Settlers of the Rochedale District

by A. Keay

Tom and **Bill Patterson** were a couple of bachelors who came out from Ireland around 1900 and settled on W 1/2 of 30, 23, 28, which is west of R. Morrison farm. They farmed there until they passed away, Bill in 1924 and Tom in 1930. They both rest in the Rochedale Cemetery.

Mr. Gray and **Jim Walker** came from Scotland in the early 1900's. Up to that time they had been in the British Navy so had pretty well seen the world. When they came to Canada, they settled in the Rochedale area on S.E. 1/4, 30, 28 and tried farming. When World War I broke out, Mrs. Grey returned to the British Isles to enlist in the Army and was never heard of again.

Jim Walker bought 1/4 section N,W, 7, 23, 28 which is on the top hill where the Shell River joined the Assiniboine River and now looks over the Lake of the Prairies. He made an attempt at farming for a number of years, then gave it up. Then he spent most of his time with the neighbors. He was a great reader and as long as the lamp was full of coal oil and lots of wood in the house. He would read all night and keep the stove stoked up all night in the winter time. He passed away in 1956 and was laid to rest in the Tummel Cemetery.

Then there was **Bert Cox**, a young chap from England, who somehow arrived in Rochedale and worked on the farm of William Skinner for a number of years. Then he too decided to try farming on his own on S.W. 1/4 20-23-28. Where he stayed until World War II broke out. Then he sold out and enlisted in the Canadian Army and went overseas. After the War, he made one trip back to Canada for a visit, then went back to England where he passed away a couple of Years later.

Ed Talbot was another man who came out from England. He was a great teamster and worked for a number of years for Dick Keay until his sudden death. He was laid to rest in Rochedale Cemetery.

Mr. and Mrs. Archie Gilchrist lived on N. W. 1/4 16-23-28 along the East side of 83 Highway whey farmed. Mrs. Gilchrist passed away in 1929. Mr. Gilchrist moved into the Shell Valley just south of the bridge on old Highway 83 going up the hill to a few acres, where he had a filling station, and kept a few sweets and smokes. It was called "Bide a Wee". Many folks did just that. He passed away in 1949 and both Mrs. and Mrs. Gilchrist rest in the Rochedale Cemetery.

Nelson Gilchrist was adopted by the Gilchrists and stayed on the farm for awhile, then moved to British Columbia and no more was heard of him. There is a Mr. Peacock in Rochedale Cemetery who was Nelson's father. But no one seems to know where he came from or how long he was in the District.

Nick Harrick came from the Ukraine as a young boy and worked with a circus and the railroad. Eventually he ended up in the Rochedale District where he worked for Dick Keay for a number of years. From all accounts, he didn't mind giving Mrs. Keay a helping hand in the house with the meals etc. He was a sort of a Jack of all trades. Then he bought some land S.W. 1/4 of 19-23-28 which he farmed for a few years, then sold. Then eventually he got another 1/4 section, east and south near the Shell River where he remained until his passing away in 1972. He is also resting in the Rochedale Cemetery.

Mr. and Mrs. John McInnis moved to the Todd Ranch in the early 1900's. This Ranch was located at the foot of the valley hills, where the Shell River met the Assiniboine. Mr. Attwood had taken this Ranch over, because it was lush with hay and pasture. He kept a large number of cattle there. Mr. McInnis was one of the cowboys who took care of the cattle. Then from there, they moved to Shellmouth and purchased the Livery Barn from R.W. Patterson.

Section Three

Historical Recollections in Photo Memory of

**Castleavery
Dropmore
Grainsby
Rochedale**

After the horse and wagon ...

1946 Chev car owned by Mickey Minchuk, used on Bill & Buryle's 40th anniversary 1986

1928 Chev. with Kay, Lawrence, Clarence Robb

Edward Bieber in front of his (Circa 1929) vehicle.

Hilliard & Marion Ferriss
1927 Chevrolet

International truck in the 50's.
Note, the heavy snowfall.

Annie keeps them running! Annie Ferriss standing in front of the gas station at Dauphin.

Ida Brown's 1949 Plymouth. Flooding over the road by Dropmore.

Buildings of the past ...

Bert Hunt home that the Munro's lived in.

The big brick house built by Ike Goodman.

The old Skinner house with Mrs. Dugan holding Joe & Jean.

The Frederick Bieber home in Dropmore. The entire Bieber Family of ten can be seen on the verandah.

Mrs. Dugan 1939. This building is the garage at the present Skinner yard.

The Cranwell home in Roblin. Lillian Ratke and Anne Wishart in photo.

Another unique 30's style home with Fred Richardson, Mrs. Lewis, Chris Anderson, Nell Richardson, Alex Skinner, Willie Skinner, Belle Dugan, Annie Robertson and Fred Skinner.

Old brick building made of bricks from the foundry near Longden Lake.

Hunting cabin in the Duck Mountains.

By-gone school days ...

Children coming to Castleavery School by horse and buggy.

Children on their way to school. Note the unique "syrup and lard pails" lunch buckets.

Children going to school by horseback.

On the way to school. Paul Dietrich with Pam, Pearle Penny and Phyllis - 1970

Hollie Andrew, Teacher at Castleavery School

Holly Andrew's first Christmas Concert.

Last day of school 1978. Picnic near slide area.
Paul Dietrich & Garry Morrison bus drivers.

Alice & Betty Goodbun going to Dropmore
School with "Paint".

Community activities ...

Castleavery Curlers: Bob Digby Rene Jennings, Ellen Rowan, Beryl Bauming, Marge Nichols, Mrs. Digby, Mrs. Dugan, Mrs. Hunter

Dropmore Chicks

Doole Farm Auction Sale 1988 on Dropmore Farm.

Children wait patiently for Santa at annual Dropmore Xmas Pary 1994

Rochedale Ladies Club (circa) 1950.

Remembrance Day at Dropmore. Paul Dietrich, Lil Hunt, Erv Young holding flag

Farming in the past ...

Bindering on Keay Farm.

Fork-lifting hay into loft on Jones farm (circa 1941). John McFadyen in front.

Harold Jones moving a granary. (circa 1940's)

Bill Doole with his home-made grain cleaning unit 1962.

Bieber Boys loading sheaves of grain for harvesting.

Fred Bieber and sons cutting wood with Titan Tractor on the farm in Dropmore.

Threshing at the A.W. Nichol's Farm.

Butchering at the Robb's.

Hauling grain to the MacNutt elevator.

Percy Jenning & John McFadyen cutting ice blocks.

Ed Bieber cutting hay with mower.

Clive Leflar dipping water.

Threshing outfit.

Wood sawing outfit.

Great Grandpa Ferriss loved his garden.

Ivan Rowan & Donnie Turta at threshing time.

Harold & Ivan Jones cutting wood on the Jones farm 1940.

A. E. Jones with Dorothy & Beth 1928.

Edith Rowan in her corn patch.

Teen Rose and Elias by Shop north of MacNutt, SK.

Threshing. Walt Ferris, Brady Cameron, Jack Ferris, Joe Ferris, Chris Carmicheal, Grandpa Bill Ferris, Herman Spees.

Our prized livestock ...

Hazel Doole with Reserve Grand Champion Steer 1980.

Les Doole 1965 Champ 4-H Beef Club at Dauphin.

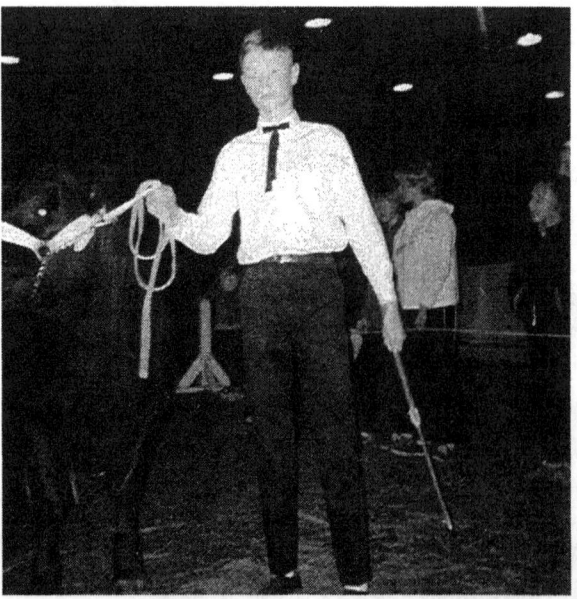
Verne Doole 4-H Beef Club 1965.

Quadruplets born at Young Farm 1995.

Calf born on the Albert Jones Farm (circa 1937) with a perfect #7 on its forehead.

Justin Jackson with the sheep on the Bauereiss Farm.

Our people tell the story ...

George & Maria (Kendal) Bieber, parents of Johann Frederick Bieber. George & Maria were among the earliest settlers in the Landestrew area. Frederick married Katherina (Wirth) Goeres and their family lived in the Dropmore area until 1934. The Johann Frederick Bieber history is found in the Family History section of this publication.

Two sets of Bieber twins. George & Mary, first set of twins born in MacNutt. Minnie & Annie born in Dropmore, MB.

Bessie Munro on her bike.

Mr. & Mrs. Archie (Janet) Morrison.

Florence Kelbert.

Minnie, Laura, & Margaret.

Victor Ferris, 1943.

Dietrich Brothers: Mervyn, Harold, Paul & George, 1944.

Helen, George Doreen, & Marie Baranet.

Fred & Mary Wright Family. (L-R) Mary Wright Violet Crib, Gordon Wright, Freda Kadlubec, (Centre) Fred Wright.

Pete Piwniuk & Fred.

Dad, Laurence & Clarence Robb.

Margaret (Babe) Comfort Handley, Christopher, and Micheal.

Dietrich in-laws 1966. Joan, Ena, Mom Dietrich, Kay, Pauley, Clara, Lucille

Anne (Rowan) Wishart.

Rabbit hunting. Walter & his cousins.

Pauley Zimmer, Barbara Hunt, Kay Robb & Mary Zimmer.

Violet Henry's wife dressed in a suit and Margaret (Nerbas) Kozak dressed in a nightgown & curtains

Wendy, Rosalyn, Noreen, Magdalena, Joan, Margaret, Charlotte, Douglas.

Harvey Munro & George Barawet checking bees.

Mr. & Mrs. E. Comfort 50th Wedding Anniversary.

Paul, Melfred, Pat Dietrich, Connie Hertlein.

Annie Ferris, Jean, Eileen, & Florence.

Family Gathering, Skinner Clan.

Reg Lewis.

The six Bieber Brothers.

"The Crew"-The Hunter Boys 1942.

Funeral of Maria (Kendal) Bieber, mother to Johann Frederick Bieber. Husband George Bieber is to right of casket resting on a cane.

Cousins Lawrence & Ivan Rowan on occasion of Anne's wedding to Albert Wishart, Nov. 5, 1952.

(Back row) John & Adolf (Front row) Henry & Phillip lived at Dropmore 1956.

Albert & Ivan in a water fight.

Walter & Gen Kurtenbach.

Patricia, Paulette, Pat & Pam Dietrich, 1965.

Bill Doole on Santa's knee 1993.

Making wood in the Duck Mts. Lloyd Shearer & Brett Bauereiss.

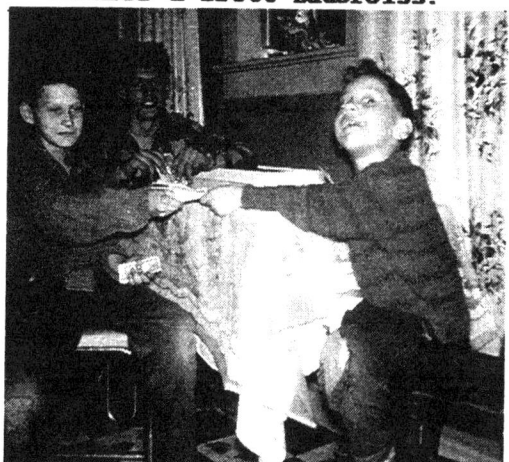
Daniel Shewchuk, Donald Rowan & Elias Shewchuk.

Pat Nichols, Tom Bauereiss, Marlene & Lloyd Shearer moose hunting in the Duck Mts. in 1980.

Harry Gilhooley, 1939.

Wedding of Garry Roloff & Tannis Shearer.

Lindsay Wagner's Confirmation.
(Back row) Eldon, Bill, Hermann,
(Front row) Wilma, Lindsay, Linda.

50th Wedding Anniversary
Joe & Maggie Simair, Mar. '87.

Gen Kurtenbach on Laddy.

Lindsay Wagner.

Kimberly Elaine Patterson.

Ivan & Anne Rowan (circa 1947).

Krystle, Riley, Chelsea Nielson, children ofl Eldon and Connie Nielson.

Santa at the Christmas Party in Dropmore.

Margaret Kurtenbach & Randy Poier wedding party, Langenburg, SK.

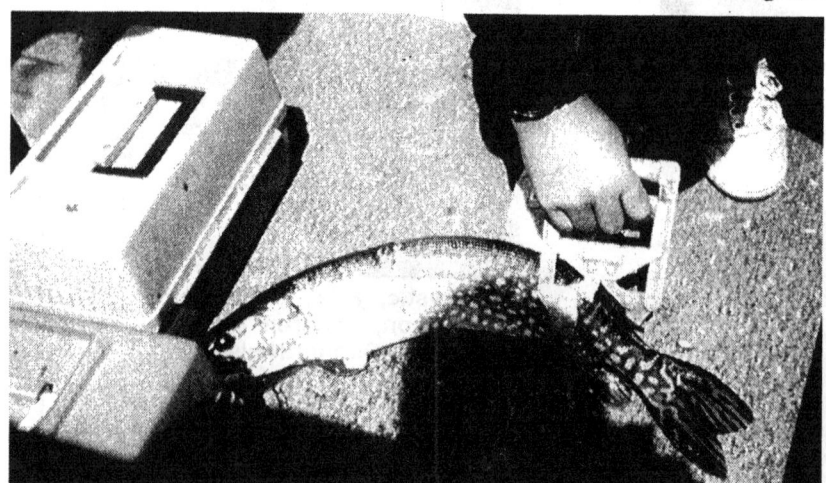
Fishing in Lake of the Prairie, not a bad catch!

When horse was King ...

Sleigh ride along the old railway bed east of Dropmore.

Dropmore trail ride.

Sleigh ride in 1985

Gen Kurtenbach & grandchildren: Tiffany Kotzer, Tyrel Poier, Angie Fatteicher, Carissa Holinaty

Fred with 'Rex' and 'Reno' at a parade.

Our first horse, Scout. Char & Rose on Scout, Roy, Adrian, Joan, Wendy, Noreen

A. E. Jones and Fritz, 1939.

Raymond Ungarian & his pony 'Darling'.

Visit our community ...

The Shellmouth Dam. The south side of the Valley.

Shellmouth Dam coming down the east side to the lake.

Asessippi Provincial Park Sign.

Wild boars near Dropmore.

Going east on #482.

Flood of '95 at the Shellmouth Spillway.

Ice fishing on Lake of the Prairies.

Overlooking the valley above the old George Dietrich place now Kilman Enterprise.

Assiniboine Bridge at Dropmore.

Dropmore from highway #482.

The Spillway.

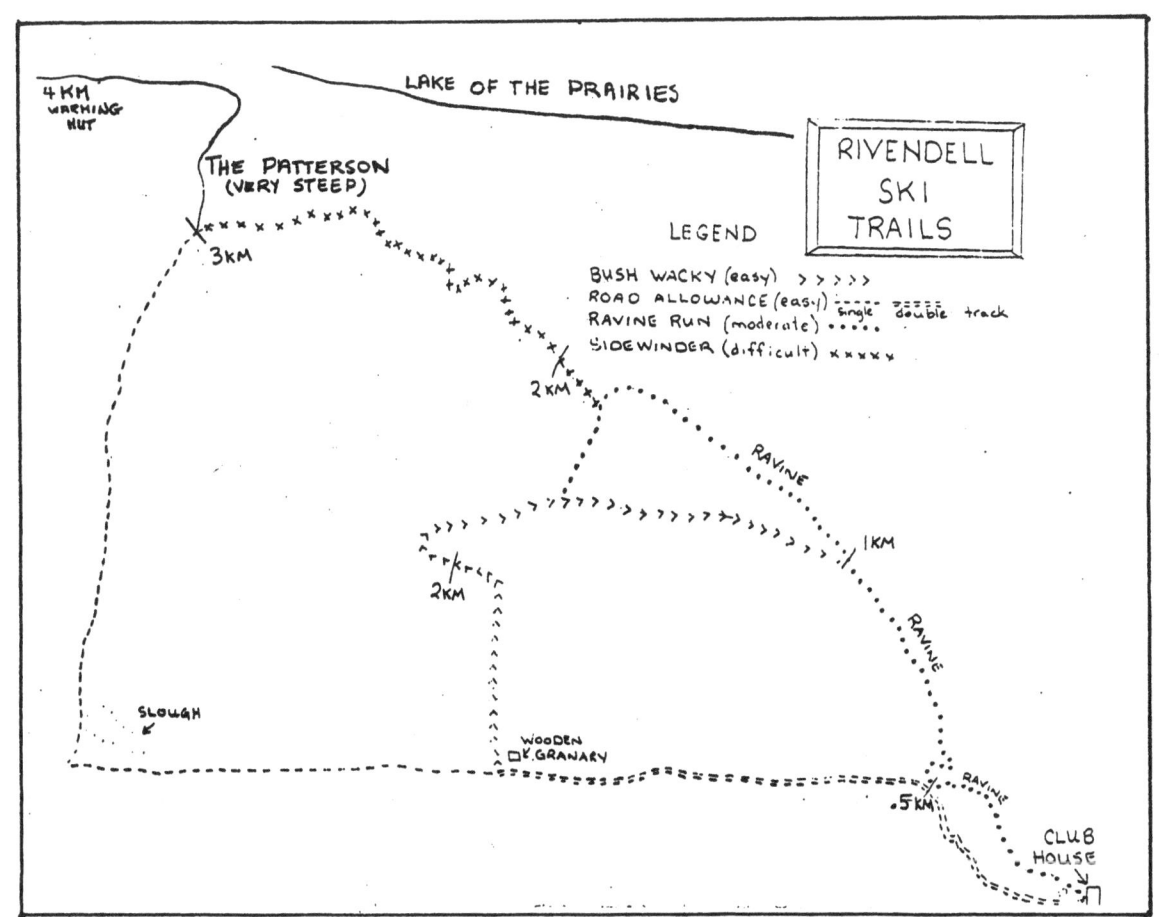

The history of Rivendell Ski Club is found in Section I of *"Then and Now"*.

We grow them big! A sunflower head 18" across grown in the Doole garden 1987.

Dropmore, a friendly community. "Helping out the neighbours".

Section   Four

Historic Archival Reprints of

Castleavery
Dropmore
Grainsby
Rochedale

A Blueprint of the Past

We have all heard it said, time and again, that a picture is worth a thousand words. This is surely true when one comes to the realization that many families have, buried in their old family chests, pictures that show how their forefathers lived and struggled. By examining these pictures closely, one can clearly identify details about their lives, work, pleasures, entertainment, anxieties and faith, as they sincerely hoped for a better tomorrow. For some, that tomorrow never came; for others, dreams became reality.

For many of our ancestors, the camera was a new invention and picture taking was in some cases a "happen stance", while for others, it was planned. For whatever reason, we are grateful to those early pioneering folk who took the time, or knew someone with a box camera ...to record their lives for future generations. These early photographs of people, lifestyles, customs and traditions, are rare finds today.

In compiling this community history, the publisher noted that all photographs in this publication are deserving of special merit. Some photographs, however, are of historic, archival importance to the memory of the Dropmore Area. These photographs warrant reproduction on a larger scale.

The Publisher,
Marcon Consulting

Reuben A. Bauer

Here is the Castleavery classroom of 1951.

The old Castleavery School with their teacher, Eva Roe of 1943.

The old country church built in Castleavery in 1896.

The most important place in the community was the home. The Bieber Family home in Dropmore.

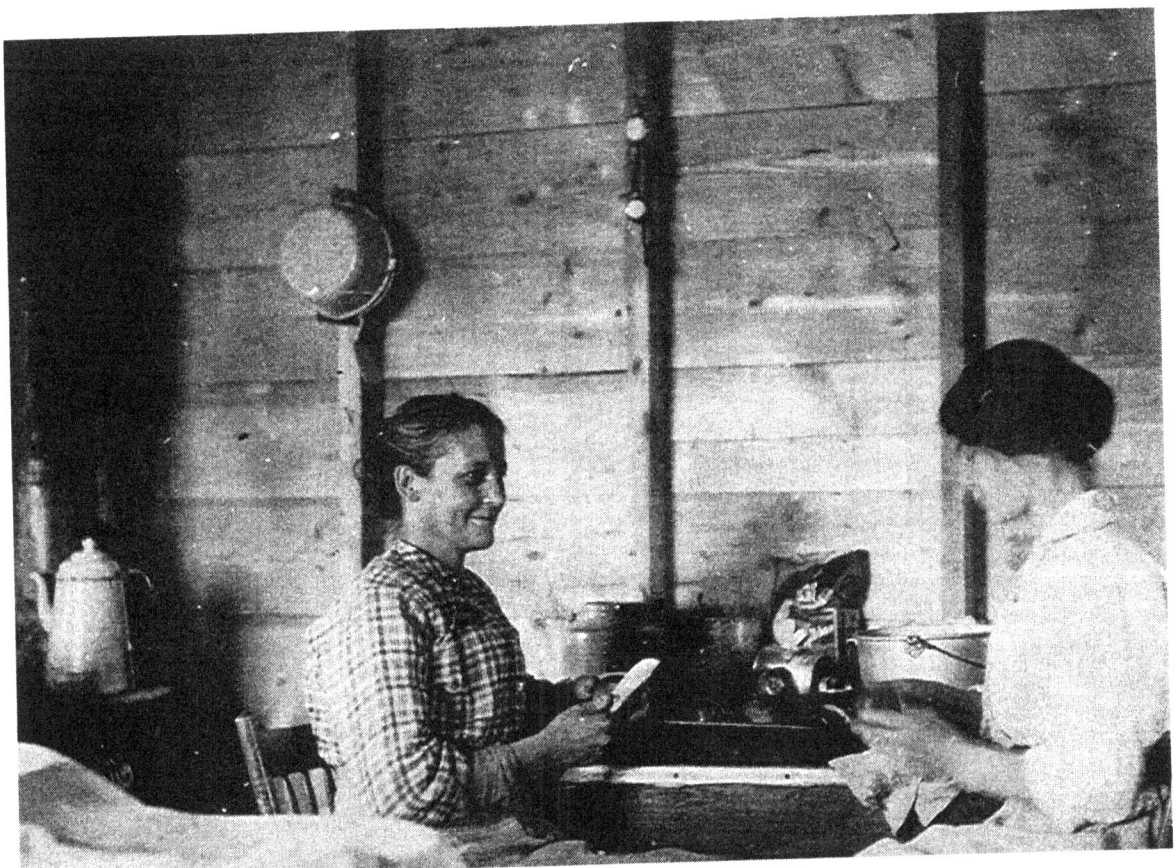
The pleasures of home... preparing for the meals.

Another pleasure... to read all about it.

Farming was a strong economic base and preparing the fields for seeding was important. At the Great Grandpa Ferriss farm at Dropmore.

Harvesting was no less a big task. Fred Bieber on his Titan tractor pulling the threshing machine (separator as they were called).

Threshing time called for many hands... old and young joined together to get that crop in.

Here loading grain into the box car at Dropmore was made easier than shovelling by hand. An invention by Grandpa Ferris speeded up the process.

Grain elevators a common site. The British American Elevator Co. at Dropmore, MB in 1909.

Drilling for water a common necessity on the prairies. Here is Britton Ferris and his water drilling operation in Dropmore.

In the spring time fertilizing the fields. Here the Bieber twins, Minnie and Annie with older brother Rudolph, hauling manure on stone boat.

Butchering time with Great Grandpa Ferriss.

Commerce and industry would not have flourished without the general merchant in town. The E.T. Lewis General Merchant in Dropmore.

Part of that commerce was tied in with the local bank. The Union Bank of Canada in Dropmore.

The "Iron Horse" a vital link to any community. The train came through Dropmore and provided a great service for grain shipment and passenger service.

Gone are the days for the old Railway Station. This one in Dropmore, MB.

Families large and small were always kept in their best attire. The Frank and Margaret Nerbas Family.

The Joseph Dugan I family and their friends.

The community gathered for special events. This is one such scene in Dropmore.

People also gathered to help one another in work "bees". The barn raising at the Keay farm in 1949.

Small and bustling communities in times past...Dropmore, MB.

Men hauling wood from the prison camp in 1945.

Although people worked hard to succeed, they also had time for entertainment. This performance by local players in Dropmore.

Another entertainment group, the Rochedale Drama Club.

The Dropmore Orchestra... real live entertainment.

There were real orchestras and then there were "make-believe" orchestras like this one.

Family History Index

Anderson, John Allan............................51
Andres, Jake and Lydia..........................51
Arnold, Minnie (Bieber).........................70
Atkinson, Elizabeth Ruth........................52
Atkinson, James.................................51
Bassil Family...................................52
Bauereiss, Tom and Betty........................53
Bauming, Andy and Noreen........................55
Beals, Harold...................................55
Beals, Walter...................................56
Bernhard, Charlie and Mary (Zimmer).............58
Bieber, Johann and Katherina (Wirth)............59
Bird, Frank & Doris.............................75
Bird, Mabel (Cook)..............................75
Birnie, John....................................75
Bradley-Hunt, Basil.............................76
Brown Family....................................77
Burgess, J. Agnes...............................80
Burla, Peter and Margaret.......................81
Carefoot, Catherine (Piwniuk)..................178
Carmicheal, Bartley and Lyla....................82
Case, Matilda (Dalle)...........................86
Chernesky, Iris.................................83
Craig, James....................................83
Cranwell, Mabel (Roe)..........................200
Dalle, Charles and Elizabeth....................84
Dietrich, Katherine.............................86
Dietrich, Mervin and Joan.......................87
Dietrich, Paul and Pauline......................87
Dietrich, Phillip and Margaret..................89

Digby, Faye..91
Digby, Garry...91
Digby, Maurice and Olive.....................................92
Digby, Robert and Elaine.....................................92
Digby, Wayne and Phyllis.....................................94
Doole, Bill and Buryle.......................................94
Doole, Hazel (Minchuk).......................................97
Doole, Les and Pam...99
Doole, Verne..100
Dougherty, Florence (Kirkpatrick)...........................100
Dugan, Joseph I...101
Dugan, Joseph II..103
Dugan, Joseph III...103
Farncombe, James Thomas.....................................105
Ferris, Henry "Britton".....................................106
Ferris, Hugh..115
Ferris, Jack..115
Ferris, Joseph Hugh...111
Ferris, Mervyn..110
Ferris, Stanley...109
Ferris, Watt..115
Ferris, William George......................................113
Ferriss Families..119
Ferriss, W.G.(Bert)...116
Finkbeiner, Margaret (Robb).................................125
Flett, Myrtle Jenny (Ferris)................................109
Gabrielson, Lillian...126
Goodbun, Archie...126
Hackman, Petro and Victoria.................................128
Hunt Family...131
Hunt, Alexander and Mary....................................129
Hunt, Robert and Edith......................................134
Hunter, James C...136
Hunter, William James.......................................138
Jennings, Percy...139
Jones, Albert...140

Keay, Harold and Alice	144
Keay, Richard and Margaret	143
Kelbert, Florence (Ferris)	109
Kelly, May (Richardson)	185
Klein, Kerry and Erla	147
Kurtenbach, Walter and Gen	148
Lewis, Edward and Clementina	152
Liske, Marilyn (Parmentier)	171
MacFarlane, John Russell	153
MacLeod, John Graham	154
Martel, Daniel	155
McFadyen, Ilene (Roe)	199
Miller, James Edward	156
Morrison, Earl	156
Morrison, Garry	158
Morrison, Wilbert	158
Munro, Harvey	159
Nerbas, Philip & Margaret	160
Nerbas, Rudolf & Louise	163
Nerbas, Sadie	164
Nerbas, Vernon - Memories	165
Nerbus, Bill	165
Nichols Family	167
Nielson, William	168
Parmentier, Fredrick & Flo	169
Paulenko, Vera (Burla)	82
Peats, Richard & Sylvia	172
Peter, Mary (Bieber)	66
Petz, George and Anne	173
Piwniuk, Bill	177
Piwniuk, Fred and Janet	178
Piwniuk, Kelly and Laurel	179
Piwniuk, Mike and Teenie	175
Piwniuk, Steve and Cathie	175
Pyott, Robert and Jessie	179
Ralston, Burnett and Annie	181

Rawlings, George and Fanny	183
Robb, Roy	186
Roberts, Hugh A.	187
Robertson, John Sr. and Ann	189
Robertson, Walter	193
Robin, Clarence	193
Robin, Don and Freda	196
Roe, Elizabeth	200
Roe, Harry George	197
Roe, James and Elizabeth	197
Roth, Annie (Bieber)	73
Rowan, George and Edith	204
Rowan, John Nelson	203
Rowan, John Nelson	203
Shearer, Albert and Dagmar	210
Shearer, James	211
Shearer, John and Barbara	210
Shewchuk, Mike and Nonie	214
Shipp, J.T.	216
Simair, Joseph and Margaret	217
Skinner, Frank Leith	219
Stauffer, Cal	221
Threinen, Edward and Katherine	222
Turta, Tony and Stella	225
Ungarian, Raymond	226
Walter, Ron and Kim	228
Wardle, William and Edith	228
Wiesner, Dave and Mary	233
Wright, Fred and Mary	234
Yaworski, Nick and Nellie	234
Young, Ervin and Viola	235
Ziebart, Gottlieb & Emily	235
Zimmer, Phil and Barbara	238
Early Settlers	240

www.ingramcontent.com/pod-product-compliance
Lightning Source LLC
Chambersburg PA
CBHW081826170426
43202CB00019B/2969